Magic in Britain

Magic in Britain

A History of Medieval and Earlier Practices

ROBIN MELROSE

McFarland & Company, Inc., Publishers

Jefferson, North Carolina

the surface by an enclosing ditch bank some 40 feet in diameter, discovered during excavations in 1960–62. A range of deposits were recovered, the earliest being Bronze Age in date, comprising a shale ring, amber beads and bone pins, along with animal bone and organic materials, including wooden containers. The excavator Paul Ashbee argued that the ring, beads and pins should be interpreted as votive deposits, of a type similar to those found as grave furniture in Wessex in the Early Bronze Age. He stresses that there is a very strong possibility that many shafts may exist adjacent to the major round barrow cemeteries of Wessex and that the chthonic (underworld) "cult" of the Iron Age and Roman periods may well have a much earlier origin.[24] Radiocarbon dating of the lower organic remains gave a date for the shaft of 1470–1290 BCE.[25]

The human bone found in Wilsford Shaft represents a minimum of five individuals (two infants, one juvenile and two adults); both adults were tentatively identified as male. The lowest bones are two adult left femurs (thigh bones), found at 8 feet 6 inches.[26] One femur was radiocarbon dated to around 370 BCE, while the other was dated to around 410 BCE.[27] Animal bone from a similar period was also found nearby. A horse calcaneum (also called hock, the equivalent of the ankle bone in humans), dated to around 500 BCE, was found at 7 feet 8 inches, while a horse cuboid/tibia (the cuboid is part of the hock, the tibia connects the stifle, or knee joint, to the hock), dated to around 530 BCE, was found at 9 feet 6 inches.

Of course, not all Iron Age Britons lived in hillforts, and in 1998–9 an unenclosed Iron Age settlement was excavated at Battlesbury Bowl outside Battlesbury Camp hillfort near Warminster in Wiltshire. The Battlesbury Bowl settlement was founded toward the end of the Late Bronze Age in the 8th century BCE and was occupied through the Early and Middle Iron Age, to the 3rd century BCE.[28] One of the most interesting features at Battlesbury Bowl was ditch 4043, a ditch at least 240 feet long. A deposit of seven cattle and three horse skulls was found in section 4105 of ditch 4043—at least some of the skulls had been carefully cleaned and possibly displayed before ending up in the ditch and it may be that it was the display, rather than any act of deposition, that was important.[29] One of the cattle skulls and the associated foreleg produced radiocarbon dates of between 790 BCE and 420 BCE. A number of the sections of ditch 4043 contained large finds assemblages. Human remains (lower limb fragments) were recovered from ditch sections 4079, 4090 and 4096 and animal bone groups from ditch sections 4090 and 4105 and all the excavated sections contained relatively large quantities of pottery and bone. Other finds included a number of quernstone and whetstone fragments as well as worked bone objects and flint hammerstones. Some of the basal deposits of the ditch had a slightly greenish tinge very similar to midden-like deposits recorded at Potterne.[30]

As the deposits from ditch 4043 show, the early inhabitants of Battlesbury Bowl buried bones or bone fragments in pits and ditches. Human bone was recovered from 29 contexts within 21 features at the settlement. Disarticulated bones, or more commonly fragments of bones, were recovered from 25 contexts, mostly Late Bronze Age to early Middle Iron Age in date, predominantly pit fills (56 percent) and, less commonly, ditch (28 percent) and post-hole fills (16 percent). The fragments mostly comprise elements of long bone (44.4 percent) and skull vault (29 percent). Of the former, femur shaft predominates (25 percent) (the femur shaft is the body of the thigh bone). Not all fragments could be sided, but 60 percent of the assemblage comprises bone from the right (including 21 percent right femur and 12 percent right humerus) compared with only 21 percent from the left side. Canid gnawing (gnawing by dogs, foxes or wolves), evident from the crenulated, worn ends of bone fragments and extant puncture marks, was observed in 28 percent of the disarticulated bone assemblage. The skeletal elements in which gnawing was observed are predominantly the larger long bones (femur, tibia, and humerus). A higher percentage of the material from the ditches (57 percent) compared with that from the pits (28 percent) show evidence for gnawing.[31] The bone specialist Jacqueline McKinley concludes[32] that the Late Bronze Age–early Middle Iron Age material "all comprises disarticulated bone fragments (representing the remains of a minimum of three individuals) with common evidence for canid gnawing and some weathering. The form and nature of the material is indicative of some level of exposure linked to deliberate human manipulation involving excarnation and possible 'curation.'" In other words, the bones show evidence of having been gnawed by dogs, foxes or wolves, and of having been "curated"—in other words, kept as souvenirs of the deceased. One intriguing finding from Battlesbury Bowl is that bones deposited in pits tended to come from the right side of the body, which links Battlesbury Bowl to the midden at Potterne.

Toward the end of its period of use, burial practices changed at Battlesbury Bowl. Two later Middle Iron Age pits (350 BCE–200 BCE) contained inhumation burials. Pit 4223 contained two crouched inhumation burials. The body of a man aged over 40 years was laid on its right side with its head to the west. A horse lower mandible had been placed over the pelvis, and a fragment of bone from another adult (aged over 18 years) was also recovered from this level. Although a layer of soil was recorded between the two inhumations, it is possible that the two burials were not separated by any great length of time. The upper skeleton, of an adult female aged 35–55 years, was more tightly crouched, lying on its left side and with the head to the east, and further fragments of horse mandible were recovered from the surrounding soil. Pit 4332 contained a crouched inhumation, a juvenile aged about 10 years, possibly a male; associated with the burial were a Neolithic flint axe, part of a chalk loomweight, and three articulated sheep/goat vertebrae.[33] Both the burial and the animal bones produced radiocarbon dates in the range 410–190 BCE.

HAMPSHIRE

Danebury hillfort at Nether Wallop in Hampshire is a hillfort on the eastern edge of Salisbury Plain, excavated by Barry Cunliffe over a period of twenty years. Cunliffe says that the settlement started life in the Late Bronze Age as a hilltop enclosure, a ritual site crowned by a circle of tall posts set in ritual pits (one with the possible sacrifice of dog). The first hillfort was built in 5th century BCE, after the ritual posts had rotted and the pits silted up; circular huts were associated with this phase. About 400 BCE, or perhaps a little earlier, there was a major change. In the interior regular rows of rectangular house structures were established along planned streets, while an impressive entrance was built on the east side, and the defenses were strengthened and remodeled. Danebury had become a major hill-town and the seat of considerable political authority. This condition continued for some 300 years with regular maintenance of the defenses and rebuilding of the houses. About 100 BCE the eastern gateway was completely rebuilt on a grand scale and with complex defensive hornworks. Soon after, however, the gate was destroyed, and the fort abandoned. Between 1971 and 1975 a continuous strip 100–140 feet wide extending across the center of Danebury from on side to the other was completely excavated revealing pits, gullies, circular stake-built houses, rectangular buildings and 2-, 4- and 6-post structures ranging in date from the 6th century BCE to the ends of the second century

BCE. About 100 BCE rectangular buildings, possibly of a religious nature, were erected. Excavations from 1976 to 1980 located further pits, houses and buildings, as well as a main road crossing the fort from the east entrance. Three more rectangular "ritual" buildings were also found. A hoard of twelve bronze axes and other objects of the 7th century BCE was discovered within the fort in 1974 and 1977, suggesting that occupation at Danebury may have begun as early as the 7th century BCE.[34] During his excavation of Danebury, Cunliffe uncovered a large number of storage pits or underground silos, and notes that they are common on all settlement sites. It had earlier been thought that they were constructed to protect the grain from raids, but Cunliffe believes they had a different function. In his view, the seed was placed in storage pits after harvesting and before sowing, so it would be protected by the "chthonic deities" (gods or goddesses of the underworld). Once the seed was sown, offerings were made to the chthonic deities in thanks for their protection of the grain.[35]

The nature of these offerings varied considerably. One offering at Danebury involved a dog and a horse which has been partially dismembered, its head and one foreleg being placed separately against the pit side.[36] In another pit were a pig and two calves.[37] Articulated horse legs were found six or seven times in a sample of 200 pits, indicating that this offering had some sort of religious significance.

But these offerings did not only involve animals. Some 300 depositions of human remains have been found at Danebury, including skulls. Fifteen complete or near complete skulls have been found in pits, together with about 30 skull fragments.[38] Two of the male skulls bear marks of sword wounds. Isolated skulls were placed in the middle or upper parts of pit fills (unlike complete bodies, which were placed toward the bottom of the pit). Humans were sometimes buried with animals. The pelvis of a young male aged between 18 and 25 was placed in the bottom, and in the center, of an elongated pit with a pig skull and the innominate (hip) bone of a child nearby. There was evidence that the legs had been hacked off and the pelvis violently severed from the trunk. Five sets of human remains were buried in pits along with a raven, a bird associated with death in Celtic mythology: there were a skull and disarticulated human bone in one pit, a female skull fragment and a male torso in another, a crouched skeleton in two further pits, and disarticulated human bone in a final pit.[39]

SOMERSET

Glastonbury Lake Village is a mile to the north of Glastonbury in Somerset and flourished between about 200 BCE and 50 BCE. It was built on an artificial island of timber, stone and clay which lay in a swampy area of open water, reeds and fenwood. In its early stages the site comprised five or six houses, one of which burnt down, and a series of clay spreads that provided bases for outdoor work. The island was later extended, and more houses built. The site appears to have been permanently occupied even though its location in a swamp meant that everything had to be brought in by boat.

At its maximum Glastonbury Lake Village consisted of about 15 houses and had a population of, perhaps, 200. The houses were circular with walls of vertical posts infilled with wattle and daub; roofs were thatched with reeds or straw. Many of the clay floors were constructed for hearths, some for cooking and warmth, others for industrial purposes. The site was surrounded by an irregular palisade which was probably more structural than defensive and there was a landing stage on the eastern side.[40]

Glastonbury was excavated between 1892 and 1908 by Arthur Bulleid and Harold St. George Gray, who comment on one particular find[41]: "One of the most interesting objects of bone from the Village is the disc or roundel … of human skull bone—part of the table of the of the occipital bone of an old person." This disc was "of concavo-convex section," measuring almost 3 inches in diameter and a third of an inch in thickness. It was "perforated centrally" by a hole a third of an inch in diameter on the external surface, but slightly larger on the inner side. Its precise use, they say, "is unknown, but it is generally regarded as an amulet or charm for superstitious purposes and may have been worn on the person. The edges are very smooth." As at All Cannings Cross, this fragment of skull bone may have performed some magical function. In addition to this disc, seven fragments of crania were found within the settlement, and nine outside the palisades, some with signs of violence.[42]

Magic and Ritual in Eastern England

GODWIN RIDGE (CAMBRIDGESHIRE)

Godwin Ridge is a sand ridge 628 yards in length, flanked on all sides by the channels of ancient streams, in the floodplain of the River Great Ouse, just above Earith, where the river flows into the southwestern Cambridgeshire peat fens. The ridge was investigated in 2008–9 as part of the Over Narrows phase of Barleycroft/Over Quarry project. In the late Bronze Age Godwin Ridge was a feasting site, but in the Iron Age it became a center of ritual activities.

These activities were focused at the western edge of the ridge, on the northern riverside and a dumped-soil platform 23 feet by 33 feet and between 6 inches and a foot thick. The platform's foundation layer contained the remains of four dismembered horses, and the disarticulated or partially articulated remains of a dog, two cows, a pig and 12 sheep, suggesting that it had a ritual purpose from the very beginning. Also associated with the platform "were the bones from at least fifteen different wild bird species, mostly coot, mallard, other ducks and great-crested grebe; swan, heron, bittern, crow and marsh harrier were also present, as was a Dalmatian pelican, a bird even larger than a swan that once bred in Britain…. The bones were disarticulated, while some were broken or displayed signs of butchery, suggesting that at least some of the birds had been eaten or otherwise utilised." Three copper-alloy brooches were found close to each other, including a Thistle and a Colchester brooch and a rare, near-complete Nauheim type of late 2nd or earlier 1st century BCE date. Nearby, at the riverside, there was "an unequivocal 'ritual package,' a discrete group of three antler weaving combs."[43]

Eighty-nine skeletal elements were found across the western half of the ridge, with the majority (fifty-six) deriving from the northwestern end, where most (forty-eight) were spread across an area measuring 49 feet by 65 feet. The vast majority of the material "was loose and disarticulated. Altogether, portions of seven skulls were recovered from at least five adults, including a male and two females."[44] Canine gnawing was recorded on one tibia. There were also cut marks on a scapula and humerus, and a chop mark on a rib. These occurred "on fresh bone, with no evidence of healing, suggesting that they were made at around the time of death, arguably in relation to dismemberment. The most marked 'modification' involved a polished occipital portion of an adult's skull found along the northern channel side. Apart from shallow knife incisions, this included drilled holes arranged in a near-four-square pattern." The holes were drilled after death with a rotating blade.[45] It seems likely that the four holes were drilled with some magical purpose in mind, and that this skull fragment may well have been an amulet.

Based on the pottery and the radiocarbon dates recovered from the Godwin Ridge riverside platform area, the "human bone deposition would appear to have been a phenomenon of the Middle to Late Iron Age and into the third quarter of the first century AD."[46]

Excarnation (De-Fleshing) in the Iron Age

It is clear from the evidence that the Iron Age Britons of Wiltshire, Hampshire, Somerset and Cambridgeshire were practicing a burial rite known as excarnation, or defleshing. Excarnation is a form of burial in which the body is allowed to decompose and the "dry" bones are given a second burial. This may seem like a macabre practice to us, but it has a very clear religious motivation. Among many people who practice this burial rite even today, or practiced it until very recently, it is believed that the soul of the deceased cannot leave the body until the flesh has decomposed. While the flesh is decaying, the deceased is neither alive nor dead, and is unable to enter the "society of the dead," and leads a shadowy existence on the fringes of human habitation. Once the flesh is decayed, the dry bones are recovered, a great feast is held, the bones are given a second burial, and the deceased is then free to enter the land of the ancestors.[47]

The osteoarchaeologist Rebecca Redfern has studied human bone from the Iron Age sites of Gussage All Saints and Maiden Castle in Dorset for evidence of excarnation. Gussage St. Michael was excavated by Geoffrey Wainwright, who recorded six contexts of disarticulated human remains recovered from a ditch and proposed hut structure, all dating to the 3rd century BCE. The human remains consisted of 11 pieces of cranium (skull) and one femur (thigh bone), all from adult individuals. The cranial material was dominated by parietal bones (the bones which form the sides and roof of the cranium), and the most frequently observed changes were cut marks and fractures that occurred around the time of death. The thigh bone shows signs of gnawing, most probably by a dog.[48]

Redfern also examined eight pieces of disarticulated human bone from Maiden Castle hillfort near Dorchester. These bones were recovered from trenches II and IV from pit, gully, or post-hole fills and soil layers, which had been created during the extended fort phase (phase 6), dating to the Early–Middle Iron Age. Three pieces were long bones, the remainder cranial (skull) material. The long bones had evidence for dry fractures, gnawing and fine cut marks. The cranial material appears to have been formed by radiating fractures produced by blunt-force trauma, and cut marks are also present. All this implies that bodies were allowed to decay, being gnawed by dogs, foxes or wolves, and the bones were then removed and buried in pits, post-holes or gullies.[49]

Fear of the Dead Returning

HORNISH POINT, SOUTH UIST (OUTER HEBRIDES)

There has long been a fear of the dead returning to haunt the living, which was first documented in England in the 12th century. There is burial evidence to suggest that the fear existed in the Roman period and in Anglo-Saxon times, and it probably existed in prehistoric times as well. At Danebury hillfort, complete bodies were buried at the bottom of pits, while skulls were buried in upper fills, suggesting that the inhabitants of Danebury feared that the complete bodies might return to haunt the living.

An extreme example of the fear of complete bodies comes from Hornish Point on South Uist in the Outer Hebrides, northwest Scotland, the site of an Iron Age wheelhouse (a type of roundhouse), possibly dating to between 69 and 240 CE. The remains of a single individual were found buried in four different pits, in a disarticulated state.[50] The individual was around 12 years old, and possibly male. Three of the four pits also contained animal remains. Pit 1 held substantial parts of the skeleton of a young ox aged 18–30 months; Pit 2 produced substantial parts of two female sheep, aged over 3 years and 18–30 months at death; while Pit 4 contained much of a second young ox slightly older than the one in Pit I.[51] It seems likely that the boy was deliberately killed, being struck from behind by an assailant using a sharp-bladed weapon with considerable force.[52] In that case, the fragmentation of his body may be to ensure that he did not come back to haunt the person who killed him.

POCKLINGTON (EAST YORKSHIRE)

In the Iron Age the people of East Yorkshire did not practice excarnation, but buried their dead in cemeteries, often with grave goods, which sometimes included chariots. Recently an Iron age cemetery has been discovered at Pocklington in East Yorkshire. The most spectacular burial was the grave of a warrior buried with his chariot. Excavating his grave, archaeologists have found the stain "imprints" left in the ground by the rotted wood of the 12 spokes of one of the chariot's wheels; the iron tire (which would have gone round that wheel); the stain imprint of the chariot's central timber pole (which connected the vehicle to the two horses pulling it); the stain imprint of the box-shaped compartment that the driver (and potentially one companion) stood in; the two horses used to pull the vehicle; the bridle bit; the iron nave hoop band (which went round the axle); and the remains of the driver himself.

But another grave seemed to show that the people of Iron Age East Yorkshire also feared that the dead might return to haunt them. This was the grave of a possible enemy warrior

> He had died very violently and had sustained serious injuries (possibly caused by a club and a sword) and was buried face down at much greater than normal depth. Interring a person face down in an unusually deeply dug grave is believed to have been seen as a way of preventing an angry, bitter or evil deceased individual, perhaps even an enemy, from rising from the dead and haunting or hurting the living. It was, potentially, a measure to combat revenants (people who return from the dead).[53]

The End of the Iron Age

The prehistoric people of Britain left behind no written records, and so we know very little about their religious beliefs. We can guess the religious beliefs of those who buried their dead in cemeteries like the one at Pocklington in East Yorkshire, but when it comes to the burial of human bones in storage pits at Danebury, or the body of the boy buried in four separate pits at Hornish Point, we can speculate but we really have no idea what the people of Danebury hillfort or Hornish Point wheelhouse believed. But then in the 1st century CE the Romans invaded Britain, and for the first time Britons acquired a voice.

2

Witchcraft, Curse Tablets
and Fear of the Restless Dead:
Magic in Roman Britain

Curse Tablets in the Roman Empire

In 43 CE, the Romans invaded Britain, and by the end of the 1st century Britain as far north as Hadrian's Wall was part of the Roman Empire. The Romans brought with them a pantheon of gods and also a belief in magic, so we need to know something about how the Romans viewed magic, starting with curse tablets.

As the historian of witchcraft Bryan P. Levack points out[1]: "In all societies there are individuals who perform harmful magic—the exercise of preternatural or occult power to bring misfortune to another person. The most common form of such maleficent magic is the utterance of a curse or hex on the intended victim.... In Roman times one form that such curses took was their inscription on leaden tablets and the dedication of these curse tablets to pagan gods. To ensure their effectiveness, a nail or sharp object was sometimes driven into the tablet, often through the name of the intended victim."

This first curse quoted below was written in Latin during the late Roman Empire. It was found at Hadrumetum (now Sousse in Tunisia):

> I adjure you, demon, whoever you are, and I demand of you, from this hour, from this day, from this moment that you torture and kill the horses of the Greens and Whites, and that you kill and smash their drivers Clarus, Felix, Primulus and Romanus, and leave not a breath in their bodies. I adjure you, demon, by him who has turned you loose in these times, the god of the sea and the air.

The following spell, found near Carthage (now Tunis), was directed chiefly against a driver of the Blues, Victoricus, "son of Earth, mother of every living thing." The curse was obviously accompanied by the sacrifice of a cock. The conclusion reveals that the writer knew something of the Hebrew scriptures[2]:

> As this cock is bound, wings and head, so bind the legs, hands, head and heart of Victoricus, the charioteer of the Blues tomorrow, and the horses he is going to drive.... I adjure you, by the God of Heaven above, who sits on the Cherubim, who divided the land and set apart the sea, by Iao, Abriao, Arbathio, Adonai Sabao, that you bind Victoricus and Dominator, so that they may not come to victory tomorrow. Now. Now. Quick. Quick.

The Cherubim are mentioned throughout the Old Testament, and the names that follow are the name of God in the Hebrew scriptures.

Witchcraft in Roman Literature

WITCHCRAFT IN *THE GOLDEN ASS*

Lucius Apuleius was a Roman writer born in Madauros (now M'Daourouch in Algeria) in the 2nd century CE. He studied Platonism in Athens, traveled to Italy, Asia Minor (Turkey) and Egypt, and was an initiate in several cults or mysteries. The most famous incident in his life was when he was accused of using magic to gain the attentions (and fortune) of a wealthy widow. He declaimed and then distributed a witty tour de force in his own defense before the proconsul and a court of magistrates convened in Sabratha, near ancient Tripoli, Libya. This is known as the *Apologia*. His most famous work is the comic novel *Metamorphoses*, better known as *The Golden Ass*, which contains a famous scene involving witchcraft. This story is told by a character called Thelyphron[3]:

When I was still a student in Miletus I sailed across to watch the Olympic Games, and since I wanted to visit this region too of the famous province, I travelled all through Thessaly and arrived one unlucky day at Larissa. Since my purse was feeling rather thin, I was wandering all over town seeking a source of funds when I saw a tall old man standing on a block of stone in the middle of the market-place announcing that anyone willing to guard a corpse for a night might bid for the work. "What's this?" I asked, of a passer-by, "Are corpses here in the habit of running off?"

"Hush, young man!" he replied. "You're an innocent stranger and it seems you don't realise you're in Thessaly where witches are always gnawing away bits of dead men's faces to use in their magic arts."

"Tell me then, if you would" I countered, "what this guardianship involves."

"Well firstly," he replied, "you need to stay wide awake all night, eyes straining unblinkingly and fixed on the corpse, and never glancing around you or letting your concentration waver, because those dreadful women have the power to change their shape and can creep up on you silently, transformed to any sort of creature they wish, defeating the sun's eye or the gaze of justice. They can look like dogs, or birds, or mice or even flies. Then they send the watcher to sleep with dreadful incantations. No one could count the number of tricks those evil women contrive to gain their wish. Yet only four or five pieces of gold are the pay for this dangerous task. Oh yes—I almost forgot to say—that if, by the morning, any piece of the body's face is damaged, the watcher must part with bits sliced from his own face to replace the portions removed."

So Thelyphron went to watch over the corpse:

Left alone to look after the corpse, I rubbed my eyes and readied them for vigil, keeping up my spirits by humming a song, as twilight fell and darkness came, then deeper darkness, and deepest hush, and at last the dead of night. Fear gradually crept over me. Suddenly a weasel appeared, halted in front of me, and fixed me with its piercing eyes. It was far too bold for such a tiny creature, and that was troubling. In the end I shouted: "Off with you, impure beast, go and hide with your weasel friends before you feel the weight of my hand, and make it quick! Off you go!"

It turned at once and fled from the confines of the room. Instantly I fell into a profound abyss of sleep. Even the god of Delphi would have had trouble deciding which of us in the room might be the corpse. I lay so motionless I was barely alive, and needed another watcher for myself.

The cockcrow from the crested ranks was sounding a truce to night when I woke at last and in a panic ran in terror to the body. I brought the lamp up close, uncovered the face, and examined it carefully item by item, but everything was there. Then the poor weeping wife entered the room with the witnesses as before. At once she fell anxiously on the corpse, kissing it long and passionately, and subjecting every detail to the lamp's judgement. Then she turned and summoned her steward, Philodespotos, and told him to give the successful guard his reward without delay. He paid me there and then. "We're extremely grateful to you, young man," she said, "and by Hercules in return for this dedicated service of yours we count you among our friends."

But then at the funeral something unexpected happened:

Statue of Pliny the Younger, author of an early ghost story, at the Dom S Maria Maggiore in Como, northern Italy. July 14, 2006 (Wolfgang Sauber, CCA-SA 3.0 Unported).

construction of the RAF airfield at Valley.[9] The finds are "primarily military" and included eleven swords, eight spearheads and parts of a parade shield. Equipment from several chariots was also present, both the harness and parts of the structure:

> Up to 22 chariots can be recognised from the wheels discovered, but this might indicate the offering of wheels alone (which are known to have been sacred to one of the Celtic gods) rather than complete

vehicles. Some items were locally manufactured, a few came from Ireland but a great many originated from southern England; a possible sign of trade, plunder captured from war or suggestive that the lake was more than a shrine of local importance. The dates of the finds are also of interest. Some of the swords are of types current in the 2nd century BC, others are of later designs, but nothing later than AD 60 can be identified.

While the Roman governor was fighting in Wales, a rebellion broke out in East Anglia (Suffolk, Norfolk and parts of Cambridgeshire) among the local tribe, the Iceni. According to Tacitus,[10] Prasutagus, the king of the Iceni "had named the emperor his heir, together with his two daughters; an act of deference which he thought would place his kingdom and household beyond the risk of injury." But this was far from the case:

> his kingdom was pillaged by centurions, his household by slaves; as though they had been prizes of war. As a beginning, his wife Boudicca was subjected to the lash and his daughters violated: all the chief men of the Icenians were stripped of their family estates, and the relatives of the king were treated as slaves.

The outraged Iceni then joined forces with the Trinovantes of Essex to revolt against the Romans. They first destroyed the nearest Roman town, Camolodunum (Colchester in Essex), then sacked London and Verulamium (St. Albans in Hertfordshire). According to Tacitus,[11] "close upon seventy thousand Roman citizens and allies fell in the places mentioned." Boudica was eventually defeated by the Roman governor, who had hastily returned from Wales—but before the final battle she addressed her troops[12]:

> Boudicca, mounted in a chariot with her daughters before her, rode up to clan after clan and delivered her protest:—"It was customary, she knew, with Britons to fight under female captaincy; but now she was avenging, not, as a queen of glorious ancestry, her ravished realm and power, but, as a woman of the people, her liberty lost, her body tortured by the lash, the tarnished honor of her daughters. Roman cupidity had progressed so far that not their very persons, not age itself, nor maidenhood, were left unpolluted. Yet Heaven was on the side of their just revenge: one legion, which ventured battle, had perished; the rest were skulking in their camps, or looking around them for a way of escape. They would never face even the din and roar of those many thousands, far less their onslaught and their swords!—If they considered in their own hearts the forces under arms and the motives of the war, on that field they must conquer or fall. Such was the settled purpose of a woman—the men might live and be slaves!"

According to another Roman historian Cassius Dio (155–235 CE), before joining battle Boudica made a stirring speech to her assembled troops[13]:

> When she had finished speaking, she employed species of divination, letting a hare escape from the fold of her dress; and since it ran on what they considered the auspicious side, the whole multitude shouted with pleasure, and Boudica, raising her hand toward heaven, said: "I thank thee, Andraste, and call upon thee as woman speaking to woman,"

Andraste was a goddess of victory, and Boudica was apparently a priestess as well as a queen.

Burial in Roman Britain

CREMATION AND INHUMATION

During the Roman period, burial was strictly controlled by the state, so everyone was either cremated or buried. Early Roman cemeteries in Britain tend to be cremation cemeteries, and it was only from the later 2nd century that cremation was gradually replaced by inhumation as the preferred rite.[14]

DECAPITATED BURIALS

The inhabitants of Roman Britain practiced a form of burial which was certainly not in line with Roman customs, the so-called "decapitated burial"—this is most commonly found in the 4th century, when the power of the Roman Empire was declining, and Christianity had not yet become established. In decapitated burials, the head is detached, presumably after death and before interment. Usually, says Dorothy Watts,[15]

> the head has been removed with care, with a sharp blade and with little damage, if any, to the bone. The cut is high, often between the second and third or third and fourth vertebrae. The body is then interred, with or without the head. If the head is present, as it usually is, it may be placed between the knees, the feet, the upper legs, outside the knees or feet, or on the pelvis. In a couple of published cases the head has been found outside the coffin or in the fill above it. Only rarely is it placed in its correct anatomical position.

Cemeteries with decapitated burials are found throughout Roman Britain, especially in the south. In 2007 Wessex Archaeology excavated a Roman cemetery at Little Keep, Dorchester (the Roman town of *Durnovaria*), 87 yards from the Roman cemetery at Poundbury, and 306 yards west of the Roman town walls. A total of 29 graves of late Romano-British date were excavated together with the remains of five truncated graves and a disturbed grave. There was clear archaeological evidence for the decapitation of five individuals, that is 17 percent of the burials; all were adults over 35 years of age, three were over 50, two were females and three were males. In each case, the skull and neck vertebrae above the point of severance had been placed at the distal end of the grave adjacent to or over the leg/ankle, though space for the head in the correct anatomical position was maintained within the grave.[16] Later, the bone specialist Jacqueline McKinley says that the "occurrence of so large a number of decapitations in one cemetery is rendered even more intriguing at Little Keep in that the practice is seen as a predominantly rural one, rarely seen and certainly far less common in large urban centres such as Roman Dorchester."

Another town where decapitated burials are found is Winchester (Roman *Venta Belgarum*) in Hampshire, at the Lankhills cemetery, just to the north of the Roman town, which dates mainly to the 4th century. In seven graves the head had been severed from the body and the skull, mandible, and uppermost vertebrae were discovered still articulated lying by the legs or feet.[17] Of the seven decapitated skeletons, three belonged to men, two to women, and one to a child.[18] The heads seem to have been severed from the front, between the third and fourth vertebrae, probably with a knife. Bone damage was minimal, suggesting a degree of precision perhaps possible only if the deceased was already dead when decapitated.[19]

One rural example of decapitated burials is the cemetery at Winterbourne Down, Pitton, to the east of the Roman town of *Sorviodunum* near Salisbury in Wiltshire. This was a 4th century Romano-British cemetery that contained 36 cremations and 14 inhumations. Of the 14 inhumations, three contained infant skeletons and one of these was accompanied by a pot containing an iron pin. Of the adults, five had been buried in coffins; two with coins, one of Constantine II (337–340), the other of Valentinian I (364–375). There were cleats and hobnails in five of the graves. Three adults had been decapitated.[20]

In 2008, human remains were recovered at Swanpool Walk, St. Johns, Worcester (Roman *Vertis*) during excavations ahead of proposed development of the land. Five grave cuts were discovered containing human skeletal remains, each representing an individual inhumation grave. Skeleton 1447 from the land off Swanpool Walk was found to have been decapitated, with the head having been placed in the grave by the feet; this burial contained the remains of a young adult, probably female.[21]

Excavations at the Roman town of Towcester in Northamptonshire (Roman *Lacto-durum*) revealed the remains of two decapitated young adult males dating from the 2nd to 4th centuries. In one case, the skull had been placed over the lower legs, while in the other the skull was in its correct anatomical position. Both males have evidence of peri-mortem trauma—trauma around the time of death—to the bones. The bodies were found in an urban Roman cemetery among the other burials, and the decapitation was not the cause of death. The cut marks show that the decapitation took place around the time of the death, but the clumsy manner of cutting and burial within the community cemetery suggest this was ritual rather than punishment.[22]

A Romano-British cemetery was excavated at Stanton Harcourt, Oxfordshire, in 1978. Thirty-four graves were identified, of which thirty-three were excavated. Thirty-four skeletons were recovered, two, an infant and an adult, from Grave 60. The graves were oriented north-south, and the majority of skeletons lay with the head to the north. Most of the skeletons were supine, but three lay face down. Three skeletons were found, each with a group of three coins from the middle of the 4th century; a further three had the head cut off and placed near the feet.[23]

There is no agreement on what the decapitated burials meant, and the archaeologist Katie Tucker lists seven of the explanations that have been put forward[24]:

- Cult of the Head. Greek and Roman writers says that the Gauls decapitated their enemies and displayed their heads, though their reports, which date from the early 1st century BC, refer to the south of France: there is evidence for such practices in the area around Aix-en-Provence, some 19 miles north of Marseille, which was annexed by Rome around 120 BC.
- Aiding passage to the afterlife
- Preventing the dead from returning. There is no written evidence for this in the Roman period, but there is evidence in the Middle Ages. For example, in the 12th century *Life and Miracles of St Modwenna*, Geoffrey of Burton (Staffordshire) wrote about the ghosts of two recently buried peasants returning to their village of Stapenhill, Derbyshire, and causing sickness and death amongst the inhabitants. In order to stop the haunting, the graves were re-opened and the heads of the corpses cut off and placed between their legs
- Punishment after death: There is a body of evidence from Roman literary sources and material culture for punishment after death in the form of decapitation of statuary of deposed and hated rulers, with the decapitation of corpses also being recorded, in one case with the head subsequently being carefully buried with the rest of the remains. The Roman poet Lucan (1st century AD) says that the head of the Roman general Pompey (assassinated in 48 BC) was removed before he had drawn his last breath; and the head of the Roman emperor Galba (assassinated in AD 69) was also cut off while he was still "half alive" (Tucker. pp.153–154).
- Human sacrifice
- Execution
- Warfare/Interpersonal violence

On the other hand, Belinda Crerar, a curator at the British Museum who specializes in Romano-British archaeology, prefers to look at decapitated burials in terms of frag-mented bodies—that is, decapitations and disarticulated bones. For her Ph.D. thesis she has studied decapitated burials in the following areas: Dorchester in Dorset, London (the Roman town of *Londinium*), and the Fen Edge in Cambridgeshire. In the case of Dorchester, Crerar can find little evidence for disarticulated bones in Roman cemeteries but points out that disarticulated bones have been found in Iron Age sites in Dorset, like the settlement at Gussage All Saints, and the hillfort of Maiden Castle near Dorchester (see Chapter 1). In London, disarticulated bone, along with decapitated burials, has been found in cemeteries in Southwark such as Lant Street and Trinity Street.[25] In addition over a hundred human skulls have been found in the Upper Walbrook Valley in Moorgate.[26]

On the Fen Edge in Cambridgeshire, Crerar studied three cemeteries—Babraham, Jesus Lane (Cambridge) and Foxton—which all contained decapitated burials. The cemetery at Foxton, some six miles south of Cambridge, contained two decapitated burials, but to appreciate the significance of these two burials, says Crerar,[27] "we must look beyond the limits of the cemetery itself. The inhumations within the bounded cemetery were not the only human remains to be discovered at Foxton. Two 'partial' human skeletons were discovered to the north of the site. One was a badly disturbed inhumation of a young adult female and nearby, in ditch [3091], the partial remains of an unsexed subadult/young adult were found. Furthermore, a nearby pit [3285] contained an articulated human arm." Overall, Goode and Bardill "record a total of 14 contexts from outside the cemetery area that contained human bone, mainly skull fragments, including individuals of all age groups and both sexes. We may add to this total the disarticulated and particularly-articulated human remains discovered within the backfill of the grave of headless female [3468], consisting of two adult male crania and an articulated left leg, as well as various other disarticulated adult and subadult bones."

Later Crerar notes[28] that "Foxton has produced the most evidence of other forms of corpse manipulation with possible evidence for exposure and excarnation." Excarnation of course was practiced at the Iron Age site of Godwin Ridge near Earith in the Cambridgeshire Fens, well to the north of Foxton.

OTHER DEVIANT BURIALS

Other deviant forms of burial haven been recorded in Roman Britain and have been explored by the archaeologist Alison Taylor. At the Roman cemetery of Guilden Morden, to the southwest of Cambridge, the archaeologist T.C. Lethbridge found the charred remains of a decapitated probable male. The individual's arms and lower legs also appear to have been removed and his skeleton was discovered lying in thick layers of charcoal. A nearby burial contained a disabled woman whose head had been severed as a consequence of a sideways cut and placed at her feet. Another woman from the cemetery had her head removed and placed in her lap[29]:

> I suggest, though this may appear fanciful, that this lame woman had been decapitated after her death to ensure that her spirit—perhaps bad-tempered owing to her infirmity—should not walk and haunt her relatives. The method of laying a ghost by decapitating a corpse was of course well known in later times ... one wonders if both of these women had been witches.

There were a number of prone (face down) burials in Romano-British cemeteries, thought to indicate outcasts of some sort. In cemeteries such as Bath Gate, Cirencester (Gloucestershire), 33 prone bodies displayed many signs of disrespect and one probably had his arms tied behind his back. In Colchester (Essex) the burials of two men located outside the cemetery boundary lay prone, with their wrists and ankles bound and the bones gnawed as if they had been left exposed for some time.[30]

There are also examples of "very secure burials, often of children with disabilities." At Poundbury in Dorchester (Dorset), a six-year-old child who was considered to have been congenitally deaf, was buried prone in a coffin that was made of, and covered by, stone roof tiles. At Arrington in Cambridgeshire a hydrocephalic infant, kept alive to about nine months of age, was buried in an oversized lead-lined coffin that lay a good six feet deep in heavy clay. The baby had been wrapped in a colored shawl, with aromatic resin packed around its face and a box of pipe clay figurines placed on top of the coffin. As the archaeologist Alison Taylor says[31]: "Loving care may have been demonstrated here, but care too was taken that the soul would pass safely to the afterlife and would not escape to trouble the living."

It seems that some Roman Britons did not have the same attitude to burial as their Roman masters. If Pliny the Younger is to be believed, a decent burial would satisfy the restless dead, while in Britain only special measures such as decapitation or prone burial would ensure that the dead stayed where they were.

The Temples, Shrines and Curse Tablets of Roman Britain

Jordan Hill Roman Temple, Weymouth (Dorset)

After the Romans occupied Britain, they established numerous towns like Dorchester, Winchester and London, and also numerous temples, most dedicated to Roman gods, but some also dedicated to British gods. Jordan Hill Romano-Celtic temple was situated on the South Dorset Downs on a south-facing chalk ridge overlooking Weymouth Bay to the south. The earliest feature on the site is thought to have been a large well-like pit or shaft, 4 feet by 3 feet and 12 feet deep. The sides were lined by roofing slabs set in clay and the fill consisted of 16 layers of ash and charcoal. Between the layers were pairs of roofing slabs, each with the remains of a bird (including buzzard, raven, starling and crow) and a bronze coin. There were also two cists within the fill, which held a range of artifacts. Based on the finds, the shaft is thought to have been constructed in the early Roman period (69–79 CE) and sealed during the Theodosian period (379–395 CE). Overlying the shaft was a structure, interpreted as the cella of a Roman-Celtic Temple, with stone footings 22 feet square and an entrance to the south. A thin concrete surface on the external sides is thought to have been the remains of a pavement for a colonnade or portico. A limestone base and Purbeck marble Tuscan capital were also found. A 275-foot-square outer enclosure with stone walls is thought to have surrounded the site and contained animal bones, numerous bull horns, pottery and hundreds of coins from Iron-Age to Roman in date.[32]

River Hamble (Hampshire)

A curse tablet was found in the mudflats of the River Hamble, to the east of Southampton. The nearest known Roman settlement to the Hamble is the small walled town of Bitterne, approximately 5 miles to the northwest. The tablet is dedicated to Neptune, the Roman god of the sea, and reads[33]:

Lord Neptune, I give you the man who has stolen the *solidus* and six *argentioli* of Muconius. So I give the names who took them away, whether male or female, whether boy or girl. So I give you, Niskus, and to Neptune the life, health, blood of him who has been privy to that taking-away. The mind which stole this and which has been privy to it, may you take it away. The thief who stole this, may you consume his blood and take it away, Lord Neptune.

Other curse tablets addressed to Neptune have been found in the River Thames at London, and in the River Tas at Caistor St. Edmund in Norfolk (Roman *Venta Icenorum*).[34] Neptune is also invoked in a folded lead tablet found in the Little Ouse at Brandon in Suffolk, near the border with Norfolk. This curses a thief who had stolen a pan, and sacrifices him to the god Neptune by hazel, a reference to drowning by holding under water with a hazel hurdle.[35]

HAYLING ISLAND (HAMPSHIRE)

There was a Late Iron Age shrine on Hayling Island near Portsmouth in Hampshire—one of the best authenticated examples of a Late Iron Age shrine in northwest Europe. The archaeologists who excavated the shrine identified two phases of use in the Late Iron Age. Three main elements formed the focus of the ritual ensemble in Phase I: "an enclosure (c. 25 × 25 m) with its entrance aligned to the east, an inner enclosure,

The River Little Ouse in Suffolk, where a Romano-British curse tablet addressed to the sea-god Neptune was found. April 5, 2009 (Bogbumper, CCA-SA 3.0 Unported).

also with an eastern entrance, and a pit set on the western margin of the inner enclosure." The coins associated with Phase I can all be dated to the early/mid–1st century BCE, up too around 30 BCE. In Phase II, the elements that replaced Phase I "used the same outer enclosure, but the inner enclosure was demolished to make way for the circular structure built around the central pit. The circular structure is made up of an inner gully, 9.2 m in diameter, with post-holes within it, presumably forming the foundation of the walling, and an outer gully of variable depth that appears to have served to drain water away from the structure's foundations."[36]

The objects deposited include a large number of coins, mainly coins of the immediate area, but also those of the peoples to the west and a significant number from Gaul, primarily from Armorica and central/northern Gaul, and some Roman republican coins. Analysis of the coins shows that they are relatively early in date, the majority being of the mid/late 1st century BCE, and that there may have been a gap in the practice of coin deposition in the early 1st century CE. Other votive material from the site includes two fragmentary "currency bars," fibulae (brooches), shield binding, iron spearheads, vehicle fittings and some fragmentary human remains. The "horse and vehicle equipment from phases I and II includes a three-link bridle-bit of cast bronze with bronze-cased iron rein rings, datable to the 1st century BC." One of the "more remarkable objects found was a bronze yoke-terminal with inlaid red enamel decoration on its terminal knob. It is without parallel in Britain, but is almost identical to examples from Mont-Beuvray," an oppidum near Autun (Saône-et-Loire) in the Burgundy region of eastern France. One significant ritual practice that the excavators noticed at the Hayling Island shrine is that many of the artifacts there were deliberately broken or bent, including several of the coins. The action of breaking or bending artifacts can be interpreted as indicating that the objects were "killed" in an act of dedication to the deity by rendering them useless.

In 55–60 CE the Iron Age shrine was replaced by a Roman temple, which continued in use until the early 3rd century. This circular structure, 47 feet in outside diameter with massive walls 4¾ feet thick, lay within a rectangular porticoed structure measuring 134 feet by 143 feet. The foundations of a square entrance porch abutted the circular building on the southeast. Excavations recorded tesserae from a mosaic or tessellated floor, painted wall plaster, plaster moldings and roof tiles. Other finds included pottery fragments, a fibula brooch, a bracelet, a gold torque, several animal bones and fourteen coins including one British issue, the rest being Roman and ranging from Augustus to Constantine II. The plan of the building and its monumental structure coupled with the small finds suggest that this was a religious center of some kind, or perhaps a mausoleum.[37]

WAYSIDE FARM, DEVIZES (WILTSHIRE)

In 1999 a small Romano-British cemetery and midden (the name that archaeologists give to an accumulation of domestic and animal waste) was excavated at Wayside Farm on the southeastern outskirts of Devizes. There were three closely spaced graves, all aligned approximately east-west. According to the archaeologists John Valentin and Stephen Robinson,[38] two of the individuals in the graves had been buried in coffins; two had been buried with hobnail boots; and complete pottery vessels were found in two graves. In one grave, the head was removed and placed toward the foot end of the grave, with a complete pottery vessel next to it.

TEMPLE OF NODENS, LYDNEY PARK (GLOUCESTERSHIRE)

The temple at Lydney Park in Gloucestershire was dedicated to the Nodens, a British god. Lydney Camp is a Late Iron Age promontory fort on the west bank of the Severn close to the Welsh border, established in or just before the 1st century BCE. In the 2nd and 3rd centuries CE the Romano-British population there were engaged in iron-mining and in the late 3rd or early 4th century the hillfort became the site of a Romano-British temple. The presiding deity at Lydney "is named as Nodens on the single curse tablet from the site and on two other metal plaques from the site as Mars Nodons and Nudens Mars." Among the votive objects (ritual deposits) found at the site are dog figurines—some are "highly schematic," but one figurine, possibly of an Irish wolfhound, is "amongst the most accomplished pieces of bronze sculpture from Roman Britain." Other ritual offerings include "the bone representation of a woman and a hollow bronze arm." The "discovery of an oculist's stamp (to be stamped into cakes of eye medicine)" suggests the presence of a healer at the temple.[55] Sea monsters and fish on the cella mosaic and bronze reliefs depicting a sea deity, fishermen and tritons suggest some connection of Nodens with the sea. A bronze object (headdress or vessel?) also shows a sea-god driving a chariot between torch-bearing putti (chubby male children) and tritons.[56]

Nodens appears in Irish mythology as Nuada, a legendary Irish king who lost a hand or arm in a battle and had it replaced by a silver hand or arm. In Welsh mythology Nodens became Nudd or Lludd and in the 11th century tale Culhwch and Olwen it is said of Gwyn son of Nudd that "God has placed [him] over the brood of devils in Annwn, lest they should destroy the present race."

One curse tablet is known from Lydney Park[57]:

> To the god Nodens: Silvianus has lost his ring and given half (its value) to Nodens. Among those who are called Senicianus do not allow health until he brings it to the temple of Nodens.
> (This curse) comes into force again.

CAERLEON, SOUTH WALES

Caerleon was a Roman legionary fort near Newport in south Wales and the single curse tablet known from Caerleon was found during excavations of the amphitheater by Sir Mortimer Wheeler in 1926 and 1927. The amphitheater was built in 80 CE, southwest of the legionary fortress. The Second Legion Augusta garrisoned the fortress from the late first to the fourth centuries CE, inscriptions demonstrating the soldiers also to be the builders of the amphitheater.

The curse tablet was found in the sand of the arena. It is addressed to the goddess Nemesis, to whom a chamber built over one of the minor entrances to the arena may have served as a shrine. In the rear wall of the chamber was a brick-built niche, perhaps housing a statue of the deity. Nemesis, a goddess of retribution, is frequently attested in Roman amphitheaters: dedications to the goddess have survived at Chester, for example. The curse tablet reads: "Lady Nemesis, I give thee a cloak and a pair of boots, let him who wore them not redeem them except with his life and blood."[58]

SPRINGHEAD, GRAVESEND (KENT)

At the heart of Springhead, at the head of the River Ebbsfleet near Gravesend in Kent, was a pool fed by eight natural springs, an unusually large number that made the

The ruins of the Roman amphitheater at Caerleon, Wales, where a curse tablet addressed to the goddess of vengeance Nemesis was found. January 14, 2007 (Greenshed at English Wikipedia).

site sacred to the Celts, who began settling there around 100 BCE. They called the site *Vagniacis* ("the place of marshes"). Excavation revealed a ceremonial way 650 yards long, sacred pits filled with animal remains and pots, as well as numerous coins. The Romans were also drawn to the site's religious significance after they invaded in 43 CE, though their first aim was to make sure their occupation was secure—they built what seems to have been a supply base at Springhead, reached by a road from the River Ebbsfleet. But the fact that the base was used only briefly, and no fort was built, suggests that Kent did not resist the invasion strongly.

It was not a military connection that made Vagniacis so important, but religion and trade. The Romans connected the area to the rest of the country when they put one of their roads, Watling Street, from Dover to London, right through Vagniacis. This would have brought to Vagniacis both travelers wanting to rest on their journey between the capital and the coast, as well as pilgrims attracted to the springs. We see this in the archaeological evidence for a succession of buildings put up on the side of the road, culminating in a complex of perhaps as many as a dozen temples established in the late 1st century CE.

By the end of the first century CE Vagniacis had a population of perhaps 1,000–2,000 and its central area was about 37 acres in area. Around the sacred pool was a walled sanctuary containing one, possibly two, shrines or temples, a large tree, a tank or bath, a small booth for baking bread, and several sacrificial pits where dead animals and pottery were placed. Overlooking the pool were platforms which may have been put up to allow visitors to view the sacred pool. Near the southern end of the pool was a structure which may have been a guest house where pilgrims were housed.

Strewn on the floors of some of Vagniacis's temples were votive offerings and religious paraphernalia, including a ceramic figurine of a goddess and a stone altar. In one temple the bodies of four children were buried: two were headless, probably decapitated after death as part of a religious ritual. In a bakery nearby were 14 other child burials. Whether these were human sacrifices or had simply died from natural causes, we cannot tell. Not far from the pool was a deep shaft filled with ritual deposits including one human and various animal skulls, perhaps buried there as part of a ritual.[59]

St. Albans (Hertfordshire)

The most interesting temple in Roman Verulamium (St. Albans in Hertfordshire) is one that was built on the site of a high-status Late Iron Age or early Roman burial. The site of the burial is approximately 500 yards northeast of Roman Verulamium. Centered on a single burial, an important cult complex with a large ceremonial enclosure (128 by 130 yards) developed in the middle of the 1st century CE, followed by a Romano-British temple on the site of the pyre in the Flavian period (late 1st century). In the first phase, an underground "funerary chamber" was constructed that probably served to display the corpse for several months. The body was exposed until the time for cremation had come. A large number of pre-burial funerary rituals seem to have taken place inside the chamber, which was accessible by a ramp. A gravel walkway around the central chamber may indicate that processions and dances took place. Funerary feasts around the displayed corpse are indicated by the conscious and ritualized deposition of pottery from the gravel walkway; pottery (Samian ware and amphorae) reflects libations and feasting. The dating of the artifacts (all burnt on the pyre) suggest that the cremation took place around 55 CE. Grave goods indicate the person's high status—these goods include luxury ivory furniture, rare pieces of horse tack, and a chain mail shirt. The cremated remains were buried just outside the site of the chamber. The buried remains weighed around 7 ounces instead of the expected 3.3–5.5 pounds, suggesting that the remaining bones were kept as "relics." All the objects associated with the funerary rituals and the burial were systematically destroyed, including all the grave goods. A Romano-British temple was constructed on the site of the pyre and remained in use until the 3rd century CE. South of the enclosure were 42 ritual shafts dated to between 150 and 250 CE. One contained a face pot, puppy bones, the bones of at least 34 cattle and, at the bottom of the shaft, a human skull that had been de-fleshed shortly after the person's death and displayed in the open prior to deposition. The ancient historian Ralph Haeussler suggests that Folly Lane "moved beyond the original meaning of a burial site to become the civic cult par excellence of Verulamium's patron 'deity' in the Principate."[60]

Cambridge

In the Roman period there was a defended settlement at Cambridge known as *Duroliponte*, centered on what is now Castle Hill, which was founded in the 2nd century and continued into the 5th century. In the late 2nd century, a timber shrine was constructed in Ridgeons Gardens just off Castle Street. It consisted of a subterranean cellar that was 26 feet long, 13 feet wide and 10 feet deep, with an apsidal end with a niche; several post-holes at the edges supported a substantial timber superstructure. Its religious associations are suggested by various finds in the immediate vicinity, including the burial of two dogs and a bull's head in the gravel flooring and an unusual sequence of animal burials in the ash layers derived from the building's early 3rd century destruction: they included a sac-rificed horse surrounded by seven complete pottery vessels, a bull and a sheep, and three dogs arranged in a triangular formation around a pot. Immediately above the ash layer a large quantity of pottery was found, including samian and color-coated wares, at least 256 flagons and a quantity of glass vessels, all suggesting some specific event such as a great feast. This was all sealed with clay and subsequent rubbish dumping. Northwest of the shrine lay a number of later 3rd and 4th century shafts. Each contained a mature dog and one or two infant burials in a wicker-work basket or on a rush mat, together with a pair of child's shoes.[61]

HADDENHAM (CAMBRIDGESHIRE)

At Haddenham in the Cambridgeshire Fens, not far from the Iron Age ritual site at Godwin Ridge, a Romano-Celtic shrine was placed on top of a Bronze Age barrow. The barrow had been deturfed in the mid–2nd century and a masonry-footed octagonal cell constructed on its southern edge, placed directly over a cluster of secondary cremations in the barrow ditch. In the floor of the octagon were many sheep mandibles with hooves laid out on either side, and in two cases a coin had been placed in the mandibles. In the northwest corner of the compound a series of intercutting pits contained four complete sheep skeletons, each accompanied by a pot. A boar burial was found in the southeast of the compound.[62] As well as the sheep, some 2,600 bird specimens were found among its 33,000 animal bones. The birds were predominantly domestic fowl, but "the assemblage also included such wild birds as pelican, coot, duck and geese," together with buzzard, heron and crow or rook. All were thought to have been sacrificed, "with the wild birds perhaps performing a role as winged messengers."[63]

RATCLIFFE-ON-SOAR (NOTTINGHAMSHIRE)

A curse tablet was found in 1960 on the lower slope of Red Hill in the parish of Ratcliffe-on-Soar (Nottinghamshire). Roman pottery, bone counters and other objects have been found on Red Hill, which appears to be a Roman site. It is at the junction of the rivers Trent and Soar (where also Nottinghamshire and Leicestershire meet). The curse tablet reads[64]:

> In the name of Camulorix and Titocuna I have dedicated in the temple of the god the mule (?) which they have lost. Whoever stole that mule (?), whatever his name, may he let his blood until the day he die. Whoever stole the objects of theft, may he die; and the (), whoever stole it, may he die also. Whoe(ver) stole it and the () from the house or the pair of bags (?), whoever stole it, may he die by the god.

Camulorix and Titocuna are both Celtic names: *Camulorix* is made up of *kamulo-* "cham-pion" and *rigo-* "king" (*Camulorix*, at the website Celtic Personal Names of Roman Brit-ain), while the second element of *Titocuna* is *kuno-* "hound" (*Titocuna*, at the website Celtic Personal Names of Roman Britain).

ANCASTER ROMAN TOWN (LINCOLNSHIRE)

Ancaster is in the south of Lincolnshire, on the site of a Roman town, and perhaps the most significant sculpture from Ancaster Roman town was discovered in 1831 while a grave was being dug in the southeastern corner of the churchyard of the parish church of St. Martin. The sculpture, which is 1 foot 7 inches long and 1 foot 4 inches high, shows three seated goddesses and represents the Romano-Celtic Mother-Goddess in triple form. When it was found the sculpture was still standing upright, facing south and had been placed on top of a rough stone block at one end of a massive 6 feet by 4 feet stone slab. At the southern end of the slab was a small, elaborately carved stone altar 1 foot high and 5 inches wide, which had been set on a stone disc 9 inches in diameter placed on top of a stone column 1 foot 8 inches high. The column itself stood on a stone block 5 inches by 15 inches by 15 inches. This somewhat curious arrangement gave the discoverers the impression that both the altar on the column, and the sculpture of the Mother-Goddesses were in their original positions and it seems possible that what the gravedigger had accidentally stumbled on was in fact the remains of a shrine or temple dedicated to the worship of the Mother-Goddess.

The three goddesses are seen here seated on a long couch with upright sides and back. They are all apparently pregnant and wear long dresses gathered under the bust and at the neck. The two surviving heads have shoulder-length hair. The goddess on the right-hand side is holding a round loaf of bread or possibly a corn measure in her right hand while the central figure holds a shallow basket of fruit, probably apples. The figure on the left holds a flat dish or tray, on which is an animal, perhaps a piglet or a lamb, in her left hand and a small "patera" or bowl in her right hand. The Mother-Goddesses are commonly depicted holding country produce of this type, and their worship was doubtless widespread among Romano-British agricultural communities.[65]

HESLINGTON EAST, YORK

Heslington East was a greenfield site approximately two miles southeast of York, owned by the University of York and designated for campus expansion. During field work carried out between 2007 and 2011, a Roman well dating to the second half of the 4th century was uncovered. In total, 1,067 animal bone fragments were recovered, at different levels of the well, here referred to as "fills." The second fill contained two adult female pig skulls, their unsophisticated butchering indicating the removal of the mandibles. Many of the other bones from this deposit, were disarticulated and appear to be associated with carcass processing and meat consumption, a total of 75 bones being butchered. These included many cattle-sized rib fragments but also eight horse bones that display marks most likely associated with carcass reduction. The presence of nine gnawed bones, unusual in the well, indicates that at least a portion of the bones were redeposited here. While this material together does not preclude structured deposition, it has the signature of redeposited refuse.

The third fill was the richest in terms of animal bones, yielding 476 fragments (although 159 were of frogs/toads, likely "pitfall" victims). It included a horse skull and two horned cattle skulls. Other, disarticulated bones are essentially those of cattle and horse. All major body parts from both are represented, while numerous paired bones for cattle and for horse suggest rapid disposal.

The fourth fill contained the majority of the bones from a red deer skeleton and two further skeletons, a dog and a calf. The deer skeleton is from a sub-adult individual between 13 and 16 months old. Based on an early summer birth, this animal was hunted in the summer or autumn of its second year. In the absence of any antlers or antler buds, it is presumably female. Cut marks to its left humerus indicate that the carcass was processed to some extent, although with all body parts present the animal was clearly not dismembered and its joints widely distributed. This fill also contained a pole-axed cattle skull from an adult animal and a large, complete red deer antler from a large mature stag.[66]

COVENTINA'S WELL, CARRAWBURGH ROMAN FORT (NORTHUMBERLAND)

Carrawburgh Roman fort near Hexham in Northumberland was probably constructed around 130 CE and remained in use until the 4th century. The most significant part of the fort is Coventina's Well (actually a spring or reservoir) which was excavated in 1876. The excavation revealed a spring encased in a rectangular basin, about 8 feet 6 inches by 7 feet 10 inches, which lay at the center of a walled enclosure or temple, measuring 40 feet north/south by 38 feet transversely within a wall 2 feet 11 inches thick. The contents of the well included at least 13,487 coins, from Mark Antony to Gratian, a relief of three water nymphs, the head of a male statue, two dedication slabs to the goddess Coventina, ten altars to Coventina and Minerva, two clay incense burners, and a wide range of votive objects.[67] Also found in the well were jewelry, bones, and many other objects. On one incense burner she is referred to as "Augusta," the only non–Roman goddess in Britain to receive this designation.[68]

Scotland in the Roman Iron Age

NEWSTEAD ROMAN FORT, MELROSE (SCOTTISH BORDERS)

Southern Scotland was only briefly part of the Roman Empire, and during this period a number of forts were established, including Newstead Roman fort near Melrose in the Scottish Borders. The fort was first excavated between 1905 and 1910 by Dr. James Curle, who revealed the outline of the Roman fort, details of internal buildings, three annex enclosures attached to the main fort, and a large temporary camp for the Roman army on the march. But the most remarkable discoveries came from an enigmatic set of deep pits. Curle records the excavation of 107 deep pits mostly in the South annex. The deepest went 36 feet down; most were cut to below the water table. From them came most of the finds that now make up the Newstead collection. The waterlogged fills of the pits preserved objects in especially fine condition. The surfaces of iron and bronze remain smooth and unpitted by corrosion. Organic materials—such as wood and leather—have survived their normal fate of decay in the soil. The range of the collection is immense. Two intricately decorated bronze wine jugs show how the refinements of Roman life reached even this remote part of the Imperial frontier. The series of three parade helmets, two with facemasks, stand for the highest quality of the display equipment of the Roman army, together with two decorated leather headpieces, or chamfrains, for the horses themselves.

In 1989, one of the annexes excavated by Curle was again excavated by the Newstead Project. A sequence of streets and wooden workshops was found, probably mostly for iron-working, and dating to the second century CE. The 1989 excavation also located the trenches dug by Curle in 1906, showing that his workmen had trenched the site very energetically, and had probably found all the deep pits in the South Annex, as he claimed. The top of one of the richest of these, Pit 22, was uncovered. It had been 23 feet deep, with a fill that contained an iron sickle, bridle pieces, leather, skulls of horse and dog, red deer antlers, and three of the four Newstead helmets. The new excavation found traces of structures around the top of this pit, and fixed its date as probably contemporary with the blacksmith's workshop next to

A new interpretation of the pits and their finds can now be proposed. They were probably dug as wells to serve the workshops, as there was a well for each workshop plot in the area examined in 1989. They were later deliberately filled in a ritual way, with rich votive deposits.[69]

SCULPTOR'S CAVE, MORAY FIRTH

Scotland north of the Forth and Clyde was never part of the Roman Empire, but it still traded with Rome. Sculptor's Cave at Covesea on the Moray Firth, northeast Scotland, takes its name from a series of Pictish symbols carved on its entrance walls. Sylvia Benton carried out the first series of excavations in 1929 and 1930, finding evidence for two major periods of activity. On the basis of associated metalwork, the earliest cultural deposits are dated to the Ewart Park phase of the Late Bronze Age, around 1000–800 BCE. A later occupation layer contained a rich assemblage of Roman Iron Age material (coins, rings, pins, beads, bracelets, toilet instruments etc.), ranging from the 2nd to the 4th centuries CE. The most striking feature of Sculptor's Cave is its substantial assemblage of human remains: Benton's excavations seem to have recovered around 1,800 human bones scattered throughout the deposits. In the late 1970s, Ian and Alexandra Shepherd carried out further excavations in the cave and found further Late Bronze Age metalwork and yet more bones, including several mandibles from juveniles, perhaps reflecting the display of the severed heads at the entrance to the cave. It has long been assumed that all the bones were of Late Bronze Age date, but radiocarbon dating of one of the bones produced a date of 231–395 CE, within the period referred to as the Roman Iron Age. It is possible the bones derive from two distinct episodes in the life of the cave: A Late Bronze Age episode in which "the remains mainly of children were deposited in the cave, with some emphasis on the placing of heads at the entrance," and a Roman Iron Age episode "represented by the remains of several decapitated individuals."[70]

The End of Roman Rule and the Arrival of the Anglo-Saxons

In 410 CE Alaric king of the Visigoths captured Rome, and around the same time the last Roman legions left Britain. The Western Roman Empire survived until the middle of the 5th century CE, when Germanic tribes like the Visigoths, the Burgundians and the Franks began occupying what was previously Roman Gaul. Meanwhile another group of Germanic people, now known as the Anglo-Saxons, were moving into the eastern parts of Roman Britain, bringing a new form of paganism to what would later become England.

3

Germanic Paganism, Magic and Witchcraft in Anglo-Saxon England

Britain After the Romans

In around 410 CE, the last Roman legions left Britain, and by the end of the 7th century, much of England and parts of southern Scotland were controlled by Anglo-Saxon kingdoms: Northumbria (England north of the Humber and southern Scotland), Mercia (the Midlands), East Anglia, Essex, Kent, Sussex and Wessex (Hampshire, Wiltshire, Dorset and Somerset). Information for the period immediately after the end of Roman rule is scarce, and most of what we know comes from one text, *On the ruin and conquest of Britain*, written in Latin by the British cleric Gildas in the first half of the 6th century.

According to Gildas, after the last Roman legions left, Britain was attacked by Picts and Scots (Irish), who occupied the north of Britain as far as Hadrian's Wall. Hoping for help from Rome, the inhabitants of Britain sent a letter (known as the "Groans of the Britons"), some time between 446 and 454 CE, to Aetius, a Roman general who was fighting insurgents in Gaul at the time. This help was not forthcoming, so a council was held "to deliberate what means ought to be determined upon, as the best and safest to repel such fatal and frequent irruptions and plunderings by the nations mentioned above."[1] The council along with the "proud tyrant" (*superbus tyrannus*) decided that "those wild Saxons, of accursed name, hated by God and men, should be admitted into the island, like wolves into folds, in order to repel the northern nations."[2]

After the "proud tyrant" invited the Saxons to settle in England, says Gildas, they arrived in three "keels" (*cyulae*) and settled in the "eastern part of the island," to be later joined by more of their countrymen. In inviting the Saxons to settle in Britain, the council and the "proud tyrant" were merely following the Roman practice of employing groups of "barbarians" to fight in their army in return for money, food and land: a treaty (*foedus*) was signed with these "barbarians," who were known as *foederati*.[3] However, the Saxons were not satisfied with the terms of the treaty, and "devastated all the neighbouring cities and lands."[4] There was constant conflict until the British united under a leader called Ambrosius Aurelianus, who defeated the Saxons at the Siege of Mons Badonicus (Mount Badon), whose location is unknown but much debated.

Gildas says that the Saxons settled in the "eastern part of the island," and the cemetery evidence supports this. The first Anglo-Saxon settlers practiced cremation, and there are early cremation cemeteries along the east coast of England, from East Yorkshire in the north to Norfolk in the south: these cemeteries include Sancton in East Yorkshire (near the Iron Age cemetery at Arras); Cleatham and Loveden Hill in Lincolnshire; and North Elmham in Norfolk. South of North Elmham there are mixed inhumation and cremation cemeteries: at Caistor St. Edmund in Norfolk (the site of the Roman town of *Venta Icenorum*, the tribal capital of the *Iceni*); West Stow in Suffolk; Mucking on the Thames Estuary in Essex; Ringlemere Farm, Woodnesborough near Sandwich in Kent; Bishopstone near Seaford in East Sussex; Highdown Hill near Worthing in West Sussex; Boscombe Down and Chessell Down on the Isle of Wight; and Winchester in Hampshire.

Horses in Germanic Paganism

Judging from the pottery and jewelry found in Anglo-Saxon cremation cemeteries in England, many of the settlers came from the Baltic coast of Germany, between the rivers Weser and Elbe, though some of them may have originated in Denmark or Sweden. We know from the Anglo-Saxon monk and historian Bede that the Anglo-Saxons were pagans when they settled in England, but we have less idea what that paganism consisted of. The Roman historian Tacitus, writing in the late 1st century CE about the "Germans" (that is, the people who lived in the Netherlands and Germany east of the River Rhine, as well as those living in Scandinavia), says that horses were important to the Germans[5]:

> It is peculiar to this people to seek omens and monitions from horses. Kept at the public expense, in these same woods and groves, are white horses, pure from the taint of earthly labour; these are yoked to a sacred car, and accompanied by the priest and the king, or chief of the tribe, who note their neighings and snortings. No species of augury is more trusted, not only by the people and by the nobility, but also by the priests, who regard themselves as the ministers of the gods, and the horses as acquainted with their will.

The importance of horses to the ancient Germans is underlined by the site known as Skedemosse bog on the island of Öland in the Baltic Sea off the southeast coast of Sweden. Excavations were conducted here in the 1950s and 1960 because gold arm rings had been ploughed up. Several depositions had been made in the former lake, starting around 2,000 years ago. Most of the oldest votive deposits at Skedemosse consist of animal bones. Common assemblages consist of horses' heads, hooves and tail bones, which have been interpreted as the result of horse-baiting or horse-racing. In several cases the bones show traces of marrow extraction, which indicates that the sacrifice was preceded by a meal. Among the bones there are also the remains of about 30 people who had been sacrificed. In the period 200 CE to 500 CE a large number of weapons, parts of weapons, and horse equipment were deposited, in several cases after having been subjected to fire, chopped into pieces, or bent. These finds are viewed as gifts to the gods for victory in battle. The most spectacular find from Skedemosse consists of seven gold arm rings, which weigh a total of almost 3 pounds.[6]

Why did the excavators find heads, hooves and tail bones? One historical account from 950 CE gives us some guidance. While visiting the Scandinavian market town of Hedeby (in modern-day north Germany), the Arab tradesman al-Tartuschi witnessed villagers placing animal heads on poles to honor their gods during a celebration. Similar practices have been recorded by anthropologists working in Central Asia where, among the Altai people, horses are often sacrificed and then skinned in a way that leaves the head, hoofs, and hide as a single piece. This hide, with its extremities, is then placed on a long pole, using the tip of the pole to support the back of the horse cranium.[7]

Horse sacrifice is also found in Denmark. At Valmose near Rislev on the large island of Zealand, one of the horses was found *in situ* with its tail placed in its mouth with the thick end first, after the animal's tongue was removed; the lower extremities of the horse were also present. Altogether eleven horses were found at Valmose—six of them were deposited with head, hooves and tail. The sacrifice was dated to the 4th or 5th century CE. The remains of four humans were also found at Valmose, two of them dated to the pre–Roman Iron Age (380 BCE and 335–225 BCE).

The Hjortspring boat, found on the island of Als off the coast of southeast Denmark, is the oldest of the Iron Age weapon sacrifices, and wood from the boat has been radio-carbon dated to 350–300 BCE. It is most famous for the find of the well-preserved boat, but at least one horse was found nearby, in the southeast corner of the excavation area. It had been deposited on its back, partly under the boat, so that ribs and long bone had perforated the board planks. Its head, which was found about 3 feet from the rest of the skeleton, was turned the right way up. The lower jaw was in its place and the tongue bone lay *in situ* in the peat. In the horse's mouth one of its splint-bones (a bone in the leg) had been deliberately placed between the mandibles in the same position as the tongue.[8]

One of the most famous Iron Age sites in Demark is Illerup Adal in the east of Jutland. Following drainage work in 1950 archaeologists found large numbers of bent swords, spears, lances and arrowheads from the Iron Age that had been sacrificed to the gods by being submerged in the lake, which at that time covered the area. Until now more than 15,000 objects have been found, mostly weapons and the warriors' personal equipment. Digging is still going on, since it is believed that at least as much material remains in the ground. Some objects have been dated, and it has been demonstrated that they date from between 200 CE and 450 CE. The first sacrifice in 200 CE was by far the largest. More than 150 personal items, nearly 1,000 spear and lance heads, about 100 swords, more than 300 shields and bows, arrows, axes, tools and more than 10 harnesses for horses were sacrificed in the water.[9] The remains of horses were also found—they show severe head injuries as a result of blows from sharp, heavy objects. The archaeologist Jorgen Ilkjaer describes how several horses were led out into the water, cut to pieces and left where they fell. A hind leg of a horse was packed together with weapons in a piece of cloth and deposited with them in the lake.[10]

Horses in Anglo-Saxon Paganism

Horses played a prominent role in the burial rites of the pagan Anglo-Saxons of East Anglia. Mound 17 at Sutton Hoo in Suffolk contained a young warrior and a horse and was excavated by Martin Carver's team in 1991. The excavation revealed two grave pits under the mound, one containing a young man and the other containing a horse. The horse was a stallion or gelding, five or six years old and about 14 hands (56 inches) high. The young man was aged about twenty-five years and had been buried in a rectan-gular wooden coffin fitted with iron clamps. At his side there was a long sword with a

The sacrificial moor at Illerup Adal in Denmark, where bent weapons were thrown into what was then a lake. April 26, 2014 (Sten, CCA-SA 3.0 Unported).

horn pommel, together with an iron knife in a leather sheath. The buckle of his sword-belt was made of bronze inlaid with garnets. A small cloth-lined leather purse or pouch had been placed by his shoulder, containing seven rough-cut garnets, a single garnet in the shape of a bird's beak, and a fragment of red and blue glass.

Underneath the coffin were two spears and a shield with an iron boss; the coffin had been laid on top of the shield boss and had canted over at the time of burial. Alongside the left (north) edge of the coffin were an iron-bound bucket, a bronze cauldron with an earthenware cooking pot stacked inside it, and a handful of lamb chops propping up a bronze bowl. The cauldron had probably contained some perishable material such as grain, which had decayed and been replaced by sand from the grave fill, and the lamb chops and the bronze bowl had originally been in some kind of haversack or kit bag, along with some other perishable food (perhaps bread or fruit).

At the west (head) end of the grave pit a splendid horse harness was found—a bit with gilt-bronze cheek pieces, joined to reins, nose-band and brow-band. The strap connectors were gilt-bronze and covered in animal ornament, decorated with ax-shaped bronze pendants. Two gilt-bronze strap-ends were decorated in the form of human faces. Fragments of leather and wood on top of the harness were probably from a saddle, and on top of that was a tapering wooden tub for feeding the horse. Leaning against the coffin side, as if it had been dropped into the grave at the last minutes, was a comb.[11]

A similar burial was found in a grave at RAF Lakenheath near Mildenhall in Suffolk. The grave contained the body of a man in his mid–30s. He was 5 feet 10 inches tall with a muscular build. There was no obvious cause of death and his bones suggest he would

Sutton Hoo Mound 2, the only Sutton Hoo tumulus to have been reconstructed to its estimated original height. October 3, 2010 (Geoff Dallimore, CCA-SA 2.5 Generic, 2.0 Generic and 1.0 Generic).

have been in pretty good health. This man was buried in a wooden coffin with his sword and his shield and spear would have been laid on top. Close by were cuts of lamb—perhaps for a meal in the afterlife. A horse wearing decorative bridle fittings was also buried with him and a wooden bucket close to the horse's head suggests that perhaps he too was left a final meal. We do not know the funeral rites of his people, but horses were valuable to Saxon people and this one was sacrificed, probably at the grave site, to join the warrior in the afterlife.[12]

The Boar in Germanic and Anglo-Saxon Paganism

According to Tacitus, the Aestii, who lived on the Baltic, possibly between present-day Poland and Lithuania, "worship the mother of the gods, and wear as a religious symbol the device of a wild boar. This serves as armour, and as a universal defence, rendering the votary of the goddess safe even amidst enemies."[13]

The importance of the boar in Germanic paganism is apparent in both Sweden and England. Helmet plates from the ship graves at Vendel (Sweden) show warriors with immense boar crests on their helmets, and one man wearing what is almost a boar mask, with huge protruding tusks. The early kings of Uppsala (Sweden) were said to have had great boar helmets as treasures, with names like *Hildisvin* ("Battle-Swine").[14]

Boars are found on a small number of Anglo-Saxon helmets in the English Midlands. The Benty Grange helmet was found in 1848 by Thomas Bateman in an early medieval barrow at Benty Grange Farm in the Derbyshire Peak District. The helmet is crested with an iron boar with bronze eyes inset with garnet that sits upon an elliptical copper plate.[15] A similar helmet, known as the Pioneer Helmet, was found in a quarry operated by Pioneer Aggregates at Wollaston near Wellingborough in Northamptonshire. A simple iron boar crest adorns the top of this helmet. The helmet accompanied the burial of a young male, possibly laid on a bed with a pattern welded sword, small knife, hanging bowl, three iron buckles and a copper alloy clothes hook[16]

Boar-helmets are mentioned in the Old English epic *Beowulf*. We are told in the saga of Finn (a legendary Frisian king)[17]:

> The pyre was heaped
> with boar-shaped helmets
> forged in gold,
> with the gashed corpses
> of well-born Danes—
> many had fallen.

Later, Beowulf dons his armor to fight Grendel's Mother, and the poet describes his helmet:

> To guard his head he had a glittering helmet
> That was due to be muddied on the mere-bottom
> and blurred in the upswirl. It was of beaten gold,
> princely headgear hooped and hasped
> by a weapon-smith who had worked wonders
> in days gone by and embellished it with boar-shapes

Anglo-Saxon Paganism and Prehistoric Monuments

The archaeologist Sarah Semple, in a 2007 paper, analyzed placename evidence and the term *hearg*, which in Old English is thought to mean temple, holy place, idol or altar, to identify potential temple sites. She found these place name types to be spatially apart from settlement, burial or the square enclosures identified by John Blair, but to be associated instead with seemingly natural features and on hilltops, low, or distinctive rises of land. By investigating three *hearg* sites—Harrow Hill (Sussex), Harrow Fields (Cheshire) and Wood Eaton (Oxfordshire)—she concluded that these places occupy dramatic topographies and also seem to be associated with long term use of a particular place from prehistory through the Roman occupation of Britain and into the early Middle Ages. The landscapes of the three case studies yielded finds to suggest these places had held their significance over long periods of time and held cultic significance to the pre–Christian occupants of 6th–7th century England. Semple argues that *hearg* does not refer to a religious structure but "a naturally significant location that formed a place of gathering and ritual for many generations…. Christianity cut short their active lives, weaving them into a mythology of landscape aligned to stories and tales of religious conversion."[18]

The three sites investigated by Semple do indeed have a long history. Harrow Hill near Patching in West Sussex, which rises 550 feet above sea level, was the site of a Neolithic flint mine and a Late Bronze Age/Early Iron Age enclosure; there was also a Romano-British settlement on the south side of the hill, and two Anglo-Saxon barrows on New Barn Down, the name given to the southeastern spur of Harrow Hill.[19]

Harrow Fields is near Thurstaston in the Wirral, northwest England. The collection of nine field names sits across low ground lying close to the estuary and marked by numerous fresh water springs. In 1992 the Field Archaeology section of Liverpool Museum undertook an extensive fieldwalking survey in advance of a proposed development. The site investigated is the ridge lying some 500 yards from the *hearg* placename cluster. Extensive Mesolithic activity is present, with lithic scatters "indicative of specialist activities being carried out across the area and some evidence for a base camp in the immediate vicinity."[20] Some Neolithic activity is evident, and the Bronze Age flint "implies settlement evidence with tools indicative of food processing or clothing production."[21] The whaleback ridge has also produced "the densest concentration of Romano-British finds in the Wirral, with the exception of the well-known first millennium AD trading site of Meols." Twelve to fourteen brooches of the 1st to 2nd centuries CE have been recovered from the fields adjacent to the Thurstaston rectory on Telegraph Road. A bronze key and seven Roman coins ranging from the 1st to the 3rd centuries CE come from the same location. A substantial settlement is implied, almost certainly in the Rectory Field, to the east of Telegraph Road. Finally, a small-long brooch, dating to 500–575 CE was also retrieved in the rectory field, the only early Anglo-Saxon find from rural Merseyside.

Middle Hill at Wood Eaton near Oxford was the site of a Romano-British cult center active throughout the Roman period. There is also clear evidence that the area around the temple was occupied from the Early Iron Age. Brooches and pins of Iron Age date "form a considerable component of the overall assemblage, along with a late La Tène scabbard chape." Bronze-working evidence recovered during excavations in the 1960s "led Harding to conclude that the site was important from at least the middle of the first millennium BC, with an industrial role and possible cultic importance."[22] In 1406 a field near Wood Eaton is recorded as *Harrowdonehyll* (Harrowdown Hill), suspected to be the hilltop location of the temple.[23]

The Anglo-Saxon settlers often buried their dead on the sites of prehistoric monuments. The most popular prehistoric monuments were Bronze Age round barrows, with communal cemeteries of over 50 burials at Abingdon Saxton Road in Oxfordshire and Bishopstone in Sussex.[24] There were also Anglo-Saxon burials in Neolithic long barrows—for example at Bowls Barrow and King Barrow in Wiltshire, Burn Ground, Hampnett (Gloucestershire) and the Poles Wood long barrows, Upper Swell (Gloucestershire). Hillforts were also reused for burials, including Blewburton Hill in Oxfordshire and Highdown Hill in Sussex. Burials have also been found in Neolithic henges, for example at Long Hanborough in Oxfordshire.[25] Early Anglo-Saxon burials have been found inside or next to Roman temples and shrines, at Maiden Castle (Dorset), Lowbury (Oxfordshire), Frilford (Oxfordshire), Benwell (Newcastle upon Tyne), and Swaffham Prior (Cambridgeshire).[26]

The Anglo-Saxons and Watery Places

Judging from Skedemosse in Sweden and Illerup Adal in Demark, watery places played a significant role in Germanic paganism, and they also exercised a strong hold on the Anglo-Saxon imagination. For example, in the Old English epic poem *Beowulf*, which may date from the 8th century, the monster Grendel and his mother live in a "mere," that is a lake. In the poem, one of the Danes tells Beowulf how to find Grendel and his mother[27]:

> They are fatherless creatures,
> and their whole ancestry is hidden in a past
> of demons and ghosts. They dwell apart
> among wolves on the hills, on windswept crags
> and treacherous keshes, where cold streams
> pour down the mountain and disappear
> under mist and moorland. A few miles from here
> a frost-stiffened wood waits and keeps watch
> above a mere; the overhanging bank
> in a maze of tree-roots mirrored on its surface.
> At night there, something uncanny happens:
> the water burns. And the mere-bottom
> has never been sounded by the sons of men.
> On its bank, the heather-steppe halts:
> the hart in flight from pursuing hounds
> will turn to face them with firm-set horns
> and die in wood rather than dive
> beneath its surface. That is no good place.

Water was a place of horrors, perhaps because of its pagan associations, and could even be the gateway to Hell. It has been recognized since the late 19th century that the description of Hell in *Blickling Homily XVII*, which dates from the 10th century, closely matches the passage in *Beowulf* that describes Grendel's Mother's mere. Here is the passage from *Blickling Homily XVII*[28]:

> Thus St. Paul was looking into the north of this middle earth, where all waters depart downwards, and there he saw over the water a certain hoary stone. And north of the stone were growing very frosty groves, and there were dark mists, and under the stone was the dwelling of monsters and water monsters. And he saw that on the cliffs in the icy woods many dark souls were hanging bound by their hands, and then the devils in the likeness of water monsters were seizing them, just as a greedy wolf. And that water was dark under the cliff below, and between the cliff and the water were approximately twelve miles. And when the branches broke, then the souls departed downward, those who on the branches were hanging, and the water monsters seized them.

In both texts the waters tumble down, there are mists, frosty groves, and trees on the cliff that overhangs the mere. In the *Blickling Homily*, the water contains water monsters, and we know that the mere in *Beowulf* contains Grendel's Mother.

This association between water and monsters, demons and pagan gods may explain why so many Anglo-Saxon churches and monasteries were sited near rivers or the sea—their location would reassure nervous Anglo-Saxons that all the monsters and demons of their pagan past were now under the control of the Church and could not harm them.

Ritual Curses in Anglo-Saxon Legal Documents

Ritual curses were widespread in the Roman Empire, including Britain, and they soon became part of Anglo-Saxon legal documents, especially charters granting land to monasteries or individuals. Here is a particularly lurid example from a grant of land in Amounderness (Lancashire) made by King Æthelstan in 934 CE[29]:

> If, however, which God forbid, anyone puffed up with the pride of arrogance shall try to destroy or infringe this little document of my agreement and confirmation, let him know that on the last and fearful Day of Assembly when the trumpet of the archangel is clanging the call and bodies are leaving

the foul graveyards, he will burn with Judas the committor of impious treachery, and also with the miserable Jews blaspheming with sacrilegious mouth Christ on the altar of the Cross in eternal confusion in the devouring flames of blazing torments in punishments without end.

Not all curses were as graphic as this—here is an early curse in a Kentish charter dated 679 CE which is simple and to the point: "Whoever dares to go against this donation shall be separated from all Christianity and suspended from the body and blood of Our Lord Jesus Christ." The same charter has a postscript which elaborates on the first curse: "if anyone acts differently, he shall know himself to be damned by God and on the Day of Judgement give account to God with his soul."[30]

These two curses threaten excommunication and damnation, and both these penalties are invoked in another Kentish charter from 765 CE[31]: "Yet if someone attempts to break my donation on account of an envious and malevolent heart, he shall be separated from participating in the body and blood of our Lord Jesus Christ in this age and he shall be separated from the union of all the saints in the future, unless he earlier corrects his presumptuousness with proper amends."

Sometimes curses spell out the meaning of damnation, as in this charter from 960 CE, in which King Edgar grants land at Bishopstoke (Hampshire)[32]: "If someone wants then to turn our donation into anything other than what we have constituted, deprived of the holy community of God's church he shall be punished perpetually as a deplorable person in the eternal fires of the abyss together with Judas, the traitor of Christ, and his accomplices, unless he make suitable amends for what he did wrong against the decree."

Another charter, from 940 CE (a grant of land in Overton, Hampshire, by King Edmund) is even more explicit about the torments of damnation[33]: "Finally, if some people, what I do not wish, oppressed by envy aspire to violate this charter of privilege, falling through the troops of hideous gloom, they shall hear the voice of the Judge, who says to them: 'Depart from me, ye cursed, into everlasting fire,' where they shall be tormented in iron cauldrons by demons with cruel punishment, unless they correct it with proper penitence before their death."

All these curses are of course written, but they may have begun as oral curses. Consider the following passage from a land grant,[34] made some time between 926 and 941 by the Archbishop of Canterbury:

And Archbishop Wulfhelm and all the bishops and abbots who were there assembled excommunicated from Christ and from all the fellowship of Christ and from the whole of Christendom anyone who should ever undo this grant or reduce this estate in pasture or in boundary. He shall be cut off and hurled into the abyss of hell for ever without end. And all the people who stood by said "So be it, Amen, Amen."

Anglo-Saxon Spells and Charms

Ritual curses are a kind of magic, but spells and charms are even more directly magical. One of the most revealing spells/charms is the *Æcerbot*, or "Field Remedy," which hints at Anglo-Saxon pagan veneration of the sun and the earth mother[35]:

Here is the remedy by which you can improve your fields, if they will not grow properly, or if any harm has been done to them by sorcery or witchcraft.
Take then at night before daybreak four sods from four sides of the land and mark how they stood before.

Then take oil and honey and yeast and milk of all the cattle that are on the land, and part of
every kind of tree growing on the land, except hard trees, and part of every well-known herb,
except burdock only, and pour holy water on them, and let it drip three times on the bottom of
the sods.

And then say these words:

Crescite, grow, *et multiplicamini*, and multiply, *et replete*, and fill, *terram*, the earth. *In nomine
patris et filii et spiritus sancti sitis benedicti.*

And Our Father as often as the other.

And afterwards carry the sods to the church and have a priest sing four Masses over the sods,
and turn the green sides to the altar. And afterwards take the sods back to where they stood
before, before the setting of the sun.

And he must have four crosses made of "quickbeam" (aspen-wood) and let him write at the end
of each: Mattheus and Marcus, Lucas and Johannes. Lay the cross at the bottom of the pit
(made by cutting away the sods).

Say then:

Crux Mattheus. Crux Marcus. Crux Lucas. Crux Sanctus Johannes.

Then take the sods and lay them on the crosses. And say then nine times these words: *Crescite*
and as often the Our Father.

And then turn to the east and bow humbly nine times, and say then these words (lines 30–42):

Eastwards I stand, for favours I pray.
I pray the great Lord, I pray the mighty prince,
I pray the holy Guardian of the heavenly kingdom.
Earth I pray and sky,
and the true holy Mary,
and heaven's might and high hall,
that by the grace of the Lord
I may pronounce this charm, by my firm will
Raise up these crops to our worldly benefit,
fill this earth by firm faith,
make beautiful these grasslands; as the prophet said
that he would have favours on earth
who dealt out alms judicially, according to the will of the Lord.

Then turn three times with the course of the sun, then stretch yourself along the ground and
say the litany there. And then say *Sanctus Sanctus Sanctus* until the end. Sing then *Benedictine* with arms outstretched and *Magnificat* and Our Father three times. And commend it
(the land) to Christ and Holy Mary, and to the Holy Rood [Cross] in praise and worship,
and to the benefit of the owner of the land and all those who are subject to him.

When all this is done, then take unknown seed from beggars and give them twice as much as you
take from them. And collect all the ploughing implements together, bore a hole in the plough-
tail and put incense and fennel and hallowed soap and hallowed salt in it.

Then take the seed and place it on the body of the plough. Say then (lines 54–69):

Erce, Erce, Erce, mother of earth,
May the omnipotent eternal Lord grant you
fields growing and thriving,
flourishing and bountiful,
bright shafts of millet-crops,
and of broad barley-crops,
and of white wheat-crops,
and of all the crops of the earth.
May the eternal Lord grant him
And his saints who are in heaven,
that his produce may be safe against every foe,
and secure against every harm

from witchcraft sown throughout the land.
Now I pray the Sovereign Who created this world
that no woman may be so eloquent, and no man so powerful
that they can upset the words thus spoken.

When you drive forth the plough and cut the first furrow, say then:

Hail to thee, earth, mother of men,
may you be fruitful under God's protection,
filled with food for the benefit of men.

Then take flour of every kind and have a loaf baked as big as the palm of your hand, and
     knead it with milk and with holy water, and lay it under the first furrow.
Say then:

Field full of food for the race of men
brightly blooming, be thou blessed
in the holy name of Him Who created heaven
and the earth of which we live.
The God Who made this earth
grant us the gift of fertility
that each grain may be profitable to us.

Then say three times: *Crescite. In nomine patris sitis benedicti, Amen.* And Our Father three
     times.

As Gotfrid Storms points out,[36] this text, which dates from the first half of the 11th century, is "unique as a specimen of Anglo-Saxon agricultural rites. Though Christian influences, in the form of texts from the Old and New Testaments, of Masses, holy names and holy objects, have penetrated everywhere, the old heathen practices and formulas have kept their ground and are recognisable throughout." The text, says Storms, "reveals something of an older religion, for the words that are spoken are hymns rather than charms. Lines 30–42 constitute a hymn to the sun and lines 54–69 constitute a hymn to mother earth."

The hymn to mother earth is easy to explain. The Roman historian Tacitus mentions an earth goddess, Nerthus, when he is discussing the *Langobardi* (Lombards) who probably lived in southern Scandinavia[37]:

The Langobardi, by contrast, are distinguished by the fewness of their numbers. Ringed round as they are by many mighty peoples, they find safety not in obsequiousness but in battle and its perils. After them come the Reudingi, Aviones, Anglii, Varini, Eudoses, Suarini and Nuitones, behind their ramparts of rivers and woods. There is nothing noteworthy about these peoples individually, but they are distinguished by a common worship of Nerthus, or Mother Earth. They believe that she interests herself in human affairs and rides among their peoples. In an island of the Ocean stands a sacred grove, and in the grove a consecrated cart, draped with cloth, which none but the priest may touch. The priest perceives the presence of the goddess in this holy of holies and attends her, in deepest reverence, as her cart is drawn by heifers. Then follow days of rejoicing and merry-making in every place that she designs to visit and be entertained. No one goes to war, no one takes up arms; every object of iron is locked away; then, and only then, are peace and quiet known and loved, until the priest again restores the goddess to her temple, when she has had her fill of human company. After that the cart, the cloth and, if you care to believe it, the goddess herself are washed in clean in a secluded lake. This service is performed by slaves who are immediately afterwards drowned in the lake.

Nerthus appears to be related to related to the Norse pagan god Njordr. The difference of sex between Nerthus and Njordr "is probably less of a barrier to the identification than it might appear at first sight; for according to the mythology, Njordr's son and daughter, Freyr and Freyja, who also have names that are closely related etymologically, were twins, so it is not inconceivable that Nerthus and Njordr represent twin sibling deities too."[38]

Nerthus' oxen-drawn cart has been linked with the chariot of the goddess Freyja, though this was pulled by a pair of cats. Carts may have had a ritual function: at Oseberg in Norway, two women were buried with a Viking ship in 834 CE, along with a richly carved four-wheel wooden cart.[39] This ritual function is underlined in a 14th century Icelandic tale. Gunnarr, a Norwegian suspected wrongly of murder, flees to Sweden where there was a vigorous cult of Freyr. He ingratiates himself with a young woman (perhaps a priestess) who is locally regarded as the god's wife. Toward the end of each year Freyr, in the form of a wooden effigy, accompanied by his "wife," was drawn by servants in a cart through the Swedish countryside to promote fertility, much like Nerthus in Tacitus' *Germania*. Gunnar joins Freyr's tour, but their progress is slowed by blizzards and Gunnarr antagonizes the god by resting in his cart. Freyr attacks him; but Gunnarr remembers the Christian God worshipped by King Olafr back in Norway and manages to defeat Freyr, who departs, leaving behind his effigy, which Gunnarr destroys.[40]

However, the cult of the sun is more difficult to account for. The sun was extremely important in the Nordic Bronze Age, as we know from the Trundholm Sun Chariot, which was found in a bog on the large island of Zealand in Demark and which dates from around 1400 BCE. However, the sun is apparently a less significant figure in the Iron Age, and Maria Kvilhaug[41] believes that the Bronze Age sun deity was a goddess who survived in the form of the Old Norse goddess Freyja (Anglo-Saxon Frige), who rode in a chariot and owned a necklace called Brisingamen ("Necklace of Flames"). Freyja can be linked to a Bronze Age goddess figurine who drives a cart, wears a necklace and has golden eyes.

There were numerous spells and charms against disease in Old English, and here is one of the better-known ones, from the Old English collection called *Lacnunga* ("Remedies")[42]:

Against Rheumatism

Boil feverfew and the red nettle that grows through [the wall of] a house and plantain in butter.

Loud they were, lo, loud, when they rode over the mound,
they were fierce when they rode over the land.
Shield yourself now that you may survive their ill-will.
One little spear, if you are in here!
I stood under linden-wood, under a light shield,
where the mighty women betrayed their power,
and screaming they sent forth their spears.
I will send them back another,
a flying arrow from in front against them.
One little spear, if you are in here!
A smith was sitting, forging a little knife,
......
Out little spear, if you are in here!
Six smiths were sitting, making war-spears.
Out, spear, not in, spear!
If there is a particle of iron in here,
the work of hags, it shall melt!
Whether you have been shot in the skin, or shot in the flesh,
or shot in the blood, [or shot in the bone],
or shot in a limb, may your life be never endangered.
If it be the shot of Aesir, or the shot of elves,

or the shot of hags, I will help you now.
This as your remedy for the shot of Aesir, this for the shot of elves,
This for the shot of hags, I will help you.
Fly to the mountain head.
Be whole. May the Lord help you.

Then take the knife and dip it in the liquid.

This charm serves as a cure for stinging pain, suddenly felt by the victim and supposedly caused by "mighty women," hags, elves and gods. Nobody knows for certain what elves were in pagan times. In Norse mythology they are often mentioned after the *Aesir*, the chief group of gods. They are also mentioned in the Old English epic *Beowulf*, in relation to the monster Grendel[43]:

> Grendel was the name of this grim demon
> haunting the marshes, marauding round the heath
> and the desolate fens; he had dwelt for a time
> in misery around the banished monsters,
> Cain's clan, whom the Creator had outlawed
> and condemned as outcasts. For the killing of Abel
> the eternal Lord had exacted a price:
> Cain got no good from committing that murder
> because the Almighty made him anathema
> and out of the curse of his exile there sprang
> ogres and elves and evil phantoms
> and the giants too who strove with God
> time and again until He gave them their reward.

Anglo-Saxon Witchcraft

DOCUMENTARY EVIDENCE OF WITCHCRAFT

It is clear from the *Æcerbot* that the Anglo-Saxons believed in witchcraft, and possibly the first reference to witchcraft comes from an Anglo-Saxon charter which dates from the years between 963 and 975 and records the execution of a widow from Ailsworth near Peterborough and the forfeiture of her lands on account of witchcraft[44]:

> they drove pins into an effigy of Wulfstan's father Ælfsige. And it was detected and the murderous instrument dragged from her chamber; and the woman was seized, and drowned at London Bridge, and her son escaped and became an outlaw.

The details here are rather scarce, and a better recorded story of witchcraft occurred in the time of Æthelric, Bishop of Dorchester-on-Thames (Oxfordshire) from 1016 to 1034. It was reported in the *Ramsey Chronicle* (Ramsey Abbey was a monastery in the Cambridgeshire Fens, not far from the Romano-British temple at Haddenham), and involved a Danish man called Thurkill[45]:

> Thurkill's wife died, leaving him with one son. He remarried, but his new wife was jealous of her husband's love for her stepson. She called in the services of a witch to make the father stop loving his child. The witch's spells were so successful that Thurkill rejected the boy, but this didn't satisfy the wife, who wanted her own children to be her husband's own heirs; so while Thurkill was away she murdered her stepson, and buried him in a meadow with the witch's help. When Thurkill returned, she told him the boy had just disappeared and couldn't be found. Thurkill believed her, and over time grew reconciled to the loss.

But after a while the witch grew very poor, and came asking Thurkill's wife for help. The woman refused her and drove her from the door (big mistake!), so the witch went to Bishop Æthelric and told him about the murder of the boy and concealment of the body. The bishop decided to investigate and summoned Thurkill and his wife to come to him, but Thurkill refused three times. At last the king had to order him to come, and to bring witnesses to a trial at the place where the child's body had been buried. The abbot of Ramsey was there, with some of his monks, and they brought with them some saints' relics. The bishop told the abbot and monks to place the relics on the child's grave.

In front of the whole crowd, Thurkill declared that he was entirely innocent—he had known nothing of the child's murder. And he was so sure of his wife's innocence that he swore an oath: he wrapped his hand in his long beard and said, "O Bishop, as God permits me to glory in this beard, so my wife is clear and innocent of the crime imputed to her." After saying this he took his hand away from his face, and the beard came away with it!

Everyone was amazed, and realised the wife must be guilty. Thurkill himself was dumbfounded. But his wife still denied the crime, so Æthelric ordered that the grave should be opened. The child's bones were brought out, and at the sight the wife broke down and confessed her guilt. Thurkill was so grateful to the bishop that he gave him part of the estate of Ellesworth, which Æthelric promptly bestowed on Ramsey Abbey.

The 12th century chronicler William of Malmesbury also tells the story of a witch from Berkeley in Gloucestershire, not far from the Romano-British temple at Lydney Park. This story dates from around the same time as the funeral of Pope Gregory VI, who died in 1048[46]:

At the same time something similar occurred in England, not by divine miracle, but by infernal craft; which when I shall have related, the credit of the narrative will not be shaken, though the minds of the hearers should be incredulous; for I have heard it from a man of such character, who swore he had seen it, that I should blush to disbelieve. There resided at Berkeley a woman addicted to witchcraft, as it afterwards appeared, and skilled in ancient augury: she was excessively gluttonous, perfectly lascivious, setting no bounds to her debaucheries, as she was not old, though fast declining in life. On a certain day, as she was regaling, a jackdaw, which was a very great favorite, chattered a little more loudly than usual. On hearing which the woman's knife fell from her hand, her countenance grew pale, and deeply groaning, "This day," said she, "my plough has completed its last furrow; today I shall hear of, and suffer, some dreadful calamity." While yet speaking, the messenger of her misfortunes arrived; and being asked, why he approached with so distressed an air? "I bring news," said he, "from the village," naming the place, "of the death of your son, and of the whole family, by a sudden accident." At this intelligence, the woman, sorely afflicted, immediately took to her bed, and perceiving the disorder rapidly approaching the vitals, she summoned her surviving children, a monk, and a nun, by hasty letters; and, when they arrived, with faltering voice, addressed them thus: "Formerly, my children, I constantly administered to my wretched circumstances by demoniacal arts: I have been the sink of every vice, the teacher of every allurement: yet, while practicing these crimes, I was accustomed to soothe my hapless soul with the hope of your piety. Despairing of myself, I rested my expectations on you; I advanced you as my defenders against evil spirits, my safeguards against my strongest foes. Now, since I have approached the end of my life, and shall have those eager to punish, who lured me to sin, I entreat you by your mother's breasts, if you have any regard, any affection, at least to endeavor to alleviate my torments; and, although you cannot revoke the sentence already passed upon my soul, yet you may, perhaps, rescue my body, by these means: sew up my corpse in the skin of a stag; lay it on its back in a stone coffin; fasten down the lid with lead and iron; on this lay a stone, bound round with three iron chains of enormous weight; let there be psalms sung for fifty nights, and masses said for an equal number of days, to allay the ferocious attacks of my adversaries. If I lie thus secure for three nights, on the fourth day bury your mother in the ground; although I fear, lest the earth, which has been so often burdened with my crimes, should refuse to receive and cherish me in her bosom." They did their utmost to comply with her injunctions: but alas! Vain were pious tears, vows, or entreaties; so great was the woman's guilt, so great the devil's violence. For on the first two nights, while the choir of priests was singing psalms around the body, the devils, one by one, with the utmost ease bursting open the door of the church, though closed with an immense bolt, broke asunder the two outer chains; the middle one being more laboriously wrought, remained entire. On the third night, about cock-crow, the whole monastery seemed to be overthrown from its very foundation, by the clamor of the approaching enemy. One devil, more terrible in appearance than the rest, and of loftier stature, broke the gates to shivers by the violence of his attack. The priests grew motionless with fear; their hair stood on end, and they became speechless. He proceeded, as it appeared, with haughty step towards the coffin, and calling on the woman by name, commanded her to rise. She replying that she could not on account of the chains: "You shall be loosed," said he, "and to your cost": and directly he broke the chain, which had mocked the ferocity of the others, with as little exertion as though it had been made of flax. He also beat down the cover of the coffin with his foot, and taking her by the hand, before them all, he dragged her out of the church. At the doors appeared a black horse, proudly neighing, with iron hooks projecting over his whole back; on which the wretched creature was placed, and, immediately, with the whole party, vanished from the eyes of the beholders; her pitiable cries, however, for assistance, were heard for nearly the space of four miles.

MAGIC, WITCHCRAFT AND DEVIANT BURIALS IN ANGLO-SAXON CEMETERIES

In Roman Britain prone (face down) burials were reserved for outcasts, and it was the same in early Anglo-Saxon times, as demonstrated by the archaeologist Andrew Reynolds in *Anglo-Saxon Deviant Burial Customs*. A 6th century woman from the cemetery at Broughton Lodge, Willoughby on the Wolds (Nottinghamshire), aged 40, was buried prone, accompanied with annular brooches of copper-alloy and iron, fragments of three wrist-clasps, glass and amber beads, a knife and ring, a copper-alloy pin, and a beaver-tooth pendant, probably an amulet or charm. At Westbury-by-Shenley (Buckinghamshire) a woman aged between 25 and 35 years was buried prone with grave goods that included a gold and garnet pendant, thirteen silver ring fragments, beads of shell and glass, a pair of shears, and an iron knife, perhaps in a bag, and a pin. Both women were thought to be "cunning women"[47] ("cunning-women is a term used from the 15th century to describe women who used magic for a variety of purposes, including healing"). As Reynolds says of prone burial[48]: "it is difficult not to accept the long-established views … that the principal desire was to limit the possibility of the corpse returning to the world of the living."

Decapitated burials were common in the late Roman period and continued in Anglo-Saxon times. At Bidford-on-Avon (Warwickshire), Grave 138 consisted of the skull of a woman surrounded with limestone slabs to form a box within which the woman's skull lay, along with a copper-alloy pin, a ring, and a pot. Grave 23 at Portway East (Hampshire) contained only the skull of a woman in the northern end of the grave, yet the beads and knife found with the burial were at the southern end of the grave.[49] Decapitation seems to have had the same motivation as prone burial: to prevent the dead from haunting the living.[50]

Reynolds made a special study of four cemeteries with an unusual number of deviant burials, including Abingdon and Lechlade. At the Saxton Road cemetery, Abingdon (Oxfordshire), in Grave 29 (6th century), a young woman was buried prone with iron objects from a chatelaine, an iron bag-ring, an ivory distaff-ring, and two tinned copper-alloy disc brooches. Her grave was packed with fifty or more large stones. The woman was clearly not overly wealthy, but the presence of a bag of objects in the grave and the combination of the prone-burial rite with stones piled over the corpse "suggests a high degree of superstition or fear of the deceased," who may have been a "cunning woman."[51]

St. Mary's Church, Berkeley, Gloucestershire, where, according to William of Malmesbury, the devil came to seize the witch of Berkeley. June 7, 2014 (Elisa.rolle, CCA-SA 4.0 International).

At Lechlade cemetery in Gloucestershire, Inhumation 71 (7th century) was buried with a bag with an iron frame, 200 hundred uncut polished garnets, and a cowrie shell. Inhumation 3 (also 7th century) was buried with a knife, silver bead and two cowrie shells. Perhaps these are burials of "cunning women," given the amuletic function sometimes attributed to cowries.[52] Inhumation 18 was the grave of a female aged 25–30, richly furnished with a wide range of objects. The grave, which lay at the southern end of the main cluster, was filled with tightly packed large stones designed either to prevent her corpse from returning to the world of the living, or to thwart potential grave robbers. Grave 18 (6th century) contained over fifty different objects, including ivory and iron bag-rings, a complete beaver-tooth pendant and a fragment of another, an iron chatelaine, several silver rings, a silver-coated tube, three Roman coins, and a fragment of a Roman altar. This burial, says Reynolds,[53] "fulfils all the criteria discussed by Dickinson with regard to her suggested class of 'cunning women'…, and compares not only with other 'amulet' burials in Graves 3 and 71, but with others elsewhere."

Not all Anglo-Saxon burials of possible "cunning women" were deviant burials, and a good example comes from the cemetery at Bidford-on-Avon (Warwickshire). This particular woman was found buried at Bidford-on-Avon, lying on her back with her head turned to one side. She lived around 550 CE, was aged between 18 and 25 and was some 5 feet 4 inches tall. Her peplos (a long gown) was fastened by two brooches—an Anglo-Saxon "small long" and a western British penannular, showing allegiance to the two main culture groups of the age. Slung between the brooches was a necklace of 39 beads of red, green and yellow glass, amber and gold-in-glass. To this was added the tools of her trade.

Cowrie shells. These are found in some pagan Anglo-Saxon burials, and may have been attributed with magic powers. February 2005 (Bricktop/Gallery/Mollusca, CCA-Share Alike 3.0 Unported).

Slung across her back was a kind of leather bib to which was sewn a dozen tiny bronze buckets with curved handles. By her right hip was a big bag and next to it a sharp knife with a stubby blade and a long, decorated bone handle.

The archaeologist Tania Dickinson studied the objects and worked out their original positions: the beads festooned around the neck; the bib with its dangling buckets hanging across the breast; the bag with its vanished organic contents suspended from the hip; and the "surgical" knife hanging beside it. Dickinson concluded that "the odd mixture of amulets and 'junk' may be both the stock-in-trade and sign of women possessed of special powers" and she identified the Bidford-on-Avon lady as a rare example of a cunning woman.[54]

Cunning-women is a term used in the late Middle Ages and Early Modern period to describe practitioners of magic (*cunning* is from Old English *cunnan* to know"). Little is known about cunning-women in the Anglo-Saxon period, and much of what we do know comes from one sermon. In the late 10th century the Anglo-Saxon priest and writer Ælfric wrote a sermon on auguries, which gives us a glimpse into the magical practices of the time. For example, Ælfric says[55] that "he who trusteth in auguries, either from birds or from sneezings, either from horses or from dogs, he is no Christian, but is an infamous apostate." He also condemns witches[56] (Old English *wicca*):

> Now a certain sorcerer saith that witches often declare even as a matter happens with a true result. Now say we of a truth that the invisible devil who flieth through these worlds, and seeth many things, revealeth to the witch what she shall say to men, that they may be destroyed who seek this sorcery.

He warns against consulting witches: "Neither shall the Christian enquire of the foul witch concerning his health, though she may be able to tell something through the devil." He also blames witches for a variety of pagan practices: "Some men are so blinded that they bring their offerings to earth-fast stones, and eke to trees, and to well-springs, even as witches teach."

It's not clear whether Ælfric's witches are male or female, but women are certainly implicated in witchcraft[57]:

> some witless women go to crossroads, and draw their children through the earth, and thus commit themselves and their children to the devil. Some of them kill their children before they are born, or after birth, that they may not be discovered, nor their wicked adultery be betrayed.... Some of them devise drinks [philtres] for their wooers, or some mischief, that they may have them in marriage.

The reference to women going to crossroads and drawing their children through the earth seems to be a ritual related to Germanic veneration of the earth-mother. What the ritual meant is uncertain, but an early 14th century Icelandic version of Ælfric's work has a similar passage which offers some explanation[58]: "And there are some women who take their children and go to the crossroads and there draw them through the earth for their health, and in order that they should get better and thrive."

The Beginning of the Anglo-Saxon Kingdoms

It was not long before the Anglo-Saxon pagans converted to Christianity. In the 5th and 6th centuries the Anglo-Saxons of the future kingdom of Northumbria in northern England and southern Scotland were pagans, but by the early 7th century, Northumbria had become Christian, and acquired its first saints' cults. It was also home to the famous Anglo-Saxon historian Bede, a monk at the twin monasteries of Wearmouth and Jarrow in northeast England, who shines a light on the so-called "Dark Ages" of English history.

4

Paganism, Christianity
and the Cult of Saints
in Early Northumbria

The Beginnings of Northumbria

Deira and Bernicia

Thanks to Bede and his *Ecclesiastical History of the English People* (730 CE) we know a great deal about early Northumbria. Bede was a monk, first at Wearmouth on the River Wear near Sunderland, and later at its companion monastery St. Paul's in modern Jarrow, both in northeast England. The name Northumbria ("The Land North of the Humber") was probably created by Bede to describe the amalgam of two early kingdoms, Deira and Bernicia, which both seemed to have British roots. It is generally thought that the name Deira is British rather than Anglo-Saxon—the Celtic scholar John Koch says[1] that the Welsh form *Deifr* may well be derived from Celtic *Dubria* "land of waters." The kingdom included east and northeast Yorkshire, between the Humber Estuary and the River Tees, and the name Deira probably referred to these rivers as well as the Ouse, the Ure and the Swale, which may have formed the western boundary of Deira. Bernicia initially covered the present counties of Northumberland and Durham in England, and Berwickshire and East Lothian in Scotland. The name Bernicia is thought to derive from Celtic *Bryneich* or *Brynaich* and may mean "Land of the Mountain Passes" (see Old Irish *bern*, "mountain pass"), referring perhaps to mountain passes through the Pennines. By the time Bede was writing his *Ecclesiastical History* in 730, Bernicia also included Cumbria in northwest England, and Dumfries and Galloway in southwest Scotland.

Early Northumbrian Paganism

There was an early Anglo-Saxon cemetery at West Heslerton near Malton in North Yorkshire, in what was then Deira. Like many Anglo-Saxon cemeteries, West Heslerton was on a site that had been sacred for millennia: the excavators found a Neolithic henge, Early Bronze Age barrows, an Iron Age square-barrow cemetery, and a Romano-British shrine or temple near a spring. The Anglo-Saxon cemetery, which re-used the site of the Neolithic henge and smaller Bronze Age barrows, contained the remains of about 250

60

people buried between the end of the 4th and middle of the 7th centuries CE; grave goods including dress fittings, weapons, pottery and wooden vessels accompanied most of the burials. The cemetery appears to have been laid out in family groups, each containing a broadly comparable group of burials. Many were well-furnished with grave goods—one burial was accompanied by a sword, shield and spears—others had relatively few accompanying objects. Analysis of trace elements absorbed from the food eaten early on in life indicates that a small percentage of the people may have come from southern Sweden, an area from which some of the dress fittings seem to originate. Another group clearly grew up locally, while a third group appears to originate elsewhere in Britain. Analysis of the ancient DNA preserved in the teeth indicates that some of the burials accompanied by weapons may be females and others with brooches and beads may be male, contrasting with the traditional method of sexing burials based generally on the type of grave goods with the burials.[2] Horses played an important role in Germanic paganism, and must have been important to the early Anglo-Saxon settlers at West Heslerton: a horse (a five-year-old mare) had been decapitated and the head placed between the legs,[3] together with a horse-bit.[4] At West Heslerton, seven percent of the burials were prone (face down) burials, the majority of them female. Among the prone burials, Graves 113 and 132 stood out as "special" burials. Both graves contained a wide array of objects, but significantly, both were furnished with walnut amulets encased within copper-alloy cradles. Both graves included amber beads, while the necklace of the woman in Grave 113 also featured a beaver tooth and an antler bead. It is possible that both these prone burials were the graves of cunning women.[5]

At the early cemetery at Norton near Stockton-on-Tees, County Durham, in the kingdom of Bernicia, there were seven prone burials (5.8 percent of all burials), including three females, two males, and two that could not be sexed. In the female prone burial in Grave 99, the hands were raised above the body and together, as if bound, and the legs were raised and appear to be similarly bound. In the female prone burial in Grave 28, the woman was accompanied by annular brooches, beads and a key set among other objects, but these objects were placed on her back after she was laid in the grave.[6]

Early Northumbrian Christianity

THE NORTHUMBRIAN CONVERSION: PAGANISM AND CHRISTIANITY IN EARLY NORTHUMBRIA

The first Northumbrian king that Bede mentions is Æthelfrith of Bernicia (593–616), who "ravaged the Britons more than all the great men of the English," for "he conquered more territories from the Britons, either making them tributary, or driving the inhabitants clean out, and planting English in their places, than any other king or tribune."[7] Æthelfrith was a pagan, and for Bede the history of Northumbria began in earnest when King Edwin, son of king Aelle of Deira, converted to Christianity in 627 CE, persuaded to do so by the Roman missionary Paulinus. Before he converted, Edwin held a meeting of his advisers, attended by Paulinus and, among others, the pagan priest Coifi. The pagan priest, says Bede,[8] played a decisive role at the meeting saying to Edwin:

> "O king, consider what this is which is now preached to us; for I verily declare to you, that the religion which we have hitherto professed has, as far as I can learn, no virtue in it. For none of your people

has applied himself more diligently to the worship of our gods than I; and yet there are many who receive greater favours from you, and are more preferred than I, and are more prosperous in all their undertakings. Now if the gods were good for any thing, they would rather forward me, who have been more careful to serve them. It remains, therefore, that if upon examination you find those new doctrines, which are now preached to us, better and more efficacious, we immediately receive them without any delay."

Coifi listened to the words of Paulinus and was apparently convinced:

Then immediately, in contempt of his former superstitions, he desired the king to furnish him with arms and a stallion; and mounting the same, he set out to destroy the idols; for it was not lawful before for the high priest either to carry arms, or to ride on any but a mare. Having, therefore, girt a sword about him, with a spear in his hand, he mounted the king's stallion and proceeded to the idols. The multitude, beholding it, concluded he was distracted; but he lost no time, for as soon as he drew near the temple he profaned the same, casting into it the spear which he held; and rejoicing in the knowledge of the worship of the true God, he commanded his companions to destroy the temple, with all its enclosures, by fire. This place where the idols were is still shown, not far from York, to the eastward, beyond the river Derwent, and is now called Godmundingham, where the high priest, by the inspiration of the true God, profaned and destroyed the altars which he had himself consecrated.

Godmundingham is Goodmanham in East Yorkshire. This is one of the few times Bede mentions Anglo-Saxon paganism, and we can see that horses played an important part in Coifi's ritual life. Goodmanham is not far from an early Anglo-Saxon cremation cemetery at Sancton. The site lies on the Yorkshire Wolds, near two Roman roads, one from the south through Brough-on-Humber (the Roman town of *Petuaria*) to Malton (Roman *Derventio*), the other one on the same line but veering off to the east of Sancton toward York (Roman *Eboracum*). The 6th century pagan cemetery was discovered sometime before 1854 at Grange Farm, near the village of Sancton. The discovery of 69 pottery urns was recorded on an Ordnance Survey map of 1854. Excavations were carried out in 1953–1957—they covered an area 24 yards by 36 yards and recorded much more carefully and accurately the urns and contents. Around 200 hundred cremations were recorded. As well as the cremated bone, the urns contained fused glass beads, objects of copper alloy, bone combs, miniature shears and spindlewhorls.[9] Nearly half of the cremation urns at Sancton contained animal remains, and horse was the most popular animal sacrifice.[10]

Edwin was baptized by the Roman missionary Paulinus in a specially constructed timber church in the old Roman city of York. Then Paulinus spent thirty-six days in Yeavering, Northumberland, baptizing people in the River Glen, after which he moved on to Catterick in North Yorkshire, baptizing people in the River Swale.

However, the *History of the Britons*, composed in Latin somewhere in Wales around 830 CE, has a different story about the baptism of Edwin and his subjects[11]:

Edwin, son of Aelle, reigned seventeen years, seized on Elmet, and expelled Cerdic, its king. Eanflaed, his daughter, received baptism, on the twelfth day after Pentecost, with all her followers, both men and women. The following Easter Edwin himself received baptism, and twelve thousand of his subjects with him. If any one wishes to know who baptized them, it was Rhun son of Urien: he was engaged forty days in baptizing all classes of the Saxons, and by his preaching many believed on Christ.

The *History of the Britons* says that Rhun was the son of Urien, a late 6th century king of Rheged, a British kingdom which probably included part of Cumbria in northwest England and Dumfries and Galloway in southwest Scotland.

Elsewhere, the *History of the Britons* says[12] that Oswiu, king of Northumbria (642–670) had two wives, Rhianmellt, daughter of Royth, son of Rhun (obviously a British princess from Rheged), and Eanflaed, daughter of Edwin. In the Durham *Liber Vitae*, which probably dates from the 9th century, a register is provided of "queens and abbesses" of Northumbria, in which a lady called "*Raegnmaeld*" is listed first, followed by Oswiu's Anglo-Saxon wife Eanflæd–*Ragnamaeld* is thought to be an Anglo-Saxon version of Rhianmellt. It is likely that Oswiu married Rhianmellt some time in the 630s, before he married Eanflaed, which occurred between 642 and 645.[13] So it does seem plausible that Rhun at least played a part in the conversion of the Saxons, especially in the west of Northumbria, despite Bede's assertion[14] that the British "never preached the faith to the Saxons, or English, who dwelt amongst them." Bede rarely had a good word to say about the British, so some of his claims should be taken with the proverbial pinch of salt.

Bede says that Paulinus baptized Northumbrians at Yeavering and Catterick, and both of these have long histories. Catterick in North Yorkshire was originally a Roman town, probably known as *Cataractonium*, which began life as a fort in the late 1st century, but soon became a civilian settlement. Timber buildings, probably shops and workshops, were erected on the main east-west road in the 2nd century. Further north, a more complex building with stone foundations covered nearly an acre and probably included a bath house. In the first half of the 3rd century some shops were rebuilt in stone, one being used as a temple podium. The late 3rd century town wall destroyed many existing buildings and the whole layout of the town was radically altered in the early 4th century. Later the temple was pulled down and the podium used for shop stalls. Building continued to the last half of the 4th century, a flourishing community still existing at the end of the century. Anglo-Saxon brooches were also found at Catterick, with occupation continuing into the 6th century.[15] Timber buildings were constructed on the site of Roman buildings, probably in the 5th century.[16] An early cemetery comprising 44 Anglian inhumations has been discovered outside the town, adjacent to a Neolithic henge—it is dated to the period 450–550 CE from the brooches associated with the inhumations.[17]

Yeavering in Northumberland is the site of an Anglo-Saxon palace which was excavated by Brian Hope-Taylor between 1952 and 1962. The site actually consists of the Iron Age hillfort of Yeavering Bell and a much smaller "whaleback hill" immediately to the north which contains the site of the Anglian palace named by Bede as *Ad Gefrin*. Hope-Taylor's excavations showed that a small henge monument was constructed on the whaleback during the late Neolithic/early Bronze Age and an early Bronze Age cremation cemetery is focused on an unusual monument which Hope Taylor interprets as a stone circle. The hillfort on Yeavering Bell is usually thought to date from the latter half of the 1st millennium BCE, though a Late Bronze Age origin is possible. It may have been during the Late Iron Age that the so called "Great Enclosure" was erected on the whaleback. This has been interpreted as a great stock enclosure, presumably of both functional and ceremonial significance. It was maintained throughout much of the life of the Anglian palace which was erected immediately adjacent to it at some point during the latter half of the 6th century CE. The palace incorporated several large buildings, most notable of which were the great hall and a unique "theatre." The name *Gefrin* is Celtic and can be translated as "Hill of the Goats." Interestingly, Hope Taylor found a goat's skull and a "ceremonial staff" decorated with what may have been a goat motif in what was apparently one of the most significant Anglian period burials at *Ad Gefrin*.[18] It seems likely that Yeavering was an important British ceremonial center that was taken over by Anglo-Saxons in the 6th century CE.

Edwin did not long survive his conversion to Christianity: in 633 he was killed by Penda of Mercia and Cadwallon ap Cadfan of Gwynedd at the Battle of Hatfield Chase, near Doncaster. Bede remarks, in a passage that helps explain his hostility to the British[19]:

> At this time a great slaughter was made in the church or nation of the Northumbrians; and the more so because one of the commanders, by whom it was made, was a pagan, and the other a barbarian, more cruel than a pagan; for Penda, with all the nation of the Mercians, was an idolater, and a stranger to the name of Christ; but Cadwalla, though he bore the name and professed himself a Christian, was so barbarous in his disposition and behaviour, that he neither spared the female sex, nor the innocent age of children, but with savage cruelty put them to tormenting deaths, ravaging all their country for a long time, and resolving to cut off all the race of the English within the borders of Britain. Nor did he pay any respect to the Christian religion which had newly taken root among them; it being to this day the custom of the Britons not to pay any respect to the faith and religion of the English, nor to correspond with them any more than with pagans.

Edwin was succeeded as king of Bernicia by Eanfrith, son of the former king Æthelfrith, who was killed by Cadwallon ap Cadfan in 634. Eanfrith in turn was succeeded as king by his brother Oswald, who led an army against Cadwallon and defeated and killed him at the Battle of Heavenfield, near Hexham.

EARLY CHRISTIANITY IN NORTHUMBRIA

Oswald had spent several years in exile in the kingdom of Dal Riata, at the hillfort of Dunadd in Argyll and Bute on the west coast of Scotland, where he converted to Christianity, no doubt under the influence of the monastery of Iona. The monastery of Iona was founded in 563 CE by the Irish monk Columba on a small island off the west coast of Scotland. The monastery existed until about the turn of the 8th–9th centuries when the wooden complex was destroyed by Norse raiders. Nothing remains above ground of the original monastery except possibly the vallum, the bank and ditch that enclosed the monastery, and the cell on Tor Abb said to have been used by St. Columba. Excavations have shown that the Columban monastery, which consisted of about a dozen huts and a small church, lay in the vicinity of the early 13th century abbey. A few grave-slabs of the 7th and 8th centuries, generally simple incised or outline crosses, still survive from the early monastery.[20] Columba died in 597 and by 700 he was being venerated as a saint.

Bede was a great admirer of Oswald, and records a pious act that Oswald performed on the eve of the Battle of Heavenfield[21]:

> The place is shown to this day, and held in much veneration, where Oswald, being about to engage, erected the sign of the holy cross, and on his knees prayed to God that he would assist his worshipers in their great distress. It is further reported, that the cross being made in haste, and the hole dug in which it was to be fixed, the king himself, full of faith, laid hold of it and held it with both his hands, till it was set fast by throwing in the earth and this done, raising his voice, he cried to his army, "Let us all kneel, and jointly beseech the true and living God Almighty, in his mercy, to defend us from the haughty and fierce enemy; for He knows that we have undertaken a just war for the safety of our nation." All did as he had commanded, and accordingly advancing towards the enemy with the first dawn of day, they obtained the victory, as their faith deserved. In that place of prayer very many miraculous cures are known to have been performed, as a token and memorial of the king's faith; for even to this day, many are wont to cut off small chips from the wood of the holy cross, which being put into water, men or cattle drinking thereof, or sprinkled with that water, are immediately restored to health.

Adomnan, in his *Life* of St. Columba, written around 700 CE, also mentions Oswald's piety, but he tells a different story. On the eve of the Battle of Heavenfield, says Adomnan,

Oswald had a vision of St. Columba, "beaming with angelic brightness, and of figure so majestic that his head seemed to touch the clouds," who announced to the king[22]:

"March out this following night from your camp to battle, for on this occasion the Lord has granted to me that your foes shall be put to flight, that your enemy Cadwallon shall be delivered into your hands, and that after the battle you shall return in triumph, and have a happy reign." The king, awaking at these words, assembled his council and related the vision, at which they were all encouraged; and so the whole people promised that, after their return from the war, they would believe and be baptized, for up to that time all that Saxon land had been wrapt in the darkness of paganism and ignorance, with the exception of King Oswald and the twelve men who had been baptized with him during his exile among the Scots.

With his ties to Dal Riata and Iona, it is no surprise that Oswald should establish a monastery and bishopric on the island of Lindisfarne in Northumberland, with the Iona monk Aidan as the first bishop. Nothing remains of the Anglo-Saxon church and monastery but a collection of 51 complete or fragmentary Anglo-Saxon carved stones. One 9th-century stone sculpture clearly shows a violent attack by armed men, brandishing Viking-style swords and battle axes,[23] no doubt inspired by the attacks of the 9th century which led to the formation of a Danish kingdom based in York.

Like his predecessor Edwin, Oswald was killed fighting against Penda of Mercia, at the Battle of Maserfield (possibly Oswestry in Shropshire) in 642. According to Bede,[24] Oswald died a pious and bloody death. As he died,

he prayed to God for the souls of his army. Whence it is proverbially said, "Lord, have mercy on their souls, said Oswald, as he fell to the ground." His bones, therefore, were translated to the monastery which we have mentioned, and buried therein: but the king that slew him commanded his head, hands, and arms to be cut off from the body, and set upon stakes. But his successor in the throne, Oswiu, coming thither the next year with his army, took them down, and buried his head in the church of Lindisfarne, and the hands and arms in his royal city.

The royal city, which "has taken its name from Bebba, one of its former queens" (Book 3, Chapter 6), is Bamburgh in Northumberland. Little remains of Anglo-Saxon Bamburgh but the Bowl Hole cemetery, 300 yards south of Bamburgh Castle, which dates from the 7th/8th century; and two 7th century artifacts—the Bamburgh Sword, a high-status sword made of six strands of iron (instead of the normal four), and the Bamburgh Beast, an animal ornament that adorns a tiny gold plaque.[25]

Oswald was succeeded as king by his brother Oswiu, who had also been brought up in Dal Riata. As a result, Oswiu's Christianity was heavily influenced by the Irish monks of Iona, whose practices differed in some respect from those of Rome, particularly in the dating of Easter. Many Northumbrians had adopted the Roman dating of Easter, which caused division even in the Northumbrian court: Queen Eanflaed, the daughter of the former king Edwin, observed Easter according to Roman custom, while King Oswiu followed the "Celtic" custom of Iona.[26] So in 664 CE, a council was held at Whitby, with Wilfrid, abbot of Ripon, arguing in favor of the Roman position, and Colman, bishop of Lindisfarne advocating the traditional "Celtic" dating. Eventually, the synod came down in favor of the Roman dating of Easter, and Colman returned to Iona.

The monastery at Whitby in North Yorkshire, where the synod was held, stands on the East Cliff overlooking the North Sea above the town of Whitby. It was founded in 657 CE by St. Hilda, and recently an Anglo-Saxon cemetery has been excavated there. The cemetery was in use for a long period of time and showed some intercutting of the graves. An Anglo-Saxon coin called a sceatta dating to 700–740 CE from a late grave and the ritual use of quartz pebbles, typical of Celtic monastic practice, suggest an early date for the cemetery.[27]The reason for the white quartz pebbles is not known, but similar pebbles have been found at an early cemetery at Llandough in the Vale of Glamorgan (south Wales), and the excavators link these white pebbles to a line in *Revelation* 2.17 (King James Version): "He that hath an ear, let him hear what the Spirit saith unto the churches; To him that overcometh will I give to eat of the hidden manna, and will give him a white stone, and in the stone a new name written, which no man knoweth saving he that received it."[28]

The quartz pebbles suggest a Celtic influence at Whitby, and there is also a Celtic connection with the religious poet Caedmon, described at length by Bede[29]:

There was in this abbess's monastery [= Whitby] a certain brother, particularly remarkable for the grace of God, who was wont to make pious and religious verses, so that whatever was interpreted to him out of Scripture, he soon after put the same into poetical expressions of much sweetness and humility, in English, which was his native language. By his verses the minds of many were often excited to despise the world, and to aspire to heaven. Others after him attempted, in the English nation, to compose religious poems, but none could ever compare with him, for he did not learn the art of poetry from men, but from God; for which reason he never could compose any trivial or vain poem, but only those which relate to religion suited his religious tongue; for having lived in a secular habit till he was well advanced in years, he had never learned anything of versifying; for which reason being sometimes at entertainments, when it was agreed for the sake of mirth that all present should sing in their turns, when he saw the instrument come towards him, he rose up from table and returned home.

Having done so at a certain time, and gone out of the house where the entertainment was, to the stable, where he had to take care of the horses that night, he there composed himself to rest at the proper time; a person appeared to him in his sleep, and saluting him by his name, said, "Caedmon, sing some song to me." He answered, "I cannot sing; for that was the reason why I left the entertainment, and retired to this place because I could not sing." The other who talked to him, replied, "However, you shall sing." "What shall I sing?" rejoined he. "Sing the beginning of created beings," said the other. Hereupon he presently began to sing verses to the praise of God, which he had never heard, the purport whereof was thus:

We are now to praise the Maker of the heavenly kingdom, the power of the Creator and his counsel, the deeds of the Father of glory. How He, being the eternal God, became the author of all miracles, who first, as almighty preserver of the human race, created heaven for the sons of men as the roof of the house, and next the earth.

This is the sense, but not the words in order as he sang them in his sleep; for verses, though never so well composed, cannot be literally translated out of one language into another, without losing much of their beauty and loftiness. Awaking from his sleep, he remembered all that he had sung in his dream, and soon added much more to the same effect in verse worthy of the Deity.

What is particularly intriguing about this story is that Caedmon is a British name meaning "Battle-Pony." The name is attested in early medieval Wales as *Catamanus*, on a stone found at Llangadwaladr, Anglesey, north Wales, commemorating Cadfan, the ruler of Gwynedd, who died around 625[30] (he was the father of Cadwallon, who wreaked such havoc in Northumbria).

Oswiu was succeeded by his son Ecgfrith, who was killed in a disastrous battle against the Picts of northern Scotland[31]:

rashly leading his army to ravage the province of the Picts, much against the advice of his friends, and particularly of Cuthbert, of blessed memory, who had been lately ordained his bishop, the enemy made show as if they fled, and [Ecgfrith] was drawn into the straits of inaccessible mountains, and slain with the greatest part of his forces, on the 20th of May, in the fortieth year of his age, and the fifteenth of his reign. His friends, as has been said, advised him not to engage in this war; but he having the year before refused to listen to the most reverend father, Egbert, advising him not to attack the Scots, who did him no harm, it was laid upon him as a punishment for his sin, that he should not now regard those who would have prevented his death.

The Irish annals name the site of the battle as *Dun Nechtain,* and recently the historian Alex Woolf has identified *Dun Nechtain* as Dunachton in Badenoch and Strathspey in the Highlands of Scotland,[32] to the southeast of Inverness.

The Saints of Northumbria

ST. OSWALD

After his death at Maserfield, Oswald soon came to be venerated as a saint, as Bede makes clear[33]:

> How great his faith was towards God, and how remarkable his devotion, has been made evident by miracles since his death; for, in the place where he was killed by the pagans, fighting for his country, infirm men and cattle are healed to this day. Whereupon many took up the very dust of the place where his body fell, and putting it into water, did much good with it to their friends who were sick. This custom came so much into use, that the earth being carried away by degrees, there remained a hole as deep as the height of a man. Nor is it to be wondered that the sick should be healed in the place where he died; for, whilst he lived, he never ceased to provide for the poor and infirm, and to bestow alms on them, and assist them.

Some time later, says Bede,[34] the Mercian queen Osthryth, the daughter of Oswald's brother Oswiu, decided to move Oswald's bones to the monastery of Bardney on the River Witham in Lincolnshire. The monastery at Bardney, which was once a slight island in marshy ground around the Witham, was probably founded some time between 675 and 697 by the Mercian king Æthelred and his wife Osthryth. Oswald's bones were taken to Bardney, but the monks refused to admit the bones of a foreign ruler (Lindsey was part of Mercia, and Oswald was Northumbrian). As a result, says Bede,

> the relics were left in the open air all that night, with only a large tent spread over them; but the appearance of a heavenly miracle showed with how much reverence they ought to be received by all the faithful; for during that whole night, a pillar of light, reaching from the wagon up to heaven, was seen by almost all the inhabitants of the province of Lindsey. Hereupon, in the morning, the brethren who had refused it the day before, began themselves earnestly to pray that those holy relics, so beloved by God, might be deposited among them. Accordingly, the bones, being washed, were put into a shrine which they had made for that purpose, and placed in the church, with due honor; and that there might be a perpetual memorial of the royal person of this holy man, they hung up over the monument his banner made of gold and purple; and poured out the water in which they had washed the bones, in a corner of the sacred place. From that time, the very earth which received that holy water, had the virtue of expelling devils from the bodies of persons possessed.

ST. CUTHBERT OF LINDISFARNE (NORTHUMBERLAND)

Bede also mentions several other Northumbrian saints, including Cuthbert and John of Beverley. Cuthbert was Bishop of Lindisfarne from 684 to 687, but before he became bishop, says Bede,[35] Cuthbert had lived the life of a hermit: "[he] had for many years led a solitary life, in great continence of body and mind, in a very small island, called Farne, distant almost nine miles from [Lindisfarne]." Inner Farne off the coast of Northumberland became an anchoritic cell with Bishop Aidan retiring there in 651. Cuthbert spent

his last years there until his death in 687. The island was used as by anchorites successively until the last anchorite, Thomas de Melsonby, who died there in 1246.[36]

Bede describes Cuthbert's death and sanctity in the following terms[37]:

> In order to show with how much glory the man of God, Cuthbert, lived after death, his holy life having been before his death signalised by frequent miracles; when he had been buried eleven years, Divine Providence put it into the minds of the brethren to take up his bones, expecting, as is usual with dead bodies, to find all the flesh consumed and reduced to ashes, and the rest dried up, and intending to put the same into a new coffin, and to lay them in the same place, but above the pavement, for the honour due to him. They acquainted Bishop Ebert with their design, and he consented to it, and ordered that the same should be done on the anniversary of his burial. They did so, and opening the grave, found all the body whole, as if it had been alive, and the joints pliable, more like one asleep than a dead person; besides, all the vestments the body had on were not only found, but wonderful for their freshness and gloss.

Bede later mentions a miraculous cure performed by the relics of St. Cuthbert[38]:

> It happened in the monastery, which, being built near the river Dacore [Dacre in Cumbria], has taken its name from the same, over which, at that time, the religious Suidbert presided as abbot. In that monastery was a youth whose eyelid had a great swelling on it, which growing daily, threatened the loss of the eye. The surgeons applied their medicines to ripen it, but in vain. Some said it ought to be cut off; others opposed it, for fear of worse consequences. The brother having long laboured under this malady, and seeing no human means likely to save his eye, but that, on the contrary, it grew daily worse, was cured on a sudden, through the Divine Goodness, by the relics of the holy father, Cuthbert; for the brethren, finding his body uncorrupted, after having been many years buried, took some part of the hair, which they might, at the request of friends, give or show, in testimony of the miracle.

Bede also has a more light-hearted story about Cuthbert's miraculous powers. Once Cuthbert was

"St. Oswald Crowned as King," from a manuscript dated to around 1220 (New York Public Library, manuscript Spencer 1, folio 89 reverse).

staying at the monastery of St. Abbs Head in Berwickshire, on the southeast coast of Scotland. While he was there, he used to go out alone at night, and one night a brother of the monastery followed him[39]:

> when he left the monastery, [he] went down to the sea, which flows beneath, and going into it, until the water reached his neck and arms, spent the night in praising God. When the dawn of day approached, he came out of the water, and, falling on his knees, began to pray again. Whilst he was doing this, two quadrupeds, called otters, came up from the sea, and, lying down before him on the sand, breathed upon his feet, and wiped them with their hair after which, having received his blessing, they returned to their native element.

Cuthbert was buried at Lindisfarne, but after Lindisfarne was attacked by Danes in 875, his body was moved to Chester-le-Street in County Durham. Symeon of Durham, writing in the early 12th century, says that Oswald's head and some of the bones of St. Aidan were placed in the same shrine as St. Cuthbert. In 995, another Danish invasion was imminent, and Cuthbert's remains were moved to Ripon in North Yorkshire. Not long after, the monks prepared to return to Chester-le-Street, but Cuthbert let it be known that he would prefer to go to Durham, where a wooden church was built to house his remains. In 1104 Cuthbert's tomb was opened again and his relics were translated to a new shrine behind the altar of the recently completed cathedral. When the casket was

The Journey, a modern sculpture by Fenwick Lawson, showing the coffin of St. Cuthbert being carried by six monks, eventually to Durham, after the Viking attacks in the 9th century. December 22, 2008 (Kaihsu Tai).

opened, a small book of the Gospel of John measuring only three-and-a-half by five inches, was found. Also recovered much later were a set of vestments of 909–916, made of Byzantine silk, with a stole and decoration in extremely rare Anglo-Saxon embroidery; these had been deposited in his tomb by King Æthelstan (927–939) on a pilgrimage while Cuthbert's shrine was at Chester-le-Street.[40]

St. John of Beverley (East Yorkshire)

John of Beverley was Bishop of Hexham and later York in the late 7th and early 8th century. Hexham monastery was founded by Wilfrid in 674 and became a cathedral in 678. Various Roman stones have been found at Hexham, including a tombstone nearly 9 feet in height constructed for Flavinus, a standard-bearer, an altar-stone bearing the inscription APOLLO MAPONO (Maponus was a Celtic god), and an imperial inscription erected by the Emperor Septimius Severus (193–211).[41] The nearest Roman town to Hexham was Corbridge, which started life in the 70s CE as a fort, but became a base for legionary soldiers after 160 CE, and then developed into a small town which survived until the late 4th century.

According to Bede,[42] John displayed his miraculous powers when he visited the nunnery at Watton, between Beverley and Driffield, East Yorkshire, where he performed a miracle by curing one of the nuns (the story was told to Bede by a priest called Berthun who was accompanying John):

> the abbess told us, that one of the virgins, who was her daughter in the flesh, labored under a grievous distemper, having been lately bled in the arm, and whilst she was engaged in study, was seized with a sudden violent pain, which increased so that the wounded arm became worse, and so much swelled, that it could not be grasped with both hands; and thus being confined to her bed, through excess of pain, she was expected to die very soon. The abbess entreated the bishop that he would vouchsafe to go in and give her his blessing; for that she believed she would be the better for his blessing or touching her. He asked when the maiden had been bled? and being told it was on the fourth day of the moon, said, "You did very indiscreetly and unskillfully to bleed her on the fourth day of the moon; for I remember that Archbishop Theodore, of blessed memory, said, that bleeding at that time was very dangerous, when the light of the moon and the tide of the ocean is increasing; and what can I do to the girl if she is like to die?"
> The abbess still earnestly entreated for her daughter, whom she dearly loved, and designed to make abbess in her stead, and at last prevailed with him to go in to her. He accordingly went in, taking me with him to the virgin, who lay, as I said, in great anguish, and her arm swelled so fast that there was no bending of the elbow; the bishop stood and said a prayer over her, and having given his blessing, went out. Afterwards, as we were sitting at table, some one came in and called me out, saying, "Coenberg" (that was the virgin's name) "desires you will immediately go back to her." I did so, and entering the house, perceived her countenance more cheerful, and like one in perfect health. Having seated myself down by her, she said, "Would you like me to call for something to drink?"—"Yes," said I, "and am very glad if you can." When the cup was brought, and we had both drunk, she said, "As soon as the bishop had said the prayer, given me his blessing, and gone out, I immediately began to mend; and though I have not yet recovered my former strength, yet all the pain is quite gone from my arm, where it was most intense, and from all my body, as if the bishop had carried it away with him; though the swelling of the arm still seems to remain."

John died in 721 and was buried in the monastery at Beverley ("Beaver-Stream"), which Bede[43] calls *Inderawuda* ("In the Wood of the Deirans"). The earliest firm evidence of settlement in Beverley comes not from the well drained north but from the lower-lying southern end of the town. Excavation south of the minster between 1979 and 1982 revealed timber structures and cobbled pathways datable to the period from the early 8th to the mid–9th century. Pollen analysis suggests that the same period saw the clearance of local woodland for cultivation. The site of the early settlement was a ridge of boulder clay bounded to north and south by undrained marshland, perhaps the home of the beavers which gave Beverley its name. The marshy land to the north of the ridge, in the area of the modern Highgate and Eastgate, seems still to have been flooded in the 9th century, which suggests that any growth in the initial settlement is likely to have been confined to the ridge and that expansion northwards was not possible until later. The archaeological evidence of 8th-century settlement near the site of the later minster provides some support for the traditional equation of Beverley's origins with the foundation of the monastery of *Inderawuda*, to which Bishop John of York retired *c.* 714 and where he was buried in 721. The topography of the site, as revealed by excavation, also fits Bede's account of Bishop John's liking for isolated religious retreats. The 8th-century settlers occupied a virtual island in badly drained wetlands and did so presumably from choice since there was higher ground nearby.[44]

St. Wilfrid of Ripon (North Yorkshire)

Wilfrid, who argued in favor of the Roman dating of Easter, was the virtual founder of the monastery at Ripon in North Yorkshire. Alhfrith, sub-king of Deira (654–664) granted land at Ripon (North Yorkshire) to the monks of Melrose in the Scottish Borders, who left around 660 when he granted the monastery to St. Wilfrid, who formed a community probably under the Order of St. Benedict. Wilfrid built a large stone church of which the crypt remains and after his death in 709 his body was brought from Oundle to Ripon for burial. The monastery was destroyed by the Danes around 875, then restored but burnt down during internal warfare around 948. It is said to have been rebuilt for secular priests after 972 by Archbishop Oswald and prebends are attributed to Archbishop Ealdred after 1061.[45]

After his death Wilfrid was venerated as a saint, though Bede only mentions one miraculous event in relation to Wilfrid[46]:

Passing through France, on his way back to Britain, on a sudden he fell sick, and the distemper increasing, was so ill, that he could not ride, but was carried in his bed. Being thus come to the city of Meaux, in France, he lay four days and nights, as if he had been dead, and only by his faint breathing showed that he had any life in him; having continued so four days, without meat or drink, speaking or hearing, he, at length, on the fifth day, in the morning, as it were awakening out of a dead sleep, sat up in bed, and opening his eyes, saw numbers of brethren singing and weeping about him, and fetching a sigh, asked where Acca, the priest, was? This man, being called, immediately came in, and seeing him thus recovered and able to speak, knelt down, and returned thanks to God, with all the brethren there present. When they had sat awhile, and begun to discourse, with much reverence, on the heavenly judgments, the bishop ordered the rest to go out for an hour, and spoke to the priest, Acca, in this manner—

"A dreadful vision has now appeared to me, which I wish you to hear and keep secret, till I know how God will please to dispose of me. There stood by me a certain person, remarkable for his white garments, telling me he was Michael, the Archangel, and said, "I am sent to save you from death: for the Lord has granted you life, through the prayers and tears of your disciples, and the intercession of his blessed mother Mary, of perpetual virginity; wherefore I tell you, that you shall now recover from this sickness; but be ready, for I will return to visit you at the end of four years. But when you come into your country, you shall recover most of the possessions that have been taken from you, and shall end your days in perfect peace." The bishop accordingly recovered, at which all persons rejoiced, and gave thanks to God, and setting forward.

ST. HILDA OF WHITBY

After her death in 680, Hilda, abbess of Whitby, was venerated as a saint. Bede reports two miraculous events associated with her death, which occurred on the night of her death at the monastery of Hackness in North Yorkshire, which had been established by Hilda[47]:

Depiction of St. Hilda (here called Hild) from the late Victorian Caedmon's Cross, Whitby—at her feet are snakes she supposedly turned into stone, according to a late medieval legend (see Chapter 8). June 6, 2015 (Wilson44691, CCO 1.0 Universal Public Domain Dedication).

There was in that monastery, a certain nun called Begu, who, having dedicated her virginity to God, had served Him upwards of thirty years in monastical conversation. This nun, being then in the dormitory of the sisters, on a sudden heard the well known sound of a bell in the air, which used to awake and call them to prayers, when any one of them was taken out of this world, and opening her eyes, as she thought, she saw the top of the house open, and a strong light pour in from above; looking earnestly upon that light, she saw the soul of the aforesaid servant of God in that same light, attended and conducted to heaven by angels. Then awaking, and seeing the other sisters lying round about her, she perceived that what she had seen was either in a dream or a vision; and rising immediately in a great fright, she ran to the virgin who then presided in the monastery instead of the abbess, and whose name was Frigyth, and, with many tears and sighs, told her that the Abbess Hilda, mother of them all, had departed this life, and had in her sight ascended to eternal bliss, and to the company of the inhabitants of heaven, with a great light, and with angels conducting her. Frigyth having heard it, awoke all the sisters, and calling them to the church, admonished them to pray and sing psalms for her soul; which they did during the remainder of the night; and at break of day, the brothers came with news of her death, from the place where she had died. They answered that they knew it before, and then related how and when they had heard it, by which it appeared that her death had been revealed to them in a vision the very same hour that the others said she had died. Thus it was by Heaven happily ordained, that when some saw her departure out of this world, the others should be acquainted with her admittance into the spiritual life which is eternal. These monasteries are about thirteen miles distant from each other.

It is also reported, that her death was, in a vision, made known the same night to one of the holy virgins who loved her most passionately, in the same monastery where the said servant of God died. This nun saw her soul ascend to heaven in the company of angels; and this she declared, the very same hour that it happened, to those servants of Christ that were with her; and awakened them to pray for her soul, even before the rest of the congregation had heard of her death. The truth of which was known to the whole monastery in the morning. This same nun was at that time with some other servants of Christ, in the remotest part of the monastery, where the women newly converted were wont to be upon trial, till they were regularly instructed, and taken into the society of the congregation.

St. Æbbe of St. Abbs Head (Berwickshire)

We know from Bede[48] that there was a nunnery at *Colodaesburg*, that is, St. Abbs Head in Berwickshire, southeast Scotland, established by Æbbe, the aunt of King Ecgfrith. Today Kirk Hill at St. Abbs Head is the site of the ruined St. Abbs Kirk, first mentioned in 1372. Limited excavations were carried out here in an attempt to locate the early fortification implied in the 7th century place name Colodaesburg. At Kirk Hill a cliff-edge site of some seven acres had been enclosed by either a double palisade or two successive palisades. This was overlaid by a massive turf rampart, with a footing of dressed blocks. There were no closely datable stratified finds, but the wickerwork of the palisade was radiocarbon dated to 630–770 CE. This may imply an Anglian construction, but in a British tradition. The turf rampart is later still and may be the monastic vallum of St. Aebbe's monastery.[49]

Just down the coast from St. Abbs Head is Burnmouth, and here an oval masonry cist was found on 26th July 1923 by James Wood, Coldingham, during work preparatory to quarrying, about 50 yards east-northeast of Catch-a-Penny farmhouse. It was built of two or three irregular courses of small boulders, with four sandstone slabs as covers, and was unpaved. It contained the slightly flexed inhumation of an adult male, aged about 35, accompanied by the bones of a pig, fragments of coal and wood, an iron knife, and a pair of bronze spoons, datable to the second half of the 1st century CE,[50] and similar to the spoons found near Bath in Somerset. Judging from the bronze spoons, the man buried there may well have been an Iron Age priest.

St. Ninian of Whithorn (Dumfries and Galloway)

The only British saint Bede mentions is St. Ninian[51]:

> In the year of our Lord 565, when Justin, the younger, the successor of Justinian, had the government of the Roman empire, there came into Britain a famous priest and abbot, a monk by habit and life, whose name was Columba, to preach the word of God to the provinces of the northern Picts, who are separated from the southern parts by steep and rugged mountains; for the southern Picts, who dwell on this side of those mountains, had long before, as is reported, forsaken the errors of idolatry, and embraced the truth, by the preaching of Ninias, a most reverend bishop and holy man of the British nation, who had been regularly instructed at Rome, in the faith and mysteries of the truth; whose episcopal see, named after St. Martin the bishop, and famous for a stately church (wherein he and many other saints rest in the body), is still in existence among the English nation. The place belongs to the province of the Bernicians, and is generally called the White House, because he there built a church of stone, which was not usual among the Britons.

St. Ninian is associated with Whithorn ("White House") in Dumfries and Galloway, southwest Scotland. Excavations at Whithorn between 1984 and 1991 concentrated on

Northumbrian remains of 700–850 CE but also found evidence for the 5th to 7th centuries. Low-lying ground revealed a complex of curvilinear ditches, pits and stakeholes inter-leaved with waterborne silts which had been severely disturbed by 7th century mould-board ploughing. A rich assemblage of finds includes high-status 6th century pottery from the eastern Mediterranean, 6th–7th century pottery from Merovingian France, and 5th–6th century glass beakers from Frankish workshops in France, Belgium or Germany. An extensive 7th century cemetery on higher ground contained at least 50 graves mostly laid out in regular rows. Graves include long cists with and without stone cover slabs.[52] One of the oldest objects found at Whithorn is the Latinus stone. Carved around 450 CE, it was erected to Latinus and his unnamed daughter, and would have stood by an early Christian church and cemetery, pre-dating the later churches on the hilltop at Whithorn. The inscription on the stone is in Latin and when translated reads: "We praise you, the Lord! Latinus, descendant of Barrovados, aged 35 and his daughter, aged 4, made a sign here."[53]

Bede calls St. Ninian's church "the White House" (Latin *Candida Casa*), and recent excavations have found spreads of burnt limestone, plaster and cement, possibly the remains of this white church. The history of Northumbrian Whithorn is complex, as excavations have shown. The early Christian site included two shrines on either side of a paved road. The eastern shrine was a circular space variously defined by a ditch, a curb, paving and graves. It overlay the remains of an earlier roundhouse and was perhaps intended to commemorate the building or more probably a revered inhabitant. A massive cist close to the center of the eastern shrine contained vestigial remains of two bodies apparently representing a "special" burial. The northern shrine comprised a platform cut into the slope and approached by stone stairs. A regular setting of four timber or stone pillars at the center of the platform subsequently became the focus of the Northum-brian church, constructed in the late 7th or early 8th century. To the east of the church was a chapel with stained-glass windows which contained four burials, three in wooden coffins with iron fittings. To the east of the burial chapel was a children's graveyard with some 45 burials, all under 10 years old.[54]

Northumbrian saints' cults were focused on the tomb of the saint and his or her earthly remains and were, in all likelihood, based on Gaulish models like the cult of St. Martin. In the late 5th century the remains of St. Martin, Bishop of Tours, were translated to a new basilica by Bishop Perpetuus and enshrined in the eastern apse of the new basil-ica. During the centuries that followed, several Gaulish bishops became saints: Gregory of Langres (mid–6th century), Leodegar of Autun, Audoenus of Rouen (7th century), and Bonitus of Clermont (early 8th century). The translation of their remains was accom-panied by elaborate ceremonies and wonders and ended in richly adorned monuments.[55]

By the 8th century the cult of Ninian had become a tomb cult. The *Miracula Nynie Episcopi*, written at Whithorn in the last quarter of the 8th century, describes several miracles at the tomb of St. Ninian: a paralytic was restored to health, a man with leprosy was cleansed of his disease, a woman had her sight restored, and a priest called Plecgils (an Anglo-Saxon name) had a vision of Christ.[56] What was once a 6th century British cult had been transformed into an 8th century Anglo-Saxon cult.

Northumbria After Bede

In the 8th century York became the seat of an archbishop, and attracted some high-status people, as we can see from the York Helmet. The York Helmet, which dates from

750 to 775 CE, is the most outstanding object of the Anglo-Saxon period ever discovered. This iron and brass helmet was found in 1982 in Coppergate, when it was nearly struck by the claw of a mechanical digger. The operator stopped to check when he hit something hard—a wood-lined pit that contained the helmet, along with an iron tool and fragments of antler, stone and glass. The decoration of the nose-piece is a beautiful example of Anglo-Saxon craftsmanship, with an intricate pattern of entwined animals. On the crest is an inscription in Latin which translates as, "In the name of our Lord Jesus Christ, the Holy Spirit and God; and to all we say amen Oshere." The helmet was undoubtedly a prized possession and a great status symbol for the owner. "Oshere" was certainly a nobleman and may well have been a member of the Northumbrian royal family.[57]

Lindisfarne continued to play a significant role in Northumbrian religious life, producing the early 8th century Lindisfarne Gospels. The Lindisfarne Gospels (Matthew, Mark, Luke and John) is the work of one man—according to a note added at the end of the manuscript less than a century after its making—the artist was a monk called Eadfrith, Bishop of Lindisfarne between 698 and 721. His skill is evident in the opening pages of each gospel. A painting of the gospel's Evangelist is followed by an intricately patterned "carpet" page. Next is the "incipit" page, that is, an opening page in which the first letters of the gospels are greatly elaborated with interlacing and spiral patterns strongly influenced by Anglo-Saxon jewelry and enamel work. Eadfrith employed an exceptionally wide range of colors, using animal, vegetable and mineral pigments. In some places the manuscript remains partly unfinished, suggesting Eadfrith's work was ended prematurely by his death in 721.[58]

Christianity and Paganism in Early Northumbria: The Franks Casket

Despite all their saints and monasteries, the Northumbrians did not entirely forget their pagan past, as we can see from the Franks Casket. The Franks Casket (early 8th century), which is held in the British Museum—from whose website this description is taken—is a lidded rectangular box made of whale bone, carved on the sides and top in relief with scenes from Roman, Jewish, Christian and Germanic tradition. The base is constructed from four sides slotted and pegged into corner uprights, the bottom plates fitted into grooves at the base of the sides. It possibly stood on four low feet. Only one decorative panel now survives in the lid, the remaining elements being almost certainly replacements. There are scars left by lost metal fittings on the exterior—handle, lock, hasps and hinges—and crude internal repairs. The five surviving decorated panels are variously accompanied by carved texts in Old English and Latin, using both conventional and encoded runes as well as Insular script, in a variety of orientations. Each side is bordered by a long descriptive text and three contain additional labels; the lid panel has only the latter, though a longer text may originally have accompanied it.

The front is divided in two: the left half shows a composite scene from the Weland the Smith legend, the right half, the Adoration of the Magi, with the label "mægi" carved above the kings. The main inscription takes the form of a riddling alliterative verse about the casket's origin. The left-hand end depicts Romulus and Remus nurtured by the wolf with an inscription describing the scene. The back panel shows the capture of Jerusalem

Portrait of St. Mark from the Lindisfarne Gospels, seated, with his symbol, a winged lion blowing a trumpet, and carrying a book (British Library Flickr Commons, Creative Commons CCO 1.0 Universal Public Domain Dedication).

in 70 CE by the Roman general, later emperor, Titus: labels on the two lower corners read *dom* ("judgment"), and *gisl* ("hostage") respectively. The main inscription is in a mixture of Old English, Latin, runes and insular script. The right-hand end poses special problems of interpretation. The apparently episodic scene is evidently from Germanic legend but has not been satisfactorily identified. Three labels read: *risci* ("rush"), *wudu* ("wood") and *bita* ("biter"). The main runic text is in alliterative verse partly encoded by substituting cryptic forms for most of its vowels and perhaps certain other letters. The lid appears to depict an episode relating to the Germanic hero Egil and has the single label *aegili* ("Egil").

Almost everything about the Franks Casket is enigmatic, including its history.

It was first recorded in the possession of a family at Auzon in the Auvergne, during which time it was dismantled. The right-hand end became separated from the rest around this time, and passed eventually into the Museo Nazionale del Bargello in Florence, where it remains. A replica of this is mounted on the original casket. The other panels were bought from a Paris dealer and presented to the British Museum by the collector and curator Augustus Franks, whose name it bears. Its history prior to its surfacing in Auzon is unknown, though one second-hand account suggests that it came from the nearby church and cult center of St Julian at Brioude, from which it could have been looted at the time of the French Revolution. How and when the casket came to France can only ever be a matter for speculation, though Ian Wood has managed to identify one early medieval candidate who in theory could have taken it from the north of England to Brioude—the Frankish scholar Frithegod who was active in both areas in the middle 10th century.[59]

Just as enigmatic is the question of where and why it was made:

The language of the inscription shows that the carver used a Northumbrian or north Mercian dialect current in the early eighth century. The style of decoration, with its many details recalling Northumbrian manuscript art of the first half of the 8th century, accords with this. A Northumbrian origin is thus probable, though not strictly necessary. Aptly characterised as "self-consciously clever" by Wood, there can however be little doubt that the casket was made in a learned community with aristocratic tastes and connections; at such a date, that can only mean a monastic milieu. Wood's own tentative suggestion that this could have been Wilfrid's Ripon is ingenious and attractive, but discounts too readily the possibility of an origin at other major Northumbrian centers of learning such as Lindisfarne or even the more consciously Romanizing Monkwearmouth/Jarrow. The Casket's mix of Roman Christian, Jewish and Germanic traditions certainly reflects an interest in cosmography recorded in 7th or 8th century Northumbrian aristocratic and monastic circles; where, as we also know from Alcuin's famous reproof to the monks of Lindisfarne, tales of Germanic heroes were also recounted. The casket's program, in so far as we understand it, is however not merely a parade of learning and of epigraphic virtuosity. Word and image enter here a new and important Anglo-Saxon life together, in an iconographic program which seems to be based on parallels rather in the manner of Biblical types (a form of exegesis certainly known at Monkwearmouth/Jarrow). The Adoration of the Magi, for example is juxtaposed with the Weland legend, in which the birth of a hero also makes good sin and suffering, while the adjacent sides symbolising the founding of Rome and destruction of Jerusalem draw an obvious contrast.[60]

The Franks Casket features the legend of Weland, or Wayland, the Smith. Part of this legend features in the 10th century Old English poem *Deor*[61]:

> Welund tasted misery among snakes.
> The stout-hearted hero endured troubles
> had sorrow and longing as his companions
> cruelty cold as winter—he often found woe
> Once Nithad laid restraints on him,

> supple sinew-bonds on the better man.
> That went by; so can this.
>
> To Beadohilde, her brothers' death was not
> so painful to her heart as her own problem
> which she had readily perceived
> that she was pregnant; nor could she ever
> foresee without fear how things would turn out.
> That went by, so can this

According to the Old Norse *Völundarkvitha*, a poem in the 13th century *Poetic Edda*, the king of the Sami people had three sons: Völundr (Wayland) and his two brothers Egil and Slagfithr. In one version of the myth, the three brothers lived with three Valkyries: Ölrun, Hervör alvitr and Hlathguthr svanhvít. After nine years, the Valkyries left their lovers. Egil and Slagfithr followed, never to return. In another version, Völundr married the swan maiden Hervör, and they had a son, Heime, but Hervör later left Völundr. In both versions, his love left him with a ring. In the former myth, he forged seven hundred duplicates of this ring. Later, King Nithhad captured Völundr in his sleep in Nerike and ordered him hamstrung and imprisoned on the island of Sævarstöth. There Völundr was forced to forge items for the king. Völundr's wife's ring was given to the king's daughter, Böthvildr. Nithhad wore Völundr's sword. In revenge, Völundr killed the king's sons when they visited him in secret, fashioned goblets from their skulls, jewels from their eyes, and a brooch from their teeth. He sent the goblets to the king, the jewels to the queen and the brooch to the king's daughter. When Bodvild (Beadohilde) took her ring to Wayland for mending, he took the ring and raped her, fathering a son. He then escaped, using wings he made.

One of the scenes from the Wayland legend carved on the Franks Casket shows Wayland offering Nithhad a drink from a bowl he had skillfully fashioned from the skull of one of Nithhad's sons; behind Nithhad is a pregnant Beadohilde. The Franks Casket juxtaposes pagan and Christian pregnancies: the next panel to Wayland, Nithhad and Beadohilde shows the Magi, the star, Mary and her child.[62]

The story of Wayland and Beadohilde apparently had a happy ending. Beadohilde bore the hero Widia and was later reconciled with Wayland. Widia is mentioned in the Old English poem *Widsith*, and in the Anglo-Saxon fragments known as *Waldere*, in a section praising Mimung, Waldere's sword that Wayland had made[63]:

> ... a better sword
>
> except the one that I have also in
> its stone-encrusted scabbard laid aside.
> I know that Theodoric thought to Widia's self
> to send it and much treasure too,
> jewels with the blade, many more besides,
> gold-geared; he received reward
> when Nithhad's kinsman, Widia, Welund's son,
> delivered him from durance;
> through press of monsters hastened forth.

According to legend, Widia was a warrior fighting with Theodoric the Great, king of the Ostrogoths (475–526), ruler of Italy (493–526), and regent of the Visigoths (511–526). Widia may be based on the Gothic national hero Vidigoia, mentioned by Jordanes in his 6th century history of the Goths.

East Anglia and Mercia

Northumbria was the dominant kingdom in the 7th century, but two other kingdoms also vied for supremacy—East Anglia and Mercia. Mercia in particular posed a serious challenge to Northumbria, and by the 8th century it had overtaken its northern neighbor and become the most powerful of the Anglo-Saxon kingdoms.

5

Paganism and Christianity in Early East Anglia and Mercia

The Kingdom of East Anglia

Early Anglo-Saxon Cemeteries in East Anglia

The kingdom of East Anglia included the modern counties of Norfolk and Suffolk, and parts of Cambridgeshire. A number of early Anglo-Saxon cemeteries have been found in East Anglia, including a very large Anglo-Saxon enclosed cremation cemetery at Spong Hill, North Elmham (Norfolk), dated to the 5th–7th century CE; some 2,322 cremations and 40 inhumations were uncovered though finds from this site have been found since the 18th century. Grave goods include cinerary urns, knives, beads, tweezers, brooches and gaming pieces. Evidence for Neolithic settlement including pottery, lithic implements and post-holes was also uncovered. In the Roman period the area was part of a farmstead, with evidence of iron smelting and pottery manufacture. A single *gruben-haus* (sunken building) and rectangular post-hole structures represent Anglo-Saxon occupation of the site.[1] At Spong Hill 46.4 percent of cremation urns contained animal bone as well as human bone, suggesting that animal sacrifice was a widespread aspect of the funerary rites. Horse and sheep/goat were the most common species of animal sacrifice. Julie Bond argues that horses were probably the most commonly sacrificed species. Animals were probably sacrificed for funerary feasting, but this was not the primary concern in their slaughter. Even though there is widespread evidence of butchery, the motivation seems to be for beasts to accompany the deceased through the ritual process. The animals' flesh may have been partly consumed by mourners, perhaps as an important ritual act, but at Spong Hill as well as at Sancton in East Yorkshire dogs, horses and cattle often accompanied the deceased as whole animals.[2] Horses were important in the Anglo-Saxon paganism of East Anglia, with horse burials at Sutton Hoo Mound 17 and Lakenheath, both in Suffolk.

A horse burial was also found in the Anglo-Saxon cemetery at Sedgeford in north Norfolk. Here a female was buried with her head resting on the pelvis of a horse, though both the skull and limbs of the horse were missing due to truncation by a later burial. Surprisingly, the cemetery was dated to the 8th/9th century, when the Anglo-Saxons had converted to Christianity.[3]

Interestingly, horses also played an important part in the life of the Iceni, the Iron

Age inhabitants of East Anglia. In 1992, a metal-detectorist was walking a field at Saham Toney, to the west of Norwich, when he unearthed a series of small decorated bronzes, later identified as a group of Late Iron Age horse-harness fittings, consisting of harness rings, worn horse-bits, and a complete set of five terret-rings. This "exceptional group of objects was accompanied by some beautifully enamelled harness decorations, all of the early 1st century AD." In 2000, a Late Iron Age bridle-bit came to light at a farm to the north of East Dereham, not far from Saham Toney. Its appearance "was so perfect that it was initially thought to be modern, if not brand new. But its end loops betray its antiquity. They are decorated with elaborate but asymmetrical Celtic-style enamelled moldings, which make this an exceptionally rare piece, again dating to the final decades of the Iron Age."[4]

We don't know much about British survival in Anglo-Saxon Norfolk, but there are clues. The second element of the placename Kings Lynn in northwest Norfolk is from British *linn*, "pool," found in the names *Lindinis* (Ilchester in Somerset) and *Lindum* (Lincoln); Brancaster in north Norfolk has been linked to the Roman fort called *Branodunum* ("Crow/Raven Fort" in Celtic), and Eccles in northeast Norfolk is connected to Latin *ecclesia*, "church" (Welsh *eglwys*, Cornish *eglos*).[5] Perhaps this Celtic presence in Norfolk explains why the focus of Anglo-Saxon activity was in Suffolk, and why the Norfolk cities of Thetford and Norwich did not develop until the late 9th and early 10th century.

This Celtic presence may have been particularly strong in the area around King's Lynn, judging from the Late Iron Age Snettisham Treasure. The Snettisham Treasure was first discovered in 1948 at Snettisham in Norfolk, nine miles to the north of King's Lynn. Excavations were carried out, and further finds were made between 1950 and 1990. The hoard was found in a number of pits, three of which were double pits with two compartments, one on top of the other. The most spectacular part of the hoard is Hoard L—the upper compartment consisted of a small nest of seven silver and bronze torcs. Then in a corner of the shallow pit, there was an opening to a larger pit which had the richest treasure of all. There were two bronze bracelets at the top, then two silver torcs and finally ten gold torcs. In 1991 a great deposit of iron slag was found in the filling of a ditch. A magnetometer survey set up to trace the ditch, and it is now apparent that it forms an enclosure, 20 acres in extent. Coins found in the hoard (234 in all) indicated that the hoard was buried around 70 BCE. Most of the coins are Gallo-Belgic coins also found in France, which pre-date Julius Caesar's conquest of Gaul.[6]

PAGANISM IN EARLY EAST ANGLIA

The first king of East Anglia of whom anything is known is Rædwald, who ruled from 599 to 624. He converted to Christianity around 605, but his Christianity was obviously lukewarm, for as Bede says,[7] "in the same temple he had an altar to sacrifice to Christ, and another small one to offer victims to devils." Bede also says[8] that Rædwald was the fourth king that "had the sovereignty of all the southern provinces that are divided from the Northern by the river Humber."

Rædwald may have been the high-status individual buried at Sutton Hoo, near Woodbridge in Suffolk, in the famous ship-burial in Mound 1. In 1939, Mrs. Edith Pretty, a landowner at Sutton Hoo, Suffolk, asked archaeologist Basil Brown to investigate the largest of many Anglo-Saxon burial mounds on her property. Inside, he made one of the most spectacular archaeological discoveries of all time. Beneath the mound was the imprint of a 88.5-foot-long ship. At its center was a ruined burial chamber packed with treasures: Byzantine silverware, sumptuous gold jewelry, a lavish feasting set, and most famously, an ornate iron and copper alloy helmet. Tiny fragments showed that rich textiles once adorned the walls and floor, along with piles of clothes ranging from fine linen overshirts to shaggy woolen cloaks and caps trimmed with fur.[9]

The Sutton Hoo helmet is made of iron and is covered with panels of tinned copper alloy sheeting. The copper alloy sheets are stamped with various patterns including animal interlace, and warrior motifs depicted in two panels. A crest runs over the cap of the helmet and leads down the face in a straight line, forming the nose, which is gilt copper alloy. The crest itself is of iron and has gilt animal terminals at the forehead and back of the head, the animals having cloisonné garnet eyes. The iron crest and copper alloy eyebrows are inlaid with silver wire; the eyebrows have gilt zoomorphic terminals consisting of boar heads, and strips of garnet cloisonné work immediately above the eye sockets. The boar, of course, was associated with Germanic and Anglo-Saxon warriors.[10]

No trace of a body was found during the 1939 excavation of the Sutton Hoo ship burial. Analyses of soil samples for residual phosphate (a chemical left behind when a human or animal body has completely decayed away), taken in 1967 during the British Museum's excavations, support the idea that a body was originally placed in the burial chamber, but had totally decayed in the acidic conditions at the bottom of the ship. A group of coins found inside the purse in the grave provide some clues about who was buried in the ship. There were 37 Frankish gold tremissis, three coin-sized blanks and two ingots. The most recent work on the coins suggests that they were struck between around 610–635 CE. This provides an approximate period during which the burial probably took place.[11] There is no evidence that the person buried at Sutton Hoo was Rædwald, but he was certainly the most powerful and most overtly pagan of the East Anglian kings of the period.

A ship burial is described in *Beowulf*, set in pagan Denmark and Sweden. When Scyld Scefing, the ancestor of the legendary Scylding kings of Denmark died[12]

> His warrior band did what he bade them
> when he laid down the law among the Danes:
> they shouldered him out to the sea's flood,
> the chief they revered who had long ruled them.
> A ring-whorled prow rode in the harbour,
> ice-clad, outbound, a craft for a prince.
> They stretched their beloved lord in his boat,
> laid out by the mast, amidships,
> the great ring-giver, Far-fetched treasures
> were piled upon him, and precious gear.
> I never before heard of a ship so well furnished
> with battle-tackle, bladed weapons
> and coats of mail. The massed treasure
> was loaded on top of him: it would travel far
> on out into the ocean's sway.

No early ship burials are known from Denmark, but they are known from Vendel in Uppland, southern Sweden. Excavations in the late 19th century revealed 14 graves in and just beyond the southeast corner of Vendel churchyard. Several of the burials were contained in boats up to 30 feet long and were richly furnished with arrangements of weapons (including fine swords), helmets, cauldrons and chains, beads, shields, and tools.

The helmets from Graves 1, 12 and 14 bear close comparison to the helmet from the early 7th century ship-burial at Sutton Hoo, with die-stamped plaques depicting scenes of warriors. The shield from Grave 12 at Vendel is also very comparable to the Sutton Hoo shield and has a stamped metal strip mount which is actually die-linked to an equivalent piece at Sutton Hoo.[13]

However, Sutton Hoo was not only used for high-status burials. During excavations carried out between 1986 and 1992, two unusual groups of flat-grave burials were found:

> The Group 1 graves were situated at the eastern periphery of the site and comprised 23 burials, ten of which showed clear signs of violence or disrespectful treatment. The body positions were varied with at least 12 supine and 5 prone burials occurring, as well as two unusual kneeling burials and the enigmatic burial 27 interred in a unique plowing position. Of the Group 1 burials, three had traces of a coffin, of which one may have been accompanied by a joint of meat, and another, the "plowman," was buried with a wooden ard and rod. The burials were centered on a pit interpreted as the rotted root-mantle of a tree and Professor Carver's 1992 interim statement sees the group as marking a ritual area contemporary with the 7th-century mounds, where human sacrifice was carried out associated with a tree. Perhaps the "plowman" was sacrificed to the earth-mother.
>
> Group 2 was associated with Mound 5, which contained a primary cremation dated to the late 6th or early-7th-century, a date broadly consistent with the primary cremations in many of the excavated mounds. The group consisted of 16 graves, some apparently arranged around the mound and some in the quarry pits of the mound. A total of nine, or possibly ten, exhibited signs of violence or disrespectful treatment Six burials were on their sides, five were supine and three were prone. Two burials contained additional human remains and one may have been bent over backwards. One burial had the head wrenched out of alignment and an organic collar, which may have been a noose, was observed around the neck. It is likely that all the Group 2 burials had been executed.[14]

CHRISTIANITY IN EARLY EAST ANGLIA

Bede says[15] that Swithhelm, king of Essex, was baptized at the East Anglian royal estate of Rendlesham near Woodbridge in Suffolk, and the site of this royal estate has recently been located. Archaeological evaluation was undertaken on the Naunton Hall Estate close to the River Deben in Rendlesham to test the character and degree of preservation of the subsoil archaeology in two fields that had previously been subject to intensive metal-detecting and geophysical survey. These surveys indicated extensive and high-status Anglo-Saxon activity which can be related to the reference in Bede to a *vicus regius* ("royal settlement") at Rendlesham in the 7th century and represent a residence of those buried at Sutton Hoo about 3.5 miles to the southwest. Suffolk County Council have been managing the survey project since 2008, in which time 350 acres have been systematically surveyed. The metal detected finds suggest the presence of high status settlement, craft working and trade dating to the Anglo-Saxon period, with particular foci across individual fields. One of the notable features of the magnetometry results was a change in the character of the apparent archaeology from a landscape dominated by linear features and enclosures south of Naunton Hall Farm, to one consisting predominantly of individual pits, with finds indicative of 5th–7th century occupation, cremation and inhumation burials in the fields north of the farm. The aim of the evaluation was to test the result of the survey and establish the quality and preservation of the archaeological features below the plowsoil. To this end seven trenches were excavated in autumn 2013 and spring 2014 within two fields. Preliminary interpretation suggested potential settlement and burial of the early Anglo-Saxon period in one field and enclosed settlement and elite activity including metal working, particularly in the 6th–8th centuries in the other, with a definite later Roman background.[16]

At around the same time Ipswich in Suffolk was created as a trading settlement. The earliest occupation in Ipswich is 7th century and consists of a settlement, north of the river crossing at Stoke Bridge, and a cemetery on the higher ground above it, south of the Buttermarket. Around 700 CE the town expanded to cover about 120 acres. The economy was based on craft production and international trade. Craft production was dominated by the Ipswich Ware pottery industry, a large-scale enterprise, concentrated in the northeast corner of the town. The importance of the Ipswich ware industry is shown by its distribution, which not only covers the entire Kingdom of East Anglia but as far as the West Country, Yorkshire, London and Kent. All sites produced evidence of international trade. Imported goods include hone stones from Norway, lava querns from the Rhineland and pottery from the Rhineland, Belgium and Northern France. The trade also included perishable goods such as wool or woven textiles going out and wine coming in. Wine was imported in wooden barrels, some of which have been found, re-used as the linings of shallow wells across the town. An example from Lower Brook Street matched the tree ring pattern of the Mainz area of Germany.[17]

Christianity did not become established in East Anglia until the reign of Sigeberht, who came to the throne around 630 and ruled for about ten years. Bede (Book 3, Chapter 18) calls Sigeberht "a good and religious man" who had been baptized in France after being exiled by Rædwald. According to Bede, he was a particularly pious man[18]:

> This king became so great a lover of the heavenly kingdom, that quitting the affairs of his crown, and committing the same to his kinsman, Ecgric, who before held a part of that kingdom, he went himself into a monastery, which he had built, and having received the tonsure, applied himself rather to gain a heavenly throne. Some time after this, it happened that the nation of the Mercians, under King Penda, made war on the East Angles; who, finding themselves inferior in martial affairs to their enemy, entreated Sigebert to go with them to battle, to encourage the soldiers. He refused, upon which they threw him against his will out of the monastery, and carried him to the army, hoping that the soldiers would be less disposed to flee in the presence of him, who had once been a notable and a brave commander. But he, still keeping in mind his profession, whilst in the midst of a royal army, would carry nothing in his hand but a wand, and was killed with King Ecgric; and the pagans pressing on, all their army was either slaughtered or dispersed.

Ecgric was Sigeberht's successor, and the monastery he founded was possibly Bury St. Edmunds in Suffolk, then called *Beodricsworth*. Sigeberht established East Anglia's first bishopric at *Dommoc*,[19] probably Dunwich in Suffolk, with Felix of Burgundy as the first bishop. During the 630s, Sigeberht also established a royal palace, the cathedral church of St. Felix, and the earliest documented English school. A school at Dunwich was last mentioned between 1076 and 1083 when it was granted to Eye Priory in Suffolk. The church was overwhelmed by the sea in 1330 and no trace of the palace, church or school remains. While Sigeberht was king, says Bede,[20] the Irish priest Fursey established a monastery at *Cnobheresburg*, possibly the Roman fort of Burgh Castle near Great Yarmouth in Norfolk.

AN EARLY EAST ANGLIAN SAINT IN THE CAMBRIDGESHIRE FENS

The next East Anglian king discussed by Bede was Anna, whom Bede calls "a good man, and happy in a good and pious offspring."[21] The most pious of his offspring was Æthelthryth (also known as Etheldreda or Audrey). She married the Northumbrian king

Ecgfrith in 660 but, according to Bede, remained a virgin throughout her marriage. Eventually she entered the monastery of St. Abbs Head near Coldingham in the Scottish Borders, but after a year she was made abbess of the monastery at Ely in Cambridgeshire, which lay on an island surrounded by fenland, not far from the Romano-British shrine at Haddenham, and the Roman settlement and temple at Stonea. Sixteen years after her death, says Bede,[22] her sister and successor Abbess Seaxburh

> thought fit to take up her bones, and, putting them into a new coffin, to translate them into the church. Accordingly she ordered some of the brothers to provide a stone to make a coffin of; they accordingly went on board ship, because the country of Ely is on every side encompassed with the sea or marshes, and has no large stones, and came to a small abandoned city, not far from thence, which, in the language of the English, is called Grantchester [= Cambridge], and presently, near the city walls, they found a white marble coffin, most beautifully wrought, and neatly covered with a lid of the same sort of stone. Concluding therefore that God had prospered their journey, they returned thanks to Him, and carried it to the monastery.
>
> The body of the holy virgin and spouse of Christ, when her grave was opened, being brought into sight, was found as free from corruption as if she had died and been buried on that very day; as the aforesaid Bishop Wilfrid, and many others that know it, can testify. But the physician, Cynefrid, who was present at her death, and when she was taken up out of the grave, was wont of more certain knowledge to relate, that in her sickness she had a very great swelling under her jaw. " And I was ordered," said he, "to lay open that swelling, to let out the noxious matter in it, which I did, and she seemed to be somewhat more easy for two days, so that many thought she might recover from her distemper; but the third day the former pains returning, she was soon snatched out of the world, and exchanged all pain and death for everlasting life and health. And when so many years after her bones were to be taken out of the grave, a pavilion being spread over it, all the congregation of brothers were on the one side, and of sisters on the other, standing about it singing, and the abbess, with a few, being gone to take up and wash the bones, on a sudden we heard the abbess within loudly cry out, 'Glory be to the name of the Lord.' Not long after they called me in, opening the door of the pavilion, where I found the body of the holy virgin taken out of the grave and laid on a bed, as if it had been asleep; then taking off the veil from the face, they also showed the incision which I had made, healed up; so that, to my great astonishment, instead of the open gaping wound with which she had been buried, there then appeared only an extraordinarily slender scar.
>
> "Besides, all the linen cloths in which the body had been buried, appeared entire and as fresh as if they had been that very day wrapped about her chaste limbs."

Miracles occurred at the tomb of the saint: "It happened also that by the touch of that linen, devils were expelled from bodies possessed, and other distempers were sometimes cured; and the coffin she was first buried in is reported to have cured some of distempers in the eyes, who, praying with their heads touching that coffin, presently were delivered from the pain or dimness in their eyes."

The Kingdom of Mercia

THE BEGINNINGS OF MERCIA

The name *Mercia* is a Latinization of Old English *mierce*, "border-people," from Old English *mearc* "border," referring perhaps to people living in Herefordshire, Shropshire and Cheshire, on the border between the Anglo-Saxons and the Welsh kingdom of Powys. The first Mercian king of whom anything is known is Penda, who first entered history in 633, when, with his Welsh ally Cadwallon ap Cadfan, king of Gwynedd, he defeated and killed Edwin of Northumbria at the Battle of Hatfield Chase. Bede calls Penda "a most warlike man of the royal race of the Mercians," who "from that time governed that nation twenty-two years with various success."[23]

In 642, Penda defeated and killed Oswald of Northumbria at the Battle of Maserfield; Welsh sources imply that this time he was assisted by Cynddylan, the ruler of the Welsh kingdom of Powys. In 655 Penda attacked King Oswiu of Northumbria with "thirty legions, led on by most noted commanders," including Æthelhere, king of East Anglia[24] (Bede, Book, and Cadfael king of Gwynedd.[25] He besieged Oswiu at *Iudeu* (location unknown), where Oswiu offered him a great deal of treasure in return for peace. Then for some reason Penda and his army moved south, and Penda was killed at the Battle of Winwaed, possibly somewhere along the River Went, which rises near Featherstone in West Yorkshire, and flows into the River Don a few miles from Doncaster in South Yorkshire. Most of Penda's leaders were killed, including Æthelhere. As Bede says[26]: "The battle was fought near the river Winwaed, which then, with the great rains, had not only filled its channel, hut overflowed its banks, so that many more were drowned in the flight than destroyed by the sword."

PAGANISM IN MERCIA

Penda was a pagan, and most of what we know of Mercian paganism come from boar helmets, like the helmet from Benty Grange (Derbyshire), and the Pioneer Helmet from Northamptonshire, and from deviant burials, like the woman buried prone (face down) at Willoughby on the Wolds (Nottinghamshire) with a number of items including a beaver-tooth pendant, thought to be an amulet or charm—she may have been buried prone to prevent her from returning to haunt the living. There were also horse burials at Broughton Lodge: horse 3 was found buried next to weapon burial 88, with the head-bridle placed in the horse's grave between its legs.[27] Grave 15/16/H1 contained two human individuals together with a horse: a male without grave goods, and an individual in female costume, with a gilt-bronze great square-headed brooch.

A number of other horse burials have been found in the Mercian region. At Wood-stone, Peterborough (in Cambridgeshire but close to Northamptonshire) inhumation burials and artifacts dating from the 5th/6th century also included a burial with a horse. At Hunsbury Hill Hardingstone (Northamptonshire) a cemetery which was in use until the late 7th century yielded a horse in a grave accompanied by a circular bronze attachment plate with a central boss and four other bosses at the points of a cruciform star with four fishes set cruciformly. At Marston St. Lawrence (Northamptonshire) a cemetery dated to the last part of the 6th century included a trail of burnt grain and a horse near a human burial.[28]

Two horse burials have been found in Leicestershire. At Wanlip, about three miles north of Leicester, an Anglo-Saxon cemetery was uncovered between 1958 and 1960. A number of horse bones were discovered beneath a patch of charcoal and ash. It would appear that the horse was buried with its bridle still in place. Two shields were then placed on top of it, and judging from the ash and charcoal, then set of fire. The cemetery dates from the 5th/6th century.[29] Wigston Magna is just south of Leicester, and an Anglo-Saxon cemetery was found there in 1795 and was visited by the Leicester historian John Thosby. Throsby says that "about twenty human skeletons were found all within a square of about 10 yards, and, by most of them, some sort of furniture." Throsby adds that they found a pile of stones—in removing these stones they found the remains of four skeletons; but, although every part might be found lying in a state perfectly undisturbed ever since their interment, yet most of them, except the leg and arm bones, were in such a state of decay, that they could not be moved by the hand without dropping instantly to pieces. These four lay nearly side by side at the depth of a yard below the surface of the gravel and with them many apparent war trappings; and near one of them part of the skeleton of a horse, and something like a bridle-bit, which I did not see; the men informed me it was much perished and in consequence threw it away.

The cemetery is difficult to date but may well belong to the 6th century.[30]

THE MERCIAN CONVERSION

In 653, while Penda was still king of the Mercians, the Middle Angles of the East Midlands, who were ruled by Penda's son Peada, converted to Christianity. As Bede says of Peada[31]:

Being an excellent youth, and most worthy of the title and person of a king, he was by his father elevated to the throne of that nation, and came to Oswiu, king of the Northumbrians, requesting to have his daughter Alchflaed given him to wife; but could not obtain his desires unless he would embrace the faith of Christ, and be baptized, with the nation which he governed. When he heard the preaching of truth, the promise of the heavenly kingdom, and the hope of resurrection and future immortality, he declared that he would willingly become a Christian, even though he should be refused the virgin; being chiefly prevailed on to receive the faith by King Oswiu's son Alhfrith, who was his relation and friend, and had married his sister Cyneburh, the daughter of King Penda.

So Peada was baptized by Bishop Finan at the royal estate called "At the Wall" (possibly Newcastle-upon-Tyne). Peada returned home, bringing with him four priests; including Cedd and Adda, and Betti, who were English, and Diuma, who was Irish. They preached to the Middle Angles, with Penda's tacit approval:

Nor did King Penda obstruct the preaching of the word among his people, the Mercians, if any were willing to hear it; but, on the contrary, he hated and despised those whom he perceived not to perform the works of faith, when they had once received the faith, saying, "They were contemptible and wretched who did not obey their God, in whom they believed."

After Penda was killed, Oswiu ruled over the Mercians, Peada ruled over the kingdom of the Southern Mercians, "divided by the River Trent from the Northern Mercians," and Diuma was made first bishop of the Mercians and Middle Angles. However, Peada did not rule for long, for he was "very wickedly killed, by the treachery, as is said, of his wife, during the very time of celebrating Easter," just a year after the death of Penda.[32] While he was king Peada founded the monastery of Peterborough in Cambridgeshire, originally called *Medehamstede*. Little is known of its history, and no details of the buildings survive, but the grandeur of the daughter church at Brixworth suggests that the church must have been large and similarly grand. *Medehamstede* was destroyed by the Danes in 870 and lay ruined until refounded around 963–6 as a Benedictine monastery.[33] The church at Brixworth in Northamptonshire was built between 670 and 720. Brixworth church is described as "probably the most impressive early Saxon building in the country." It is likely that it was the church of a Mercian monastery and that St. Wilfrid was the builder. There are indications of a pre-existing (presumably Roman) building under the tower and west end of the present church. The major part of the surviving building is 7th century with re-used Roman brick.[34]

Peada was succeeded by Wulfhere, another son of Penda, who was a Christian. He was as aggressive as his father and conquered the Isle of Wight and the Meon Valley in Hampshire, giving them to Æthelwealh, king of the South Saxons. He died in 675 and was succeeded by Æthelred, another son of Penda, who ruled until 704. Æthelred invaded Kent and destroyed the city of Rochester; he defeated Ecgfrith of Northumbria at the Battle of the Trent; and he took permanent possession of Lindsey in Lincolnshire, which until then had alternated between Northumbria and Mercia. In 704 Æthelred abdicated to become a monk at Bardney in Lincolnshire in favor of his nephew Coenred, the son of Wulfhere. Coenred abdicated in 709 and went to Rome. He was replaced by Ceolred, the son of Æthelred, who died in 716. Ceolred was succeeded by Æthelbald, who was the grandson of Eowa, the brother of Penda.

St. Chad of Lichfield

The most famous early Mercian bishop was Chad, the brother of Cedd, one of the priests who first preached to the Middle Angles. Chad was probably born in Northumbria but is likely to have come from a British background—his name apparently derives from Celtic *cad*, "battle, war-band."[35] He studied with the Irish monk and bishop Aidan at Lindisfarne in Northumbria, some time between 635 and 651, then spent some time in Ireland. In 664 he became abbot of the monastery of Lastingham in North Yorkshire. Not long after, he was ordained bishop of the Northumbrians by Wini, bishop of Winchester, and two British bishops. This ordination was judged invalid, and Chad retired to Lastingham. But a bishop was soon required in Mercia, so Chad took up an appointment as Bishop of Lichfield (Staffordshire), but died of the plague after only two and a half years, in 672.

Lichfield is close to the Roman Ryknild and Watling Streets, and recent work close to Stowe Pool in the center of Lichfield has revealed evidence of a two-celled structure, partially built of reused Romano-British rubble, dating to the 5th/6th century CE. The Romano-British material may have come from the nearby Roman settlement of *Letocetum*, and the two-celled structure may have been an early British church.[36]

Not long before he died, says Bede,[37] Chad had a sort of vision when he was alone but for one monk called Owini:

> One day when he was thus employed abroad, and his companions were gone to the church, as I began to state, the bishop was alone reading or praying in the oratory of that place, when on a sudden, as he afterwards said, he heard the voice of persons singing most sweetly and rejoicing, and appearing to descend from heaven. Which voice he said he first heard coming from the southeast, and that afterwards it drew near him, till it came to the roof of the oratory where the bishop was, and entering therein, filled the same and all about it. He listened attentively to what he heard, and after about half an hour, perceived the same song of joy to ascend from the roof of the said oratory, and to return to heaven the same way it came, with inexpressible sweetness. When he had stood some time astonished, and seriously revolving in his mind what it might be, the bishop opened the window of the oratory, and making a noise with his hand, as he was often wont to do, ordered [Owini] to come in to him. He accordingly went hastily in, and the bishop said to him, "Make haste to the church, and cause the seven brothers to come hither, and do you come with them." When they were come, he first admonished them to preserve the virtue of peace among themselves, and towards all others; and indefatigably to practise the rules of regular discipline, which they had either been taught by him, or seen him observe or had noticed in the words or actions of the former fathers. Then he added, that the day of his death was at hand; for, said he, " that amiable guest, who was wont to visit our brethren, has vouchsafed also to come to me this day, and to call me out of this world. Return, therefore, to the church, and speak

to the brethren, that they in their prayers recommend my passage to our Lord, and that they be careful to provide for their own, the hour whereof is uncertain, by watching, prayer, and good works."

As promised, the "angelic spirits" who had sung to him, returned within seven days and took Chad away:

Chad died on the 2nd of March, and was first buried by St. Mary's Church, but afterwards, when the church of the most holy prince of the apostles, Peter, was built, his bones were translated into it. In both which places, as a testimony of his virtue, frequent miraculous cures are wont to be wrought. And of late, a certain distracted person, who had been wandering about everywhere, arrived there in the evening, unknown or unregarded by the keepers of the place, and having rested there all the night, went out in his perfect senses the next morning, to the surprise and delight of all; thus showing that a cure had been performed on him through the goodness of God. The place of the sepulchre is a wooden monument, made like a little house, covered, having a hole in the wall, through which those that go thither for devotion usually put in their hand and take out some of the dust, which they put into water and give to sick cattle or men to drink, upon which they are presently eased of their infirmity, and restored to health.

ST. GUTHLAC OF CROWLAND (LINCOLNSHIRE)

One Mercian saint not mentioned by Bede is Guthlac of Crowland in Lincolnshire. Guthlac (673–714) was born into the Mercian nobility and became a soldier at the age of 15. After nine successful years, he rejected the warrior life and became a monk at the monastery of Repton in Derbyshire. After living under monastic rule for several years, he withdrew to Crowland, a secluded, desolate, spot on an "island" (actually, a gravel peninsula) in the fens of south Lincolnshire, to pursue the life of the religious hermit. About 740, scarcely twenty-five years after the saint's death, Ælfwald, King of the East Angles (713–749), commissioned Felix to write Guthlac's *Life*, which was translated into Old English in the 11th century. Here Guthlac's Lincolnshire retreat is described in some detail[38]:

There is in Britain a fen of immense size, which begins from the river Granta [Cam] not far from the city which is named Grantchester [Cambridge]. There are immense marshes, now a black pool of water, now foul running streams, and also many islands, and reeds, and hillocks, and thickets, and with manifold windings wide and long it continues up to the north sea.

Guthlac decided he would settle there and asked the inhabitants about a suitable place to live:

Whereupon they told him many things about the vastness of the wilderness. There was a man named Tatwine who said he knew an island especially obscure, which ofttimes many men had attempted to inhabit, but no man could do it on account of manifold horrors and fears, and the loneliness of the wide wilderness; so that no man could endure it, but every one on this account had fled from it. When the holy man Guthlac heard these words, he bid him straightway show him the place, and he did so; he embarked in a vessel, and they went both through the wild fens till they came to the spot which is called Crowland

There Guthlac made his home[39]:

There was on the island a great mound raised upon the earth, which some of yore men had men had dug and broken up in hopes of treasure. On the other side of the mound a place was dug, as it were a great water-cistern. Over the cistern the blessed man Guthlac built himself a house at the beginning, as soon as he settled in the hermit-station. Then he resolved he would use neither woollen nor linen garment, but that he would live all the days of his life in clothing of skins, and so he continued to do.

Guthlac's "great mound" sounds like a Neolithic or Bronze Age barrow, or burial mound. It is known that there was a Bronze Age barrow cemetery constructed along the axis of the gravel peninsula, on a line running northeast from Crowland Abbey to Anchorage Field.[40]

While he was at Crowland, Guthlac gave sanctuary to Æthelbald, who at the time was fleeing from Ceolred. Guthlac predicted that Æthelbald would become king, and Æthelbald promised to build him an abbey if his prophecy became true. Æthelbald did become king and, even though Guthlac had died two years previously, kept his word and started construction of Crowland Abbey on St. Bartholomew's Day (August 24) 716 CE.

St. Guthlac, tormented by demons, is handed a scourge by St. Bartholomew. *Guthlac Roll*, dating from AD 1210. The British Library Board Harley MS Roll Y.6 (British Library, London, UK © British Library Board. All Rights Reserved/Bridgeman Images).

THE STAFFORDSHIRE HOARD

Very little was known about 7th century Mercia until the recent discovery of the Staffordshire Hoard. The Staffordshire Hoard, the largest collection of Anglo-Saxon gold and silver metalwork ever found, was discovered in a field near the village of Hammerwich, near Lichfield, in Staffordshire, on July 5, 2009; it consists of more than 3,500 items, that are nearly all martial or warlike in character. The Staffordshire Hoard totals over 11 pounds of gold, 3 pounds of silver and 3,500 cloisonné garnets. There is nothing comparable in terms of content and quantity in the UK or mainland Europe. It is remarkable for being almost exclusively war-gear, with an extraordinary quantity of weapon hilt fittings, that is, decorative items from the handles of swords and knives. Many feature beautiful garnet inlays or animals in elaborate filigree. The artifacts have tentatively been dated to the 7th or 8th centuries, placing the origin of the items in the time of the Kingdom of Mercia.

The hoard was discovered very near Watling Street. One of the major thoroughfares of Roman Britain, it ran for about 250 miles from Dover in Kent past Wroxeter in Shropshire and was probably still in use when the hoard was buried. The average quality of the workmanship is extremely high, and especially remarkable in view of the large number of individual objects, such as swords or helmets, from which the elements in the hoard came.

The hoard contains mainly military items, including sword pommel caps (the pommel cap is the tip of the hilt of a sword that anchors the hilt fittings to the sword blade). Single pommel caps from this period are extremely rare archaeological finds, and to find this many together is unprecedented. It is possible that the red garnets in the hoard came from as far away as India or even Sri Lanka—scientific analysis is being carried out to discover more. There are hundreds of pieces of silver foil in the hoard, which are thought to come from one or more helmets.[41]

One of the few non-martial items from the hoard is a silver gilt strip bearing a Biblical inscription in Latin. Rivet holes show that it was originally fastened to another, larger object, possibly a reliquary or the cover of a Bible. A decorative stone, possibly a garnet, was set into the now empty mount at one end of the strip, while an animal head adorns the other end.

Incised into each face of the strip is a verse from the Latin Bible (Numbers 10:35). The text is slightly different on the two sides, but it is clear that the outer side is the most important one since the incisions for the letters have been filled with a dark, silver compound known as niello. The text, when translated into English, reads: "rise up, o Lord, and may thy enemies be scattered and those who hate thee be driven from thy face."[42]

This text is a prayer for spiritual protection invoked against the torment of demons by the desert father St. Anthony, and was re-employed for this purpose by St. Guthlac, and by St. Dunstan, the 10th century Archbishop of Canterbury, as recorded in their Lives. Of great relevance in this context, it was also quoted around 700 in a consoling prophecy by Guthlac to King Æthelbald, whose reign signaled the rise of Mercia's fortunes. Æthelbald was at that time in exile and was comforted by the hermit saint who assured him that he would come to power without bloodshed, quoting the passage from Numbers 10.35 which was the plea of the Israelites to the Lord in the Wilderness invoking God to rise to protect them, through the Ark, the following of which would bring them restoration and renewal. The wording of this prophecy closely parallels the inscription on the Staffordshire hoard strip.[43]

It is likely that the hoard was buried in the late 7th or early 8th century. The Anglo-Saxon scholar Nicholas Brooks points out that most of the hoard is gold and sees the gold in terms of gift-giving. Whoever composed *Beowulf* thought of the king as a *goldwine gumena*—the gold-friend of the warriors—or as the *goldwine Geata*—the gold-friend of the Geats. He is a *gold-gyfa*, a giver of gold, a *beag-gyfa*, a giver of rings. The royal hall of Heorot is the *gifhealle*—the gift hall. The importance of the king's gifts of gold, to his wives and to his followers and warriors, is emphasized again and again throughout the poem. And in return, both from his wife and from his followers, the king expects faithful service. The practice of giving a heriot, *here-geatu*, war-gear, to the king, at death, was well-established in Anglo-Saxon law, and is attested from the middle of the 10th century.[44] So it is possible that the hoard represents a series of gifts to Mercian kings like Penda (after all, Oswiu offered a great deal of "treasure" to Penda before his final battle), which were accumulated as potential gifts from a Mercian king to his followers. It could have been buried after the death of Penda in 655 or his son Peada a few months later, or in the early 700s after the death of Æthelred and before the accession of Æthelbald (who was not a descendant of Penda).

The Last Anglo-Saxon Kingdom

The kingdom of Wessex in southern England was a long way from Northumbria, and Bede has relatively little to say about the kingdom. In fact, Wessex was insignificant in Bede's time, and did not emerge from obscurity until the late 9th century, when became in effect the last Anglo-Saxon kingdom. Then King Alfred ordered the writing of the *Anglo-Saxon Chronicle*, with a new version of the Wessex foundation story in which Wessex appears as the least Anglo-Saxon of the Anglo-Saxon kingdoms.

6

Paganism and Christianity
in the Early Kingdom of Wessex

Early Wessex in Bede's Ecclesiastical History

THE HISTORY OF EARLY WESSEX

The core of the kingdom of Wessex lay in the modern counties of Hampshire, Wiltshire, Somerset and Dorset. The first Wessex king that Bede mentions[1] is Ceawlin, who was pagan and apparently ruled all the lands south of the Humber in the late 6th century. Intriguingly, Ceawlin is a Celtic name, shared with Caelin, the brother of Cedd who preached to the Middle Angles, and Chad, the saintly bishop of Lichfield in Mercia. The next ruler that Bede mentions is Cwichelm, who tried to assassinate Edwin of Northumbria in 626 CE. However, for Bede, the first notable event in the history of Wessex was the conversion in 635 of the Wessex king Cynegils[2]:

> At that time, the West Saxons, formerly called Gewisse, in the reign of Cynegils, embraced the faith of Christ, at the preaching of Bishop Birinus, who came into Britain by the advice of Pope Honorius; having promised in his presence that he would sow the seed of the holy faith in the inner parts beyond the dominions of the English. where no other teacher had been before him. Hereupon he received episcopal consecration from Asterius, bishop of Genoa; but on his arrival in Britain, he first entered the nation of the Gewissae, and finding all there most confirmed pagans, he thought it better to preach the word of God there, than to proceed further to seek for others to preach to.
>
> Now, as he preached in the aforesaid province, it happened that the king himself, having been catechized, was baptised together with his people, and Oswald, the most holy and victorious king of the Northumbrians, being present, received him as he came forth from baptism, and by an alliance most pleasing and acceptable to God, first adopted him, thus regenerated, for his son, and then took his daughter in marriage. The two kings gave to the bishop the city called Dorcas, there to settle his episcopal see; where having built and consecrated churches, and by his labor called many to the Lord, he departed this life, and was buried in the same city; but many years after, when Hedda was bishop, he was translated thence to the city of Winchester, and laid in the church of the blessed apostles, Peter and Paul.

From this we learn that Cynegils was baptized by Birinus at *Dorcic* (Dorchester-on-Thames, Oxfordshire), that Oswald of Northumbria was his godfather, that Birinus was bishop of Dorchester until his death, and that his body was later translated to Winchester by bishop Hedda (also known as Hædde). Dorchester-on-Thames was an old Roman town, and by 600 CE it had become the stronghold of a prominent Anglo-Saxon ruler or leading family[3]:

Excavations within the town disclosed Byzantine and early Anglo-Saxon gold coinage, along with gold ornaments and personal jewelry dated c. 600–625AD. Another "princely" or royal site of the early Thames Valley Saxons has been identified at Cuddesdon, some 6 miles north of Dorchester. The unusually rich finds there were contemporary with those within Dorchester and probably represent a rural *villa regalis* [royal estate center] of the same family. It has also been observed correctly that some place in this region, probably Dorchester, was serving as a central, perhaps royally controlled redistribution or production centre for early Anglo-Saxon prestige items and raw materials. The sum of the archaeological evidence thus strongly points to Dorchester as an important multifunctional central place of the Thames Valley Saxons and a likely headquarters of their kings by the opening of the seventh century.

The Byzantine gold coin found in Dorchester was a *solidus* of Mauricius Tiberius, Byzantine Emperor from 582 to 602 CE.[4] The rich finds from Cuddesdon were found in a 7th century cemetery in front of the gateway of the 17th century episcopal palace at Cuddesdon—the finds included a "Coptic" bronze bucket and blue glass vases.[5]

Cynegils was succeeded by his son Cenwalh, who was apparently a pagan[6]:

The king also dying, his son Cenwalh succeeded him in the throne, but refused to embrace the mysteries of the faith, and of the heavenly kingdom; and not long after also he lost the dominion of his earthly kingdom; for he put away the sister of Penda, king of the Mercians, whom he had married, and took another wife; whereupon a war ensuing, he was by him expeled from his kingdom, and withdrew to Anna, king of the East Saxons, where living three years in banishment, he found and received the true faith, and was baptized.

Having been expelled from his kingdom by Penda of Mercia, Cenwalh abandoned Dorchester-on-Thames (which was uncomfortably close to Mercian territory) and relocated the bishopric to Winchester in Hampshire (the old Roman city of *Venta Belgarum*). As Bede says[7]:

But when Cenwalh was restored to his kingdom, there came into that province out of Ireland, a certain bishop called Agilbert, by nation a Frenchman, but who had then lived a long time in Ireland, for the purpose of reading the Scriptures. This bishop came of his own accord to serve this king, and preach to him the word of life. The king, observing his erudition and industry, desired him to accept an episcopal see, and stay there as his bishop. Agilbert complied with the prince's request, and presided over those people many years. At length the king, who understood none but the language of the Saxons, grown weary of that bishop's barbarous tongue, brought into the province another bishop of his own nation, whose name was Wini, who had been ordained in France; and dividing his province into two dioceses, appointed this last his episcopal see in the city of Winchester.

The name *Cenwalh* means "Bold Briton" suggesting that Cenwalh, like Ceawlin, had a British background.

The next Wessex king to attract Bede's attention was Cædwalla, who has the same name as Cadwallon of Gwynedd, the Welsh ruler who wreaked such devastation in Northumbria. In 685 Cædwalla attacked Aethelwealh king of Sussex, which at the time was under Mercian control[8]:

Meanwhile Caedwalla, a young and vigorous prince of the Gewisse, being an exile from his own land, came with an army and slew King Aethelwealh, wasting the kingdom with fierce slaughter and devastation. But he was quickly driven out by two of the king's ealdormen, Berhthun and Andhun, who from that time held the kingdom. The former was afterwards killed by Caedwalla when he was king of the Gewisse and the kingdom reduced to a worse state of slavery. Ine, who ruled after Caedwalla, also oppressed the country in the same harsh way for many years.

Not long after says Bede,[9] Cædwalla also attacked the Isle of Wight, which was controlled by the kingdom of Sussex:

After Caedwalla had gained possession of the kingdom of the Gewisse he also captured the Isle of Wight, which until then had been entirely given up to idolatry, and endeavoured to wipe out all the natives by merciless slaughter and to replace them with by inhabitants from his own kingdom, binding himself, or so it is said, by a vow, though he was not yet Christian, that if he captured the island he would give a fourth part of it and of the booty to the Lord. He fulfilled his vow by giving it for the service of the Lord to Bishop Wilfrid, who happened to have come there from his own people at that time.

The name *Gewisse* means "The Sure Ones, The Certain Ones," and suggests that the Gewisse, with their Celtic names, were originally British allies of the Saxons. Wilfrid was abbot of the monastery at Ripon (North Yorkshire) and Bishop of Northumbria, until he fell out with the king; while he was exiled from Northumbria, he founded a monastery at Selsey in West Sussex.

Cædwalla reigned for only a short time, as Bede explains in an entry for 688[10]:

In the third year of the reign of Aldfrith, Caedwalla, king of the West Saxons, having most honorably governed his nation two years, quitted his crown for the sake of our Lord and his everlasting kingdom, and went to Rome, being desirous to obtain the peculiar honor of being baptized in the church of the blessed apostles, for he had learned that in baptism alone, the entrance into heaven is opened to mankind; and he hoped at the same time, that laying down the flesh, as soon as baptized, he should immediately pass to the eternal joys of heaven; both which things, by the blessing of our Lord, came to pass accord. mg as he had conceived in his mind. For coming to Rome, at the time that Sergius was pope, he was baptized on the holy Saturday before Easter Day, in the year of our Lord 689 and being still in his white garments, he fell sick, and departed this life on the 20th of April, and was associated with the blessed in heaven.

Cædwalla was succeeded by King Ine, says Bede:

When Cædwalla went to Rome, Ine succeeded him on the throne, being of the blood royal; and having reigned thirty-seven years over that nation, he gave up the kingdom in like manner to younger persons, and went away to Rome, to visit the blessed apostles, at the time when Gregory was pope, being desirous to spend some time of his pilgrimage upon earth in the neighborhood of the holy place, that he might be more easily received by the saints into heaven.

ANGLO-SAXONS AND BRITONS IN EARLY WESSEX

Native Britons obviously played a significant role in early Wessex, and this is particularly evident during the reign of King Ine. Ine drew up a code of laws which recognized the rights and obligations not only of Englishmen but also of "Welshmen" (that is, Britons) in the kingdom of Wessex. The code states (24.2) that a Welshman who owns five hides of land has a *wergeld* of 600 shillings; and (23.3) that a Welsh taxpayer (*gafolgelda*), or the owner of a single hide of land, has a *wergeld* of 120 shillings, and his son a *wergeld* of 100 shillings (a hide is the amount of land sufficient to support a household). This compares unfavorably with the equivalent English ranks which have *wergelds* of 1,200 and 200 shillings respectively. The property qualification of five hides is that which was required to qualify as a member of the nobility, and one of the most significant pieces of information we are given here is that there were "Welsh" nobles within Ine's kingdom.[11] *Wergeld* is a concept that comes from the early 6th century Salic Law drawn up by the Frankish king Clovis I, and is the value placed on every human being and every piece of property.

CHRISTIANITY IN EARLY WESSEX

Bede gives us details of only one saint from Wessex, Hædde of Winchester. Hædde was Bishop of the West Saxons from 676 to 705 and Bede says of him[12]:

In the year of the incarnation of our Lord 705, Aldfrith king of the Northumbrians, died just before the end of the twentieth year of his reign. His son Osred, a boy about eight years of age, succeeding him in the throne, reigned eleven years. In the beginning of his reign, Hædde, bishop of the West Saxons, departed to the heavenly kingdom; for he was a good and just man, and exercised his episcopal duties rather by his innate love of virtue, than by what he had gained from learning. The most reverend prelate, Pechthelm, of whom we shall speak in the proper place, and who was a long time either deacon or monk with his successor Aldhelm, is wont to relate that many miraculous cures have been wrought in the place where he died, through the merit of his sanctity; and that the men of that province used to carry the dust from thence for the sick, which, when they had put into water, the sprinkling or drinking thereof restored health to many sick men and beasts; so that the holy earth being frequently carried away, there was a considerable hole left.

Bede tells us that after the death of Hædde, Wessex was divided into two dioceses: one diocese (Winchester) was given to Daniel, the other (Sherborne in Dorset) was given to Aldhelm:

Aldhelm, when he was only a priest and abbot of the monastery of Malmesbury, by order of a synod of his own nation, wrote a notable book against the error of the Britons, in not celebrating Easter at the proper time, and in doing several other things not consonant to the purity and the peace of the church; and by the reading of this book he persuaded many of them, who were subject to the West Saxons, to adopt the Catholic celebration of our Lord's resurrection.

Indeed, in around 672, when he was abbot of Malmesbury in northwest Wiltshire, Aldhelm wrote to Geraint, king of Dumnonia (Devon and Cornwall), exhorting him to fall in line with Wessex and the other Anglo-Saxon kingdoms on the dating of Easter. It seems that relations between Wessex and Dumnonia were cordial, for at some point Aldhelm visited Dumnonia, and Geraint gave a grant of five hides of land at Maker in Cornwall, at the mouth of the Tamar, to the monastery and bishopric of Sherborne in Dorset.[13] Evidently relations with Dumnonia were much better than relations with Dyfed in southwest Wales: Aldhelm explains that the priests or bishops of Dyfed, who "glory in the special individual purity of their way of life,"

detest our communion to such a great extent that they disdain equally to celebrate the divine offices in church with us and to take courses of food at table for the sake of charity. Rather, they cast the scraps of their dinners and the remains of their feasts to be devoured by the jaws of ravenous dogs and filthy pigs, and they order the vessels and flagons [i.e., those used in common with clergy of the Roman Church] to be purified and purged with grains of sandy gravel, and with the dusky cinders of ash. No greeting of peace is offered, no kiss of affectionate brotherhood is bestowed…. But indeed, should any of us, I mean Catholics, go to them for the purpose of habitation, they do not deign to admit us to the company of their brotherhood until we have been compelled to spend the space of forty days in penance.

Aldhelm's letter might suggest that relations between Anglo-Saxons and British were strained, but this was not necessarily the case. Bede tells us[14] that in around 665 Chad was consecrated bishop of Northumbria by Bishop Wini of Winchester and "two bishops of the British nation, who kept Easter Sunday according to the canonical manner."

Winchester was probably chosen as the first bishopric because it was an old Roman town, and because there were Anglo-Saxons living nearby, judging by the Anglo-Saxon cemeteries to the east and north of the town—at St. Giles Hill, Winnall, Kings Worthy and Itchen Abbas. The best known of these was the cremation and inhumation cemetery at Worthy Park, Kings Worthy, to the north of Winchester. It included 94 inhumations and 46 cremations. The majority of the inhumations were accompanied by grave goods which included beads, brooches, buckles, knives, latchlifters, pursemounts, rings, shield bosses, spearheads and tweezers. Wood stains indicating traces of either coffins or wooden lining were recorded in eight of the graves. All the cremations were placed in urns. A number also had grave goods including miniature toilet implements.[15]

An indication of Winchester's new status is shown by a late 7th century burial in Lower Brook Street. Here a female was buried with an elaborate necklace. The young woman wore as many as thirty rings of silver wire, two strung with beads, six assorted *bullae* (amulets) and a gold ring, which together formed a collar encircling the neck, resting on the clavicles of the skeleton and perhaps originally stitched to the woman's garment.[16]

At Oliver's Battery, two miles southwest of Winchester and near the Roman road that ran to Old Sarum, a young male was buried in the late 7th century with a hanging bowl, a seax (dagger) and a spear or javelin. He was buried in the bank of an earthwork enclosure, thought to be an Iron Age or Romano-British hilltop enclosure. The body was oriented north-south, in the pagan fashion, the hanging bowl was cradled in its arms.[17] Hanging bowls are "thin-walled bronze vessels, rendered capable of suspension by the provision of three or four hooks mounted round the circumference of the bowl at equal intervals." The bowls vary from 5 to 18 inches in diameter, and proportionally in depth. The hooks "project from bronze plates or frames, known as escutcheons, generally circular or oval-shaped, which are attached to the bowl either by riveting or soldering, and occasionally by both." Nobody knows what the bowls were used for, either by their manufacturers or their users. Although the bowls are found in Anglo-Saxon graves, it is clear that "the great majority of the bowls are of Celtic manufacture."[18] A hanging bowl escutcheon mold has been found at Craig Phadrig in Inverness, northeast Scotland, and an unfinished escutcheon has been discovered at Seagry in northwest Wiltshire, suggesting that hanging bowls were made at these two locations.[19] The Oliver's Battery hanging bowl was around 12 inches in diameter, with a height of 5 inches. The hook takes the form of stylized bird heads with long beaks, described variously as swan- or heron-like.[20]

Malmesbury, where Aldhelm was abbot, is an Iron Age hillfort in the far northwest of Wiltshire, near the border with Gloucestershire. The monastery of Malmesbury first entered the historical record in around 675, when the scholar, poet, and later Bishop of Sherborne, Aldhelm, became abbot there. But according to tradition a religious community was founded there at a much earlier date by a certain Maildub, who was apparently one of those Irish citizens of post–Roman Britain "whose pioneering missionary work among the Anglo-Saxons may have been obscured in the standard account of the Conversion."[21] The best evidence for Maildub's existence is the name Malmesbury, which means "Maeldub's fortification." In Bede's *Ecclesiastical History* Malmesbury is *Maildubi urbs*, a Latin form of the name *Maldubesburg* in some of the abbey's earliest records.[22] According to the early 12th century historian William of Malmesbury, Maildub established a hermitage there, but was later forced to accept a group of disciples, among them Aldhelm. He is said to have built a small church there, which could still be seen a few years before the date William was writing (1125).

Sherborne in northwest Dorset became a bishopric in about 705, with Aldhelm as bishop, and in a late 14th century manuscript which lists royal benefactors of Sherborne and the lands they granted, the first name on the list is that of the 7th century Wessex king Cenwalh. He is said to have granted 100 hides at a location called *Lanprobi*.[23] This document may be a forgery, though the name *Lanprobi* may well be genuine. The first element of this name, *lan*, is the equivalent of Welsh *llan*, "enclosure, church," a word related to English *land*. The second element appears to be Probus, presumably the name of the saint who is also commemorated at Probus in Cornwall. Nobody knows for certain where *Lanprobi* was, but it may have been on the hill overlooking Sherborne where the ruins of the 12th century castle now stand. A bull issued by Pope Alexander III and dated 1163 mentions "The church of St Mary Magdalene situated next to Sherborne castle with the chapels of St Michael and St Probus." Early Christian burials have been uncovered during excavations at the Castle, along with five grass-tempered pottery shards dating from the 5th–8th centuries.[24]

There was also an early monastery in Exeter (Devon), attended by St. Boniface, the Anglo-Saxon apostle of the Germans, who was born around 675.[25] The early monastery has long since disappeared, but excavations at St. Mary Major Church in Exeter have revealed a Saxon cemetery in use from the early 8th century; two Saxon phases were identified. From the 12th–17th centuries, the site was part of the Close cemetery of the Cathedral–272 inhumations were revealed, the majority being medieval.[26] The earliest burials on the site are six unfurnished burials cut into the remains of the Roman forum and basilica. Two of the burials were radiocarbon dated to the 5th century and are thought to be part of a much larger cemetery destroyed by grave digging. Four of the graves were arranged in a row indicating they were part of a well laid out cemetery. All were orientated northwest to southeast, the same alignment as the demolished Roman buildings. It is possible that grave orientation was determined by extant features or structures outside the excavated area.[27]

Early Wessex in the Anglo-Saxon Chronicle

CERDIC, CYNRIC AND CHARFORD (HAMPSHIRE)

In the late 9th century, King Alfred of Wessex ordered the writing of the *Anglo-Saxon Chronicle*, which continued to be recorded until the Norman Conquest and beyond (the Peterborough version of the *Chronicle* did not cease until 1154). Bede implies that the kingdom of Wessex started around Dorchester-on-Thames in Oxfordshire, but the *Chronicle* has a very different story. According to the *Chronicle*, Wessex was founded in 519 by two chieftains called Cerdic and Cynric. Cynric may be a Saxon name meaning "Kin-Ruler," but Cerdic is a British name, the Anglo-Saxon version of Caratacus, the name of the chief of the Catuvellauni of Hertfordshire who resisted the Roman invasion of Britain between about 43 and 50 CE. The name is found in various forms in post–Roman Britain: a certain *Coroticus* was excommunicated by St. Patrick for taking some of his converts into slavery[28]; a Ceretic Guletic, king of *Alt Clut* (Dumbarton on the River Clyde in Scotland), is mentioned in Welsh and Irish sources; while Bede says[29] that Hereric, the father of Abbess Hilda of Whitby was killed at the court of a certain "Cerdic, king of the Britons," where he lived in banishment (this *Cerdic* may have been king of Elmet in West Yorkshire).

The foundation story is confused, but it involves the Isle of Wight, together with the old Roman fort of Portchester near Portsmouth, Netley Marsh near Southampton, and Charford, all in Hampshire. There is evidence for early Anglo-Saxon settlement on the Isle of Wight, with 5th and 6th century cemeteries at Chessell Down in the southwest and Carisbrooke Castle in the center of the island. There is also evidence for early Anglo-Saxon settlement at Portchester in the mid–5th century CE, with sunken floored huts, timber houses and ancillary buildings.[30] There is no evidence for early settlement in the Southampton region, nor at Charford. But south of Charford is Breamore, and Breamore has recently emerged as a significant site in the early Anglo-Saxon period.

THE EARLY ANGLO-SAXON CEMETERY
AT BREAMORE (HAMPSHIRE)

In October 1999, metal detectorist Steve Bolger reported an unusual find to the Hampshire Finds Liaison Officer for the Portable Antiquities Scheme. Among the early medieval objects he had uncovered at Breamore was a rare copper alloy Byzantine bucket in a field by the River Avon. The body of the bucket was made from a single sheet of metal, hammered and then hand-decorated by stamping and incising with punches and a chisel. The resulting frieze, which runs around the bucket, depicts three naked warriors armed with spears, shields, swords and a discus, fighting a leopard and a mythical beast or bear. An inscription in ancient Greek around the top of the bucket reads *"Use this, lady, for many happy years."* The bucket handle was threaded through two raised lugs with holes punched through them. The flat base of the bucket had become detached from the body.

This bucket is one of only three known in England and belongs to a closely related group of which a further three were found in Turkey, Italy and Spain, with three more having unknown find spots. All of these buckets are decorated with a hunting frieze and most have an inscription. Their manufacture is so similar that it is thought that they were produced at the same workshop, or group of workshops, in the eastern Empire possibly at Antioch in Asia Minor (now Turkey), in the 6th century CE. The precise use of such buckets is not certain but several of the inscriptions refer to good health and suggest a personal domestic setting, probably related to bathing. The rarity of these buckets may be seen as an indicator of the high status of the owners. The other two examples from England come from Bromeswell, Suffolk, within half a mile of the Sutton Hoo cemetery, and from Chessell Down on the Isle of Wight, where the bucket was part of a rich female grave excavated in the 19th century,[31] believed to have been that of a Kentish princess.[32]

An initial geophysical survey of the area where the bucket was found revealed a number of anomalies and led to a small-scale excavation, which revealed that the bucket was part of an important early Anglo-Saxon cemetery. The site attracted the attention of the British television program *Time Team*, and in August 2001 they broadcast a three-day *Time Team Live* event from Breamore. They hoped to determine the extent of the cemetery and relate the Byzantine bucket to the broader picture of the burials. Surprisingly, a further six burials with buckets (though not Byzantine) were found and there were a higher than expected number of weapon burials.[33] The six further buckets were copper-alloy wood staved buckets and not Byzantine in origin. The Byzantine bucket was not the only imported find—other finds included a glass bowl, likely imported from Cologne or northeast France/Belgium, and a Frankish buckle.[34] Breamore is near an Iron Age hillfort, Whitsbury Castle Ditches, which may have been fortified in the 5th century, and near Rockbourne Roman villa, so the Anglo-Saxons of Breamore, with their Byzantine bucket, may well have been British allies of the Anglo-Saxons living on the Isle of Wight, who were on good terms with the Anglo-Saxon kingdom of Kent, and may have obtained their luxury goods through their Kentish connection.

Paganism in Wiltshire: Early Cemeteries

SALISBURY

According to the *Chronicle*, Cerdic died in 534 and in 552 his son Cynric "fought against the Britons at the place which is named Salisbury, and put the Britons to flight."[35] Salisbury of course was the Roman town of *Sorviodunum*, to the north of modern Salisbury, and there are several Anglo-Saxon cemeteries around Salisbury, many of them on the River Avon or its tributary the River Bourne.

The cemetery at Petersfinger, on the eastern outskirts of Salisbury, was first recorded in 1846 when a cutting for the South-Western Railway at Petersfinger was under construction. Further inhumations were discovered after a fall of chalk which necessitated a widening of the cutting. Excavations also took place between 1948 and 1951 revealing 70 inhumations lying both north-south and east-west and accompanied by grave goods. The bulk of the associated grave goods are Frankish, perhaps mid–6th century onwards, and later Saxon goods.[36] Inhumations lying north-south are likely to be pagan Saxon, while inhumations lying east-west may be Romano-British or Christian.

An Anglo-Saxon inhumation cemetery in the Low Field, Harnham, in the south of Salisbury, was excavated by Akerman during 1853/4. Excavations revealed sixty-four shallow graves, containing 73 skeletons, accompanied by a variety of Saxon ornaments and weapons, including a fork and a bronze-bound wooden dish. A bronze Roman coin accompanied one burial and Akerman claimed that the burials had abraded Romano-British shards deliberately placed over them. The burials were mainly extended and orientated east to west; no traces of coffins were found, but most of the bodies were protected by large flint stones, placed to form a coffin-like cist. Frankish grave goods appear to the earliest present, suggesting a mid–6th and 7th century date.[37] The east-west orientation of the burials suggests a Romano-British or Christian influence.

WINTERBOURNE GUNNER

Winterbourne Gunner lies near the River Bourne to the east of Old Sarum, and the Anglo-Saxon cemetery was discovered in 1960. Salisbury Museum Archaeological Research Group excavated ten 6th century graves. Watching briefs and excavations in 1992–4 by Wiltshire County Council staff and AC Archaeology on three bungalows have located 72 graves. Those to the east dated to the 8th century. Archaeologists from the television program Time Team in 1994 uncovered the graves of two adult females and one child which had been placed around the edge of the site of a Bronze Age round barrow. Grave goods include an encrusted bronze saucer brooch, an amber bead and an iron pin. The Time Team archaeologists also found two Bronze Age cremation urns in the barrow.[38]

COLLINGBOURNE DUCIS

To the north of Winterbourne Gunner, on the River Bourne, is Collingbourne Ducis, and the Anglo-Saxon cemetery there is one of the largest cemeteries in Wiltshire. Dating to between the 5th and 7th centuries CE, it was investigated in 1974 and, in 2007, by Wessex Archaeology. In all over 120 burials have been found, including 114 inhumations and around 13 cremations. The grave goods are fairly typical of Anglo-Saxon cemeteries in Wessex. A range of weapon types is present and the jewelry is predominantly Saxon in character. The humble knife is the most common object, closely followed by the buckle. Many buckles are simple iron loops, but an exception is the rare iron kidney-shaped buckle with rectangular cellwork plate. It is significant that two of the other three known examples (from graves) come from Wiltshire (Petersfinger and Pewsey). Twelve weapon burials were found. There are no particularly elaborate assemblages—in contrast to both Petersfinger and Pewsey, no sword/shield/spear combinations were found. Overall 24 inhumations contained jewelry, mainly brooches, and the range is again typical for southern England, especially the Saxon area. Among the brooches was a pair of unusual bow or equal-armed brooches and a small group of penannular brooches. An important discovery was a rare gilded "face brooch" decorated in Style 1 animal art. No exact parallels have so far been found, although a pair of roughly similar brooches was found in the Upper Thames Valley in Grave 136 at Lechlade, Gloucestershire.[39]

There was one prone (face down) burial at Collingbourne Ducis. The male prone burial in grave 11 had a Roman disc brooch, possibly fastening a cloak in classical fashion, and his grave was incorporated into the main part of the cemetery. Because prone burial was also practiced in the Roman period, it is possible that the individual was signaling his allegiance to a non–Germanic cultural tradition through both position and costume.[40]

BULFORD

Recently an Anglo-Saxon cemetery has been found at Bulford, around 2 miles to the north of Amesbury—the cemetery is sited on a ridge overlooking Nine Mile River, close to where it joins the River Avon. Excavations on Ministry of Defence land in Bulford uncovered 150 Anglo-Saxon graves spanning the later 7th to early 8th century. Containing the remains of men, women, and children, the burials were arranged in neat rows, packed closely together—though as none of the graves intercut, the team from Wessex Archaeology suggests that they may once have been picked out in some way, with markers. Many of the individuals had been laid to rest with personal items, from jewelry (including glass beads and brooches) and knives to more unusual prestigious objects such as a large antler comb decorated with patterns of rings and dots, and chevrons. Some items, such as cowrie shells from the Red Sea, speak of the community's far-reaching trade connections, while others hint at their owners' social status. Another rare object, found placed on the chest of a young woman, was a "work box"—a small cylindrical container so called because previous finds have sometimes contained pins. While no such items were discovered within the Bulford example, x-rays suggest it holds a number of as-yet unidentified copper-alloy fragments. The young woman with the "work box" was also buried with a cowrie shell, suggesting that like the female burials at Lechlade in Gloucestershire, she was a cunning-woman, and that the "work box" held the tools of her trade. Another possibly high-status individual was a man found in the largest grave on the site, who had been interred with an unusually large spear, its haft decorated with bronze bindings—perhaps a ceremonial object belonging to an important individual.

Two prehistoric "hengiform" monuments, possibly ring ditches or barrows, have been identified a short distance from the graves, and preliminary dating evidence suggests that these were in use from the Neolithic period into the Bronze Age. Further signs of Neolithic ceremonial activity came with the discovery of a series of large pits, into which a range of unusual objects seem to have been deliberately placed. Most were found to contain shards of Late Neolithic Grooved Ware pottery, and axes or fragments of axes (including one of a distinctive green stone thought to come from Cornwall). Carved pieces of chalk—forming a bowl and a little ball—and flint hammerstones, as well as antler and aurochs bone were also found, but for Wessex Archaeology prehistory expert Phil Harding, a highlight was the discovery of a rare discoidal knife—a delicate, oval flint blade, of which only two other examples are known from the Stonehenge area.[41]

An Execution at Stonehenge

Very little is known about early Anglo-Saxon Amesbury, but there is a story to tell about nearby Stonehenge. Between 1919 and 1926 William Hawley carried out excavations at Stonehenge, and among other things he discovered a skeleton, numbered 4.10.4 in 1938 by the Royal College of Surgeons. Hawley believed that the skeleton was Neolithic, while Arthur Keith, of the Royal College of Surgeons, thought that it was Roman, and that it was male. The College was bombed in 1941 and archaeologists believed that the skeleton was lost. In fact, most of the College's collection of human remains had been taken to country houses around London, and after the war had been given to the Natural History Museum. Skeleton 4.10.4 was eventually discovered by the archaeologist Mike Pitts, who brought the osteoarchaeologist (bone specialist) Jacqueline McKinley to examine the skeleton. Traumatic spinal lesions showed that the man had been decapitated, the head apparently being removed by a single blow from the rear-right side. The skeleton was radiocarbon dated to 600–690 CE, in the Anglo-Saxon period. Further tests showed that the man came from southern England, to the north and east of Stonehenge. It seems that the man had been executed, and it may be relevant that one possible interpretation of the name *Stonehenge* is "stone gallows."[42]

Pewsey

The Early Anglo-Saxon cemetery at Blacknall Field (also known as Black Patch) near Pewsey lies on the southern edge of the Vale of Pewsey, in the upper Avon valley.[43] The cemetery was discovered in 1968 and excavated by Ken Annable between 1969 and 1976. It contained over 100 graves, all of them inhumations bar four cremations, and was in use from 475 to 550 CE.[44] Ken Annable died in 2002 and the report on the cemetery was published in 2010 under the editorial oversight of Bruce Eagles.

The cemetery is remarkable for the number of high-status graves, both male and female. There are four sword burials, all with male adults; in each case the sword was at the left side. In addition to the sword, Grave 1, which was very disturbed, contained a possible drinking horn and wooden vessels, all to the right of the skull, and a bone dress pin; Grave 22 a sword bead (an amulet attached to the scabbard by a small strap), spear with ferrule, a silvered buckle with Style 1 animal ornament, possibly a bucket by the skull, and a knife; Grave 47, a spear with ferrule, a shield, a wooden belt with iron fittings, a wooden vessel right of the skull, a knife, and toilet items. The most richly furnished female burials, both of adults, were Grave 21, the deepest grave in the cemetery, with a great square-headed brooch, saucer brooches, an amber bead, an iron buckle, a bucket left of the skull, another wooden vessel left of the bucket, a wooden box by the right foot and a knife; and Grave 31, with a pair of Style 1 ornamented square-headed brooches, amber and rock crystal beads, a knife, toilet items, and a purse.[45] Some of the graves contained lumps of iron pyrites; it is possible that the radiating crystalline structure of this mineral encouraged a belief among the Anglo-Saxon inhabitants that the mineral possessed magical powers—indeed, the term "thunderbolt" is still commonly applied to describe pyritic nodules by local people.[46]

There are "intriguing differences" between male burials with and without weapons. Male adults with weapons had an average of 4.6 artifacts in their graves; male adults without weapons only 1.0. Males with weapons measured on average 1.741 meters (5.7 feet) in height, while males without weapons measured 1.718 meters (5.6 feet), a difference of almost exactly 1 inch. This difference is remarkably close to the overall averages for early Anglo-Saxon males and Romano-British males, respectively,[47] suggesting that, like many cemeteries in Wiltshire, native Britons were buried alongside Anglo-Saxon settlers.

There was one prone burial at Pewsey, which had also been mutilated. The left forearm of the male in Grave 71 had been severed and had healed but his feet had been cut off at the ankles at or shortly after death, presumably to prevent him from returning to haunt the living.[48]

The cemetery is on the site of a Late Bronze Age/Early Iron Age midden, which left its mark on the soil (thus the name Black Patch).[49]Little is known about the Pewsey midden, but presumably, like the middens at All Cannings Cross and Potterne, it was a feasting site where the de-fleshed bones of a small number of people were buried during important celebrations.

Paganism in Early Wiltshire: Individual High-Status Burials

ROUNDWAY DOWN, DEVIZES

A number of high-status individual burials have been found in Wiltshire, dating to the late 7th century, and comparable to the burials in Lower Brook Street, Winchester and at Oliver's Battery near Winchester. In 1840 a Bronze Age barrow on Roundway Down, to the north of Devizes, was opened, revealing a female inhumation in an iron bound coffin or chest, accompanied by a cabochon garnet and gold necklace, a composite gold pin-suite, and a wooden bucket with bronze mounts. The burial was dated to the late 7th century, "based largely on the stylistic attributes of the artefactual assemblage."[50]

FORD, SALISBURY

Another late 7th century rich burial was found in the remains of a barrow near Ford, to the east of Old Sarum. It was found next to an Early Bronze Age burial mound, and near the Roman road from Old Sarum to Winchester. The Anglo-Saxon grave contained the skeleton of a man equipped with a hanging bowl, seax, a shield, two spears, a buckle and a bone comb. The seax is a rare object and its presence suggests that the deceased was a man of some importance.[51]

WILTON

In 1860 a hanging bowl was discovered in the grounds of Wilton House at Wilton, to the west of Salisbury, near the site of the medieval Wilton Abbey. Four plates (escutcheons) are attached to the body of the bowl—each one is decorated with a simple cross design. There are hooks attached to the escutcheons shaped like dragons' heads, and the copper alloy rings attached to each hook were used for suspending the bowl.[52] Wilton became a royal estate in the 9th century with a monastery by the 10th century— since hanging bowls were used in late 7th century burials, it is likely that the bowl marks the last resting place of a member of the Wessex elite.

SWALLOWCLIFFE DOWN

In August 1966 Faith Vatcher excavated an extremely rich female grave at Swallowcliffe Down between Swallowcliffe and Ansty in southwest Wiltshire. The burial, which dated to the late 7th century, was located in a chamber inserted into the center of an Early Bronze Age burial mound. At the west end of the grave were two vessels, an iron pan or skillet and a large yew-wood iron-bound bucket, while at the foot end of the grave was a bronze-mounted bucket placed on a ledge on the side of the grave. Beside the right forearm were two glass palm cups. By the left leg was a maple-wood casket containing a range of items, including a bronze sprinkler, a silver spoon, four silver brooches, a strap mount, one amber and two glass beads, an iron spindle, two knives with horn handles and a comb of bone or antler. By the right leg was a satchel of wood and leather decorated with an openwork disc mount of copper alloy with gold and silver repoussé foils. Some of these items were connected with feasting (the buckets, pan and cups), while some were connected with Christian ritual practices (the sprinkler).[53] The body was placed on an iron bed, orientated west-east in Christian fashion.[54]

Early Christianity in Wiltshire

TISBURY

Tisbury on the River Nadder, to the west of Salisbury and not far from the rich burial on Swallowcliffe Down, was certainly occupied at an early date by the West Saxons who, by 759, named it *Tissebiri*—Tysse's Burh. A monastery was here by 700 and may have been established by 674. An early, if not the first, abbot was Wintra who is mentioned in land documents. In 705 the Synod of the Nadder was held here, which was attended by a young monk named Winfrith, who is better known, particularly in continental Europe, as St. Boniface. The fact that Tisbury hosted this synod is a good indication as to the importance of the monastery here. The monastery was probably one large building, with a separate church and outbuildings. It was razed to the ground in the 9th century during the early Viking raids and the monks were slain.[55]

BRADFORD ON AVON

The earliest documented mention of Bradford on Avon, on the Bristol Avon in the west of Wiltshire, is in the *Anglo-Saxon Chronicle* as the scene of the battle of Witgenesburg in 652, a possible indication of the Celtic name for Bradford. A monastery existed at Bradford in 705, when St. Aldhelm, having become Bishop of Sherborne, agreed at the request of the monks to remain as their abbot. Aldhelm then referred to Bradford, Malmesbury, and Frome as "my monasteries," and William of Malmesbury in his life of Aldhelm mentions the foundation of the monastery by Aldhelm and adds that there was

The Anglo-Saxon church at Bradford on Avon in the west of Wiltshire. The church dates from the 10th century but may be on the site of Aldhelm's original church. May 26, 2005 (BlendsinWell at English Wikipedia).

in his own day (around 1125) a little church at Bradford that was said to have been dedicated to St. Laurence.[56]

This may be the 9th or 10th century Saxon church which stands opposite the Norman Holy Trinity Church in Bradford.

Early Christianity in Somerset

CELTIC CHRISTIANITY

While Anglo-Saxons were settling along the Salisbury Avon and the River Bourne in Wiltshire, Celtic Christianity was flourishing in Somerset. Cadbury Congresbury is an Iron Age hillfort near Weston-super-Mare. After 400 CE it was refortified on a minor scale, and large quantities of eastern Mediterranean pottery have been found there, together with evidence of several buildings.[57] Nearby is Henley Wood, where Roman temple was excavated. When the temple was partly in ruins, "graves were cut through it, of a cemetery of over 50 west-east graves extending over the eastern forecourt and over and into the temenos ditch. Radiocarbon dates from the skeletons gave a range in the later 5th–6th centuries." The general belief is that Congresbury was the site of a British monastery, perhaps dedicated to Congar, a 5th–6th century Welsh saint. Congresbury is first mentioned in Asser's *Life of Alfred* as a derelict Celtic monastery which was assigned to Asser, a Welsh monk from St. David's in southwest Wales who became bishop of Sherborne in Dorset. Little is known of St. Congar, except that he may have come from near St. David's in Pembrokeshire, where there is a place name *Llanungar* ("Church of Congar").[58]

There was probably a British monastery or hermitage on Glastonbury Tor. Excavations in 1964–6 uncovered timber buildings, evidence of bronze-working, evidence of much meat-eating (food bones), and 14 shards of imported Mediterranean pottery dating to the 6th century.[59] Given its isolated position, it is more likely to have been a hermitage than a secular site–Aldhelm abbot of Malmesbury, writing in the late 7th century, refers to British monasticism disparagingly as "a life of contemplative retirement away in some squalid wilderness,"[60] and Glastonbury Tor would certainly have qualified as a wilderness in the 6th century.

At Lamyatt Beacon on the top of Creech Hill near Bruton in Somerset, a Romano-British temple was excavated, which was in use from 250 to 375 CE. After the temple went out of use it became a Christian cemetery—sixteen inhumations were discovered, all orientated west-east or southwest-northeast. Two of the burials were dated to between the 6th and the 8th century.[61]

A Christian cemetery was excavated at Cannington near Bridgewater in Somerset which may have been in use from around 350 to 800 CE. 542 burials have been located, though over 1000 burials may have been lost through quarrying. A small proportion of the graves contained grave goods, including knives, coins, combs, glass beads, brooches and pins. Two graves were unusual. One grave, dated to between 465 and 518 CE, consisted

Glastonbury Tor in Somerset, where there may have been a 6th century British monastery or hermitage. The tower on the summit belongs to the 14th century Church of St. Michael. May 19, 2014 (Rodw, CCA-Share Alike 3.0 Unported).

of a circular rock-cut trench with a single extended inhumation in the middle, the whole covered by a low mound. The other, also beneath a mound, was dated to around 620 CE and contained the skeleton of a young girl surrounded by a structure of slabs set in the surface. Other graves were cut into this one and a well-defined path led to it. The circular rock-cut trench had traces of a red sandstone revetment and was possibly the site of a religious building such as a mausoleum.[62] It has been suggested that the grave of the girl was a saint's grave. The path leading to the grave shows continuous visitation of the grave over a long period of time, which suggests the grave was a site of pilgrimage. The dense concentration of burials surrounding the grave, indicating a desire to be buried as close as possible to the grave, suggests *ad sanctos* burial[63] (that is, burial beside a saint). The cemetery was near the Iron Age hillfort of Cannington Camp, which may have been re-occupied in the Roman period.

Carhampton is a village near Exmoor in west Somerset, and excavations there in the 1990s revealed an occupation site dating from the 5th to 8th century CE. Ditches, pathways and structural features such as post holes and mortar layers were revealed by excavation, though the trenches were too narrow to provide a plan of any of the structures. Metalworking hearths, and quantities of metal slag and charcoal were present. Several shards of eastern Mediterranean pottery were found, dating from the 5th or 6th centuries CE. This pottery is usually associated with high-status sites like defended settlements or monasteries. A Medieval cemetery was discovered and 18 burials were recorded. The number of burials in the cemetery is estimated at several hundred, when account is taken of those found in the 19th century.[64] Carhampton is associated with St. Carantoc, and a church dedicated to the saint was recorded in Norman times.

ANGLO-SAXON CHRISTIANITY

It is thought that a minster church was established around 704 at Wells in Somerset. The most important feature of Wells is the spring (St. Andrew's Well), and excavations have shown that there may have been a Roman villa close to the spring, "probably at the centre of an affluent estate with mining interests," possibly under the eastern end of the medieval Cathedral.[65] By the late or sub–Roman period

> there was a mausoleum west of St Andrew's Well, the sacred spring. This may have been in origin a private mausoleum attached to the villa. The building itself was of a common late Roman type, a square building with a central burial vault. However, its position and history suggests that it was of some religious importance, probably of Celtic origin: it may have contained a shrine to a Christian martyr.

When the Saxon minster was established, "the mausoleum was replaced by a mortuary chapel: the vault was cleared out and used as an ossuary, and the site formed a focus for 8th century burials."[66]

According to the *Anglo-Saxon Chronicle*, in 688 King Ine "succeeded to the kingdom of Wessex and held [it] 37 years; and he built the minster at Glastonbury."[67] We know from William of Malmesbury[68] that there was already a church at Glastonbury, dedicated to St. Mary, when Ine established his monastery. This church, known as the Old Church, was of "wattle-work," and extremely ancient, since "No other hands than those of the disciples of Christ erected the church of Glastonbury." William associated the church with the disciples of Christ, but most archaeologist "consider it more likely that the Old Church itself was originally a 7th century building." The dimensions of the church given in the medieval period "are too large for a wattled church but comparable with major

Irish timber churches of the 7th century … and there does appear to have been a considerable Irish influence at Glastonbury."[69] William of Malmesbury says that Glastonbury "possessed the relics of several Irish saints, St Brigit and St Benignus among them. More important, the remains of St Patrick and St Indract were said to be housed in stone shrines within the Old Church of St Mary of Glastonbury—St Patrick on the south side of the high altar, St Indract on the north."[70] The church that Ine built, to the east of the Old Church was a stone church dedicated to St. Peter and St. Paul which was extended eastwards and later, probably by 760, was joined to the Old Church by means of an atrium. The first cloister, on the model of St. Gallen in Switzerland, was probably begun by St. Dunstan in the 10th century. Dunstan further extended the abbey church by adding a porticus (side chapel) and building a tower over its east end as well as an aisled eastern arm. His church was described as a basilica.[71]

The early history of Glastonbury is obscure, but recently a team from the University of Reading and the Trustees of Glastonbury Abbey has been reviewing excavations carried out at Glastonbury between 1904 and 1979. This review has discovered 21 shards of Dark Age pottery, mainly from below the west range of the cloisters. These shards come from amphorae (storage jars) of the type called in the Mediterranean "Late Roman A1" and in the British Isles "Class B2": utilitarian red earthenwares of the east Mediterranean, with rilled bodies (decorated with parallel channels), known to have been made at Antioch (Syria) and in Cyprus. One vessel shows "pitching" (coating of the inner surface to reduce leakage); another has a scratched ("graffito") line. They demonstrate occupation on the site at some stage in the period 450–600 CE.[72] Such pottery is associated with high-status sites, in this case perhaps the early church hinted at by documentary sources, and links Glastonbury to Glastonbury Tor, where 14 shards of 6th century Mediterranean pottery were uncovered.

Excavation by Ralegh Radford in 1955-7 discovered glass furnaces thought to date from just before the Norman Conquest. However, radiocarbon dating has now revealed that they date approximately to the 680s and are likely to be associated with a major rebuilding of the abbey undertaken by King Ine of Wessex. Glass-making at York and Wearmouth is recorded in historical documents in the 670s but Glastonbury provides the earliest and most substantial archaeological evidence for glass-making in Saxon Britain. The extensive remains of five furnaces have been identified, together with fragments of clay crucibles and glass for window glazing and drinking vessels, mainly of vivid blue-green color. It is likely that specialist glassworkers came from Gaul to work at Glastonbury.[73] They may well have been the same glassworkers who helped to build Wearmouth and Jarrow—in any case, the use of glass underlines the close ties between Northumbria and Wessex at the time.

From Obscurity to Triumph

At the time of Bede, Wessex appears to have been an insignificant kingdom, and remained so during the 8th and the early 9th centuries. During the 9th century Vikings began attacking England and eventually destroyed the kingdoms of Northumbria, East Anglia and Mercia, leaving Wessex as the most powerful Anglo-Saxon kingdom. Initially the Vikings were pagans, and they brought with them pagan beliefs and their own form of magic, as I show in the next chapter.

7

The Kingdom of Wessex, the Vikings, and Pagan Amulets and Christianity in the Danelaw

Wessex and Mercia

After King Ine of Wessex abdicated in 726, Wessex was dominated by Mercia, which for over a hundred years was ruled by three strong kings, Aethelbald (716–757), Offa (757–796), and Coenwulf (796–821). There is no indication that Wessex was ever occupied by Mercia, except for Somerton in Somerset. According to the *Chronicle* entry for 733, Aethelbald of Mercia (716–757) captured the royal estate at Somerton, implying that, for a time at least, all of Somerset, from Bath in the north (which was in the kingdom of the Hwicce, a sub-kingdom of Mercia) to Somerton in the south, was under Mercian control.

This period came to an end in the early 9th century, with the reign of Egbert (802–839). Egbert's predecessor was Beorhtric, who was close to Offa of Mercia, and in its entry for 839, the *Chronicle* says of Egbert that before he was king[1] "Offa, king of Mercia, and Beorhtric, king of Wessex, put him to flight from the land of the English to the land of the Franks for 3 years"—which suggests that Offa and Beorhtric saw Egbert as a threat. On his accession in 802, the *Chronicle* reports[2]:

> Ealdorman Aethelmund rode from the Hwicce across at Kempsford; the Ealdorman Weohstan met him with the Wiltshire men; and there was a big battle, and both ealdormen were killed there and the Wiltshire men took the victory

The Hwicce, as I said, were a sub-kingdom of Mercia, based in Winchcombe, Gloucestershire, and Kempsford is in Gloucestershire on the Thames, on the border with Wiltshire. The "Wiltshire men" are in Old English the *Wilsaete*, literally, "those who dwell by the River Wyle," referring to the old Wiltshire capital of Wilton. Wilton is again mentioned in 838 when a concordat between the King of Wessex and the Archbishop of Canterbury, made at Kingston on Thames, was confirmed at Wilton. Wilton, a short distance to the west of present-day Salisbury, lies at the confluence of the River Wylye and the River Nadder, and was presumably the Anglo-Saxon successor to the Roman town of Sorviodunum (Old Sarum).

The first years of Egbert's reign were otherwise uneventful, apart from the entry for 815, when the *Chronicle* notes: "King Egbert spread devastation in Cornwall from east to west." In 821, Coenwulf, the last of Mercia's three great rulers, died and Mercia entered a period of instability with two short-lived kings, Ceolwulf and Beornwulf. In 825, says the *Chronicle*, King Egbert and King Beornwulf fought at Ellandun ("Elder-bush Down"), and "Egbert took the victory; and a great slaughter was made there." The location of Ellandun is not known for certain, but it is generally thought to be somewhere near Swindon in Wiltshire. After Egbert defeated the Mercians at Ellandun,[3]

> he sent his son Aethelwulf from the army, and Ealhstan his bishop, and Wulfheard his ealdorman, to Kent with a great troop, and they drove Baldred the king north over the Thames; and the inhabitants of Kent turned to him—and the Surrey men and the South Saxons and East Saxons—because earlier they were wrongly forced away from his relatives. And, for fear of the Mercians, the same year the king and the nation of the East Angles sought King Egbert as their guardian and protector; and that year the East Angles killed Beornwulf, king of the Mercians.

Æthelwulf was Egbert's only known son, and Ealhstan was bishop of Sherborne in Dorset.

In 829, says the *Chronicle*, Egbert "conquered the Mercian kingdom, and all that is south of the Humber, being the eighth king who was sovereign of all the British dominions" (the first seven being the kings listed by Bede). The *Chronicle* also says that Egbert "led an army against the Northumbrians as far as Dore, where they met him and offered terms of obedience and subjection" (Dore is a village in south Yorkshire), probably then on the border between Mercia and Northumbria). Egbert's domination of Mercia did not last long, for two years later, says the *Chronicle*, "Wiglaf recovered his Mercian kingdom."

Wessex, the Vikings and the Creation of the Danelaw

EARLY VIKING ATTACKS

It was during Egbert's reign that the Danes (Vikings) began attacking Wessex. In 834 the Danes attacked the Isle of Sheppey in Kent, and the following year, says the *Chronicle*, Egbert fought with the Danes at Carhampton in west Somerset, but the Danes "remained masters of the field." In 838, according to the *Chronicle*[4]:

> Here a great raiding ship-army came to Cornwall, and they turned into one and were fighting against Egbert, king of Wessex. Then he campaigned against them and fought with them at Hingston, and there put to flight both the Britons and the Danish.

It appears from this that the Danes landed somewhere in Cornwall, presumably Plymouth Sound, and joined forces with the local British. Hingston is thought to be Hingston Down in east Cornwall, not far from Gunnislake, and close to the River Tamar, which later became the border between Cornwall and Devon.

Egbert died in 839 and was succeeded by his son Æthelwulf who, according to the *Chronicle*, immediately gave Kent, Essex, Surrey and Sussex to his son Æthelstan. The Viking attacks continued, with skirmishes at Southampton (Hampshire), Portland (Dorset), Carhampton (Somerset), Wembury (Devon), and Sandwich (Kent). In 850, the Danes "for the first time stayed over the winter." In the same year, 300 ships sailed into the mouth of the Thames, and the Danes stormed Canterbury and London, putting to flight Beorhtwulf, king of the Mercians. The Danes then marched south into Surrey, and Aethelwulf, with his son Aethelbald, fought with them at Ockley in Surrey, on the Roman road from London to Chichester, and there made "the greatest slaughter of a heathen raiding army that we have heard tell of up to this present day."[5]

Æthelwulf died in 858 and was buried in Winchester. He was succeeded by his son Æthelbald, with his brother Æthelberht ruling over Sussex, Kent, Essex and Surrey. Æthelbald died in 860 and was buried at Sherborne; he was followed by his brother Æthelberht who "succeeded to the whole kingdom, and held it in good order and great tranquility." However, at the beginning of his reign, says the Chronicle,[6] "a great raiding ship-army came up and destroyed Winchester." But alderman Osric, with the command of Hampshire, and alderman Ethelwulf, with the command of Berkshire, fought against the enemy, and putting them to flight, made themselves masters of the field of battle (the *Chronicle* does not identify the "ship-army," but the *Annals of St-Bertin*, produced in the 9th century and named after the Abbey of Saint Bertin in Saint-Omer, northeastern France, say that Danes on the Somme launched the attack[7] (the Danes under a leader called Weland had arrived on the Somme in 858 and had taken the city of Amiens and burnt it to the ground[8]).

THE VIKINGS IN EAST ANGLIA: ST. EDMUND OF BURY ST. EDMUNDS (SUFFOLK)

Æthelberht died in 865 and was buried in Sherborne; he was succeeded by his brother Æthelred. In the same year, according to the *Chronicle*, "came a large heathen army into England, and fixed their winter-quarters in East Anglia." The Great Heathen Army crossed into Northumbria and in 866 captured York. In the following year the Danes went into Mercia and fixed their winter headquarters at Nottingham. The Mercian king Burgred appealed to Æthelred for help, and the two besieged Nottingham, and made peace with the Danes. In 870 the Danes conquered the kingdom of East Anglia and destroyed the monastery of Medhamstede (Peterborough). According to the *Chronicle*,[9] "King Edmund fought against them, and the Danish took the victory, and killed the king and conquered all the land."

In around 986 the monks of Ramsey Abbey in Cambridgeshire commissioned Abbo of Fleury, from Fleury Abbey on the River Loire near Orléans, to write a *Life* of St. Edmund. According to Abbo, one of Edmund's killers was Hinguar (possible Ivar the Boneless). The Danish leader captured Edmund at a place called *Hægelisdun*, had him tied to a tree, scourged, shot at with arrows, and finally beheaded. To prevent a decent burial, the Danes threw the head into a thicket in *Hægelisdun* wood. As Edmund's followers went seeking, calling out "Where are you, friend?" the head answered, "Here, here, here," until at last they found it, clasped between a wolf's paws, protected from other animals and uneaten. The people then took the head back to their village and fitted the head back on the body— the two miraculously reunited. The villagers buried the perfect uncorrupt body, which began to work miracles, and built a simple church over it. Later the body was taken to *Beodricsworth*, now Bury St. Edmunds in Suffolk. Abbo says the body was perfect but had, as a sign of martyrdom, a thin red line like a thread of silk around its neck.[10]

THE VIKINGS IN MERCIA: PAGAN BURIALS IN REPTON (DERBYSHIRE)

Then in 871 the Danish army entered Reading. King Æthelred and his brother Alfred led their army to Reading and fought the Danes but could not defeat them. Four nights later, Æthelred and Alfred again fought the Danes at Ashdown in Berkshire, and the

Danes were defeated. Then two weeks later Æthelred and Alfred fought with the Danes at Old Basing near Basingstoke in Hampshire, and this time the Danes were victorious. Two months later Æthelred and Alfred again engaged the Danes at *Meretune*, the location of which is uncertain. Heahmund, bishop of Sherborne was killed, and Aethelred died shortly after, though it is not clear whether this was a result of the battle. He was buried in Wimborne Minster (Dorset). Æthelred was succeeded in 871 by his brother Alfred, and within a month, as the *Chronicle* records, "King Alfred fought against all the Army with a small force at Wilton, and long pursued them during the day; but the Danes got possession of the field."

After this the Danish army headed north, and in 873 they seized the royal Mercian town of Repton (Derbyshire). Repton was the site of a monastery where St. Guthlac studied before he moved to Crowland in Lincolnshire. Several Mercian kings were buried there, including Æthelbald. In 849 Wigstan (Wystan) was brought to Repton for burial after his murder in a struggle over the succession to the throne. Wigstan was buried in the mausoleum of his grandfather Wiglaf, who was king between 827 and 840. This mausoleum is almost certainly the crypt which survives to this day. Miracles took place at the tomb of Wigstan, the church became a place of pilgrimage, and before the end of the 9th century Wigstan had come to be regarded as a saint.

When the Danish forces arrived in Repton, they fortified the monastery for the winter of 873–4. In 875 the army divided, one part going north into Northumbria and the other south toward Cambridge. Little was known about their winter quarters until the 1970s and 80s when Martin Biddle and his wife, Birthe Kjølbye-Biddle excavated the site of St. Wystan's.

A series of burials were excavated to the east of the church—the most striking of these was Grave 511, lying to the north of the church, inside the line of defenses. This was the burial of a man aged at least 35–40 who had been killed by a massive cut into the head of the left femur. He lay with his head to the west, the hands together on the pelvis, and wore a necklace of two glass beads and a plain silver Thor's hammer, with a leaded bronze fastening, A copper-alloy buckle with traces of textile and leather from a belt lay at the waist. By the left leg was an iron sword in a wooden scabbard lined with fleece and covered with leather, with a second copper-alloy buckle for a suspension strap. An iron folding knife and a wooden-handled iron knife lay by the sword hilt, and halfway down the blade was an iron key. Carefully placed between the thighs was the tusk of an adult wild boar, and lower down between the thighs was the humerus of a jackdaw.

To the west of the church is the site of a sunken two-celled stone building of late 7th or 8th century date, probably in origin a mortuary chapel. This was later cut down to ground level to serve as the chamber of a burial mound. When the mound was first opened in 1686 the east compartment contained the stone coffin of a "Human Body Nine Foot long" surrounded by a hundred skeletons "with their Feet pointing to the Stone Coffin."[11] Re-excavation in 1980–6 revealed the disarticulated remains of at least 249 people, whose bones had been stacked charnel-wise against the walls. The central burial did not survive, but the deposit contained many objects which may have originally accompanied it. An iron ax of early medieval type, a fragment of a two-edged sword, two large seaxes, a series of smaller seaxes and other knives, a chisel, a barrel-padlock key and other iron objects were found among the bones, together with seven fragments of precious metalwork (including a tiny circular silver band, the interior divided into four quadrant cloisons each containing a garnet), and six pins and tacks of gilded copper alloy. There were also five silver pennies, four of which were struck no earlier than 872 and the fifth of which may belong to 873/4.

Anthropological study of the main burial deposit shows that it was 80 percent male in the age range 15–45, of a massively robust non-local population type, parallels for which can be found in Scandinavia. The females were of a different type, possibly Anglo-Saxon. It seems likely that this mass grave was a burial of kingly status to which the bodies of those of the Viking Great Army who had died in the season of 873–4 had been gathered from graves elsewhere.[12]

The Biddles believe that the man buried with 249 soldiers was Ivar the Boneless. Ivar was noted as a man of exceptional cruelty and ferocity, and his nickname may indicate that he lacked legs, or may simply mean that he was long-legged or tall. The Viking force split into two in 874 and the occasion may have prompted the high status, elaborate and complex burial in the cairn placed on the bluff above the River Trent at Repton. The entombment is without parallel in Europe during the Viking age, and it is interesting that one saga notes that Ivar died and was buried in England "'in the manner of former times,' an allusion to the fact he was interred in a barrow."[13]

This was not the only Viking burial ground in the Repton area. Some 2 miles from Repton is the Viking barrow cemetery in Heath Wood, Ingleby. The cemetery was in use during the late 9th to early 10th centuries CE and includes 59 barrows laid out in four spatially distinct groups. The barrows are circular or sub-circular in shape and vary in height from 8 inches to over 4 feet and in diameter from almost 20 feet to over 42 feet. Some were constructed with an encircling ditch and others without. Approximately a quarter of the mounds have been partly excavated. The excavations have shown that although cremation burials are contained within some of the mounds, others are empty. The most common artifact to be found during excavation was nails, being found in five of the 15 mounds excavated and all but one of the cremation burials. The nails represent what remained of ships planking, upon which some of the burials were laid. This was a traditional, early Viking custom and ranks the burials among the earliest Viking graves in the British Isles. The Viking cemetery in Heath Wood is the only known example in England. It was used at a time of instability and insecurity within the period of Viking occupation. The use of the cemetery spans the conversion from pagan to Christian beliefs. The mounds containing cremation burials are characteristic of pagan burial rites, while the empty mounds are thought to be cenotaph graves constructed to commemorate those Vikings given Christian burials in the churchyard at nearby Repton. The conversion to Christianity was a gradual one and certain pagan traditions continued in use during this time.[14]

King Alfred Triumphant

In 878, the Danes launched a surprise attack on the royal estate at Chippenham, northwest Wiltshire, where Alfred was staying. Alfred managed to escape and sought refuge at Athelney, an island in the Somerset Levels, where he later established a monastery. The placename Athelney has been translated as "isle of the aethelings" and is traditionally the place where Æthelwine (son of Cynegils and brother of Cenwalh) lived as a hermit in the mid–7th century. From there Alfred was able to rally local militias from Somerset, Wiltshire and Hampshire. In May 878 Alfred met the combined militias of

The Alfred Jewel, which dates from the late 9th century and is inscribed in Old English: "Alfred ordered me made." It is likely that the jewel's function was to be the handle for a pointer stick for following words when reading a book (*Dresses and Decorations of the Middle Ages*, by Henry Shaw, 1843).

Somerset, Wiltshire and "that part of Hampshire which is on this side of the sea"[15] (that is, west of Southampton Water), at *Egbert's Stone* east of Selwood, and fought the Danes at *Ethandun* (possibly Edington, near Westbury in Wiltshire). He defeated them and pursued them to Chippenham, where he starved them into submission. Guthrum, the leader of the Danes, surrendered to Alfred, and agreed to convert to Christianity. Some weeks later, according to the *Chronicle*, Guthrum and 29 of his men were baptized at Aller near Athelney, and this baptism was further celebrated at the royal vill of Wedmore in Somerset. Following this celebration, Guthrum and the Danes left Wessex and returned to East Anglia.

THE CREATION OF THE DANELAW

In the same year, or perhaps in 880, after the death of the Mercian king Ceolwulf II, Alfred and Guthrum signed a treaty which divided up the kingdom of Mercia: Alfred would rule West Mercia, while Guthrum would incorporate East Mercia into an enlarged kingdom of East Anglia—the Danish lands now included Essex, East Anglia, the Kingdom of York (Northumbria between the River Tees and the Humber), the so-called Five Boroughs (the Mercian towns of Derby, Leicester, Lincoln, Nottingham and Stamford in the East Midlands), and some towns to the south like Northampton, Bedford and Cambridge. Alfred also had control of the Mercian city of London. After this Alfred began styling himself "King of the Anglo-Saxons" as well as King of Wessex.

Edward the Elder and the Five Boroughs

RECAPTURING THE FIVE BOROUGHS

After Alfred had signed a treaty with Guthrum and taken control of West Mercia, he persuaded a Welsh monk Asser, from St. David's in the kingdom of Dyfed, southwest Wales, to write his biography. The biography, in Latin, dated to 893, gives us information about Alfred not found in the *Chronicle*. For example, Asser tells us that Alfred had five children, Æthelflæd the eldest, Edward, Æthelgifu, Ælfthryth and Æthelweard. His daughter Æthelflæd, says Asser, was married to Æthelred, lord of the Mercians, probably some time in the 880s.

Alfred died in 899 and was succeeded by his eldest son Edward, usually referred to as Edward the Elder. From the time of Edward and well into the 11th century, the history of England is marked by almost continuous conflict between English and Danes. Edward's succession did not happen smoothly. Edward's cousin Æthelwold, the son of King Æthelred, rose in revolt and seized Wimborne and Christchurch, both in Dorset. Edward marched to Badbury near Wimborne and offered battle, but Æthelwold refused to leave Wimborne. Then under cover of night, Æthelwold left Wimborne and joined the Danes in Northumbria, who "received him as king."[16] In 901, Æthelwold came with a fleet to Essex, which submitted to him. The following year he encouraged the Danes of East Anglia to rise up, so that they "raided across all the land of Mercia, until they came to Cricklade, and there went over the Thames" (Cricklade is in the far north of Wiltshire). Edward then ravaged East Anglia and ordered his forces to return home. But the Kentish men refused to obey the order and engaged the Danes in battle: the Danes were victorious, but Æthelwold was killed.

Æthelred, lord of the Mercians, died in 911 and was replaced by Alfred's daughter Æthelflæd, who is commonly referred to as the Lady of the Mercians. For the next several years, the Lady of the Mercians and Edward concentrated on regaining lands lost to the Danes. In 913, according to the *Chronicle*, Edward went with some of his forces into Essex, to Maldon, and "camped there the while they made and built the stronghold of Witham; and a good part of the people who were earlier under the control of Danish men submitted to him."[17] In 917, Æthelflæd, Lady of the Mercians, conquered the town of Derby, one of the Five Boroughs which had been under Danish control, and in 918 she conquered Leicester, another of the Five Boroughs. In 919, Edward conquered Bedford, which had also been under Danish control.

But Edward's greatest successes came in 920 and 921. In 920, he captured Towcester (Northamptonshire) and the Danish fortress of Colchester (Essex). Then as the *Chronicle* records: "And there returned to him Earl Thurferth, and the captains, and all the army that belonged to Northampton northward to the Welland, and sought him for their lord and protector" (in other words, the Danes of Northamptonshire and south Lincolnshire submitted to Edward). Later that year, Edward went with the West Saxon army to Colchester and "repaired and renewed the town." Then many people "turned to him, both in East Anglia and Essex, that were before under the power of the Danes."[18]

In 921 Edward went with his army to Stamford (Lincolnshire), and "ordered the town to be fortified on the south side of the river. And all the people that belonged to the northern town [= the Danes] submitted to him and sought him as their lord." In the same year he went to Nottingham (one of the Five Boroughs) and "secured that borough and ordered it to be repaired and manned both with English and Danes. And all the population turned to him that was settled in Mercia, both Danish and English."[19]

THE FIVE BOROUGHS UNDER DANISH CONTROL

The Danes occupied the Five Boroughs for around forty years, and during this time some settlements flourished. Before 878 there was only one urban center in East Anglia

(Ipswich), but by the early years of the 10th century Norwich and Thetford in Norfolk had become urbanized. There are no documentary references to Norwich at this period (*Norwic* appeared for the first time on coins of Athelstan between 924 and 939), but *Theodford* had been named in the *Anglo-Saxon Chronicle* as the place where the Danish army had spent the winter of 869/70. Norwich and Thetford both grew with enormous speed from modest Middle Saxon beginnings. In the late 10th century Thetford covered some 185 acres—a colossal size for the period—while by the time of Domesday (1086) the population of Norwich had overtaken that of Thetford and the two towns ranked fifth and sixth in England after London, York, Lincoln and Winchester.[20]

In the Anglo-Saxon period Lincoln was an administrative and ecclesiastical center, but the late 9th century saw the revival of Lincoln as an urban center which accompanied its establishment as one of the Five Boroughs. The evidence from pottery finds shows that the development started in the southeast quarter of the lower city. By the middle of the 10th century there had been rapid expansion including the suburb of Wigford south of the river and into the upper city by the end of the century. The Flaxengate excavations of the 1970s have provided a sequence for the development of the southeast part of the city. Remains of rectangular wooden domestic buildings dating from the late 9th century, and buildings of both domestic and industrial use from the late 10th century onwards were revealed.[21]

As one of the Five Boroughs, Stamford in the south of Lincolnshire also flourished, on the north bank of the Welland (the "northern town" mentioned in the *Chronicle*). There is no evidence of any substantial occupation in the Middle Saxon period, but in the late 9th century, a pottery industry developed in Stamford, with pots that "display influences and parallels with northern France, particularly the Beauvais area"[22] (there were Danish armies in northern France at the time).

DANISH PAGANISM IN THE FIVE BOROUGHS

The Vikings were initially pagans, and in 1994 a metal detector found a decorated gold alloy Thor's hammer pendant at South Lopham in Norfolk, near the border with Suffolk. Thor's hammers, the symbol of the god Thor in Norse mythology, were worn as amulets by Vikings of pagan belief to invoke his protection.[23]

The Vikings of Lincolnshire also left behind some traces of their pagan beliefs. Two Viking pendants have been recovered from Lincolnshire recently which give us an insight into these beliefs. The first of these is a gold Viking pendant in the form of "Thor's hammer," which dates from around 850–950 CE and was found near to Spilsby in 2013. "Thor's hammers" are believed to be amuletic pendants which resembled Mjölnir, the hammer of the Norse god Thor, and they have often been considered to reflect a pagan reaction to the spread of Christianity. In addition to the general symbolism of the item, this pendant is interesting in two regards. First, it is made of gold, whereas most known "Thor's hammers" are made of other metals, notably silver and copper-alloy; in fact, only one other gold example is known from England (the one from South Lopham in Norfolk). Second, it is decorated with punched motifs resembling quatrefoils or miniature axes, whereas most English examples are plain or only minimally decorated.

The second pendant was found in 2014 at Wintringham, north Lincolnshire. It is a cast silver pendant with a gilded face that depicts the Norse god Odin and his attendant ravens, Huginn and Muninn ("Thought" and "Memory"). Odin and his ravens are

Thor's Hammer or Mjölnir. The Stenkvista runestone in Södermanland, Sweden, showing Thor's hammer instead of a cross. March 23, 2008 (Berig, CCA-Share Alike 4.0 International, 3.0 Unported, 2.5 Generic and 1.0 Generic).

Thor's Hammer from Spilsby, Lincolnshire (Portable Antiquities Scheme, CCA 2.0 Generic).

depicted skeletally, with Odin shown with one sighted and one blind eye, clasping the two birds to his chest while they appear to whisper into each of his ears. It has been suggested that this 10th-century pendant "proudly proclaims a militant paganism" in an era that saw the Christianization of the Scandinavian inhabitants of the Danelaw. Further, the possibility has been raised that the tripartite grouping of Odin, Huginn and Muninn might be "a deliberately offensive pastiche of the Christian Trinity or of Christ crucified flanked by thieves," an intent that could also lie behind the resemblance of "Thor's Hammer" pendants to Christian crucifixes, according to Kevin Leahy (cited in the Portable Antiquities Scheme record).[24]

CHRISTIANITY IN WESSEX

Meanwhile in Wessex, Edward the Elder did not neglect the religious needs of his subjects, creating three new bishoprics in Wells (Somerset) and Crediton (Devon), which already had monasteries, and Ramsbury (Wiltshire). Ramsbury is near Marlborough and also near the Roman town of Cunetio (Mildenhall). The present church of the Holy Cross at Ramsbury dates from the 13th century, but during the restoration of the church in 1891 substantial masonry foundations were observed to the south of the present building. These are thought to relate to the Anglo-Saxon church. Also recovered during this work were large fragments of an intricately carved Saxon cross shaft—possibly of 9th century date—and pieces of stone coffin lid, one of which is thought to depict a bishop.[25]

The Fight for Northumbria

RECAPTURING NORTHUMBRIA

Edward died in 924 and was succeeded by his son Æthelstan. In 925 "King Æthelstan and Sihtric king of the Northumbrians came together at Tamworth ... and Æthelstan gave away his sister to him." The following year Sihtric, the Danish king of York, died and "King Æthelstan took to the kingdom of Northumbria."[26] Sihtric's cousin Guthfrith led a fleet from the Viking settlement of Dublin to retake York, but was unsuccessful. In 937, Æthelstan and his half-brother Edmund defeated Anlaf (Olaf Guthfrithsson, King of Dublin), at the Battle of Brunaburh (possibly Bromborough in the Wirral, northwest England).

Æthelstan died in 939 and was succeeded by his half-brother Edmund. Anlaf (Olaf Guthfrithsson), the King of Dublin who was defeated at Brunaburh, invaded and occupied Northumbria and the Five Boroughs of Mercia. Anlaf/Olaf died in 942 and Edmund reconquered the Five Boroughs. In 944, Edmund reconquered Northumbria and expelled King Anlaf (Olaf III) Sihtricsson, also known as Amlaib Cuaran, and King Raegnals Guthfrithsson. In 946 Edmund was murdered, stabbed by a certain Leof at Pucklechurch, south Gloucestershire.

Edmund was succeeded by his brother Eadred. In 948 he launched an attack on Northumbria because "they had taken Eric for their king"[27] (this was Eric Bloodaxe, a Norwegian who may have been King of Norway). Another version of the *Chronicle* says that Eric replaced Amlaib Cuaran, who had become king in 949. At any rate, in 954 the Northumbrians expelled Eric, and Eadred became undisputed ruler of Northumbria.

NORTHUMBRIA UNDER DANISH RULE

Like Thetford, Norwich, Lincoln and Stamford, York flourished under Danish rule. It is uncertain where the Danish king resided, but according to Richard Hall,[28] the "location of a royal residence is hinted at by the place-name Kings Court (*Konungsgurtha*) recorded in the late 14th century in relation to an area immediately outside the site of the *porta principalis sinistra*, the west gatehouse of the Roman legionary fortress, which might, perhaps, have formed the most defensible nucleus of a palace." Hall also notes[29] that the excavations of 1967–73 at York Minster "revealed forty-eight pieces of sculpture which allowed Lang ... to define a York Metropolitan school of Anglo-Scandinavian stonecarving. The sculptured stones took a variety of forms, including cross-shafts, recumbent graveslabs and hog-backed tomb-stones. The choice of decorative motifs, such as animal interlace, often in the form of a beast chain, suggested to Lang a date of c.900 and he attributed the *floruit* of the York Metropolitan school to the early tenth century."

One area of York that was developed during the period of the Danelaw was Coppergate, to the south of York Minster and near the River Ouse. Hall says that in the opening decades of the 10th century the site "underwent at least the initial stages in a process of subdivision which defined all subsequent land-use hereabouts. Indeed, it may be that buildings were laid out and occupied. This was represented by greater quantities of pottery being deposited on the site ... and by the growth of industrial-scale activity across a range of craft specialisms." Among these specialisms were textile-making, woodturning, ferrous and non-ferrous metalworking, leatherworking, and aspects of bone- and antlerworking. Hall adds that judging by the foreign objects recovered at Coppergate, "York's overseas contacts were at their furthest flung in these decades." Exotic artifacts found at Coppergate include amber imported from the Baltic to be made into pendants, beads and rings, a large walrus ivory die, a walrus ivory ring, a large smithing hammer of the type common in Scandinavia, large copper alloy ringed pins of a type common in Ireland, rotary querns made of lava stone from the Mayen area in the Eifel Mountains of what is now southwest Germany, a silk cap made of silk from Byzantium, a Scandinavian woolen sock, and a metal weight with a decorative triskele motif from Scandinavia.[30]

DANISH PAGANISM AND CHRISTIANITY IN NORTHUMBRIA

The Danes of Northumbria soon converted to Christianity, but they left behind some Christian monuments that reflect their former pagan beliefs. The 15-foot high cross at Gosforth in the Lakes District of Cumbria is one of the finest monuments left by the Vikings in the British Isles and is a mixture of Christian scenes and scenes from Norse mythology. "A crucified Christ on the bottom of the east shaft is attended by both a man with a spear (probably the Longinus of medieval Christian legend) and a woman with a sweeping gown, who may represent Mary or Mary Magdalen but resembles iconographically similar valkyrie or queen figures on the pre–Christian picture stones of Gotland [in Sweden]." The rest of the scenes on the cross appear to be "references to Ragnarök, the pagan version of the last judgement, in which the Æsir and their allies do final battle with against the unleashed forces of Loki and his ilk."[31]

A number of Thor's hammers have also been discovered in the area controlled by the Vikings of Cumbria or the Kingdom of York. A silver Thor's hammer pendant was found at Longtown in Cumbria, near the border with Scotland; another silver Thor's hammer pendant was found at Leconfield near Beverley in East Yorkshire; and yet another silver Thor's hammer pendant was uncovered at Wetwang near Driffield in East Yorkshire.[32] Interestingly, Wetwang was the site of a large Iron Age cemetery, and in 2001 an Iron Age chariot burial was found there, to add to the three chariot burials excavated in 1984.

The most distinctive contribution of the Danes to Anglo-Saxon culture were the so-called hogback stones. Hogbacks are stone-carved Anglo-Scandinavian sculptures from 10th to 12th century England and Scotland, generally accepted as grave markers, or stylized "houses" for the dead. The hogback was derived from a variety of sources, the two most influential being Anglo-Saxon and Scandinavian in origin. Although hogbacks are not found in Scandinavia, they are considered a unique invention made by the Viking settlers in Northern England. It has been suggested that the monument type was invented in the late 9th century, at a time when Viking warlords had seized power at York. However, a 10th-century date has been generally accepted due to the ornament on hogbacks, largely influenced by the Borre (Norway) and Jellinge (Denmark) styles which appeared in Scandinavia in the late 9th and early 10th centuries.

The resemblance of so many early hogbacks to Viking-Age long houses is brought about not only by the shape and lines of the monuments but also on occasion by the depiction of architectural details, often stylized or modified by accompanying ornament. The ornament of hogbacks varies widely with some featuring large, three-dimensional end-beasts, often in the shape of bears. Hogbacks without end-beasts often resemble longhouses and their ornament consists only of architectural features. Some hogbacks are also decorated with "shingles" on either side of the central ridge, known as tegulation.[33]

One of the largest collection of hogback stones in England is at St. Thomas' church at Brompton near Northallerton in North Yorkshire, some with muzzled bear end-beasts, some decorated with shingles. This is not the full number from Brompton, since six hogbacks were purchased by Canon Greenwell in the 19th century and installed in the Monk's Dormitory at Durham Cathedral.[34]

Later Anglo-Saxon Saints and Monasteries

GLASTONBURY ABBEY (SOMERSET) AND ST. PATRICK

In the second half of the 10th century, English monasteries were reformed to bring them under the Benedictine rule—a reform most closely associated in Wessex with Dunstan, Archbishop of Canterbury, and Æthelwold, Bishop of Winchester. Dunstan was born around 910, probably at Baltonsborough near Glastonbury in Somerset, and studied at Glastonbury Abbey. Some time during the reign of King Edmund (939–946) he became Abbot of Glastonbury and brought Glastonbury under the Benedictine rule. King Edmund was murdered in 946 and replaced by Eadred, who was an ardent supporter of Dunstan and made him one of his principal advisers. When Eadred died in 955, he was succeeded by Eadwig, who was suspicious of Dunstan and forced him into exile; however, in 957 Eadwig's brother Edgar was made king of England north of the Thames, and Dunstan returned from exile to become Bishop of Worcester. When Eadwig died in 959 and

Hogback Stone from Dalserf churchyard, Lanarkshire, Scotland. September 10, 2006 (Supergolden, GDFL, CC-BY-SA).

was succeeded by Edgar, Dunstan was appointed Archbishop of Canterbury. He died in 988 and was soon venerated as a saint. Æthelwold was born in Winchester and studied under Dunstan at Glastonbury. He subsequently founded a Benedictine monastery at Abingdon in Oxfordshire and was made Bishop of Winchester in 963. In the following year, Æthelwold had the clerics of the Old and New Minsters expelled and replaced by monks from Abingdon.

Both Dunstan and Æthelwold were associated with Glastonbury, and it may have influenced their attitude to the cult of saints. The earliest *Life* of Dunstan was written between 995 and 1004 by a secular cleric known only by the first letter of his name, B., and it tells us a little about Glastonbury. The early 10th century monastery was presumably of modest extent, for as a boy Dunstan had a vision of the greater buildings he was subsequently to construct there. B. also refers to an Irish community at Glastonbury, and the Irish seem to have long played a role there. In the 7th century, Aldhelm criticized a certain Heahfrith for succumbing to the allure of Irish learning. Under the year 891 the *Anglo-Saxon Chronicle* refers to an Irish presence in England as the result of the travels of Irish pilgrims[35]:

> And three Scots came to King Alfred in a boat without any oars, from Ireland, from where they had stolen away because they wanted for the love of God to be abroad—they did not care where. The boat in which they set out was made of two-and-a-half skins, and they took with them food for seven days; and after 7 days they came to land in Cornwall, and immediately went to King Alfred.

Glastonbury was a center for Irish pilgrims because, according to B., St. Patrick "the Elder" was buried there. In his late 11th century *Life* of St. Dunstan, Osbern of Canterbury, who had visited Glastonbury, makes a similar point[36]:

> Many distinguished scholars, eminent both in sacred and profane learning, who quitted Ireland to embrace a life of voluntary exile in England, chose Glastonbury for their habitation, as being a retired but convenient spot, and one famous for its cult—a point of special attraction, this, for the exiles—of Patrick, who is said to have come after a lifetime of miracleworking and preaching the gospel, and to have ended his days there in the Lord.

As B. and Osbern make clear, it was believed that the remains of St. Patrick were buried there, though nobody was sure whether it was the famous St. Patrick who brought Christianity to Ireland, or another St. Patrick. Even the Irish themselves had an early hagiographical tradition that there had been more than one Patrick. In the 8th century, for example, a hymn was composed which stated that "When Patrick departed this life, he went first to the other Patrick: together they ascended to Jesus the Son of Mary." The Elder Patrick, according to some scholars, might have been Palladius, the Roman deacon who was sent to Ireland in 431 by Pope Celestine. It may be that the earlier tradition at Glastonbury concerned Palladius/Patrick, but it was later transformed when the monks realized that they might actually possess the relics of the greater and more prestigious saint. Just how early that tradition may be is uncertain. However, there was a high-status site at Glastonbury in the Dark Ages, possibly an Irish church, and the monastery that King Ine built in the late 7th century was the equal of the finest monasteries in Northumbria, so there may have been a saint's cult there from the earliest times.

By the 10th century there was also a cult of St. Brigit at Glastonbury. It was believed that Brigit, the Irish saint celebrated in the church of Kildare, had made a pilgrimage to Glastonbury in 488, that she stayed for some time on the nearby island of Beckery and that she left various objects behind when she ultimately returned to Ireland: a wallet, a collar, a bell and assorted weaving implements. Excavations confirm that a chapel did exist at Beckery in the Middle Ages: there was an outer building dating from the 14th century, enclosing a similar chapel of late Saxon or early medieval date, which may even have been built by St. Dunstan.

St. Swithun of Winchester (Hampshire)

In the 10th century Carolingian world (France, Belgium and Germany) large numbers of local saints were translated into lavish shrines and their translations recorded by hagiographers. For example, in 914 the remains of St. Eugenius were translated to Brogne abbey in Belgium; in 935–7 St. Maximinius was translated at Trier in Germany; and the remains of St. Hunegund, the 7th century founder of Homblières in Picardy were translated in 946 and the translation and accompanying miracles were recorded by Abbot Berner of Homblières in 964.[37]

Perhaps inspired by these Continental cults and his time at Glastonbury, Æthelwold set about creating a saint for Winchester. Swithun was an obscure bishop of Winchester between 852 and 863 and it is not clear why he was chosen to become the patron of the Old Minster. In 971 his relics were lifted from a prominent stone sarcophagus outside the west door of the Old Minster and translated into the Old Minster itself. King Edgar commissioned a lavish gold and silver reliquary to house the saint's relics, and within a few years Æthelwold began reconstructing the minster on a vast scale in order to incorporate the site of Swithun's original tomb and to make it the focal point for the saint's cult.[38]

The best-known account of his life was written by Ælfric, who was educated in the Old Minster at Winchester, and later became abbot of Eynsham in Oxfordshire. In the *Lives of the Saints*, written between 992 and 1002, Ælfric tells us[39] that Swithun appeared in a vision to "a certain faithful smith" and asked him to tell a priest called Eadsige to inform the bishop that "he must himself open my grave and bring my bones within the church." The smith duly conveyed Swithun's message to Eadsige, one of the secular clerks expelled from the Old Minster by Æthelwold; unsurprisingly, perhaps, no further action was taken. Then, says Ælfric,

> there was a poor peasant, awfully humpbacked,
> painfully stooped as a consequence of the broad hump.
> To him was revealed in a dream as truth
> that he should obtain his bodily health at Swithin's
> sepulchre, and [recovery from] his crippledness.
> He arose then in the morning, greatly rejoicing,
> and crept to Winchester with two crutches
> and sought the saint as it was told to him,
> praying for his health on bended knees.
> Whereupon he was healed by the holy bishop
> so that thereafter it could not be seen on his back
> where the hump had stood that had oppressed him till then.

Finally, says Ælfric

> A certain man was afflicted with a very bad disease
> so that he could open his eyes with difficulty only,
> and he could hardly utter a single word,
> but lay thus tormented, despairing of his life.

> Then all his friends wished to carry him to the New Minster
> to Saint Judoc that he might give him health;
> but someone told them that it would be better for them
> to take the sick man to the Old Minster
> to Swithin's grave, and thereupon they did so.
> That night they then kept vigil at the grave with him,
> praying Almighty God that He would grant to the sick man
> his health through Saint Swithin.
> The infirm man also watched until it was becoming day,
> then he fell asleep, and the worshipful tomb,
> as it seemed to them all, was all rocking,
> and to the sick man it seemed as if some man was dragging
> his one shoe off his foot, and he suddenly awoke.
> He was then healed by the holy Swithin,
> and they sought for the shoe very carefully,
> but no man was ever able to find it there; and then
> they went home with the man who had been healed.

St. Judoc was a Breton saint whose relics had been taken from his shrine at the Abbey of St-Josse to the New Minster in 903 by monks fleeing Norman raiders. After the remains of St. Swithun were translated into the Old Minster, says Aelfric,

> there were healed by the holy man
> four sick men within three days,
> and during five months there were only few days
> when there were healed less than three sick persons,
> sometimes five or six, or seven or eight,
> ten or twelve, sixteen or eighteen.
> Within ten days two hundred men were healed,
> and so many within twelve months that no man could count them.
> The burial-ground lay filled with crippled folk,
> so that people could hardly get into the Minster;
> and they were all so miraculously healed
> within a few days, that one could not find there
> five unsound men out of that great crowd.

St. Edward of Shaftesbury (Dorset)

Edward the Martyr was born in 962 and became king in 975 on the death of his father Edgar. The succession was disputed, with some supporting his half-brother Æthelred, and in 978 Edward was murdered at Corfe Castle in Dorset, probably by supporters of Æthelred. The *Chronicle* has a very colorful report of the murder[40]:

> This year was King Edward slain, at eventide, at Corfe-gate, on the fifteenth day before the calends of April. And he was buried at Wareham without any royal honour. No worse deed than this was ever done by the English nation since they first sought the land of Britain. Men murdered him but God has magnified him. He was in life an earthly king—he is now after death a heavenly saint. Him would not his earthly relatives avenge—but his heavenly father has avenged him amply. The earthly homicides would wipe out his memory from the earth—but the avenger above has spread his memory abroad in heaven and in earth. Those, who would not before bow to his living body, now bow on their knees to his dead bones. Now we may conclude, that the wisdom of men, and their meditations, and their counsels, are as nought against the appointment of God.

In its entry for 980, the *Chronicle* reports[41] that "Alderman Aelfhere fetched the body of the holy King Edward at Wareham, and carried him with great solemnity to Shaftesbury," a monastery in Dorset founded in the late 9th century and closely associated with King Alfred. Aelfhere was a supporter of Æthelred, and his reburial of Edward's remains was perhaps a gesture of reconciliation.

The *Passio Eadwardi*, written in the 1080s or 1090s, tells of how Edward's body was recovered from the swamp in which it had been hidden, brought to Wareham, and then taken to Shaftesbury for burial by Aelfhere, alderman of Mercia (956–983). It also recounts a second translation of the saint's relics in 1001. The saint's desire to be raised from his resting-place was made known by his appearance in a vision to "a certain religious." This unnamed intermediary was ordered to go to Shaftesbury, to make known the saint's will to the abbess, and to urge her to pass on the information to the king. These instructions were followed and Aethelred, "hearing how boundless was his brother's glory, was filled with great joy and, had he been granted the opportunity, would gladly have … been present at his elevation." The king, hemmed in by the Danes, sent messengers to Wulfsige, bishop of Sherborne, and to another prelate called Aelfsige, "instructing and commanding them to raise his brother's body from the ground and to lay it in a worthy resting-place."[42] Edward's sanctification is specifically alluded to by Aethelred in a charter of 1001 which records a grant of land at Bradford on Avon in Wiltshire to Shaftesbury Abbey for the construction of a refuge for Edward's relics, where they could be kept safe from the Danes.[43]

According to legend, miracles at Edward's grave began to happen the night after his murder: an old blind woman, in whose poor hut Edward's body awaited burial, suddenly gained her sight. Soon, a healing spring burst forth near the martyr's first grave at Wareham and became a site of pilgrimage. As he was being taken to Shaftesbury, two cripples "were made all whole, and followed the holy body with great joy and mirth, thanking God and the holy saint of their health."[44]

St. Melor of Amesbury (Wiltshire)

The most unusual saint in late Anglo-Saxon Wessex is St. Melor. In 979 Ælfthryth, the widow of King Edgar, founded a Benedictine abbey at Amesbury dedicated to St. Mary and St. Melor. Melor, it seems, was the son of the Duke of Cornouaille in the west of Brittany. When Melor was seven, his father was killed by his brother who wished to seize the throne. Melor's life was spared by his uncle at the request of the clergy, but his right hand and left foot were cut off. The mutilated Melor was fitted with a silver hand and bronze foot and confined to a monastery. At the age of fourteen, Melor began to work miracles. His artificial limbs came to life and functioned as though natural, and he worked other miracles as well, such as calling forth a fountain from the earth by throwing a stone on the ground. On hearing of these events, the uncle bribed Melor's guardian to behead him. After the beheading, angels appeared with lights to guard the body until the deed was discovered. The assassins brought Melor's head to the uncle; during the journey the head spoke to the assassins and produced a fountain to quench their thirst. When the uncle touched the head, he died; white bulls were used to carry the body to its grave. The cult of Melor at Amesbury did not generate much income, and William of Malmesbury said very little about it.[45] The dedication is a most unusual one in Anglo-Saxon England: there are probably only two other churches in Britain dedicated to him, both in Cornwall, at Mylor near Falmouth, and Linkinhorne, between Callington and Launceston. The story of Melor has obvious similarities to the story of the Irish king

Nuada, whose namesake Nodens was worshipped in the Romano-British temple at Lydney Park in Gloucestershire. Nuada was a legendary Irish king who lost his arm in a battle and had it replaced with a silver prosthetic.

St. Aldhelm of Malmesbury (Wiltshire)

By the 10th century Aldhelm, abbot of Malmesbury and bishop of Sherborne, was being venerated as a saint. William of Malmesbury, writing in the early 12th century, says of Aldhelm[46]:

> There is a village in the county of Somerset called Doulting, and it was here that Aldhelm ended his life. He had long ago given the village to the monks of Glastonbury, though arranging to have the usufruct of it himself. The building which witnessed his end was a wooden church. As he was drawing his last breaths he gave orders for his body to be carried into it, so he might die in that particular spot, as succeeding generations, down to the villagers of today, have asserted he did. Later on the church was rebuilt of stone. A monk from Glastonbury was attending to its consecration in the name of God, when a woman who had been blind in both eyes for a long time, came up to the packed crowd and with remarkable faith pushed her way through the mass, shouting for someone to lead her to the altar, as she had a total belief that the saint, whose church was being consecrated, would cure a widow's blindness, seeing that throughout his life he had always given the customary alms to widows. Her bold belief brought down help from the sky and a clear light filled her widowed eyes. A miracle performed before so many people could not be hidden, especially as the woman and her blindness were very well known in the area. It is also said that the saint as he was dying rested on a stone in this church, which is known to have cured many sick people with the water in which it had been washed

According to William, Aldhelm's body was taken from Doulting to be buried in the church of St. Michael in Malmesbury. In the mid–9th century King Aethelwulf of Wessex (the father of Alfred the Great) presented a reliquary to Malmesbury to house the relics of St. Aldhelm. According to William of Malmesbury, the reliquary was embellished on the front with images of the saint in solid silver, and on the back with scenes in relief showing miracles performed by the saint.[47]

The Return of the Vikings

Early Attacks

Northumbria may have returned to English control, but it was not long before Vikings began attacking England once more. In 978 Æthelred became king, and in 980, Southampton (Hampshire) was plundered by the "pirate army, and most of the population slain or imprisoned." In the same year, the Isle of Thanet (Kent) was overrun, and Cheshire "was plundered by the pirate army of the North." In 981 Padstow (Cornwall) was plundered, and there were raids along the coasts of Devon and Wales. In 982, "three ships of the pirates" plundered Portland (Dorset). In 991, Anlaf (Olaf Tryggvason, later King of Norway) launched an attack: Ipswich (Suffolk) was plundered, and "very soon afterwards was Alderman Britnoth slain at Maldon. In this same year it was resolved that tribute should be given, for the first time, to the Danes, for the great terror they occasioned by the sea coast. That was first 10,000 pounds."[48]

In 993 the Vikings attacked Bamburgh in Northumberland and the River Humber, which separates Yorkshire from Lincolnshire. In 994 Anlaf/Olaf and King Swein Forkbeard of Denmark attacked London, but they suffered heavy losses and left, attacking instead the coasts of Essex, Kent, Sussex and Hampshire. King Æthelred and his councilors agreed to offer the Vikings tribute and supplies if they would stop their attacks. They agreed, and took up winter-quarters in Southampton, where "they were fed by all the subjects of the West Saxon kingdom" and given "16,000 pounds in money" (that is, 16,000 pounds of silver). Then King Æthelred sent Bishop Ælfheah of Winchester and Alderman Æthelweard, who "led Anlaf with great pomp to the king at Andover. And King Æthelred received him at episcopal hands, and honoured him with royal presents. In return Anlaf promised, as he also performed, that he never again would come in a hostile manner to England" (although the *Chronicle* is unclear on this point, it seems that Anlaf/Olaf was confirmed as a Christian in the ceremony at Andover in Hampshire).

However, in 997 a Viking army attacked the coast, from Cornwall to the Severn Estuary and Wales. In the same year they entered the River Tamar, on the border between Cornwall and Devon, attacking the fortified town of Lydford (Devon) and destroying Tavistock Abbey in Devon. In 998 the Viking army entered the River Frome, which flows into Poole Harbour near Wareham, and attacked Dorset. The Vikings made the Isle of Wight their base and took supplies from Hampshire and Sussex. In 999 the Vikings sailed up the Thames and the Medway to Rochester (Kent), and laid waste most of west Kent. In 1001 there was "a great commotion in England in consequence of an invasion by the Danes, who spread terror and devastation wherever they went, plundering and burning and desolating the country with such rapidity, that they advanced in one march as far as the town of Alton; where the people of Hampshire came against them, and fought with them." Then the Vikings went west into Devon, and were joined by Pallig, a Dane in the service of Æthelred who deserted his lord. After this, they burned Kingsteignton in the south of Devon, and attacked Pinhoe and Broad Clyst (both in Devon), after which they proceeded east to the Isle of Wight and burned down Waltham in Hampshire. In response to this, the king made peace with the Vikings and paid them a tribute of 24,000 pounds.

THE ST. BRICE'S DAY MASSACRE

Then on St. Brice's Day (November 13) in 1002, Æthelred ordered the killing of all Danes in the kingdom, because he believed they were plotting to kill him. Contemporary historians believe that the massacre was limited to recent migrants and members of the Danish elite outside the Danelaw (where a massacre would have been unlikely), but no one knows just how many people died. Politically, the order achieved little for the king. Its main outcome was the alienation of Danes working for him and, the following year, a brutal retaliation by Forkbeard. According to later literary sources, Forkbeard was particularly enraged by the death of his sister, her husband, and their child in the massacre. The story goes that they and other fleeing Danes had sought sanctuary in St. Frideswide's Church in Oxford (now Christ Church Cathedral). As Æthelred recorded in a royal charter, "When all the people in pursuit strove, forced by necessity, to drive them out, and could not, they set fire to the planks and burnt, as it seems, this church with its ornaments and its books." Those who did not die inside, sources state, were killed by their pursuers as they tried to escape.

Almost exactly 1,000 years later, archaeologists in England discovered a mass grave containing the remains of dozens of young men who had been slaughtered or executed. The mass grave was found in 2008 by archaeologists digging on the grounds of St. John's

College in Oxford. The team first found the previously unknown remains of one of Britain's largest Neolithic henges, almost 500 feet in diameter. The find immediately changed the perception of prehistoric Oxford from a rather insignificant ford across the Thames to potentially one of the most important ritual sites in southern England. The henge's eight-foot-deep ditch had become, by the medieval period, a dump for waste, including broken pottery and food scraps. It was there, in the garbage-filled ditch, that the team found the remains of 37 people.

All the bodies in the grave appear to have been male (though two were too young for their sex to be determined), and most were between 16 and 25 years old. As a group, they were tall, taller than the average Anglo-Saxon at the time, and strong, judging by the large muscle-attachment areas of their bones. Despite their physical advantages, all these men appear to have met violent ends. One had been decapitated and attempts at decapitation had seemingly been made on five others. Twenty-seven suffered broken or cracked skulls. The back and pelvic bones of 20 bodies bore stab marks, as did the ribs of a dozen others. A number of the skeletons had evidence of charring, indicating that they were burned prior to burial.

Bone specialist Ceri Falys began piecing together the fragmented skulls and skeletons. Falys saw that the damage to the bones revealed a frenzied attack, but not the sort one would expect from a traditional medieval battle. Instead, her meticulous work revealed that many of the men appear to have been attacked from all sides. For example, one victim suffered wounds to both his skull and pelvis, suggesting he had been attacked both from behind and from the side, by at least two different people. "The injuries I observed were not the result of men involved in hand-to-hand combat," says Falys. "In such cases, we would expect to find cut marks on the forearms and hands as the person raises their arms to defend. Instead, I believe these wounds were the result of undefended people running away from their attackers."

Radiocarbon analysis of the bones dates them to around 960 to 1020—England's later Anglo-Saxon period, including the reign of Æthelred. The archaeologist Sean Wallis and his excavation team were convinced, in part because of the evidence of the burning of the remains, that they had discovered a mass grave from St. Brice's Day 1002.

In 2009, to extract yet more information from the bones, scientists from the Research Laboratory for Archaeology and the History of Art at the University of Oxford, led by Mark Pollard, carried out chemical analysis of collagen from the bones and enamel from the teeth of some of the individuals. Pollard concluded that the victims had diets with a substantial amount of seafood—somewhat more than is found in the diets of the local population at the time. This supported the notion that the dead were indeed foreign to the British Isles and were Viking victims of the St. Brice's Day massacre.[49]

King Swein Forkbeard attacked England in 1003, destroying Exeter, and plundering and burning the royal town of Wilton in Wiltshire. The following year Swein returned, plundering and burning Norwich and Thetford (Norfolk). In 1006 the Vikings returned after midsummer and sacked Sandwich in Kent; Æthelred recruited an army from Wessex and Mercia, which fought against the Vikings throughout the autumn, but without success. After November 11, the Vikings returned to their base on the Isle of Wight; at Christmas they proceeded through Hampshire into Berkshire, and burned Wallingford in Oxfordshire, then returned to their ships, passing through Winchester. In 1007, a tribute if 36,000 pounds was paid to the Viking army, together with provisions supplied from all parts of England.

In 1009 the army of the Swedish Viking Thorkell the Tall came to Sandwich and headed for Canterbury, but the men of Kent made peace with them and gave them 3,000 pounds. The army then turned toward the Isle of Wight, and burned and plundered widely in Sussex, Hampshire and Berkshire. After November 11, the army returned to Kent and took up winter quarters along the Thames, receiving supplies from Kent and Essex. From there they attacked London and burned Oxford. In 1010, the army marched into East Anglia, which they plundered and burned for three months. By 1111, the army had overrun East Anglia, Essex, Middlesex, Oxfordshire, Cambridgeshire, Hertfordshire, Buckinghamshire, Bedfordshire, half of Huntingdonshire, much of Northamptonshire and, to the south of the Thames, Kent, Sussex, Surrey, Berkshire, Hampshire, and much of Wiltshire. Finally, in 1012, the king paid the Viking army 48,000 pounds in tribute.

SWEIN FORKBEARD AND CNUT

In 1013, Swein Forkbeard of Denmark came with his fleet to Sandwich, and soon entered the Humber and River Trent, and sailed up the Trent to Gainsborough (Lincolnshire). Earl Uhtred and all the Northumbrians submitted to him, as did the people of Lindsey (north Lincolnshire), the people of the Five Boroughs, and "all the army to the north of Watling Street" (that is, in the old Danelaw). Swein then moved south to Oxford and Winchester, which submitted to him; London at first refused to submit but submitted after Swein went to Bath (Somerset) and received the submission of all the western shires of Wessex. Æthelred went into exile in Normandy, the homeland of his wife Emma, the sister of Richard II, Duke of Normandy.

Swein died in early 1014 and the Danes declared his son Cnut as king. Meanwhile, the English recognized Æthelred as king, and he landed in Lindsey with an army which "plundered and burned, and slew all the men that they could reach." After the death of Swein, Olaf Haraldsson, the future king of Norway (1015–1028), apparently attacked London and destroyed London Bridge. The event is not mentioned in the *Anglo-Saxon Chronicle*, but the oldest Norse saga about Olaf Haraldsson does mention it[50]:

> Yet you broke [destroyed] the bridge[s] of London,
> Stout hearted warrior,
> You succeeded in conquering the land.
> Iron swords made headway
> Strongly urged to conflict;
> Ancient shields were broken,
> Battle fury mounted.

After his death Olaf was venerated as a saint, and six churches in London were dedicated to him, including one in Southwark, very close to the bridge he is supposed to have pulled down.[51]

After Swein died, Cnut then fled to Denmark, but returned in 1015 and conquered most of England. Æthelred died in 1016 and the English recognized his son Edmund Ironside as king. Edmund and Cnut clashed at the Battle of Assandun in Essex, and Cnut was victorious. The two kings met at Alney near Deerhurst in Gloucestershire and made a treaty: Edmund was to rule over Wessex, and Cnut would govern the rest of England. Shortly afterwards, Edmund Ironside died in mysterious circumstances, and Cnut married Emma, the widow of King Æthelred.

The End of Anglo-Saxon England

Cnut died in 1035 and was succeeded in Denmark by his son Harthnacut, and in England by his younger son Harold Harefoot. Harold died in 1040 and Harthnacut assumed the throne of England as well as Denmark. He died in 1042 and was succeeded by Edward the Confessor, the son of Æthelred and Emma of Normandy, who was virtually the last Anglo-Saxon king. Edward died childless in 1066, prompting the invasion by William, Duke of Normandy, who was distantly related to Edward and claimed to be the heir to the throne.

Anglo-Saxon England was no more, but the cult of Anglo-Saxon saints continued, with hagiographers from the Continent writing the Lives of saints who may have been venerated before the Norman Conquest but only took on historical form in the late 11th century.

8

Saints and Magic
After the Norman Conquest:
Anglo-Saxon Saints

The Norman Conquest

In 1066 William of Normandy, who was distantly related to Edward the Confessor through Edward's mother Emma of Normandy, invaded England, killed Edward's chosen successor Harold at the Battle of Hastings, and was crowned king in Edward's newly completed cathedral, Westminster Abbey. William replaced Anglo-Saxon aristocrats with his own Norman followers, built Norman castles throughout England, replaced senior English churchmen with French ones, and rebuilt many cathedrals and churches. English was replaced by Norman French as the language of the elite, and very little was written in English for over a century, apart from the Peterborough version of the *Anglo-Saxon Chronicle*, which continued until 1154.

English Resistance to the Norman Conquest

HEREWARD THE WAKE

Not all English people accepted the Norman Conquest, and among these was Hereward, also known as Hereward the Wake. According to the Peterborough version of the *Anglo-Saxon Chronicle*, in 1070[1]:

came King Sweyne from Denmark into the Humber; and the landsmen came to meet him, and made a treaty with him; thinking that he would overrun the land. Then came into Ely Christien, the Danish bishop, and Earl Osbern, and the Danish domestics with them; and the English people from all the fen-lands came to them; supposing that they should win all that land. Then the monks of Peterborough heard say, that their own men would plunder the minster; namely Hereward and his gang: because they understood that the king had given the abbacy to a French abbot, whose name was Thorold;— that he was a very stern man, and was then come into Stamford with all his Frenchmen. Now there was a churchwarden, whose name was Yware; who took away by night all that he could, testaments, mass-hackles, cantel-copes, and reefs, and such other small things, whatsoever he could; and went early, before day, to the Abbot Thorold; telling him that he sought his protection, and informing him how the outlaws were coming to Peterborough, and that he did all by advice of the monks. Early in the morning came all the outlaws with many ships, resolving to enter the minster; but the monks withstood, so that they could not come in. Then they laid on fire, and burned all the houses of the monks, and all the town except one house. Then came they in through fire at the Bull-hithe gate; where the monks met them, and besought peace of them. But they regarded nothing. They went into the minster, climbed up to the holy rood, took away the diadem from our Lord's head, all of pure gold, and seized the bracket that was underneath his feet, which was all of red gold. They climbed up to the steeple, brought down the table that was hid there, which was all of gold and silver, seized two golden shrines, and nine of silver, and took away fifteen large crucifixes, of gold and of silver; in short, they seized there so much gold and silver, and so many treasures, in money, in raiment, and in books, as no man could tell another; and said, that they did it from their attachment to the minster. Afterwards they went to their ships, proceeded to Ely, and deposited there all the treasure. The Danes, believing that they should overcome the Frenchmen, drove out all the monks; leaving there only one,

Sweyn II of Denmark (1047–1076), who was the nephew of King Cnut of England, captured York, but left England after being paid off by King William. Then in 1071,

Earl Edwin and Earl Morkar fled out, and roamed at random in woods and in fields. Then went Earl Morkar to Ely by ship; but Earl Edwin was treacherously slain by his own men. Then came Bishop Aylwine, and Siward Barn, and many hundred men with them, into Ely. When King William heard that, then ordered he out a naval force and land force, and beset the land all about, and wrought a bridge, and went in; and the naval force at the same time on the sea-side. And the outlaws then all surrendered; that was, Bishop Aylwine, and Earl Morkar, and all that were with them; except Hereward alone, and all those that would join him, whom he led out triumphantly. And the king took their ships, and weapons, and many treasures; and all the men he disposed of as he thought proper. Bishop Aylwine he sent to Abingdon, where he died in the beginning of the winter.

Earl Edwin was earl of Mercia and his brother Earl Morcar was earl of Northumbria; Morcar joined Hereward's rebellion at Ely, but later surrendered to William and was imprisoned in Normandy, while Edwin was killed by the Normans in 1071 while making his way to Scotland, where Edgar Ætheling, the Anglo-Saxon pretender to the throne, was living in exile. Æthelwine was bishop of Durham—he was initially loyal to William, but later rebelled.

The real Hereward seems to have been a small south Lincolnshire squire, holding lands from the abbeys of Crowland and Peterborough, and thus very much "the monk's man," although regularly in dispute as to tenancy agreements. In the spring of 1070 the Danish king Swein Estrithson arrived in the mouth of the Humber and was expected to make a bid for the crown. He dispatched a unit of housecarls (bodyguards) under Jarl Asbjorn and Bishop Christian of Aarhus to secure a base on the Isle of Ely, a tract of fertile land capable of supporting six hundred households, some twelve by ten miles, in the middle of the swampy fenland of Cambridgeshire. Ely was admirably suited for defense; sea-going vessels could reach it via the Wash and River Ouse, but landwards it was cut off by swamps and a network of hidden waterways.

Here the Danes were immediately joined by local people (many of whom were of Danish extraction), including Hereward. At Peterborough Abbey, on the western edge of the Fens two dozen miles away, the abbot Brand, perhaps Hereward's uncle, had recently died, and now the monks were warned that Hereward and his companions wanted to remove the monastery's valuables prior to the arrival of the Norman abbot Turold. The monks resisted Hereward and his men, who set fire to the town, forced the precinct gate and looted the monastery. Soon afterwards the Danes returned to Denmark, taking this loot with them.

Ely now became a notorious refuge for anti–Norman dissidents, including, among the better known, Earl Morcar of Northumbria, Bishop Æthelwine of Durham, and Siward

Bearn, a substantial Midlands landowner. At last William himself led an expedition against Ely. He bottled up the defenders, placing a naval blockade on the seaward side and then constructing a lengthy causeway to allow his land forces to advance through the swamps. Eventually the defenders surrendered to William who "did with them what he wanted." Florence of Worcester says that some he imprisoned, others he let go free, having cut off their hands or put out their eyes. But Hereward slipped away with some of his followers and is heard of no more in any official record.[2]

HEREWARD AND THE WITCH

By the first quarter of the 12th century Hereward had become the hero of a Latin tale, *Gesta Herewardi* ("The Deeds of Hereward"). This contains a number of fantastical episodes, including one involving a witch[3]

> Then when the war-engines were prepared as he had arranged, and in furtherance of which he had travelled there, the king began the attack, leading his entire army to Aldreth. He had also brought heaps of wood and stone and all materials for building ramparts there. And he ordered all the fishermen in the district to come with their boats to Cottenham so that they could ferry across what had been brought there, and with it construct mounds and hillocks at Aldreth from the top of which they might fight. Among these came Hereward, like a fisherman with a boat along with the rest. They diligently ferried across everything that had been brought there. Finally on the same day—the sun not going

The 8th/9th century Hedda Stone from Peterborough Cathedral. The figures may represent Christ's disciples. March 21, 2010 (NotFromUtrecht, CCA-Share Alike 3.0 Unported).

down without some damage done–Hereward finished his work and before he left set fire to it. As a result it was entirely burnt, and several men killed and swallowed up in the swamp. He had shaved his beard and head so as not to be recognized, employing various disguises to encompass the death of enemies and the destruction of foes, preferring to look bald for a while and forego his finely-styled locks, rather than spare his opponents. When it was learned that Hereward had again escaped with impunity, the king declared that it was shameful to be so frequently ridiculed by him. However, the revered king, among other things, gave instructions commanding his men that above all Hereward should be brought to him alive, and that they should keep him unharmed. And taking warning from the damage done on this occasion, they set a day-and-night guard over all their property and operations.

Thus struggling for a week they just about completed one mound and set up four wooden bastions on which to site the war-engines. But those in the Isle resisted vigorously, building outworks and ramparts to oppose them. And then on the eighth day they all advanced to attack the island with their entire force, placing the witch I mentioned earlier, in an elevated position in their midst, so that being sufficiently protected on all sides, she might have space in which to practice her art. Once mounted, she harangued the Isle and its inhabitants for a long time, denouncing saboteurs and suchlike, and casting spells for their overthrow; and at the end of her chattering and incantations she bared her arse at them. Well, when she had performed her disgusting act three times as she wished, those who had been concealed in the swamp all around to right and left among the sharp reeds and brambles of the marshland, set fire to part of it so that, driven by the wind, the smoke and flames surged up against the king's camp. Spreading for as far as two furlongs, the fire ran hither and thither among them, making a horrible sight in the swamp, and the roar of the flames and crackling of twigs in the brushwood and willows making a terrible noise. As a result, stupefied and greatly alarmed, the king's men fled, each man for himself. But they could not go far along those watery paths through the wastes of the swamp, and they could not keep to the track easily. In consequence very many of them were suddenly swallowed up, and others, overwhelmed with arrows, drowned in the same waters, for in the fire and in their flight they were unable to use their lances against the bands of those who came cautiously and secretly out from the Isle to repel them. Among them the aforesaid woman who practiced her abominable art, fell down in the greatest terror head-first from her exalted position and broke her neck.

The Monastery of Peterborough and the Wild Hunt

Clearly the English of 12th century Peterborough believed in witches, so it is not surprising that they should believe in other supernatural events. In 1127 King Henry I (1100–1135) gave the abbacy of Peterborough to a certain Henry of Poitou, a relative of the king, who was also abbot of Saint-Jean-d'Angély in southwestern France. The monks of Peterborough strongly objected to this and recorded their objections in the Peterborough version of the *Anglo-Saxon Chronicle*[4]:

He had his abbacy of St Jean d'Angely in hand, and all the archbishops and bishops said that it was against the law, and that he could not have two abbacies in hand; but the same Henry gave the king to understand that he had left his abbacy because of the great hostility that was in that land, and he did that through the advice and leave of the pope of Rome and of the abbot of Cluny, and because he was legate about the Rome-tax. But despite that it was just not so; but he wanted to have both in hand—and had so, for as long as it was God's will. While in his clerk's orders he was bishop in Soissons; afterwards he became a monk in Cluny, and later became prior in the same minster; and later he became prior in Savigny. After that, because he was relative of the king of England and of the earl of Poitou, the earl gave him the abbacy of St Jean d'Angely. Afterwards through his great tricks he then got hold of the archbishopric of Besancon, and then had it in hand for three days; then he lost it, justly, because earlier he had got hold of it unjustly. Then afterwards he got hold of the bishopric of Saintes, which was five miles from his abbacy; he had that in hand well-nigh a week; the abbot of Cluny got him out from there, just as he earlier did from Besancon. Then it occurred to him that, if he could get firmly rooted in England, he could get all his own way; then besought the king, and said to him that he was an old man and a broken-down man, and that he could not endure the great injustices and the great hostilities there were in their land; and then, personally and by means of all his well-known friends, begged for the abbacy of Peterborough. And the king granted it to him because he was his relative, and because he had been a principal in swearing the oath and witnessing when the son of the earl of Normandy and the daughter of the earl of Anjou were divorced for consanguinity. Thus wretchedly the abbacy was given, between Christmas and Candlemas at London; and so he travelled with the king to Winchester, and from there he came to Peterborough, and there he stayed exactly as drones do in a hive. All that the bees carry in, drones devour and carry off; and so did he. All that he could take, inside or outside, from clergy and lay, he sent across the sea, and did nothing good there nor left nothing good there.

Henry of Poitou's arrival in Peterborough was greeted with an ominous supernatural event:

Let it not be thought remarkable, the truth of what we say, because it was fully known over all the land, that immediately after he came there (that was the Sunday when they sing Awake, why sleepest thou, O Lord?) then soon afterwards many men saw and heard many huntsmen hunting. The huntsmen were black and huge and loathsome, and their hounds all black and wide-eyed and loathsome, and they rode on black horses and on black billy-goats. This was seen in the very deer-park of the town of Peterborough, and in all the woods there were from that same town to Stamford; and the monks heard the horns blow that they blew in the night. Honest men who kept watch in the night said that it seemed to them there might well have been about twenty or thirty horn-blowers. This was seen and heard from when he came there, all that Lenten-tide right up to Easter. This was his entrance: of his exit we cannot yet say. May God provide!

This supernatural event was the Wild Hunt, which was supposed to occur in advance of a catastrophic event. The best early description we have of the Wild Hunt is from Orderic Vitalis, an English Benedictine monk who was born in Shropshire but spent most of his life in the Abbey of Saint-Evroul in Normandy.

In Book 8 of his Latin *Ecclesiastical History* (1141 CE), Orderic pauses from discussing the warfare between William Rufus (the son of William the Conqueror) and his rebellious count Robert of Belleme, and states, "I am sure that I should not pass over in silence or consign to oblivion something that happened to a priest in the diocese of Lisieux on January 1st." Orderic explains that the priest was named Walchelin, and "he was a young man, strong and brave, well-built and active." On the night of January 1, 1091, he was returning home after a visiting a sick man at the far end of his parish. He was traveling along the road, far from any homes, when he heard the sounds of a great army coming toward him.

Walchelin believed that these were the soldiers of Robert of Belleme, and he decided it would be best for him to hide behind the trees and let the army pass by. Orderic relates what happened next:

But a man of huge stature, carrying a great mace, barred the priest's way as he ran and, brandishing the weapon over his head, cried out, "Stand; go no further." The priest obeyed at once and stood motionless, leaning on the staff he was carrying. The stern mace-bearer stood beside him without harming him, waiting for the army to pass by.

Walchelin stayed at the side of the road as he watched thousands of people walk by. First came the peasants, who were carrying across their necks and shoulders their clothes, animals, furniture and other worldly goods. To the priest they seemed to be a mob of people who were carrying off the plunder from an attack. Then came hundreds of women, riding side-saddle on horses, but the saddles were marked with red hot nails. As the women rode, they would jump off their saddles and into the air, and then land back on

Ruins of the Abbey of Saint-Evroul in Normandy, where Orderic Vitalis spent most of his life. August 20, 2012 (Giogo, CCA-SA 4.0 International).

the nails, leaving them burned and stabbed. After them came a crowd of priests, monks, even bishops and abbots, all dressed in black cowls and groaning and lamenting as they passed by. "Next followed a great army of knights in, which no colour was visible save blackness and flickering fire. All rode upon huge horses, fully armed as if they were galloping to battle and carrying jet-black standards."

Walchelin recognized many of these people—they were his neighbors and fellow clergy, but they had all died in recent years. There were even people that Walchelin and others thought to be good Christians, even considered saints. But they were here too, walking with this army of the dead. The worst of this group were those being carried on biers, suffering terrible punishments:

> On the biers sat men as small as dwarfs, but with huge heads like barrels. One enormous tree-trunk was borne by two Ethiopians, and on the trunk some wretch, tightly trussed, was suffering tortures, screaming aloud in his dreadful agony. A fearful demon sitting on the same trunk was mercilessly goading his back and loins with red-hot spurs while he streamed with blood. Walchelin at once recognized him as the slayer of the priest Stephen, and realized that he was suffering unbearable torments for his guilt in shedding innocent blood not two years earlier, for he had died without completing his penance for the terrible crime.

As Walchelin watched them pass by he realized this was Hellequin's Army, which apparently had been a folktale for many years (Hellequin's Army is the French version of the

Wild Hunt). The name *Hellequin* is originally Germanic, and can be compared to German *Heer* ("army") and Old English or Old Frisian *thing* ("assembly of free men").[5]

The origins of the Wild Hunt are obscure but may lie in Germanic paganism. In his *Germania*, Tacitus mentions a tribe called the *Harii*[6]:

> The Harii, besides being superior in strength to the tribes just enumerated, savage as they are, make the most of their natural ferocity by the help of art and opportunity. Their shields are black, their bodies dyed. They choose dark nights for battle, and, by the dread and gloomy aspect of their death-like host, strike terror into the foe, who can never confront their strange and almost infernal appearance.

The Harii have been linked to the *einherjar* ("lone fighters") of Norse mythology, mainly attested in the 13th century Icelandic texts known as the *Poetic Edda* and the *Prose Edda*. The *einherjar* are those who have died in battle and been brought to Valhalla by valkyries. The *einherjar* prepare daily for Ragnarök, the final battle in which many gods will be killed and the world will be submerged by water. The emphasis in the sources is twofold: "the eternal fighting and revival of the einherjar, and their special relationship with Odin, which is manifested in part by their feasting endlessly with him and in part by their sharing in his grace. Many scholars think there may be a basis for the myth in an ancient Odin cult, which would have centered on young warriors who entered into an ecstatic relationship with Odin."[7] Significantly, Peterborough was under Danish control in the late 9th and early 10th centuries.

Old Saints and Monasteries After the Norman Conquest

ST. MICHAEL'S MOUNT (CORNWALL)

St. Michael's Mount is a small tidal island close to the town of Marazion in southwest Cornwall. Recent excavations on St. Michael's Mount, on the summit and close to the harbor, found shards of 5th and 6th century CE amphorae of eastern Mediterranean origin, suggesting that St. Michael's Mount, like Tintagel, may have been a "citadel," the court of a Cornish ruler.[8] Later, there may have been a Celtic monastery there: John Capgrave, writing in the 15th century, said that St. Cadoc "made a pilgrimage to St Michael's Mount."[9] In the recent excavations a grave was found in the village—it was oriented east-west and radiocarbon dated to 818–1030 CE, so it was probably Christian.[10]

In 1050 Edward the Confessor granted St. Michael's Mount to the Norman Benedictine Abbey of Mont-Saint-Michel. However, it was not until 1135–1150 that a Benedictine Monastery was built here. It started off with only 12 monks. The Benedictine community here survived until 1425 when it was suppressed by Henry VI and given to a Brigittine community of nuns.[11]

According to the early 19th century antiquarian Lysons, who was quoting the 15th century chronicler William of Worcester, Pope Gregory VII (1073–1085) granted to all visiting the church on St. Michael's Mount with alms and oblations "a remission of one third part of a penance." Lysons adds that the pardon was discovered in an old register of the convent about the year 1440.[12]

ST. PIRAN OF PERRANPORTH

Another well-known Cornish saint is Piran of Perranporth, on the north coast of Cornwall, 6 miles southwest of Newquay. St. Piran's Oratory at Perranporth is an early

Christian chapel consisting of a small stone-built nave and chancel located on the wind-blown Gear Sand one mile from the coast line at Perran Bay. Burials, some in stone and slate cists lie within an associated graveyard which surrounds the chapel. The oratory, a Grade II Listed Building, has been deliberately buried in sand for its own protection. The oratory chapel is thought to have been erected probably in the 7th century CE and remained in use perhaps until the 11th or 12th centuries. The construction is of rough local stone with the walls surviving to a height of almost 8 feet when last recorded in 1953.

The association of St. Piran with the area is provided by the Domesday Book (1086 CE) entry of a monastery at Lanpiran denoting an early Christian foundation, and by the placename Perranzabuloe (*Perranus in Sabulo*, or "Piran in the Sand"). It is uncertain how much of the surviving chapel masonry dates to the earliest periods; an inscribed stone, largely illegible but believed to be an early Christian memorial stone, was recorded by Warner, built into one of the walls. The east doorway may have been added when the oratory became a place of visitation for early medieval pilgrims and an arched doorway on the south side with a cat's head carved on the keystone is considered to be 11th or 12th century date. The south doorway may have replaced an earlier original doorway and this work may represent the last addition before the site was abandoned due to engulfment by shifting sand dunes, although worship is believed to have continued at St. Piran's Church some 350 yards east-northeast of the oratory. St. Piran's Church is also known as the "new" or "second church" but the "old" church, that is the oratory chapel, may have continued to attract pilgrims who believed that St. Piran's bones were buried there; documentary evidence (now lost) of the 15th century appears to support the view that it became a pilgrim shrine.[13]

The "new" church of St. Piran grew from a small church to a collegiate church by the 12th century. By 14th century hundreds of pilgrims visited the church on their way to the shrine of St. James at Compostella in Spain, no doubt attracted by the head of St. Piran, which was kept in a silver casket in the church. By the 17th century sand was caus-ing major problems to the church, and applications were made to the canons of Exeter Cathedral to remove the church to a secure site. After much opposition this was agreed and in 1795 the last wedding was held there.[14]

St. Piran is the patron saint of tin-miners. His feast day was a traditional holiday for Cornish miners, and parades by tinners showing off the saint's relics or emblems were an early feature of the day across Cornwall. The Cost Book of Great Work Mine near Breage in southwest Cornwall shows that in the mid–18th century, every man and boy working there was paid an "allowance for Perrantide."[15]

St. Petroc of Bodmin (Cornwall)

Cornwall's best-known saint is Petroc, originally associated with Padstow on the north coast of Cornwall. According to tradition, the Celtic monastery of Lanwethinoc at Padstow was founded by Bishop Wethinoc, who was replaced by Petroc in the 6th cen-tury. No trace remains of the monastery, but a small cemetery dating to the 8th or 9th century was found nearby. Seventeen graves were exposed, arranged in two rows; they were all lined and capped with slate, and aligned broadly east–west.[16]

Later the cult of St. Petroc moved to Bodmin, to the southwest of Bodmin Moor. The 11th and 12th century Lives of St. Petroc attributed the origins of a settlement at

Bodmin to the saint having gone into a "remote wilderness" inland from his earlier foundations at Padstow and Little Petherick and there taking over the dwelling of a hermit, St. Uuron. However, it seems likely that a monastic settlement may actually have been established much later at Bodmin, around 800 CE: it has been suggested that Bodmin was the site of a monastery or church named as *Dinuurrin* in a documentary source dated between 833 and 870 CE. At this time the monastery was the seat of a bishop named Kenstec, the document recording his pledge of allegiance to the Anglo-Saxon church centered on Canterbury. This part of Cornwall appears to have already come under Saxon control by this period: much of the land formerly held by the earlier monastic foundation dedicated to St. Petroc at Padstow had been granted away by King Egbert in the wake of his military actions in Cornwall in the early 9th century; removal from Padstow to Bodmin may have occurred because the latter was a more convenient base from which to manage the remaining monastic estates.[17]

The monastery of St. Petroc was re-established as a foundation of Augustinian canons in the 1120s or 1130s, one of a number of such changes in the southwest at this period whereby former monastic settlements of "secular canons" were converted to priories. At Bodmin a new priory complex was developed on a site a short distance southeast of the earlier monastic site (now St. Petroc's church). This may not have occurred immediately: excavations in the mid–1980s uncovered the northwest corner of the aisled priory church and dated it to the late 12th or early 13th century.

The shrine of St. Petroc which had previously been kept in the monastery was removed to the priory, representing a considerable asset, in terms of both the popular legitimacy it conferred on the new institution and the offerings it attracted from visitors. The saint's relics are said to have been stolen from the priory within a few decades of its foundation and taken by a monk to his home monastery at St. Méen in Brittany; they were restored in 1177, housed in an ivory reliquary (now in St. Petroc's church).[18]

ST. SIDWELL OF EXETER (DEVON)

St. Sidwell of Exeter was venerated at Exeter from early times: by 1000 CE pilgrims visited her shrine, which was mentioned by William of Worcester in the 15th century and John Leland in the 16th century. The earliest surviving account of the saint dates from the 14th century. The late medieval catalogue of English saints describes her thus: "Born at Exeter, she was killed by her stepmother inciting the reapers to behead her; where her head fell, a well gushed forth. She was buried outside the city, where by her merits God heals the sick." Sidwell's church just outside Exeter's east gate survives (this is a modern version—the earlier church was bombed in World War II); formerly there was a well where presumably the cures took place. In art she is represented with a scythe and a well at her side, as in stained glass at Exeter Cathedral and All Souls College, Oxford, and on seven painted rood-screens in Devon.[19] By 1420 the spring known as St. Sidwell's well was used to supply the city of Exeter. The water was credited with miraculous therapeutic powers for curing diseases of the skin and eyes.[20] Recently St. Sidwell's well was discovered during building work at 3 Well Street, Exeter. The high quality of the workmanship suggests that the medieval cathedral masons were involved in building it, and it also reflects the importance of the site as a place of pilgrimage.[21] In 2009 a metal detectorist found a lead ampulla near Whimple, 9 miles to the east of Exeter, which would have been used to carry water from a holy well, possibly St. Sidwell's Well in Exeter.[22]

St. Augustine's Well, Cerne Abbas (Dorset)

Cerne Abbas is in Dorset, to the north of Dorchester. According to William of Malmesbury, writing around 1125, Eadwold, the brother of Edward the Martyr, lived a hermit's life at Cerne Abbas on nothing but coarse bread and water; he had, they say, grown tired of the luxuries of this world, for he and his brother had met with hard luck. After a life devoutly lived, Eadwold was buried at Cerne with a high reputation for sanctity. In 987 an abbey was founded at Cerne by Æthelmær the Stout, who translated the relics of St. Eadwold to the old church at Cerne "where now the parish church is."[23]

St. Augustine's Well is on the south side of the churchyard at Cerne Abbas. It is named after St. Augustine (who was buried at Canterbury in Kent) because of a tale in Goscelin's *Shorter Life of St. Augustine*, composed around 1090[24]:

> Augustine and his worthy companions were wandering through an empty land, where no water was. Heat and drought and weariness weighed on them…. True, Augustine had drunk too copiously of that sweet well which flows to eternal life for him to hanker after those earthly wells where those who drink will thirst again; nor did he take much pains for the food that decays, being nourished instead by that which endures in life eternal…. But then he thought how good it would be for the land to be flooded by the goodness of heaven, sparkling with the true spring of life. He fixed his staff in the ground, and when he drew it forth, out surged a stream of pure water. All gave praise to God as they tasted of these waters, and drank till they were satisfied. This is the spring which today feeds many streams, so that a district which was once barren is now thickly populated.

Goscelin further notes:

> one of the brethren at Cerne Abbey was a parish priest, whose business it was to celebrate the sacred mysteries for the laity. He was worn down by such weakness that he was given up for dead. The onset of night, and of exhaustion, brought some sleep to the poor wretch. Then, in his sleep, he saw the merciful figure of Augustine standing before him, in archbishop's vestments, shining with bright embroidery. He spoke to the trembling invalid, putting him at his ease with kindly words, and told him to get up and go to St Augustine's well. When he got there, he was to say the fiftieth psalm three times over with true devotion, and three times, after each psalm, he was to dip himself in the well and wash in its waters. Do this, he said, and you will be restored to life and health. And you can be sure that it is I, Augustine himself, who is telling you to repair to my spring. Now comes the miracle! The priest awoke immediately, and half-dead as he was, he threw himself out of bed. Leaning on a stick, he hobbled off to take the bath as instructed. The men of the infirmary thought he had lost his wits with the onset of death. They tiptoed after him, making no attempt to stop the man, but wondering where he was heading. The sick man bathed himself with a threefold washing in the waters of the well, saying the psalm three times, as he had been told to. And, so rapid was the remedy of his holy doctor, that the man who had set out as an invalid went home again healthy, snatched from the jaws of death.

St. Edward of Shaftesbury (Dorset)

The site of the Abbey Church of St. Mary and St. Edward, Shaftesbury was excavated on five occasions between 1816 and 1955, revealing the remains of a late 11th/early 12th century cruciform structure; the eastern arm of three bays had a central apse and was flanked by chapels with smaller apses. Early in the 14th century a chapel with crypt beneath, was built in the angle between the north chapel and north transept with entrance to the crypt by a canted flight of stairs. A leaden casket was unearthed in 1931 at the chapel and contained the fractured remains of a young man, plausibly identified as the relics of St. Edward.[25]

Shaftesbury Abbey was already wealthy by the time of the Norman Conquest, and the Norman and Plantagenet kings by their gifts and privileges added enormously to the power and wealth already enjoyed by the abbey. The endowment of the monastery was so considerable and the extent of its possessions so vast that in the Middle Ages there was a popular saying, "If the abbot of Glastonbury could marry the abbess of Shaftesbury their heir would hold more land than the king of England."[26]

ST. EDITH OF WILTON (WILTSHIRE)

By 934 there was a nunnery at Wilton, the Anglo-Saxon capital of Wiltshire, which by the 11th century had acquired a royal saint. Edith (Eadgyth) was a daughter of King Edgar (959–975) and the noblewoman Wulfthryth, born in 961. When her mother retired from secular life to become abbess of Wilton, Edith also entered the foundation and remained there until her death at the age of twenty-three. Edith apparently chose the religious life at an early age. According to Goscelin, who wrote her *Life* in the late 11th century, at the age of two, Edith was visited at Wilton by her father, who placed before her "regal dignity and ladies' finery, golden coronets, cloaks woven with gold, jewelled robes, bracelets, rings and necklaces." Her mother, in contrast, laid out "the black veil of purity, the chalice and paten, vessel of Our Lord's Passion, and the Psalter of Holy Scripture." The infant moved at once to the latter objects: "without hesitation, from the middle of the splendid colours, she picked out the veil alone, and set it in place of a crown upon her head."[27]

While a nun, Edith built a church at Wilton dedicated to St. Denis, which was consecrated by Dunstan, Archbishop of Canterbury. According to Goscelin, the ceremony of dedication provided the occasion for Dunstan to make two prophecies. Toward the end of the ceremony the archbishop, weeping, foretold the imminent death of Edith. Then, observing how assiduously the saint made the sign of the cross, he clasped her right hand and exclaimed: "Never shall this thumb which makes the sign of our salvation know corruption."[28]

In fact, Edith died on September 16, 984, 43 days after the consecration of the church of St. Denis. She was recognized as a saint 13 years after her death when she appeared in visions to Aethelred, the nobleman Ordwulf, and a further unnamed secular magnate. Finally, she approached Dunstan, who was reminded of his prophecy concerning her incorruption and was ordered to travel to Wilton, where he would find the body not only incorrupt but also raised up, "as though already prepared to leave the tomb."[29] For many years miraculous events were connected with her tomb. A woman who attempted to steal the linen frontal from Edith's tomb was miraculously stopped in her tracks and rendered immobile. On another occasion, a Glastonbury monk who attempted to remove a fragment of her clothing was duly terrified when his knife slipped and touched the holy body: immediately "a wave of blood gushed forth, as if drawn from a living vein, and spattered the snow-white garments and the flow with its rosy drops."[30] Finally King Cnut (1016–1035) ordered the manufacture of a golden shrine to house the relics of St. Edith. The workmen, however, appropriated the king's gold and made the shrine from gilded silver. Divine vengeance followed quickly: "they were punished with instant blindness of the eyes which had coveted the gold; those whose minds were dark were cast into outer darkness." Goscelin writes that King Cnut, when imperiled by a storm at sea, was saved by the intercession of St. Edith, and "when after his return to England he came to Wilton he offered up to God, through the holy intercessor Edith, his thanks with solemn gifts."[31]

According to Goscelin,[32] Edith was a rather eccentric saint, and did not wear the black habits expected of a nun. She wore fine clothes, but senior nuns testified that she wore a hairshirt "which gave a false appearance of inner delicacy by a purple exterior, although observance of the rule would have required black." Indeed, bishop Æthelwold "once warned this pearl of such sweet devotion, with her rather ornate habit, thus: "O daughter, not in these garments does one approach the marriage chamber of Christ, nor is the heavenly bridegroom pleased with exterior elegance"; she, conscious of her indwelling guest, and conscious perhaps of her harsh inner garment, is reported to have replied in these words: "Believe, reverend father, a mind by no means poorer in aspiring to God will live beneath this covering than beneath a goatskin. I possess my Lord, who pays attention to the mind, not the clothing."[33]

In the matter of clothing, it seems that Edith had the last laugh. Once a serving woman dropped a still burning candle into a chest full of Edith's clothes, and the chest caught fire. As Goscelin says: "When they unfolded the garments, made of skin or purple, and examined them separately..., by the marvellous grace of the everlasting guardian, all the things were found to be as they had been before the fire, unharmed by all the burning."

Edith also kept a menagerie of wild animals. As Goscelin tells us[34]:

> Standing with the open doorway of the enclosures, she would call by a pet name the ferocious branching-antlered stag. He would spring forward at the well-known voice and laying aside his ferocity would accept with a gentle mouth bread from the hand of the virgin lady. The rest of the animals would run together for the blessing of the lady whose kindness they sensed.

This is intriguing because Celtic saints are often associated with wild animals. St. Petroc of Bodmin had an affinity with wild animals and is often portrayed with a stag as his emblem, in memory of the one he sheltered from huntsmen. St. Brynach of Nevern in Pembrokeshire (southwest Wales) could tame wild animals and used a wolf to herd his prize cow; and St. Cuthbert, although an Anglo-Saxon saint, was educated at the Irish monastery of Melrose in the Scottish Borders, and once had his feet dried by otters after he had spent the night in the sea praising God.

Why so many Celtic saints were associated with animals is unclear, but we know that in the Iron Age people were sometimes buried with animals, as happened at Battlesbury Bowl near Warminster in Wiltshire, not far to the west of Wilton.

AMESBURY ABBEY (WILTSHIRE)

Amesbury Abbey was appropriated by Henry II in 1177 and refounded as a priory belonging to the order of Fontevrault. Between 1177 and 1186 a very extensive program of building took place—the new buildings were of high status, and "considered sufficiently grand for members of the royal house of Angevin to lodge and worship in."[35] The Welsh-Norman priest and chronicler Gerald of Wales explains the circumstances of the refoundation as follows. In 1174 Henry had vowed to make a pilgrimage to Jerusalem; three years later he sent to Rome to ask for absolution from it; he would found instead three monasteries; the Pope assented to the compromise and the king thereupon expelled the nuns of Amesbury and replaced them with others from overseas. With "characteristic rancour" Gerald adds that by this and like acts the king was able to carry out his pledge with little cost to himself.

Links with the royal house of a more personal kind began to be forged. Before 1233

Alpesia, the king's cousin, had been admitted as a nun. In 1241 Eleanor of Brittany, who had died a nun of St. James's, Bristol, bequeathed her body to Amesbury. It was translated there in the same year. The renown of Amesbury reached its peak with the accession of Edward I, who retained the family affection for Fontevrault. Edward first went to Amesbury in 1275. In 1285 Mary, his sixth daughter, then aged seven, entered the convent, and was ceremoniously veiled with thirteen noble ladies in the presence of her father and the whole royal family.[36]

St. Aldhelm of Malmesbury (Wiltshire)

After Osmund became bishop of Old Sarum (Salisbury) in 1078, he presided over the translation at Malmesbury Abbey of the bones of St. Aldhelm. Within a year of two, Osmund obtained a relic of the saint for his new cathedral (a fragment from Aldhelm's left arm). In his *Deeds of the Bishops,* William of Malmesbury recounts many miracles carried out by the saint in his own church. After one miracle, involving the cure of a deformed youth called Folkwine, an account was sent to Abbot Warin who was at the royal court. Lanfranc, Archbishop of Canterbury, heard of the affair and, says William, ordered that Aldhelm should henceforth be revered as a saint.[37]

Glastonbury Abbey (Somerset) and St. Joseph of Arimathea

The later medieval history of Glastonbury Abbey is obscured by the many legends that were promoted by the Glastonbury monks. One of these legends starts with the late 12th century work by the French poet Chrétien de Troyes, entitled *Perceval, the Story of the Grail.* This work was extremely popular, but was unfinished, and spawned a number of works around the theme of the Grail and the quest for the Grail. The most influential early work was Robert de Boron's *Joseph of Arimathea* (late 12th or early 13th century), the first work to link the Grail to the cup used at the Last Supper. Joseph of Arimathea is mentioned in all four gospels, and his story is developed in the apocryphal *Gospel of Nicodemus.* In Mark 15: 43 Joseph of Arimathea is described as "a prominent member of the Council, who was himself waiting for the kingdom of God"; in Matthew 27: 57 he is described as "a rich man," "a disciple of Jesus"; in John 19: 38, he is a "disciple of Jesus, but secretly," who with Pilate's permission took away the body of Jesus. The Bible also refers to a cup used at the Last Supper—for example in Matthew 26: 27: "Then he took a cup, and when he had given thanks, he gave it to them, saying, "Drink from it, all of you. This is my blood of the covenant, which is poured out for many for the forgiveness of sin."

Chrétien de Troyes made it clear that the Grail was a serving dish containing a mass wafer, but in his poem *Joseph of Arimathea*, Robert de Boron transformed the Grail into something much more significant. In *Joseph of Arimathea*, Joseph is imprisoned, accused of stealing the body of Jesus, and Jesus visits him in prison; he gives Joseph the cup used at the Last Supper (the Holy Grail), telling Joseph that the cup would provide him with sustenance. After Joseph is released, he and his brother-in-law Bron become leaders of a Christian community dedicated to protecting the Holy Grail. Robert tells us that the final destination of the Holy Grail was "in the land to the West, which is very wild, in the Vales of Avaron."

In 1184 Glastonbury Abbey was destroyed by fire, and in 1191 the supposed tomb of King Arthur and Queen Guinevere was found close to the site of the Old Church. This discovery was witnessed by the Welsh Norman priest and historian Gerald of Wales, who writes of it in his work *De principis instructione* ("On the instruction of a prince").[38] In the same work he notes that Glastonbury "used, in ancient times, to he called the Isle of Avalon," adding in another work, *Speculum Ecclesiae* ("Mirror of the Church"), that it was called Avalon "from the Welsh word 'aval,' which means apple."[39] It was not long before Robert de Boron's Avaron was being interpreted as Avalon, and Glastonbury became linked to the story of Joseph of Arimathea.

William of Malmesbury said in his *Chronicle of the Kings of England* that "No other hands than those of the disciples of Christ erected the church of Glastonbury." William of Malmesbury also wrote a history of Glastonbury, *De Antiquitate Glastoniensis Ecclesiae* ("On the antiquity of the church of Glastonbury"). William's original text does not survive, and all we have is a copy made by the Glastonbury monk Adam of Damerham around 1250. In this copy there are interpolations which claim that the head of the band of apostles who founded the church of Glastonbury was none other than Joseph of Arimathea, the secret disciple of Jesus who donated his own tomb for the burial of Jesus. This story was amplified in the 14th century by John of Glastonbury, who wrote a history of the Abbey, some time between 1350 and 1400—John says that when Joseph of Arimathea came to Glastonbury, he brought with him cruets containing the blood and sweat of Christ, and that Joseph was buried at an unknown spot in the monks' cemetery.[40]

However, the cult of St. Joseph was not promoted until the time of Richard Bere, abbot of Glastonbury (1494–1525). Around 1500 a crisis arose because of a rebellion against the crown in the west country which resulted in a punitive taxation of Glastonbury properties[41]:

> While the abbey's involvement had been strictly limited to the charitable care of the rebels, in keeping with their monastic rule, such assistance occasioned not only the tax burden but also the threat of royal displeasure. Bere fostered a new economic impulse, and openly acknowledged the myth of the abbey's Arimathean origin. He established a shrine to St Joseph [in the Lady Chapel] and, for the first time in abbey history, promoted St Joseph of Glastonbury.

ST. FRIDESWIDE OF OXFORD

St. Frideswide was an Anglo-Saxon saint, but her *Life* was not written until the 12th century, when her monastery became a priory of Augustinian canons. According to this account, the area around Oxford was ruled in the late 7th century by a sub-king under Mercian overlordship called Dida of Eynsham. He endowed a number of minster churches in the region, and his daughter Frideswide was abbess of the double monastery in Oxford. The Mercian king Æthelbald attempted to seduce her, but she fled into a forest retreat at Binsey near Oxford. He was temporarily blinded but cured at Bampton by her intercession.[42] In one version of her life, the nuns in Binsey complain of having to fetch water from the distant River Thames, so Frideswide prays to God and a well springs up. The well water has healing properties and many people come to seek it out.[43]

Excavations at the later priory of St. Frideswide near the River Thames in Oxford found a number of pre–Conquest graves which confirm that the cemetery was in use during the 9th or, at the latest, by the 10th century.[44] A large sub-oval earthwork enclosure at Binsey, associated with St. Margaret's chapel and its graveyard is identified with Thornbury

("Thorny Fortress"), named in the late 12th century *Life* of St. Frideswide as one of her places of refuge. It was regarded as a holy place from the 12th century onwards, and the canons of St. Frideswide's priory may have maintained a cell there.[45] The most important part of Frideswide's cult was the well at Binsey. St. Margaret's well at Binsey is in the Churchyard, to the west of the church. It clearly predates the mid–12th century, and despite its later restoration, its original fabric must substantially survive.[46] The well is named after St. Margaret because Frideswide prayed to St. Margaret of Antioch to restore Æthelbald's sight. In 1639. Anthony Wood, the Oxford historian, relates how many pilgrims came to Binsey in the Middle Ages to seek cure at the well before visiting the relics of St. Frideswide in the Priory. Pilgrims would enter the Diocese of Lincoln from the Diocese of Salisbury through the village of Seckworth (Seacourt) and would resort to the well. Here they would say their devotions, and leave symbols of their cure, such as crutches under the dome of the well. Henry VIII is known to have visited.[47]

St. Kenelm of Winchcombe (Gloucestershire)

The historical Kenelm (Cynhelm) was the son of Coenwulf, king of Mercia (796–821). Kenelm signed a number of charters from 803 to 811; already in 798 Pope Leo III had confirmed to him the ownership of Glastonbury. But Kenelm died before his father, possibly in a battle against the Welsh, and was buried at Winchcombe Abbey. When bishop Oswald revived Winchcombe in the second half of the 10th century, Kenelm was regarded as a martyr and figured as such in liturgical books, including a sacramentary, written at Winchcombe and presented to Fleury Abbey in France, where he ranks next to Stephen.

By the 11th century Kenelm had become a child martyr. According to the legend, first recorded in the 12th century, Kenelm was only seven years old and reigned for a few months as his father's successor but was put to death by his tutor at the instigation of his jealous sister, the princess Quendreda (actually, Cwenthryth, the abbess of Minster in Kent). The chapel of St. Kenelm at Clent near Halesowen (Hereford and Worcester) was believed to mark the site of his murder. The body was discovered when an Anglo-Saxon document was dropped by a dove on to the high altar of St. Peter's in Rome and deciphered by English pilgrims. The body was accordingly translated to Winchcombe and while the evil Quendreda was reciting a psalm backwards (presumably for magical purposes), her eyes fell out. The crypt of the church of St. Pancras has recently been identified as the shrine of Kenelm, buried there with his father.[48] St. Pancras of Rome was in fact a child martyr beheaded for his faith at the age of fourteen in 304 CE and it is possible that this was why Kenelm was believed to be a child martyr.

The legend of Winchcombe further relates that when the Clent monks removed the body of Kenelm, a miraculous spring gushed forth. They carried the body to Winchcombe, and where the funeral cortège rested, more miraculous springs appeared. Of these springs, only two remain, at Clent and Winchcombe. The *Annals of Winchcombe*, related in the *South East Legendary*, which dates from around 1280, tell the story of the Winchcombe well[49]:

> These men towards Winchcombe the Holy body bear,
> Before they could it thither bring, very weary they were,
> So they came to a wood a little east of the town,
> And rested, though they were so near, upon a high down,

Athirst they were for weariness, so sore there was no end,
For St Kenelm's love they bade our Lord some drink send,
A cold well and clear, there sprung from the down,
That still is there, clear and cold, a mile from the town,
Well fair, it is now covered with stone as is right,
And I counsel each man thereof to drink, that cometh there truly,
The Monks, since, of Winchcombe have built there beside,
A fair Chapel of St Kenelm, that man seek wide.

Caxton's 15th century *Golden Legend* states:

for heat and labour they were nigh dead for thirst, and anon they prayed to God, and to this holy saint to be their comfort. And then the abbot pight his cross into the earth, and forthwith sprang up there a fair well, whereof they drank and refreshed them much.

The story of St. Kenelm was still current in the late 14th century when Geoffrey Chaucer wrote his *Canterbury Tales*. In the *Nun's Priest's Tale* the cook Chaunticleer is trying to demonstrate the reality of prophetic dreams to his wife Pertelote[50]:

"Lo, I read in the life of St. Kenelm the son of Kenulph, the noble king of Mercia, how he dreamed a dream; one day a little before he was murdered, he saw his murder in a vision. His nurse expounded his entire dream and warned him to beware of treason; but he was no more than seven years old and paid little heed to any dream, so holy he was in spirit."

St. Æthelberht of Hereford

Æthelberht was an 8th century king of East Anglia—at the time East Anglia was dominated by Mercia and in 794, according to the *Anglo-Saxon Chronicle*, Offa of Mercia "ordered Æthelberht's head to be struck off."[51] His body was brought to Hereford Cathedral soon after he died. By the 12th century his place of death was said to be Sutton (*Villa Australis*, or "Southern Vill," in Latin), to the north of Hereford, where Offa had a palace. This has been identified as the Iron Age hillfort of Sutton Walls, occupied from the 1st century BCE till the 4th century CE; or, more plausibly, as Freen's Court at Sutton St. Michael,[52] a medieval moated site to the west of St. Michael's church, which became the location of a 16th century manor house.[53] The earliest Lives of the saint were written in the 11th or 12th century.

St. Chad of Lichfield (Staffordshire)

The Anglo-Saxon cathedral at Lichfield was replaced after the Norman Conquest. Building is known to have taken place from 1085 to 1126. The Norman cathedral was probably completed by Bishop Clinton shortly before 1140.[54] Chad's relics were translated in 1148 and moved to the Lady Chapel in 1296. An even more splendid shrine was built by Robert Stretton, bishop of Lichfield (1360–1385), of marble substructure, with the feretory adorned with gold and precious stones. Rowland Lee, bishop of Lichfield 1534–1543, pleaded with Henry VIII to spare the shrine: this was done, but only for a time.[55] At the time of the Reformation, the jeweled embellishments of St. Chad's shrine were seized by the Crown, and the shrine itself was destroyed. Some at least of the relics of the saint were removed by Canon Arthur Dudley, and for the next three hundred years they were concealed in various Catholic houses in Staffordshire, including Swynnerton, the home of the Fitzherberts and Aston Hall near Stone, where they came to light again in 1840, contained in a velvet-covered box of 16th century date. A year later the six bones were enshrined above the altar in the new Catholic Cathedral of St. Chad at Birmingham, their final resting-place. In 1995 a forensic investigation revealed that five of the bones are of 7th century date, but they do not all belong to the same body.[56]

ST. ALBAN OF ST. ALBANS (HERTFORDSHIRE)

The earliest British saint for whom any information survives is Alban, who has been described as the proto-martyr of Britain. The traditional narrative of Alban holds that he was a citizen of Verulamium, the Roman settlement adjacent to modern St. Albans, and was martyred in the third or fourth century. This narrative derives from the *Passio Albani* ("Passion of Alban") and later sources that repeated and expanded the story in the *Passio*, such as Gildas' *On the ruin and conquest of Britain* and Bede's *Ecclesiastical History of the English People*.

The *Passio Albani* relates the tale of Alban's martyrdom and a visit to his tomb by Germanus of Auxerre. According to all extant recensions of the *Passio*, Alban harbored a Christian fleeing persecution and presented himself in place of the Christian when the authorities came seeking him. Alban was then sentenced to execution. On his way to the execution, the waters of the river parted for him because the bridge was too crowded to walk across. This miracle seems to have made such an impression on Alban's appointed executioner that rather than execute him, he joined him in martyrdom. Once Alban reached the site of his execution on top of a hill outside town, another miracle was performed when Alban prayed for water and a spring appeared. When Alban was beheaded, the new executioner's eyes popped out of his skull. After the execution, the *Passio* describes a visit to his tomb and place of execution by Germanus of Auxerre, who placed some relics into Alban's tomb and took a bit of dust from the site of Alban's martyrdom.[57]

It has been assumed that the cult of St. Alban began in Roman times, but it is more likely that the cult was instigated by Germanus in the 5th century, as part of his campaign against the Pelagians, who believed that Christians could obtain salvation by their own efforts, without God's grace, and were skeptical of miracles.[58]

The history of St. Albans Abbey is said to begin with the visit of St. Germanus to the tomb of St. Alban the Martyr in 429. St. Germanus left relics of other saints with the body of Alban, and these are said to have been rediscovered in 793 by Offa, King of Mercia. To preserve them, he founded a monastery which came under Benedictine rule which was soon laxly practiced or abandoned. Both monks and nuns were admitted throughout the 9th and 10th centuries, in separate houses, the latter placed further away in the almonry before 940. King Edgar reformed it to Benedictine rule in about 970. After 1077, Abbot Paul made regulations for the nuns who lived near the almonry and they were apparently moved to Sopwell around 1140. There were 50 monks at the Abbey in 1190 and about the same number at the Dissolution in 1539. The church is Norman erected in 1077–88 and built of flint and Roman brick.[59]

ST. EDMUND OF BURY ST. EDMUNDS (SUFFOLK)

In 1020 King Canute replaced the community of secular priests with 20 Benedictine monks which was increased by a further sixty by William the Conqueror, who also increased the monastery's privileges. In 1095 St. Edmund's remains were re-interred, this time in a stone church which replaced an earlier, timber church. The first half of the 12th

St. Albans Abbey before the dissolution of the monasteries, from a painting in St. Albans Cathedral. June 20, 2011 (LepoRello, CCA-Share Alike 3.0 Unported).

century saw the construction of the cloister, chapter house, refectory, dormitory, infirmary, and, walls to the forecourt. In around 1150 fire caused damage to all of these except the cloister, and they were subsequently rebuilt. In the second half of the 12th century the church continued to be extended and the abbot's and guest houses were rebuilt.[60]

We have no real idea what St. Edmund's shrine looked like. However, in Jocelin's *Chronicle of the Abbey of Bury St. Edmunds,* written in the 12th century, Jocelin reports a fire at the shrine, and from his description of the fire we know that St. Edmund's shrine was formed of gold plates, decorated with colored stones. A canopy, which was commissioned by Abbot Samson (1182–1211), surmounted the structure.[61]

St. Edmund was a favorite of English kings. Henry III's eldest son was named for St. Edward, and his second for St. Edmund. As the king informed the abbot and monks of Bury on the child's birth in January 1245, the saint had responded to his supplications and the queen's. Bury was included in the East Anglian tour Henry undertook in the period immediately following Lent, and on May 30, he instructed the sheriff of Buckingham to have a window in the royal bedchamber at Brill (Buckinghamshire) neatly blocked up and an image of "St Edmund standing" painted in the space. Henry was at Bury for the saint's feast-day (November 20) in both 1235 and 1248. When he visited Bury in early September 1252 he had already (while at St. Albans) commissioned a crown with four floral finials, which was to cost £10 and in November he gave instructions that it was to be sent, with a quantity of gold coin and some cloth, to arrive at Bury if possible on the feast of St. Edmund.[62]

On 9 May 1300 Edward II came to Bury "in order to dedicate his life to the blessed martyr with deep devotion. Never had he appeared more gracious to the church and convent." He directed justices not to infringe the privileges of the church, and expressed his confidence that the saint would be with him in Scotland in "flashing armour" (this was on the eve of one of his many Scottish campaigns). A few days after he had left the abbey he sent back his standard so that a mass of St. Edmund might be said over it and all the relics in the abbey touched to it.[63]

The most enduring sign of the medieval monarchy's devotion to St. Edmund and Edward the Confessor is the late 14th century Wilton Diptych, so-called because it was

St. Edmund being shot, from John Lydgate's *Metrical Lives of St. Edmund and Fremund*, dating from between 1434 and 1439. The British Library Board Harley 2278, f.61 (British Library, London, UK © British Library Board. All Rights Reserved/Bridgeman Images).

kept at Wilton House by the Earls of Pembroke until it was purchased by the National Gallery in 1929. The left-hand panel shows Richard II (1377–1399) kneeling before the Virgin and Child; he is presented to them by his patron saint John the Baptist, and by Edward the Confessor and St. Edmund. The right hand panel shows the Virgin and Child surrounded by eleven angels, wearing badges with Richard's livery, the White Hart.[64]

St. Ivo of Ramsey (Cambridgeshire)

Ramsey in Cambridgeshire was an island in the Fens, known as Bodsey Island, and a monastery was founded there in 969 when the site was offered by Ailwine to St. Oswald, Bishop of Worcester.[65] In about 1001 the monks of Ramsey discovered the relics of Ivo, supposedly a Persian bishop who lived and died as a hermit at Slepe, on the River Ouse near Huntingdon (now called St. Ives), with three of his companions, and translated them to Ramsey.[66]

To judge from the account written by Goscelin for the monks of Ramsey between 1087 and 1090, "it was an important part of the monks' strategy to promote Ivo as a popular, wonder-working saint whose power was displayed not just at his new burial-place at Ramsey, but even more at the place of his life, death and discovery at Slepe, and especially at the spring which flowed there." Abbot Ednoth built a church at Slepe which was so designed that half the spring was inside and half outside, "so that whether the door was open or locked, the boon of the water was available to visitors."

Goscelin details a number of miracles attributed to Ivo. Abbot Ednoth (992–1008) was cured of gout, and Goscelin himself was cured of gout and toothache. A boy from Hampshire, congenitally weak in his hands and feet, was partially cured by St. Edward the Martyr at Shaftesbury before coming to Ramsey where he was completely cured and remained to "serve the saint."[67] A monk in the entourage of an unnamed foreign abbot who paused to drink the water objected that

> It did not become a prudent and religious man to lend himself to the folly and superstition of rustics; they are often known to frequent springs, being deceived by pagan error and, seduced by the illusory marvels of demons, to venerate the bones of all sorts of dead people, as if they were the relics of saints.

Having uttered this "ill-advised criticism the monk promptly fell ill." To William of Malmesbury, writing in the 1120s, St. Ivo was the "most efficacious saint in all England" and the easiest to invoke. The monk who said there was something pagan about the spring had a point: the waters of the Cambridgeshire Fens were venerated in the Iron Age and Roman times, at the Iron Age site at Godwin Ridge near Earith, where the bones of dead people played an important part in religious ritual, and at the Romano-British shrine at Haddenham, which are both close to Slepe (St. Ives).

A fair of national importance grew up under the control of the monks of Ramsey in association with the shrine of St. Ivo at Slepe. About a century after the original translation of the relics to Ramsey, inhabitants of Slepe were reported to have seen a brilliant ray of light extending from the village as far as Ramsey, seven miles away. As a result, the relics of Ivo's three companions were restored to the church at Slepe[68] "so that the church should be more honorably regarded and better known, and better and more devoutly frequented by the people, by the intercessions of their patrons [who were] now present."

The abbot and monks created a new town at Slepe, building a mile-long road on a huge causeway across the floodplain of the Ouse and a new bridge (already in existence in 1107) to link the settlement more effectively into the communications network. An Easter fair was granted in 1110 and the new town gradually came to be known as St. Ives. The church that Abbot Ednoth founded at Slepe must have been St. Ives Priory, established in 1008 and dissolved in 1539. There is no sign of a spring at St. Ives Priory, but nearby is Holywell. Here there is a holy well to the south of the church; it is not clear how old the well is, but it was substantially altered in 1845 with the construction of a brick curb and arch over the top. It appears that a 13th or 14th century stone corbel is re-used on top of the well.[69]

ST. JOHN OF BEVERLEY (EAST YORKSHIRE)

The church of St. John at Beverley was enriched by successive Archbishops of York between about 1023 and 1069, especially with the addition of monastic buildings. The Normans apparently rebuilt the church, but the East end was badly damaged by fire in 1188 and the tower fell in 1213, necessitating the complete rebuilding from 1225 onwards.[70]

During the time that Ælfric was Archbishop of York (1023–1051), John's relics were translated from an elaborately carved wooden shrine to a magnificent gold and silver shrine encrusted with jewels.[71] The mention of a wooden shrine indicates that John had been made a saint much earlier, possibly in the second half of the 8th century, at the time of Alcuin of York, who promoted the cult of John and put Bede's account into verse. In the medieval period St. John's Minster Church was a college for secular canons; this was dissolved in 1548 and it then became a parish church. In 1664, "the sexton, digging a grave in the church of Beverley, discovered a vault of freestone, in which was a box of lead, containing several pieces of bones, with some dust, yielding a sweet smell; with inscriptions, by which it appeared that these were the mortal remains of St. John of Beverley."[72]

There is a tradition, first recorded in the early 12th century by William Ketell, a monk at Beverley, that the Anglo-Saxon king Athelstan (924–939) was on his way north to deal with the Scots when he encountered "a sizeable crowd of poor and middling persons" in the province of Lindsey (Lincolnshire) and discovered they were on their way to Beverley for their health. He thereupon decided to join them in petitioning the saint and with many tears left his knife upon the altar, promising to redeem it with rich gifts if he was victorious. Of course, he was victorious, and returned to redeem his knife. In another more elaborate version of the story, Athelstan also bore St. John's banner into battle, at the suggestion of the *custodes* (wardens) of the church, saw several visions of the saint and offered his arms at the shrine on his return.[73]

In his Scottish campaign of 1296, Edward I carried the banner of St. John into battle against the Scots, and in September, at Berwick, the king granted gifts and privileges to both St. Cuthbert and St. John. He visited Durham briefly on October 5, and Beverley on the 14th. In 1298 he visited St. John again in early June, before making his way to Roxburgh to find his army duly assembled at the appointed time. In 1301 the banners of both St. John and St. Cuthbert were carried into battle against the Scots. Edward was by now sufficiently well-informed to be able to tell the pope, in May 1301, that King Athelstan had invoked St. John against the Scots, with miraculous success which was remembered every week in the church at Beverley.[74]

It is puzzling that John of Beverley should have become warrior-saint, but perhaps it has something to do with William of Malmesbury. In his 12th century *History of the English Bishops*, he relates this story of John[75]:

> John, a man of exemplary virtue, finds a well-known eulogist, Bede, in his *History of the English*. But he lives up to his praise even now, and his miracles are not yet over. The most noteworthy is the one made into a show by the inhabitants of Beverley, where he lies buried. Savage bulls are brought up, tied fast, by strong men sweating profusely; but as soon as they enter the churchyard they lose all their ferocity and become, you might suppose, no more than innocent sheep. So they are untied and left to frolic in the yard though previously they used to go for anything in their way with horns and hooves.

ST. HILDA OF WHITBY

St. Hilda's monastery at Whitby was refounded as a Benedictine Priory by 1077, but lapsed, and then again as a Benedictine Abbey by 1109. In the late Middle Ages St. Hilda became associated with the ammonites (fossilized marine mollusks) of Whitby. The geological formation there is the Lias, and in certain zones of this deposit large numbers of the fossil cephalopods, known as ammonites occur. The old idea was that these were petrified snakes, turned into stone by the patron saint of Whitby, St. Hilda. This legend is referred to in Sir Walter Scott's *Marmion*, published in 1808, in Canto ii, 13, when Whitby's nuns[76]

> told, how, in their convent cell,
> A Saxon Princess once did dwell,
> The lovely Edelfled;
> And how of thousand snakes, each one
> Was changed into a coil of stone,
> When holy Hilda prayed;
> Themselves within their holy bound,
> Their stony folds had often found;
> They told how seafowls' pinions fail
> As over Whitby's towers they sail,
> And, sinking down, with flutterings faint,
> They do their homage to the saint.

ST. CUTHBERT OF DURHAM

The main body of Durham Cathedral was constructed between 1093 and 1130 and the Galilee chapel was built in 1189. In 1104 Cuthbert's tomb was opened again and his relics were translated to new shrine behind the altar of the recently completed cathedral. As I said before, when the casket was opened, a small book of the Gospel of John measuring only three-and-a-half by five inches, was found. Also recovered much later were a set of vestments of 909–916, made of Byzantine silk, with a stole and decoration in extremely rare Anglo Saxon embroidery; these had been deposited in his tomb by King Aethelstan (927–939) on a pilgrimage while Cuthbert's shrine was at Chester-le-Street.[77]

When the tomb was opened, the body of Cuthbert was found to be still uncorrupt. The translation of 1104 and the verification of incorruption gave an immense stimulus to the cult, which spread over much of England and Scotland. No fewer than 135 churches are dedicated to Cuthbert in England, besides seventeen in Scotland.[78]

In the second half of the 12th century, the Benedictine monk Reginald of Durham wrote a book (*Libellus*, or "Little Book") in which he recorded a large number of St. Cuthbert's miracles. One of these miracles occurs at Bellingham on the River Tyne in Northumberland, and is summarized here[79]:

> A poor, pious man called Sproich, employed by Almoner of Durham to build bridges over Tyne at Bellingham, has a daughter named Ede who is making a dress on the eve of St Laurence's day and is warned by her mother to stop. She continues and her left hand becomes paralysed. They take her to the local church dedicated to Cuthbert, give her water from the well and spend the night in the church. Cuthbert appears and touches her hand, which relaxes slightly. It is cured when, as the priest Samuel suggests, she repeats the Lords Prayer and an invocation nine times. Cuthbert and Laurence cooperate here. The Priest and the village witness.

The present church of St. Cuthbert in Bellingham dates from the 13th century, and St. Cuthbert's or Cuddy's Well still stands outside the churchyard wall. Today, the water is contained in a picturesque Georgian [18th/19th century] pant with its ever flowing spout directing the water down through a grill and away to the River Tyne[80] (the term *pant* refers to the pan or trough for collecting water; a pant is technically not a well but a cistern). Bellingham is not far from Coventina's Well at Carrawburgh Roman fort, suggesting that veneration of water continued over a long period.

9

New English Saints
and Monasteries, and Late
Medieval Ritual Curses

Cornwall

GLASNEY COLLEGE, PENRYN (CORNWALL)

Penryn near Falmouth on the south coast of Cornwall was created as a planted town during the early 13th century by the Bishop of Exeter. Penryn's creation was a speculation designed to stimulate economic activity, and the first market and fair charter was granted in 1259. In 1265 the collegiate church of St. Thomas of Glasney was founded on the southern outskirts of the new town. An important place of ecclesiastical learning and significant in Cornish culture because of its links with the Cornish language and documentation of many of the Cornish mystery plays, this foundation was to play an important part in the evolution and character of the town.[1] The college complex included religious and administrative buildings, the bishop's palace and deer park, a precinct of canon's houses and gardens, and substantial defenses to the estuary side. Glasney College was dissolved in 1548. Although the Royal Commissioners suggested that the college should be retained as a grammar school this was not acted upon. The establishment was lost and Cornwall lost its chance of a university for several hundred years.[2]

The secular college was founded by Bishop Bronescombe of Exeter following vivid dreams while he was ill in Canterbury in which he saw Thomas Becket, who foretold he would recover and should establish a college to the glory of God and in the name of "St. Thomas the Martyr" at Penryn. As a result, the college was endowed for thirteen canons and thirteen vicars.[3]

Wiltshire

SALISBURY CATHEDRAL AND ST. OSMUND

A motte and bailey castle was founded by William I soon after the Conquest and constructed on the site of the Iron Age hillfort at Old Sarum, to the north of present day Salisbury. Additions to the castle were made during the reign of King Henry II, especially between 1170 and 1179. Repairs were documented between 1201 and 1208 and the last known main phase of building took place during the early 13th century. Further repairs were also documented in 1247. During the 13th century, the military importance of the castle declined. Repairs to the castle took place during the 14th century, but it was demolished by 1514.[4]

The cathedral at Old Sarum, situated within the northwest section of the bailey of Old Sarum Castle, was first constructed between 1078 and 1092 CE and consisted of an apsidal east end, narrow north and south aisles and an aisled nave. Between 1110 and 1125 the east end of the cathedral was enlarged to include an aisled presbytery, three chapels, a tower and aisled north and south transepts. This phase may have also included construction of the cloister. The Bishops Palace was constructed between 1102 and 1139 and consisted of four ranges enclosing a courtyard. Further additions at the western end of the cathedral took place between 1142 and 1200.[5]

Because of the location of the cathedral, there was constant friction between castle and cathedral, which culminated in 1215 with the Constable of the castle barring the gates to the returning Rogationtide procession (this was procession around the boundaries of the parish to pray for its protection in the forthcoming year). Bishop Herbert Poore began negotiations for a transfer of the site and papal consent was given on March 29, 1218. The new site was near the confluence of the River Nadder and the River Avon, a short distance to the east of nunnery at Wilton.

This move may have been made for purely practical reasons, but the location of the new cathedral was later linked to a story involving the Virgin Mary. The story, which survives in two documents dating from the 15th century, begins by describing an incident where the canons were refused entry into Old Sarum by the King's office after a Rogation procession to the nearby St. Martin's Church, which now lies to the east of the present cathedral (this church is first documented in 1091, before the foundation of Salisbury). When the canons reported this event to Bishop Richard Poore, who was at the time staying at Wilton, he is said to have replied tearfully: "When they persecute in one city, flee ye to another," and then vowed to build a new cathedral for the Virgin away from the king's castle. However, after the bishop had received the necessary permissions from King John (1199–1216) and from the pope in Rome, he was traveling home only to be greeted by a messenger who informed him of the death of the king. Troubled by this news, he fell asleep and had a vision of the Virgin Mary who told him to persevere in his wish for a new cathedral. On his return to England he was granted permission to build the new cathedral by King John's successor Henry III but was still unsure where he should place the building. Initially, Wilton was considered but was later rejected following an incident when the bishop overheard a seamstress suggesting that his frequent visits to Wilton betrayed his amorous interest in the abbess there. The situation was not resolved until the Virgin Mary spoke to the bishop in a second dream, "There appeared to him the Blessed Virgin Mary, telling him that he should choose as his site whereon to build his church a place called *Myrifield*. The bishop much comforted by the vision, gave thanks to God." A few days later, the bishop discovered that a part of his estate to the south of Old Sarum was called *Myrifield* and subsequently began the construction of the cathedral and city there.[6]

Osmund was a Norman aristocrat and Bishop of Salisbury from 1078 to 1099. The see had been formed by uniting those of Sherborne (Dorset) and Ramsbury (Wiltshire) and making the new center at the hillfort of Old Sarum to the north of Salisbury, where

Statue of Bishop Richard Poore, founder of Salisbury, at Salisbury Cathedral, 2007 (LordHarris at English Wikipedia, CCA-Share Alike 3.0 Unported).

the cathedral was built in the same enclosure as the royal castle. Osmund died on December 4, 1099, and was buried in his cathedral at Old Sarum. His chasuble and staff were among the treasures there in 1222; but in 1226 his body and its tomb were translated to the new cathedral of Salisbury. In 1228 Gregory IX authorized preliminary enquiries into his life and miracles with a view to canonization, but these came to nothing. Further attempts to obtain the canonization were made in 1387 and 1406. In 1412 Robert Hallam, Bishop of Salisbury, took up the cause, and in 1416 his canons allocated a tenth of their income for seven years for this purpose. Further petitions were made, supported by Henry V and Henry VI; further commissions investigated more miracles, and the canonization was finally pronounced by Callistus III in 1456.

A new shrine was set up in the Lady Chapel of Salisbury cathedral in 1457, parts of which, as well as the original tomb, still survive. In the early 15th century a lunatic, John Bemyster, was brought chained and bound to the shrine of St. Osmund in in the Lady Chapel in Salisbury Cathedral, while a Mass of the Virgin Mary was being celebrated. His head and hands were placed in one of the niches of the tomb, so as to be as near to the saint as possible. He remained in this position until the "Agnus Dei," the moment in which Christ is invoked as giver of peace, and the paxbred was passed about among all present to be kissed as a sign of peace (the paxbred, or pax-board, was a little plaque of metal, ivory, or wood, generally decorated with some pious carving and provided with a handle, which was first brought to the altar for the celebrant to kiss at the proper place in the Mass and then brought to each of the congregation in turn at the altar rails). At this point Bemyster's bonds fell away, and he was found to be whole and in his right mind. When Richard Wodewell carelessly threw a heavy metal quoit in the village of Laverstock and brained a little girl standing by to watch the game, he had to seek sanctuary in Salisbury Cathedral from her friends and family. He invoked St. Osmund and the girl recovered. She duly brought the quoit to the shrine as an offering, and Wodewell and the girl's family joined together to testify to the saint's goodness.[7]

Herefordshire

ST. THOMAS DE CANTILUPE OF HEREFORD

Thomas de Cantilupe was Bishop of Hereford from 1275 to 1282. A series of confrontations with the Archbishop of Canterbury, John Pecham, led in 1282 to the excommunication of Thomas, who, although in poor health, decided to lay his case before the papal court and made the long journey to Orvieto. He was well received by Pope Martin IV but developed a fever, possibly malaria, and died far from home. His bones were prepared as relics in the customary way, separating them from his flesh by boiling, and were brought back to Hereford for burial in the Lady Chapel of the cathedral. Five years later they were moved to a shrine in the north transept, and miracles, which had already been associated with them in small numbers, increased enormously, bringing numerous pilgrims to Hereford and great wealth to the cathedral treasury.[8]

A number of miracles were ascribed to Thomas de Cantilupe and were recorded in 1307 by three commissioners appointed by Pope Clement V to report on the deeds and reputation of Thomas. One concerns a young boy by the name of William de Lorimer. At about 9 a.m. on September 18, 1305, Thomas, aged 14, was crossing the Summergill brook near New Radnor (now in Powys) to gather wild apples for sauce making when he noticed a bundle of red clothes in the water. At first, he thought that they had been left there by the washerwoman but soon realized that he had found the body of William De Lorimer, aged two-and-a-half, from Donnington (now Downton) farm, which lay "the distance of an arrow's flight" from the stream. He took the boy out of the water and shouted for help. The occupants of the farm came running out, moved the body to a dry area, and were soon praying to Thomas Cantilupe to revive the child. They "measured" him (determined his height with the intention of lighting a candle or taper of that length at the Bishop's tomb). While they were busy with Ave Marias and Paternosters a certain Hugh de Adforton left the crowd, opened the boy's mouth, and, separating the teeth with a stick, turned him upside down. Water poured out, but he did not obviously show signs of life. William was taken into the farmhouse, where a fire was lit to warm him "first on one side and then on the other." During the afternoon Hugh de Adforton examined him again. When he put a finger in the child's mouth he was bitten and realized that recovery was occurring. There was steady improvement although "he remained a strange colour for some time."

Another miracle concerns a teenage girl with a infected foot and partial paralysis. In 1293 William de Lonsdale was journeying from the north of England to London with his 5-year-old daughter Alice. He was on his way to Spain to honor a vow to visit the shrine of St. James at Santiago de Compostela. Alice tripped over a hole in the road near Stamford in Lincolnshire and broke bones in her right foot. William carried her on his shoulders to London, where they crossed London Bridge and lodged in Southwark. She became ill on their first night there, lost power and sensation in her left limbs, and was able to use only her right hand. Life became very difficult and father and daughter were reduced to living in doorways and begging, the child dragging herself along on her thighs. The broken foot became swollen with putrefaction, with a discharge below the ankle, where bones could be seen protruding. Alice told the commissioners in 1307 that she had washed the infected foot in the well of the church of St. Clement Danes, there being no other remedy for a beggar such as her, but she was also seen by Master Gilbert, a surgeon, who had put plasters on the foot and told her that the disorder was incurable. Her father must have heard of the fame of Thomas Cantilupe in London for he prayed to him for a cure, "measuring her and putting a penny on her head." He vowed to visit the tomb in Hereford and to dedicate Alice to St. Mary if she was restored to health. He then pushed her to Hereford in a "one wheeled cart" and arrived there on the night of Pentecost in 1303. They visited the tomb and on the third night there Alice had a vision in which "a beautiful old man in white clothes, silvery like a lily, with a large ring on a finger and a rich head covering with streamers hanging from it, anointed her body with a milky substance from a little box, touching her from her breasts downwards, including the right foot with its three discharging ulcers and the withered and paralysed left leg." The wounds subsequently dried up and she could walk but only with the aid of a stick as "the sinews of the foot were drawn up and scarred." She was much more active within a week.[9]

However, the most fascinating miracle attributed to Thomas de Cantilupe is one that was rejected by the three commissioners. In 1291 Welsh rebels William Cragh and Traharn ap Howel were taken from the dungeons of Swansea Castle and hanged on the nearby gallows. Except that William Cragh did not die and appeared before the Thomas de Cantilupe commissioners in 1307, along with eight other witnesses. William Cragh ("William the Scabby"), also known as William ap Rhys, was a supporter of Rhys ap Maredudd, lord of the lands of Ystrad Tywi in Carmarthenshire, in his rebellion against Edward I of England. Captured in 1290 by the son of William de Briouze, the Welsh-Norman lord of Gower, he was tried and found guilty of killing thirteen men. The witnesses included Marie de Briouze, the widow of the late William de Briouze, William de Briouze's son, also called William, William de Codeniston, former chaplain of William de Briouze senior, and John of Baggeham and Henry the Tanner, who were among the soldiers sent to supervise the hanging.[10]

All the witnesses were sure that William Cragh died on the gallows. John of Baggeham and Henry the Tanner both told the commissioners that soon after the hanging William lost control of his lower muscles and let *natural superfluities* come out of the lower parts of his body (this was thought to be a sign of death in hangings).[11] After a time, the body was taken to the house of Thomas Matthieu, next to the church of St. Mary. A number of witnesses testified that William Cragh was indeed dead. The younger William de Briouze testified that William Cragh's face was all black and partly covered with blood. His eyes were hanging out of their proper places and they were filled with blood. His mouth, throat, neck, and even his nostrils were filled with blood in such a manner that it would have been impossible for him to breathe. His neck was swollen beyond normal measures and his tongue was hanging out of his mouth. It was also black, bloody and swollen to the size of two hands held together. Even if William Cragh had been alive it would have been impossible for him to draw his tongue back into his mouth and breathe.[12]

At some time during the evening, William Cragh was measured with a thread for St. Thomas of Cantilupe. Most witnesses recall that it was done by a household maid of Marie de Briouze. Marie de Briouze, who was extremely devoted to Thomas de Cantilupe, testified that she and her servants prayed for Thomas de Cantilupe to intervene on behalf of William Cragh. Then she sent one of her maids to measure him. Nobody witnessed the actual awakening of William Cragh. William Cragh testified about his awakening that everyone said that he moved his tongue a little and after a while also one of his feet. This took place around cockcrow, though he said that after hearing a noise when the other man was hanged, he did not feel anything before the next day around the time of nones (3 p.m.). The miracle of William Cragh was only partial. He did recover but was not totally cured. All the witnesses who saw him during the next day and days following agreed that he still looked extremely bad, although better than he had been on the evening after the execution.[13]

When William Cragh was completely recovered, the lord of Briouze and his wife took him to Hereford to thank Thomas de Cantilupe for his miraculous resuscitation. He did this pilgrimage barefooted with the rope with which he had been hanged around his neck. In Hereford they visited the shrine and donated the rope and a wax image of a hanged man on the gallows to St. Thomas.[14]

The connection between William Cragh, a Welsh-speaking rebel, and Thomas de Cantilupe, an English bishop from the Anglo-Norman nobility, seems very slight, but Marie de Briouze also testifies that when he was taken to the gallows,

> the said William begged God that He would release him from such a vile death because of the merits of Saint Thomas of Cantilupe, the aforementioned bishop of Hereford. Furthermore he reported that when he was hanged a certain bishop, as it appeared to him, held his feet and prevented him from being hanged.[15]

This is a variation on an old story which originates in a collection of miracles attributed to the Holy Virgin written by William of Malmesbury in the early 12th century.[16] The 13th century French Dominican priest, Stephen of Bourbon, told the best-known version in his book *De septem donis spiritus sancti* ("On the Seven Gifts of the Holy Spirit"):

> We read that there was a certain thief who had this one merit, that he fasted with bread and water on the vigils of Mary's feast days. Also when he went out to rob, he always read the Hail Mary and begged

the Virgin not to allow him to die in this state of sin. He was caught and hanged, and he hung on the gallows for three days not able to die. He shouted to the passers-by and asked them to fetch a priest. The priest came along with several others and when they took him down from the gallows he said that a most beautiful virgin had held him by his feet for three days. The thief promised to mend his ways and was set free.

When William Cragh spoke to the commissioners, he denied having seen any vision at all while he was hanging on the gallows. In fact, he testified to having been unconscious, or as he believed it, dead from his hanging until late that night. Instead he told the commissioners of a miraculous vision, but in a completely different version from that told to the Briouze family. According to William, the Holy Virgin had appeared to him in prison early in the morning of the execution. Accompanying her was a certain lord. She told William that the other person was Saint Thomas who would save him from the gallows. William described to the commissioners the clothing of the Holy Virgin which, hardly surprisingly, was similar to her iconographic representations. He did not, however, remember anything about the clothing or appearance of the other person. When the commissioners asked how William knew it was Thomas of Cantilupe, not St. Thomas the apostle, or Thomas of Canterbury, he replied that he had made a pilgrimage to the shrine of Thomas de Cantilupe and furthermore he had bent a coin for him.[17]

MARDEN (HEREFORDSHIRE)

The church of St. Mary at Marden near Hereford is said by Leland, writing in the 16th century, to have the dedication of St. Ethelbert (Æthelberht), Hereford's Anglo-Saxon saint. Within the church "at perhaps, about twenty feet from the western wall, is preserved an uncommon relique, the well of St. Ethelbert…, whose shrine was at Marden, until translated to Hereford Cathedral. There can be no doubt that the well occupied the focus of the original small sanctuary that was first raised over the reliques of the martyr."[18]

There is a miracle that involves both St. Ethelbert at Marden and St. Thomas Cantilupe at Hereford, recorded by the three commissioners sent to investigate St. Thomas. The five-year-old Joanna, daughter of Adam Sheriff of Marden, some 7 miles north of Hereford, followed her parents to the tavern one Sunday evening "before St. George" (April 23) in 1287. As there were many other children about, the parents thought nothing of it but, while playing in the garden of the house where the tavern was, she fell into a ditch or pond. There was some delay in raising the alarm, for fear of involvement in legal proceedings, but when Joanna was finally extracted her father measured her to St. Thomas with his belt, while all the bystanders prayed. The parents took her home and put her by the fire. Some movement was detected, and the child began to expel "humours and superfluities" and spoke. Around sunrise, her mother took her to the parish church and laid her on the altar of St. Ethelbert. Against the will of the neighbors, because the child was weak, her father lifted her up and rode with her to Hereford, accompanied by thirty or so neighbors as witnesses. Here the bells were rung, a procession was held and the miracle "published." The wax image made in her likeness remained for many years hung up near the tomb, but then fell to bits with age. Every year thereafter the father, with his household, came at least once barefoot with offerings to the tomb, especially on the feast of St. Ethelbert (May 20).[19]

Kent

St. Thomas Becket of Canterbury

The most celebrated English martyr of the Middle Ages was undoubtedly Thomas Becket, Archbishop of Canterbury. Thomas Becket was appointed Archbishop of Canterbury in 1162 and soon came into conflict with Henry II over the power of the Church versus the power of the King. In 1164 Henry convened a meeting of the English clergy at Clarendon Palace near Salisbury and drew up the Clarendon Constitutions, which restricted ecclesiastical privileges and curbed the power of Church courts and the extent of Papal authority in England. Becket was convicted of contempt of royal authority, but fled to France, where King Louis VII offered him protection. In 1170, after mediation by Pope Alexander III, Henry invited Becket to return to England. Not long after, the Archbishop of York, along with the Bishops of London and Salisbury, crowned Henry the Young King at York. This was a breach of Canterbury's privilege of coronation, and in November 1170 Becket excommunicated all three. While the three clergymen fled to the king in Normandy, Becket continued to excommunicate his opponents in the church. Upon hearing reports of Becket's actions, Henry is said to have uttered words that were interpreted by his men as wishing Becket killed. Four of Henry's knights traveled to Canterbury, and famously murdered Becket in the cathedral on December 29, 1170. Edward Grim, a clerk from Cambridge, witnessed the murder and gave this vivid account[20]:

> the impious knight, fearing that [Thomas] would be saved by the people and escape alive, suddenly set upon him and, shaving off the summit of his crown which the sacred chrism consecrated to God, he wounded the sacrificial lamb of God in the head; the lower arm of the writer was cut by the same blow. Indeed [the writer] stood firmly with the holy archbishop, holding him in his arms—while all the clerics and monks fled—until the one he had raised in opposition to the blow was severed. Behold the simplicity of the dove, behold the wisdom of the serpent in this martyr who presented his body to the killers so that he might keep his head, in other words his soul and the church, safe; nor would he devise a trick or a snare against the slayers of the flesh so that he might preserve himself because it was better that he be free from this nature! O worthy shepherd who so boldly set himself against the attacks of wolves so that the sheep might not be torn to pieces! and because he abandoned the world, the world—wanting to overpower him—unknowingly elevated him. Then, with another blow received on the head, he remained firm. But with the third the stricken martyr bent his knees and elbows, offering himself as a living sacrifice, saying in a low voice, "For the name of Jesus and the protection of the church I am ready to embrace death." But the third knight inflicted a grave wound on the fallen one; with this blow he shattered the sword on the stone and his crown, which was large, separated from his head so that the blood turned white from the brain yet no less did the brain turn red from the blood; it purpled the appearance of the church with the colors of the lily and the rose, the colors of the Virgin and Mother and the life and death of the confessor and martyr. The fourth knight drove away those who were gathering so that the others could finish the murder more freely and boldly. The fifth—not a knight but a cleric who entered with the knights—so that a fifth blow might not be spared him who had imitated Christ in other things, placed his foot on the neck of the holy priest and precious martyr and (it is horrible to say) scattered the brains with the blood across the floor, exclaiming to the rest, "We can leave this place, knights, he will not get up again."

Benedict of Peterborough, who was the chancellor (record-keeper) of Becket's successor Richard, adds this gory detail[21]:

> While the body still lay on the floor of the Cathedral, the townsfolk smeared their eyes with blood, other brought and carried off secretly as much of it as they could. Others cut off shreds of clothing and dipped them in the blood. At a later time, no one was thought happy, who had not carried some-

thing from the precious treasure of the Martyr's body. Some of the blood left over was carefully and cleanly collected and poured into a clean vessel and treasured up in the church.

Becket was canonized by Pope Alexander III in 1173 and in 1174 Henry II went on a pilgrimage to Canterbury[22]:

"The Assassination of Thomas Becket," from a medieval *Book of Hours* probably written for the De Grey family of Ruthin (Denbighshire, north Wales) around 1390 (National Library of Wales, CCO 1.0).

For the last part of the journey, he donned a hair shirt and the woollen shift of the pilgrim and walked barefoot in the rain from St Dunstan's Church to the Cathedral. He kissed the "stone of martyrdom," knelt before Thomas's tomb, wept and then prayed there. Gilbert Foliot [Bishop of London], for his own penance, had to speak for the King, declaring Henry's regret that he unwittingly prompted the murder and announcing various grants to the monastery, so that lamps might burn forever at the tomb. The Prior of Christchurch gave the King a kiss of peace. Then Henry submitted to flagellation from the Bishops, the Abbott, and each one of the eighty monks. All night long he stayed in the crypt, fasting and praying.

Within twenty-four hours, the new saint rewarded Henry with a miracle. The penance had taken place on Saturday 12 July. On Sunday night, back in London and trying to sleep off the effects of his exhausting vigil, Henry was awakened by a loud knocking on the door. A messenger brought word that William the Lion, King of the Scots, had been taken prisoner on Saturday, just after Henry had completed his penance. The capture of King William broke the back of the rebellion in the North. "God be thanked for it," Henry exclaimed, "and Saint Thomas the Martyr and all the saints of God."

The monarchy continued to reverence the shrine of St. Thomas throughout the 13th century. King John, after his coronation, went on a pilgrim-

age to the shrines of St. Thomas Becket, St. Alban and St. Edmund. Henry III was among
the witnesses when on July 7, 1220, the remains of Becket were translated to a new shrine
in the Cathedral. In 1285 Edward I, the queen, the little Lord Edward and his five sisters
traveled from Westminster to Canterbury by water and by road, reaching Canterbury on
July 6. Edward made a major contribution to the refurbishment of the shrine by present-
ing four elaborate statuettes in gold set with emeralds, sapphires, garnets and pearl.[23]

Some time before 1519 the Dutch theologian Erasmus visited Canterbury and
described the shrine of St. Thomas[24]:

> In a chest or case of wood was "a coffin of gold, together with inestimable riches, gold being the mean-
> est thing to be seen there; it shone all over, and sparkled and glittered with jewels of the most rare
> and precious kinds and of an extraordinary size, some of them being larger than a goose's egg"; most
> of them were the gifts of monarchs.

John Stow, in his *Annals*, written in the late 16th century, says of the shrine of St.
Thomas[25]:

> It was built about a man's height all of stone; then upward of plain timber, within which was an iron
> chest containing the bones of Thomas Becket, as also the skull, with the wound of his death, and the
> piece cut out of his skull laid in the same wound. The timber-work of this shrine on the outside was
> covered with plates of gold, damasked and embossed, garnished with brooches, images, angels, chains,
> precious stones and great oriental pearls; the spols of which shrine in gold and jewels of an inestimable
> value, filled two great chests, one of which six or eight men could do no more than convey out of the
> church. All which was taken to the kings use, and the bones of St Thomas, by command of lord Crom-
> well, were there burnt to ashes, in September 1538, of Henry VIII, the thirtieth.

Suffolk

OUR LADY OF WOOLPIT

The church of Woolpit in Suffolk, which belonged to the monks of Bury St. Edmunds,
became a center of devotion to the Virgin Mary. Indeed, the Chapel of Our Lady of Woolpit was a popular place of pilgrimage in medieval times, and many people from Woolpit
and further afield gave money and valuable items to enrich both the statue or image of
the Virgin and the chapel. The earliest reference to pilgrims at Woolpit occurs in a man-
date of the Bishop of Norwich issued between 1211 and 1214 directing that the monks of
Bury Abbey should have the pilgrims' offerings. This could refer to pilgrims passing
through Woolpit on their way to shrines such as Bury and Walsingham but seems more
likely to refer to pilgrims' donations to the image at Woolpit. Woolpit fair, first mentioned
in 1286, was held on September 8, the Feast of the Nativity of the Virgin Mary, and no
doubt grew up to serve and profit from the pilgrims.

The image of the Blessed Virgin Mary was probably similar to the present one at
the Anglican Shrine at Walsingham. It would have been dressed in rich clothes, decorated
with brooches, jewels and strings of rosary beads given by pilgrims; in front would have
been banks of burning candles representing the pilgrims' prayers, and the chapel would
probably have been lit by colored lights. Priests and wealthy inhabitants seem to have
been able to claim the privilege of burial within the chapel.[26]

The church at Woolpit was rebuilt in the middle of the 15th century, when it received
many benefactions, and the image of the Virgin became sufficiently famous to be made

the butt of a satirical Lollard (early Protestant) who referred to it as "Our Lady of Foulpit." Henry VI is known to have visited it in both 1448 and 1449 from Bury St. Edmunds.[27]

Norfolk

OUR LADY OF WALSINGHAM

There were many shrines to the Virgin Mary in medieval England, but the most famous was the shrine to Our Lady at Little Walsingham in the north of Norfolk. In a Book of Hours now in the University Library, Cambridge, a note claims that the original chapel at Walsingham was founded in 1061 and this is elaborated in a ballad published by Richard Pynson in or soon after 1496. But this very late evidence is contradicted by earlier and much more reliable material, which shows that the origins of the shrine belong to the early half of the 12th century. The cartulary of Walsingham Priory now in the British Museum furnishes a list of priors, giving both their names and the length of their periods of office which establishes that the priory at Walsingham began in or about 1153 and this is attested by other evidence. The Pynson ballad tells us that the priory at Walsingham was preceded by a chapel built in honor of Our Lady by one Richelde of Fervaques whose son, Geoffrey, converted the place into a priory. Little is known of Richelde, but we have in the Pipe Roll of 1130–31 a note which suggests that Richelde was a widow in that year. Richelde's erection of the Holy House may have been inspired by her son's visit to the Holy Land (which is mentioned in his foundation charter). When this journey took place is not known, but as Geoffrey was under age in 1131 it may well have been as late as the forties of the century, possibly at the time of the Second Crusade (1147–8). A connection with Geoffrey's visit to the Holy Land is perhaps borne out by the almost certain fact that Richelde's chapel was no ordinary one but was planned as a reproduction of the House of Nazareth where Our Lady had been greeted with the news of her part in the Incarnation by the Archangel Gabriel. This origin of the chapel is very clearly stated in the Pynson ballad which may well be accurate enough here, if not on other details. Such a view receives very strong support from the remarkable fact that this early chapel at Walsingham was regarded with such tremendous veneration that it was preserved intact till the Reformation.

The statue which made Walsingham famous was one of Our Lady and the Holy Child. It was burnt at the time of the Reformation1 but what is almost certainly a representation of it is preserved on a seal of the priory and on certain pilgrim badges. There can be no doubt that the statue was of mid- or late–twelfth century date and bears a close resemblance to that of Our Lady of Rocamadour in France.[28]

The shrine became prominent during the reign of Henry III, who visited Walsingham on eleven occasions between 1226 and 1272. Henry III's son Edward I visited Walsingham on twelve occasions between 1277 and 1305. There were also eminent visitors from abroad including John, Duke of Brittany (1361) and Guy, Count of Pol (1363). In the 15th century Henry VI visited Walsingham at least three times. In 1487, according to the Italian historian Polydore Vergil, when Henry VII was faced with a rebellion, he "came to the place called Walsingham where he prayed devoutly before the image of the Blessed Virgin Mary..., that he might be preserved from the wiles of his enemies."[29]

The shrine of Our Lady was destroyed at the time of the Reformation in the 1530s,

Modern statue of the Virgin Mary in the Slipper Chapel at Walsingham. September 27, 2008 (Thorvaldsson, CCA-Share Alike 3.0 Unported).

and the statue of Our Lady was taken to London where it was burnt. The loss of the shrine was keenly felt, as we can see from this anonymous ballad, composed around 1600, which ends with these haunting lines[30]:

> Weep, weep, O Walsingham,
> Whose days are nights,
> Blessings turned to blasphemies,
> Holy deeds to despites.

Sin is where Our Lady sat,
Heaven is turned to hell,
Satan sits where Our Lord did sway—
Walsingham, O farewell!

BROMHOLM PRIORY

Bromholm Priory near Bacton on the north Norfolk coast was a Cluniac priory founded in 1113 by William de Glanville. What made this remote Norfolk priory celebrated throughout England, and through many parts of continental Christendom, for upwards of three centuries, was its possession of a famous cross made from fragments of the true cross. It was brought to England in 1223 and its story is told with some detail by Matthew Paris. An English priest who served in the emperor's chapel at Constantinople, having in his charge a cross made of the wood of our Savior's cross, absconded on the emperor's death and brought it to England, and made it a condition of bestowing it on any monastery that he and his two sons should be admitted as monks. To this condition the skeptical monks of St. Albans and other great houses demurred, but at last the monastery of Bromholm, poor in worldly goods but rich in faith, believed the priest's story and agreed to his terms, and the cross was set up in their church. Its fame rapidly spread, and it soon became a place of pilgrimage. In the *Vision of Piers Plowman* (late 14th century) occur the lines: "And bidde the Roode of Bromholm,/Bryng me out of dette." In the *Reeve's Tale* of Chaucer is the pious ejaculation: "Helpe, holy cross of Bromeholme." The miracles associated with this pilgrimage were numerous. It is mentioned in the annals of Dunstable and Tewkesbury, and by other early chroniclers.[31]

Lincolnshire

ST. HUGH OF LINCOLN

Hugh of Lincoln was born in Avalon in southeastern France around 1140. In around 1165 he became a monk at the Grande Chartreuse near Grenoble, the chief monastery of the Carthusian order, and by 1175 was its procurator. In 1179 he was made prior of the Witham Charterhouse in Somerset, the first Carthusian house in England. In 1186 Henry II chose him as Bishop of Lincoln, but he refused to accept because he believed the election was uncanonical. Eventually he accepted the job, but only in obedience to the prior of the Grande Chartreuse. Hugh died in London in 1200 and miraculous powers began to be attributed to his body immediately after his death. During the four days' journey from London to Lincoln, though the weather was wet and stormy, the wax torches borne before his bier were never all extinguished at once, and when the corpse rested for the night at Biggleswade, a man who had had his arm broken in the crush believed that the saint appeared to him in a vision and by a touch restored the fractured limb. On reaching Lincoln miraculous cures at once began to testify to his sanctity. While the body lay in the Minster before burial, a knight of Lindsey was healed of a cancer by placing his diseased arm upon it; at the mere touch of the sacred corpse a blind woman received sight, while a thief who had relieved a woman of her purse as she knelt in prayer was struck with instant blindness.[32]

Hugh directed that his tomb be placed in the chapel of St. John the Baptist, close to the side wall to the south, where there would be less danger of persons tripping over it and falling.[33] The chapel was enlarged, possibly around 1220 when Hugh was canonized.[34] In 1280 the body was translated to the newly constructed Angel Choir.[35] At the time of this translation, the head was removed and taken back to the St. John the Baptist chapel, and replaced there by the altar.[36] The head was subsequently enclosed in a case of metal, adorned with plates of gold and silver and beautified with precious stones.[37] In 1364 the head was stolen by thieves, who stripped the case of its gold and silver and precious stones and threw it down in a field. Here, to their astonishment, a crow or raven miraculously appeared as its protector, and kept guard over the sacred relic until it was picked up and carried back to Lincoln.[38]

OUR LADY OF LINCOLN

During the Middle Ages the city of Lincoln was regarded as the most Marian City of the most Marian county in the whole of England, surpassed only by Walsingham (in Norfolk) in attracting pilgrims. In his *History of Lincoln in the Middle Ages* Sir Francis Hill refers to devotion to Our Lady. She was chosen as Patroness of the city on the occasion of the victory of the citizens over the forces of the Earl of Chester in 1147, during a period of civil war between the followers of King Stephen and the supporters of the Empress Matilda. From Dugdale's 17th century work *Monasticon* (Volume 6) we have a description of the original statue of Our Lady of Lincoln, found in Lincoln Cathedral:

> A great image of Our Lady, sitting in a chair of silver and gilt with four polls, two of them having arms in the front, having upon her head a crown, silver and gilt, set with stones and pearls; and one bee (metal torque) with stones and pearls about her neck, and an ouche (brooch) depending thereby, having in her hand a sceptre with one flower, set with stones and pearls and one bird in the top thereof; and her Child sitting upon her knee, with a crown on his head, with a diadem set with pearls and stones, having a ball with a cross of silver and gilt in his left hand and at either of his feet a scutcheon of arms.[39]

South Yorkshire

OUR LADY OF DONCASTER

The Carmelite friary—"a right goodly house in the middle of the town"—was founded in 1350 by John son of Henry Nicbrothere of Eyum with Maud his wife and Richard Euwere of Doncaster, who gave the friars a messuage and six acres of land. The priors of the order asked permission of the Archbishop of York to have the place consecrated in 1351. The Carmelite friary is best known for its image of the Virgin Mary. In the 15th and early 16th century many bequests were made to "Our Lady of Doncaster," a wonder-working image of the Virgin, before which the hair shirt of Earl Rivers was hung after his execution in 1483. To this image Sir Hugh Hastings left a taper of wax in 1482, Katherine Hastings, his widow, "her tawny chamlett gown" in 1506, Alice West her best beads in 1520, John Hewett of Friston-super-aquam one penny in 1521, the sister of Geoffrey Proctor of Bordley a girdle and beads about 1524, while the Earl of Northumberland gave 13 shillings and 4 pence a year to keep a light burning before Our Lady. On July 15, 1524, William Nicholson of Townsburgh attempted to cross the Don with an iron-bound wain in which were Robert Leche and his wife and their two children; being overwhelmed by the stream they called on our Lady of Doncaster and by her help came safely ashore; they came to the White Friars and returned thanks on St. Mary Magdalen's Day, when "this gracious miracle was rung and sung in the presence of 300 people and more."[40]

William of York

William FitzHerbert was Archbishop of York from 1141 to 1147 and 1153 to 1154. He was first elected Archbishop in 1141, against the opposition of the Cistercian monasteries of Yorkshire. He was deposed in 1147 and replaced by Henry Murdac, the Cistercian abbot of Fountains Abbey near Ripon in North Yorkshire. However, York's cathedral chapter refused to acknowledge the appointment, so Murdac carried out his duties at Ripon. He died in 1153 and was replaced as Archbishop by William. After less than a month back in York, William died, allegedly from poison at the hands of Osbert de Bayeux, archdeacon of York (though death by poisoning was never mentioned during the canonization process).[41] William was canonized in 1226 and the document lists a great many miracles: oil flowing from the tomb which had healed many people of their infirmities; three dead people brought back to life; blind people given their sight; and new eyes given to a man who had been unjustly defeated in a duel and blinded. The earliest recorded miracle is in the 1150s, when a fire broke out in the city and spread to the Minster. A huge burning beam fell on William's tomb and broke the grave-cover in half. The lower part of it fell away exposing the body of the saint; but the silk vestments were not in the slightest bit burnt, nor was the body damaged, and a sweet smell of burning incense or the most precious unguent was observed.[42] The tomb was resealed, and holy oil began to flow out from it.[43] A number of miracles are recorded from Pentecost (12 June) 1177. For example, girl from the parish of Leeds, blind since the age of three, fell asleep at the tomb of William. As she recounted, a man came to her who was dressed in venerable clothes and shining with remarkable brightness. He touched her eyes with his hand, and in this way, she regained her sight.[44]

North Yorkshire

AELRED OF RIEVAULX

Rievaulx Abbey on the North York Moors was founded in 1131 by Walter Espec. Because of the site's topography the church and the rest of the abbey was orientated north-south. It was intended to be a Cistercian mission center from which Cistercian colonies were sent out to found daughter houses throughout the north of England and Scotland. The abbey underwent expansion from 1145 to 1165, with further building in the late 12th century (for example in the refectory area). It reached the peak of its power around 1200, but costly building programs in the first half of the 13th century (for example the addition of the presbytery) left the abbey heavily in debt. There is also evidence that the economic production of the Abbey, which was heavily dependent on wool production, suffered in the late 13th century, partly due to epidemics among the estate's flocks of sheep. Some further smaller alterations including the sacristy were made in the 14th century, but in the 15th century parts of the abbey were demolished, indicating that it had declined in numbers as well as wealth. By 1538 when the abbey was suppressed during the Reformation, there were only 22–23 monks and just over 100 lay people, whereas there had been 140 monks and over 500 lay brothers during St. Aelred's charismatic abbacy in the 1160s.[45]

Aelred was abbot of Rievaulx from 1147 until his death in 1167. Aelred wrote several influential books on spirituality, among them *Speculum caritatis* ("The Mirror of Charity," reportedly written at the request of Bernard of Clairvaux) and *De spiritali amicitia* ("On Spiritual Friendship"). He also wrote seven works of history, addressing three of them to Henry II of England, advising him how to be a good king and declaring him to be the true descendant of Anglo-Saxon kings. Aelred was never formally canonized but became the center of a cult in the north of England which was recognized officially by the Cistercians in 1476. As such, he was venerated as a saint, with his body kept at Rievaulx. In the 16th century, before the dissolution of the monastery, John Leland saw Aelred's shrine at Rievaulx containing Aelred's body glittering with gold and silver.[46]

County Durham

GODRIC OF FINCHALE

The holy man Godric of Finchale, who died in 1170, was born in Walpole (Norfolk), the son of poor parents. After a period as an itinerant hawker, he bought a share in a

Rievaulx Abbey, North Yorkshire, with the Chapter House ruins in the foreground. 2012 (Antony McCallum, CCA-Share Alike 3.0 Unported).

ship and, drawing on his knowledge of winds and tides, became a steersman. Although he earned his livelihood "trading in diverse wares," he never hesitated to interrupt his voyages in order to visit churches and saint's shrines. Yet what fascinated him most of all was the holy island of Lindisfarne, where St. Cuthbert had lived and worked, and the even lonelier Inner Farne where Cuthbert had his retreat. His seafaring life had lasted sixteen years when he decided to follow the example of St. Cuthbert. After deciding to live the life of a hermit, he gained the minimal education required for liturgical prayer at a school in Durham. On a location at a bend in the River Wear at Finchale, not far from the city of Durham, Godric found a sheltered site for the hermitage in which he would spend the next sixty years living under harsh conditions. According to his biographer Reginald of Durham, it took Godric forty of those years to conquer his passions and attain peace in his new life. Central to his devotion was his focus on Jesus's humanity. In a vision he saw the Christ child emerge from the lateral wound on the crucifix in his cell, which made him weep tears of joy.[47]

The place where Godric settled was then exceedingly wild, overrun with snakes, and used by the bishop merely as a hunting-ground. Here St. Godric lived for half a century, accompanied at first by a poor sister, but after her death entirely alone; and here he cultivated the ground and erected a chapel which he dedicated to St. John the Baptist, an oratory of St. Mary, and other buildings, and when this had been done Bishop Flambard granted the reversion of the hermitage, its fishery, and its possessions to the prior and convent of Durham. Godric died in 1170 and soon afterwards Bishop Pudsey confirmed to the monks the gift of his predecessor, and conferred upon Reginald and Henry, the two Durham monks in possession, and their successors, the tract of land near the hermitage which now chiefly constitutes the Finchale farm.

As the revenues of Finchale Priory increased, the monks, no longer content with St. Godric's chapel, resolved in 1241 to build a new church, and the archbishop of York granted an indulgence of thirty days to all who should contribute to this work. In the following year the church was begun, and it appears to have been completed in or about 1264. In 1266 the monks added a chapel dedicated to the honor of St. Godric, in the south transept.[48]

There was a close link between Finchale and Durham. As a saint, Godric catered for the women who could not obtain access to Cuthbert, thanks to the legend of the saint's prohibition on women entering his shrine or church. In one instance, a woman possessed by demons went to Durham to seek Cuthbert's help and was guided by the saint himself to Finchale; in another Godric restored the sanity of a young girl who had thoughtlessly wandered into the precinct of St. Cuthbert.[49]

Finchale Priory is long gone, but Godric lives on in the religious songs he wrote in Middle English. One song is said to have come to Godric when he had a vision of his sister Burhcwen, also a solitary at Finchale, being received into heaven. She was singing a song of thanksgiving, in Latin, and Godric renders her song in English thus[50]:

> *Crist and sainte marie swa on scamel me iledde*
> *þat ic on þis erðe ne silde wid mine bare fote i tredie*
>
> Christ and St Mary so carried me with a crutch
> That I never had to tread upon this earth with my bare foot.

Godric's most famous song also came to him in a vision: the Virgin Mary told him to sing it whenever he was tempted, weary or in pain, and she would come to his aid:

> *Sainte marie uirgine*
> *moder ihesu cristes nazarene*
> *onfo schild help þin godric*
> *onfang bring heȝilich wið þe in godes riche*
>
> *Sainte marie xristes bur*
> *maidenes clenhad moderes flur*
> *dilie min sinne rix in min mod*
> *bring me to winne wið þe selfd God*

That is:

> Saint Mary, Virgin,
> Mother of Jesus Christ of Nazareth,
> Receive, shield, help your Godric;
> Received, bring him on high with you in God's kingdom.
>
> Saint Mary, bower of Christ,
> Purest of maidens, flower of mothers,
> Efface my sins, reign in my mind,
> Bring me to joy with that same God.

In the first verse, Godric is playing on the meaning of his own name: *godes riche* means "God's kingdom." These verses already have some of the motifs which would later become so popular in Middle English devotional poetry, especially the romance tinge of Mary as "bower of Christ," and the flower image.

Ritual Curses in the Late Medieval Church

Ritual curses were common in Anglo-Saxon ecclesiastical documents, so it is not surprising that the medieval church after the Norman Conquest should have continued to believe in the efficacy of ritual cursing. It is common to find medieval manuscripts belonging to the church inscribed with individual "book curses" against those who would steal or deface the work.[51] For example, in a manuscript from Evesham Abbey in Worcestershire, a colophon that praises the scribe's work—and requests high-quality wine for him as a reward—ends with a curse in Latin in which the book's thief is wished a "death from evil things: may the thief of this book die." A curse found in a manuscript from St. Albans Abbey in Hertfordshire is explicit about the punishment to anyone who steals it: "This book is given in use to the brothers of Oxford by John Wethamstede, father of the flock of the proto-martyr of the English [St. Alban]; if anyone secretly tears this inscription or removes it, may he feel Judas's noose [around his neck] or forks [presumably handled by demons!]."[52]

The medieval church also entered curses into the formal litany of everyday service, most particularly with the reading out of Chapter 28 of the Book of Deuteronomy. The chapter specifically deals with blessings and curses, including this comprehensive curse: "Cursed shall be the fruit of thy body, and the fruit of thy land, the increase of thy kine, and the flocks of thy sheep."

The church could also, upon a very few significant occasions, actually fall back upon using the General Great Curse. The ceremony was usually only performed by those of the rank of bishop and above and was carried out using "bell, book and candle." The ceremony is thought to date back as far as the 9th century and appears to have developed out of the elaborate excommunication ceremonies of the church, when individuals would be formally denied the comfort of the sacraments and Christian worship. However, the General Great Curse took this a large step further, stating that they were to be "accursed of God, and of his church, from the sole of their foot to the crown of their head."

One of the best recorded examples of this formal curse being actually carried out took place in Westminster Hall in 1253, when no less than thirteen fully robed bishops cursed the violators of the Magna Carta and all transgressors of the liberties of the church. At the end of the ceremony, the bells were rung, the book closed with a sound like a small thunderclap, and the candles were extinguished and cast aside—at which point the bishops cried, "So let them be extinguished and sink into the pit of hell which run into the dangers of this sentence."[53]

However, it was not only the Church and its priests who uttered ritual curses. Recent studies centered on the county of Norfolk have shown that the walls of surviving medieval churches are covered in many thousands of pre–Reformation inscriptions. Although loosely termed "graffiti" many of these inscriptions appear to have had both meaning and function that places them apart from modern perceptions of graffiti as being destructive and anti-social. The vast majority of inscriptions recorded to date appear to have been devotional in nature and to have functioned as "apotropaic" or ritual protection markings. The presence of such markings in such large quantities, with churches such as Swannington, Ludham and Litcham each containing many dozens of examples, and the fact that they have remained both visible and un-defaced suggests that they were both an accepted and acceptable aspect of lay piety in the late medieval parish. They were, in effect, prayers made solid in stone.

The graffiti survey of Norwich cathedral began in 2012 as a part of the wider Norfolk Medieval Graffiti Survey. Initial inspection of the ground floor surface areas indicated that the main body of the cathedral contained a very large number of graffiti inscriptions. Current estimates suggest that the number may well be as high as between 2500 and 4000 individual and identifiable inscriptions. The main body of pre–Reformation inscriptions consist of pictorial representations or symbols, including ships, faces, music, merchant's marks, geometric designs, animals birds and fish. Although many of these early inscriptions appear to be devotional in nature, such as the many examples of late medieval ships depictions, by far the largest single type of inscription are those which are considered "apotropaic" or ritual protection markings.

Among the many thousands of inscriptions recorded in Norwich cathedral were three individual inscriptions that were, even among the jumble of animals, faces and medieval ships, highly unusual. Had there been a single inscription then it is quite likely that it may have been overlooked, but the fact that there were three such inscriptions, located in very different areas of the cathedral, meant that they stood out as a small and distinct group. Each of the inscriptions was clearly pre-reformation text but, highly unusually, in all three the text had been inverted. One of the inscriptions, while clearly being inverted lettering, was too degraded to identify any more than a few individual letters. The second, while also heavily abraded, was sufficiently intact to allow groups of letters to be identified, although the full text of the inscription must remain conjectural. Only the third inscription appeared complete.

Located in the southern thoroughfare between the Ambulatory and Presbytery, the inscription was created at approximately 20 inches above the earlier floor height on the eastern side of the entranceway. The inscription in itself is discrete, measuring less than

4 inches across, and is almost invisible to the naked eye unless subjected to particular light conditions. In natural light it is best viewed in the mid-morning, when the sunlight casts across the surface. However, at all other times of day it is difficult to locate without the aid of a separate light source. In a very clear, neat and accurate hand is spelled out the name "Keynfford," albeit inverted. Centered directly below that is a clearly inscribed symbol which appears not to have been inverted in the same manner as the lettering.

Matthew Champion, who discovered these graffiti, compares them to the curses on Roman curse tablets. A common feature of many of these early curses, says Champion, is the fact that the text, in particular the name of the intended target, is reversed. Although Ralph Merrifield, an authority on ritual and magic, suggests that such a strategy might well be intended to hide the identity of the victim from the casual observer it would appear unlikely that such an action would delude even the semiliterate for more than a moment. It would appear more likely that the reversal of the text had an added function that created a spiritual environment whereby the malignancy of the curse could become manifest. With inversion of normal practice playing a key part in spiritual practices from the Bronze Age to the early modern period it is likely that this reversal of names was fundamental to the effectiveness of the curse itself.

Cloister ceiling statue at Norwich Cathedral showing a group of the faithful. July 24, 2011 (Fæ, CCA-Share Alike 3.0 Unported).

The symbol beneath the "Keynfford" inscription would appear to be an astrological symbol associated with the moon. Many early curses were also accompanied by a variety of symbols that appear to be related to astrology and astrological practices. Merrifield describes them as "the 'signacula' [signs] of the planets, and the 'characters' of the Intelligences and Daemons that were believed to inhabit them." These symbols were perhaps designed to add strength and potency to the curse, in much the same way as a spiritually important location might strengthen an apotropaic marking.

Perhaps the closest known parallel to the curses found on the walls of the cathedral is that found on a 17th century lead tablet found in 1892 at Wilton Place, Dymock, Gloucestershire, not far from the Lydney Park Roman temple. Although much more complex than the Norwich examples, and including a full invocation of banishment, it does share the same key elements. Across the top is the name of the intended victim, "Sarah Ellis," written backwards rather than fully inverted, and below this are a whole series of strange astrological symbols. It has been demonstrated that almost all of these symbols appear to relate to the moon, or one of its aspects, suggesting that the moon had replaced Saturn as having a particular association with the function of the curse. That such a similarly formed inscription should be discovered in a 17th century context, over two centuries after the creation of the Norwich curses, would most certainly suggest a continuity of practice of some duration.[54]

Wales and Scotland

Most of Wales remained independent of England until the late 13th century, and Scotland was an independent kingdom throughout the Middle Ages. Both of course had their own saints, and I consider these in the next chapter.

10

The Saints of Wales
and Scotland: Holy Islands,
Ritual Curses and Healing Waters

St. David of St. Davids (Pembrokeshire)

Wales' best-known male saint is David, but very little is known about the historical David. It seems that St. David and his monastic community followed the desert fathers and led an ascetic way of life. The earliest *Life* of David, composed by Rhygyfarch, dates to the late 11th century. Rhygyfarch says of David's community[1]:

> Therefore they would work with their feet and hands with more vehement zeal; they would place the yoke upon their shoulders; they would push spades and shovels into the earth with their unfailing arms; they would carry hoes and saws in their holy hands for cutting, and they would, by their own efforts, provide for all the needs of the community. They despised possessions, they rejected the gifts of the wicked, and they detested riches.

As for St. David himself, after matins[2]

> he would go alone to talk with angels. Immediately afterwards he would seek cold water; by remaining in it long enough and pouring it over himself he would tame every passion of the flesh. After that he would spend the whole day teaching, praying, genuflecting, and caring for the brethren; also in feeding a multitude of orphans, wards, widows, needy, feeble, sick, and pilgrims; he did this invariably and untiringly. In this way he began, continued, and finished. The intended brevity of this short account, however, prevents us from explaining the remaining aspects of the severity of his discipline, although they are necessary as an example; but he imitated the monks of Egypt and lived a life like theirs.

David's name is closely associated with that of his mother Non or Nonnita, who was also venerated as a saint. Unusually, David's birth was the result of a rape—according to Rhygyfarch, Sanctus king of Ceredig was one day in the kingdom of Dyfed[3]:

> And the king came across a nun named Nonnita, who was a virgin, an exceedingly beautiful girl and modest. Lusting after her, he raped her, and she conceived his son the holy David. Neither before or after did she know a man, but continuing steadfastly in chastity of mind and body, she led her life most devoutly; for, from the very time she conceived, she lived only on bread and water. In the place where she had been raped and had conceived, there lies a small meadow, pleasant to behold and filled with the gift of heavenly dew. In that field, at the moment she conceived, there appeared two large stones that had not been seen before, one at her head and the other at her feet; for the land, rejoicing at his conception, opened its bosom, that it might both preserve the modesty of the girl, and declare the significance at her offspring.

175

Little is known of the cult of David before the 11th century. In 999, Danish pirates killed Morgeneu, the bishop of Mynyw (St. Davids)—according to Gerald of Wales, this was a "judgement for having been the first bishop since Dewi himself to eat meat." In 1080 another bishop Abraham was killed by Vikings, and his predecessor Sulien was brought out of retirement. In 1081 Gruffudd ap Cynan, pretender to the kingdom of Gwynedd, landed at Porth Clais near St. Davids, and was met by Sulien along with Rhys ap Tewdr, the dispossessed king of Deheubarth. Gruffudd and Rhys accompanied Bishop Sulien the short distance to the church of Mynyw to swear an oath on the relics of St. David. This solemn action was the prelude to a successful military push, which fairly quickly gave Gruffudd and Rhys victory at the battle of Mynydd Carn: a decisive triumph over Trahaearn ap Caradog of Gwynedd, Caradog ap Gruffudd of Glamorgan, and Meilir ap Rhiwallon of Powys, all of whom fell on the battlefield.[4]

In 1090, the bodily remains of David were lost when the shrine was stripped bare in an attack by the Vikings. All that remained were secondary relics: an altar covered with skins and veils, a bell renowned for its miracles, a pastoral staff *gloriosis choruscus miraculis*, "lustrous with glorious miracles," and a tunicle (a type of liturgical vestment) made from cloth of gold.[5] It was around this time that Rhygyfarch wrote his *Life* of David.

Gerald of Wales, writing in the early 1190s, mentions another secondary relic of David.[6] Gerald tells how David was busy copying the gospel of St. John; when the church bell rang, David jumped up and rushed to church without closing the book or completing the page. When he returned to the scriptorium he found the column which he had already begun completed in gold letters by the work of an angel. David therefore "closed the book and removed it from the sight of human eyes, making no addition whatsoever."

> This is why, even to this day, the inside of the book, which was closed and bound into a volume becomingly adorned with silver and gold, is not shown to human eyes. No one is said to have dared look inside the book or to open its seal since St David's time almost to the present. But in these recent days some people have presumed to try it … but grievously and suddenly struck down by heaven's anger, they were called back from their rash daring. That text, moreover, is called by the inhabitants of this district the Imperfect Gospel, and even to this day it is renowned for its miracles and virtues, and is not undeservedly held in the highest reverence by everyone.

St. Non's chapel and holy well are on the south coast of St. Davids, overlooking the rocky coastline above St. Non's Bay. The chapel is first mentioned in 1335, but an early excavation reports "stone coffins" which might in fact have been slab-lined graves of the early Christian period. Also, the presence here of the pillar-stone with its incised Latin cross, roughly dateable to the 7th to 9th century, is suggestive of an early medieval foundation for the chapel, although unfortunately, there is no firm evidence that the stone originally came from the site. The holy well, just to the east of the chapel, continued to be a famous place for healing even after the Reformation, and there are antiquarian references to the pious offering pins and pebbles at the well on March 2, St. Non's Day. In the 18th century, the present stone vault was built over it, though this may have replaced an earlier well building.[7]

St. Brynach of Nevern (Pembrokeshire)

St. Brynach is associated with the small village of Nevern on the River Nevern in Pembrokeshire. His 12th century *Life* tells us that he was something of an ascetic[8]:

Ruins of the chapel of St. Non (the mother of St. David) on the Pembrokeshire coast near the city of St. Davids. July 30, 2009 (Thruxton, CCA-Share Alike 3.0 Unported).

Saint Brynach, being a devoted performer of divine service, strove so much to restrain the superfluities of bodily affection, as he aimed to live pleasing to the divine will. He wasted his body with continual fastings, and reduced it with frequent vigils. He checked the insolence of the flesh with the roughness of his garments, and in the chilliness of cold water which he entered daily.

He could also tame wild animals:

a cow, which he had segregated from the others, as if unique and singular for his need, both on account of the size of her body, because she was larger than the rest, and also on account of the abundance of her milk, he deputed to the custody of a wolf, which in the manner of a well-trained herdsman drove the cow in the morning to the pastures, and in the evening brought her home in safety.

There is a church at Nevern dedicated to St. Brynach—it dates from the 15th century but has a 12th century tower. In the churchyard is a late 10th or early 11th century cross, and a stone with a 5th or 6th century Latin inscription that reads VITALIANA/EMERETO, "(The stone) of Vitalianus Emeritus." Vitalianus and Emeritus were common names of this period. Along the left angle of the face is an Ogam inscription: VITALIAN(o). Inside the church, built into the sills of the southern transept windows, are two further stones. One has a Latin inscription reading vertically down: MAGLOCVN(i) FILI CLVTOR, "(The stone) of Maglocunus, son of Clutorius." The Ogam form of the inscription on the left angle of the face reads upwards: MAGLICUNAS MAQI CLUTR[]. It is 5th or early 6th century in date.[9]

Bardsey Island (Gwynedd) and Islands in Welsh Mythology

BARDSEY ISLAND

Bardsey Island is off the Llyn Peninsula in northwest Wales, and the earliest reference to a monastery on Bardsey is the record of the death of a monk in 1011. St. Cadfan is said to have founded a monastery there, though it may have been a retreat used by monks living on the mainland at Aberdaron or at nearby Capel Anelog, on the eastern slope of a hill called Mynydd Anelog, where two gravestones were found dating from the 5th or early 6th century.[10] The gravestones are in Latin—one reads "here lies the priest Veracius," while the other reads "Here lies the priest Senacus with a multitude of his brothers."[11]

In the later medieval period, Bardsey became a renowned place of pilgrimage. Many well-known saints, bishops, and princes were, according to tradition, buried under the shadow of the venerable monastery on this remote island, including St. Beuno, the founder of Clynnog and the uncle of St. Winifred; St. Padarn, the founder of Llanbadarn Fawr, in Cardiganshire; and Deiniol, first Bishop of Bangor.

Bardsey was then called the Rome of Britain, according to the *Book of Llandaf*, on account of its remoteness and the dangerous character of the passage across the narrow strait that separated it from the coast of the Llyn Peninsula. In the time of Edward II, the monastery was given immunity from taxation; and it is most interesting to note that even to the present day a farmhouse not far from Ffynnon Fair, or Mary's Well, on the mainland, enjoys immunity from tithe, a privilege given in return for hospitality shown to the pilgrims on their way to the island monastery. Of Bardsey itself it was said that the ground around the old abbey was as thick with graves as the cells in a honeycomb.

Meilir, one of the earliest of the bards of the Norman era, refers with affection to Bardsey as a center for pilgrims and to himself as a "pilgrim to Peter." It was then called the Island of Mary[12]:

> A place that is solitary
> By wayfarers untrodden
> Around its graveyard
> Heaves the bosom of the deep,
> The fair Island of Mary
> The Holy Isle of Saints.

THE SECOND BRANCH OF THE MABINOGION

Islands play a significant role in the *Mabinogion*, a set of Welsh mythological tales written between 1060 and 1200. In the Second Branch, entitled *Branwen, Daughter of Llyr*, Bran the Blessed, the king of Britain, is forced to make war on the Irish to protect his sister Branwen. In the battle, the British were victorious, but only seven survived, along with Bran, wounded in his foot with a poisoned spear. Then, because of his poisoned foot, Bran ordered the survivors to sever his head[13]:

"Take the head" said he "and bring it to the White Hill in London, and bury it with its face towards France. And you will be on the road a long time. In Harlech you will be seven years in feasting, the birds of Rhiannon singing to you. The head will be as good company to you as it was at its best when it was ever on me. And you will be at Gwales in Penfro for eighty years. Until you open the door facing Aber Henvelen on the side facing Cornwall, you will be able to abide there, along with the head with you uncorrupted. But when you open that door, you will not be able to remain there. You will make for London and bury the head."

The survivors duly cut off Bran's head, and set off with the head, landing at Aber Alaw in Anglesey. There Branwen died of a broken heart and was buried in a "four-sided grave," popularly believed to be the Bronze Age funerary mound known as Bedd Branwen. The men then set off for Harlech and learned that Caswallwn son of Beli had overrun the island and was now the crowned king in London. They reached Harlech and

> began a feast, and the indulgence in food and drink was begun. And [as soon as] they began to eat and drink there came three birds, which began to sing a kind of song to them; and when they heard that song, every other [tune] seemed unlovely beside it. It seemed a distant sight, what they could see far above the ocean yet it was as clear as if they had been right next to them. And they were at that feast for seven years.

At the end of the seven years they moved to Gwales in Penfro (possibly the island of Grassholm, off the coast of Pembrokeshire) and a "beautiful kingly place high above the ocean," with two open doors and one closed one, the one they must not open. There they "were completely free of care. Of all the grief that they had witnessed or experienced themselves—there was no longer any memory, or any of the sorrow in the world." At the end of eighty years, one of the seven survivors, Heilyn son of Gwyn, became curious and opened the door and looked out to Cornwall:

> And when he looked, suddenly everything they had ever lost—loved ones and companions, and all the bad things that had ever happened to them; and most of all the loss of their king—became as clear as if it had been rushing in towards them.

After Heilyn opened the door, the seven survivors left Gwales and made for London, where they buried Bran's head at White Hill, thought to be the site of the Tower of London.

St. Beuno's Church, Clynnog Fawr (Gwynedd)

In medieval times the church of St. Beuno at Clynnog Fawr on the Llyn Peninsula was an important stopping place for pilgrims heading for Bardsey Island. To this day important artifacts are to be found at St. Beuno's Church including an ancient wooden chest hollowed out of a single piece of ash and used to keep alms donated by the pilgrims. The chest is believed to date from the Middle Ages and the padlocks from around 1600. The choir stalls and screen are believed to be 16th Century. A barrel-vaulted passageway leads to the 16th century chapel that is believed to have been built on St. Beuno's cell. A stone known as Beuno's Stone has markings reputed to be those of Beuno's fingers and outside in the churchyard there is a sundial dated between the late 10th century and the early 12th century.[14]

In his 14th century *Life*, St. Beuno is associated with a very special oak tree[15]:

> Beuno lived on the land he had inherited from his father and built a church there, consecrating it in the name of Christ the Lord. He planted an acorn by the side of his father's grave, which grew into an oak tree of great height and thickness. From the crown of this tree there grew a branch right down to the ground and from the ground back up to the top of the tree so that the bend in the branch was touching the ground. This is how it always remained. If an Englishman passes between the branch and the trunk of the tree, he shall drop dead on the spot, but if a Welshman does so, he shall be none the worse.

St. Cybi of Holyhead (Anglesey)

There was an early monastery at Holyhead on Holy Island, off the west coast of Anglesey, not far from Llyn Cerrig Bach, the lake where weapons were offered to the gods in the later Iron Age. Caer Gybi is a stoutly walled rectangular enclosure that crowned a low cliff overlooking Holyhead harbor. It is thought to be a late Roman (3rd or 4th century CE) strongpoint presumably concerned with maritime activities. At some point in the medieval period a monastery was established within the walls and this later became a large collegiate church.[16] The monastery was established by the 6th century Cornish saint Cybi. Nothing remains of Cybi's monastery (it was attacked by Vikings in the 10th century), but recently a cemetery of long-cist graves dating to the 6th–8th century CE, was discovered during construction of the A55 expressway, to the northwest of Ty Mawr farm near Holyhead. At this site the graves were located around, and cut into, the remains of a Bronze Age barrow.[17]

There were a number of holy wells associated with St. Cybi, but the most famous are the Clorach wells near Llanerchymedd in the center of Anglesey. St. Cybi's monastery was on the west of Anglesey, at Holyhead, and on the east of the island at Penmon was the monastery of St. Seiriol. According to tradition, St. Cybi and St. Seiriol would regularly trek across the island and meet at the well near Llanerchymedd. The story tells us that Seiriol walking westwards in the morning and eastwards in the evening always had his back to the sun and thus never got a tan (regardless of how he spent the rest of his time). Cybi on the other hand always walked toward the sun.

The account has been set in verse by the English poet Matthew Arnold (1822–1888) and also by the Welsh-language poet Sir John Morris Jones (1864–1929). Here is the first verse of the English version of Morris Jones' poem[18]:

> Seiriol the fair and Cybi the tawny
> Met as it is said
> Daily by the well of Clorach
> In the centre of Anglesey

At the point where they met were two strongly flowing wells directly opposite to each other, one on either side of the road. These wells have had a reputation as an important site which is documented back into at least the 18th century and probably long before that.

St. Winefride of Holywell (Flintshire)

In the later Middle Ages, Wales' best-known female saint was Gwenfrewi (also known as Winefride), who came to be associated with Holywell in Flintshire, northeast Wales. However, Gwenfrewi was originally abbess of the monastery at Gwytherin in Conwy, where she died—her grave there was a place of pilgrimage until her body was taken to Shrewsbury in 1138.[19] Recently a fragment of an 8th-century reliquary from Gwytherin, the Arch Gwenfrewi (Winifred's Casket), was found, witnessing her status as a recognized saint almost from the moment of her death, around 650–the earliest such surviving evidence for any Welsh saint.[20] On the north side of St. Winifred's Church is an east-west line of four stones, generally 3 feet high, the westernmost of which bears the vertical

Mural of St. Cybi in Holyhead, Anglesey. June 25, 2016 (Cls14, CCA-Share Alike 4.0).

inscription: VINNEMAGLI FILI/SENEMAGLI. This inscription is thought to signify "of Vinnemaglus son of Senemaglus" and probably dates from the 5th to the 6th century CE. The stones, in particular the inscription, have been associated with an early medieval monastic complex.[21]

The first *Life* of Gwenfrewi was written in the 12th century by a monk from Shrewsbury in Shropshire. According to this and subsequent Lives, Winefride was the only child of noble parents, and a virgin. One Sunday, while her parents were at church, the local ruler Caradog tried to rape her. Escaping, Winefride fled toward Beuno's church; but Prince Caradog caught her on the hillside and cut off her head. Beuno cursed the unrepentant Caradog, who melted away. In the words of the chronicler[22]:

> As she reached the door of the church, he caught her up and struck off her head with his sword, which fell into the church while her body remained outside. Beuno and her mother and father saw what had happened, and Beuno stared into the face of the king and said: "I ask God not to spare you and to respect you as little as you respected this good girl." And in that moment the king melted away into a lake, and was seen no more in this world.

However, Winefride miraculously survived this fatal blow:

Beuno took the girl's head and placed it back with the body, covering the body with his cloak and saying to her mother and father who were mourning for her: "Be quiet for a little while and leave her as she is until the Mass is over." Then Beuno celebrated the sacrifice to God. When the Mass was finished, the girl rose up entirely healed and dried the sweat from her face; God and Beuno healed her. Where her blood fell to earth, a spring was formed, which even today still heals people and animals from their illnesses and injuries.

The spring formed from the girl's blood is St. Winefride's well in Holywell, a popular center of pilgrimage in the Middle Ages, and still a center of pilgrimage today. The legend of Winefride is fantastical, but there was a real Winefride. She was related to the royal family of Powys: Beuno was actually her uncle; and St. Tenoi, whom she succeeded as abbess at Gwytherin, her great-aunt. Most revealingly, she had a brother Owain, who killed Caradog in revenge: indicating that, whatever the exact truth of her death-and-resurrection legend, it does have a basis in historical fact.[23]

Holywell was first mentioned as a place of pilgrimage in 1115 and from 1240 to the dissolution it was part of the possessions of Basingwerk Abbey. Henry V made the pilgrimage in 1415 before his victory at Agincourt, as did Edward IV before Towton Moor in 1461. The future Henry VII, too, is thought to have made a secret visit before winning his crown at Bosworth in 1485.

The present building, set into a hillside, dates from the late 15th century. It was

St. Winefride's Well, Holywell, Flintshire (late 15th century). September 29, 2009 (Nabokov at English Wikipedia, CCA-Share Alike 3.0 Unported).

probably built for Margaret Beaufort, Henry VII's mother, to replace an earlier structure, and is richly ornamented on the exterior with a frieze of animals, and the badges of Henry VII and Thomas Stanley (Margaret Beaufort's third husband); the quality of the workmanship suggests that royal masons may have been employed.

Among the miracles related of Winifred's well by her biographer is one characterized as "stupendous," concerning three bright stones which were seen in the middle of the bubbling up of the fountain, ascending and descending, "up and down by turns, after the manner of stones projected by a shooter." They so continued to dance for many years, but one day an unlucky woman was seized with a desire to play with the stones. So she took hold of one; "whereat they all vanished, and the woman died." This miracle was supplemented by that of a man who was rebuked for theft at the fountain; and on his denying his guilt, the goat which he had stolen and eaten became his accuser by uttering an audible bleating from his belly. But the miracles of Winifred's well are for the most part records of wonderful cures from disease and deformity. Withered and useless limbs were made whole and useful; the dumb bathed in the water, came out, and asked for their clothes; the blind washed and received their sight; lunatics "troubled by unclean spirits" were brought to the well in chains, "tearing with their teeth and speaking vain things," but returned homeward in full possession of their reason.[24]

St. Cadoc of Llancarfan (Vale of Glamorgan)

The monastery of Llancarfan, dedicated to St. Cadoc, was in the Vale of Glamorgan in south Wales. An abbot of Llancarfan is first mentioned in a charter of 7th century date *Iacob abbas altaris Sancti Catoci* ("Iacob abbot of the altar of St. Cadog"),[25] and there is persistent independent evidence for its existence from the 9th century onwards. The Llandaff charters are witnessed by abbots, *magistri* ("masters"), *doctores* ("teachers"), *lectores* ("readers"), and priests from Llancarfan. In a charter from around 1075, Bishop Herewald's son, Lifris, is named as *magister* of Llancarfan and archdeacon of Glamorgan. Another charter, with a date of around 980, includes a statement that the abbot of Llancarfan should always be worthy of episcopal honor. A "Lann Gharban" is mentioned in the 9th–10th century Irish Lives of St. Finnian implying a monastic settlement, and a late 9th century pillar-cross, preserved in Llancarfan churchyard, also suggests the site of an ecclesiastical community.[26]

St. Cadoc was one of the most important saints of south Wales. Born into the royal families of Gwynllwg and Brycheiniog, he worked miracles even before his birth. Strange lights shone in his parents' house and the cellars were miraculously filled with food. An angel announced his birth and summoned the hermit Meuthi to baptize and teach him. A holy well sprang up for his baptism and afterwards flowed with wine and milk. He grew up to be a great leader: churches all over South Wales were dedicated to him, and he founded the great monastery of Llancarfan in the Vale of Glamorgan.[27]

Our Lady of Penrhys (Rhondda Valley)

One of the best-known Welsh shrines to the Virgin Mary was at Penrhys in the Rhondda Valley, south Wales. Nine Middle Welsh poems survive praising the Virgin's image and holy well at Penrhys. The shrine appears to have been situated in a clearing in a dense steeply sloping woodland. According to Llewys Morgannwg, who flourished between 1520 and 1565[28]:

> Then you came, great blessing,
> To this place from heaven to the ground.
> Your image, which came previously from heaven,
> Is alive [and] seen every day.

As is often the case with miraculous images of the Virgin, it was claimed that the figure was not a man-made image but a gift sent directly from heaven. It was found, according to Llewys Morgannwg, in the hollow trunk of an oak tree and refused to be removed. Judging from the poetry of Penrhys, the image was probably a gilded and painted wooden figure of the Virgin, crowned, enthroned, wearing a cloak and depicted holding her Son.

It is likely the statue stood in the chapel which was erected on the summit of the mountain ridge, with the well further down the slope. The site was owned by the Cistercian abbey of Llantarnam in Monmouthshire, and no doubt provided the abbey with a considerable source of income: other building included a grange (manor-house), a hostelry where pilgrims could stay, a brewery, a bake-house and a malt-house.

The poet Llywelyn ap Hywel, who is thought to have flourished around 1480, describes how all visitors were healed of both spiritual and physical afflictions at the well[29]:

> She causes the body and soul
> of every righteous man to become vey healthy.
> She gives [the power of] hearing and speech
> to the deaf and dumb.
> A blind man goes to commune with her,
> and, as a result, gains [his] sight.

Rhisiart ap Rhys, who was active between 1495 and 1510, says of the well[30]:

> There are rippling waters at the top of the rock
> Farewell to every ailment that desires them!
> White wine runs in the rill,
> That can kill pain and fatigue!

In 1538 Hugh Latimer, Bishop of Worcester, wrote to Thomas Cromwell condemning the statue in his own cathedral and suggesting that the Worcester image, along with others including Penrhys, be destroyed. In September of the same year the image at Penrhys was sent to London and burned—probably in the courtyard of Cromwell's house at Chelsea.[31]

The Saints of Wales and Ritual Curses

St. Cadoc

St. Cadoc of Llancarfan may have been a holy man and a great leader, but he had his dark side. In many of the stories about Cadoc, he is vengeful and unforgiving in the extreme. He blinded King Rhun of Gwynedd, who had tried to burn one of Cadoc's barns. At his command the earth opened and swallowed Sawyl Benuchel, who had plundered the monastery at Llancarfan, and some soldiers who had demanded food from him with menaces.[32] As a boy Cadoc cursed a peasant and caused him to be burnt alive[33]:

One day, their hearth being cold, the aforesaid presbyter bade his disciple, Cadog, to fetch fire to cook the food. He, obeying his master's command without question, went immediately to a threshing-floor, or winnowing place for corn, where in that hour was a servant of his teacher, Tidus by name, drying oats, and demanded of him firmly that he would give him fire for the master's need. But that boorish rustic, rejecting his petition, refused to give him any, unless he would carry the burning coals in his cloak. He, trusting in the Lord and taking the coals of fire in his garment, brought them to his instructor with clothing unconsumed.

Enraged at this treatment, Cadoc cursed the peasant:

'I beseech thee, God, almighty Father, Maker of heaven and earth, who givest to thy servants on earth the power of treading on scorpions, making poisons harmless, putting demons to flight, giving sight to the, blind, cleansing lepers, healing the sick, taming savage sinners, and subduing the impious, receive into thy ears my prayers, that, that rustic may, by the kindling of his own fire-brands, with the threshing-floor and grain be burnt together, and that his threshing-floor may be cursed by God, so that none other after his death may use it for ever, and that his progeny may be subject to other folks. I do not, O Lord, by these entreaties, so supplicate thy goodness that I should wish the aforewritten sinner to be condemned in his wickedness, since the Lord says, "I will not the death of a sinner, but rather that he should be converted and live." And Paul, "Not rendering evil for evil, nor cursing for cursing, but contrariwise blessing"; but that the divine virtue and power might be made manifest in this world to the wicked, and that they might the more fear thee, and that they might shrink from resisting those who minister to thee, as it is read in Daniel, "Let all who inhabit the earth fear the God of Daniel, because he is a Deliverer and Saviour, performing wonderful things in heaven and in earth." The supplication finished, and he looking back, lo, the threshing-floor anathematized by him together with the boorish villein mentioned above is fired and utterly burnt. In that place too where that thresh-ing- or winnowing-floor was situated, a horrid fountain arose after its burning in memory of this divine vengeance, which, causing there a black bog, remains to this day in memory (or record) of that event.

St. Eilian and St. Cybi

Llaneilian in the northeast of Anglesey was supposedly founded by St. Eilian. It is said that Eilian came to Wales from Rome, arriving in the 5th century with oxen and other animals, landing on the Anglesey coast to start a mission. Caswallon, the local lord, father of Maelgwn Gwynedd, offered him land on which to establish a church. His generosity extended to granting an area to be determined by the distance Eilian's pet doe could cover in a day. Unfortunately, while the doe was measuring out the land it was attacked and killed by a greyhound. Elian was so upset that he immediately cursed the place such that no man would be able to keep a greyhound on that land ever again.[34]

St. Cybi of Holyhead also occasionally resorted to ritual curses. One day King Mael-gwyn of Gwynedd went out hunting[35]:

Seeing a she-goat, he incited his molossian (i.e., dog) to seize her. Then the she-goat ran quickly for protection to saint Cybi's cottage. And saint Cybi said to his disciple Caffo, "Withdraw from me; we cannot be together." And he came to the town, which is called to-day Merthyr Caffo, and there the herdsmen of Rhosyr kill Caffo. And so the blessed Cybi cursed the herdsmen of Rhosyr with their mistress. And the she-goat found protection.

Unfortunately, we learn nothing more of the curse and its possible outcome.

Ritual Cursing in the Fourth Branch of the Mabinogion

Ritual cursing has a long history in Wales—as we know from the Romano-British curse tablet found at Caerleon near Newport, and the curse tablets found at nearby Bath and Uley—and it also features in the Fourth Branch of the *Mabinogion*, entitled *Math, Son of Mathonwy*, the longest and most complex of the four branches. As the Fourth Branch opens, we are told that Math had an unusual disability[36]:

> At that time, Math son of Mathonwy could not live except when he had his feet enfolded in the lap of a maiden, unless the commotion of war prevented him. The maiden that was with him was Goewin daughter of Pebin of Dol Pebin in Arfon. She was the most beautiful woman known [around] there in her day.
>
> Caer Dathyl was his constant abode. He could not do the circuit of the land, but Gilfaethwy son of Don and Gwydion son of Don—his nephews, sons of his sister, and the household with them—would go on the circuit on his behalf.

It turns out that Gilfaethwy was in love with Goewin, and so Gilfaethwy, with the help of his brother Gwydion, stirred up a war with the neighboring kingdom of Dyfed. While Math was away preparing for battle, Gilfaethwy returned and raped Goewin. Now that Goewin was no longer a virgin, Math needed a new footholder, and Gwydion suggested his sister Arianrhod. The name *Arianrhod* is usually translated as "Silver Wheel," and Arianrhod linked to the moon. However, in the Fourth Branch the name consistently appears as *Aranrot*; the word *Aran* survives independently in the mountain names *Yr Aran Fawr* (*Arenig Fawr* in Snowdonia to the east of Porthmadog), and *Aran Benllyn*, also in Snowdonia near Dolgellau, as well as in the name of the Isle of Arran in the Firth of Clyde, Scotland. The authority on medieval Welsh literature Rachel Bromwich says that the meaning of *aran* is uncertain, but "huge," "round" or "humped" would be possible interpretations.[37]

Arianrhod was brought to Math, who asked her to step over his wand to see if she was a virgin:

> Then she stepped over the magic wand, and in that step she dropped a large boy with curly yellow hair. What the boy did was give a loud cry. After the boy's cry, she made for the door, and in the process a little something [dropped] from her. Before anyone could get second look of it, Gwydion picked it up and wrapped a sheet of brocaded silk around it, and hid it away. [The place] where he hid it was in a small chest at the foot of his bed.

The boy with the yellow curly hair was given the name Dylan, and he made for the sea, where he became in effect a sea-god. As for the "little something":

> As Gwydion was waking up in his bed one day, he heard a cry in the chest at his feet. Although it wasn't loud, it was loud enough for him to hear it. He quickly got up and opened the chest. As he opened it, he could see a little boy thrusting his arms out of the folds of the sheet, pushing it away. He took the boy between his hands, and made for the township with him, where he knew there was a woman with [milk in her] breasts. He made a deal a woman to nurture the boy. The boy was reared for that year. And [he grew so fast that] after the period of a year, they would have been impressed by his size even if he had been two years old.

Within a year he was large enough to go to court, and Gwydion acknowledged him when he came to court, and the boy "got to know him, and loved him more than any other person."

One day Gwydion and the boy made for Caer Arianrhod, a rocky island off the coast of Caernarfonshire, opposite the hillfort of Dinas Dinlle ("Fort of Lleu") near Llandwrog and was welcomed by Arianrhod. She then enquired who the boy was:

> This boy is a boy of yours."
> "Alas, man! What has come over you, shaming me [like this], and continuing my shame, and keeping it with you for as long as this?"

"If your shame is nothing more than my having reared a boy this fine, then a small thing is your shame."

"What is the name of your boy?" said she.

"God knows," said he "there is no name upon him yet."

"Aye," said she "I will swear an oath upon him: he will not get a name until he gets it from me."

Gwydion, not surprisingly, reacted with fury to Arianrhod's oath, and swore that the boy would get a name. The next day he and the boy walked along the ocean and conjured up a ship out of dulse (a kind of red alga that has long been used as a food) and sea-girdle (a variety of brown kelp), and conjured dovan leather out of sea-weed and dulse. He and the boy then sailed to Caer Arianrhod disguised as shoemakers. When Arianrhod discovered they were shoemakers, she ordered some shoes—but the first pair were too large, and the second pair too small. Finally, she went out to the boat:

When she came, he was cutting-out, and the boy was stitching.

"Aye, Lady," he said "good day to you."

"God give well to you," said she "it seems strange to me that you are not able to adjust the shoes to my measure."

"I couldn't," he said "[but] now I can."

At that, suddenly, there was a wren alighting on the deck of the boat. The boy took aim and hit it between the sinew and the bone of its leg. She laughed.

"God knows," said she "the fair one strikes it with a skilful hand!"

"Aye," he replied "and the wrath of God upon you! He has obtained a name, and the name is good enough "Lleu Skilful Hand" he will be from now on."

Arianrhod was furious at being deceived by Gwydion and swore another oath on the boy—that he "never take arms until I arm him myself." Some time later Gwydion and Lleu walked as far as Brynn Aryen (Brynaerau, between Llandwrog and Clynnog Fawr), then at the top of Cefyn Cludno (Cefn Clydno) near Capel Uchaf, to the south of Clynnog Fawr, they kitted out some horses and went to Caer Arianrhod. There they disguised themselves as bards, and entertained Arianrhod and her court, and a room was prepared for them. The next morning,

At cock-crow, Gwydion arose. Then he invoked his enchantment and his powers. At the first light of day, there was a multitude of trumpet blasts and shouting resounding throughout the country-side. When day-break came they heard a knocking on the chamber door, and (at that) Aranrhod asking them to open it. The youth got up and opened it. She came inside, a maiden with her.

"Good men," said she "we are in an evil position."

"Aye," he replied "we can hear trumpets and shouting. What do you suppose from that?"

"God knows," said she "we can't even see the colour of the ocean for all the boats crammed-up together [out there]. And the bulk [of them] are heading for land as fast as they can. What should we do?"

At Gwydion's suggestion, Arianrhod got some weapons and armed Lleu. Once Lleu was fully armed, Gwydion told her that they no longer had any need of the weapons—there was not a single boat to be seen. Angry at being tricked again, Arianrhod swore another destiny on Lleu—"that he will never get a wife, from any race that is in the world today!"

Gwydion then approached Math and told him of Arianrhod's oath. Math had a solution:

"Aye," said Math "we must endeavour, you and I, to conjure a wife for him out of flowers, using our magic and enchantment."

[Lleu], for his part, was a fully grown man, and the most handsome youth anyone had ever seen.

Then they took the flowers of the oak, the flowers of the broom, and the flowers of the mead-
owsweet—and from those they called forth the fairest and most beautiful woman anyone had
ever seen. She was baptised with the baptism they practiced [back] then, and [the name of]
"Blodeuedd" was put upon her.

It is possible that Arianrhod is linked to the goddess Sulis of Roman Bath in Somerset, who was the recipient of over a hundred curse tablets. Like Sulis, Arianrhod is
associated with water: Caer Arianrhod appears to be an island (at least some of the time),
and Arianrhod's son Dylan is a sea god. And although Arianrhod does not punish wrong-
doers, she does curse her son three times (he of course can be seen as a substitute for
whoever it was who made her pregnant). If Arianrhod was originally Aranrot, then "enormous wheel" or "round wheel" might refer to the sun, just as Sulis ("Eye") is indirectly
linked to the sun.

St. Ninian of Whithorn (Dumfries and Galloway)

The last known Northumbrian bishop of Whithorn was Beadwulf (790–803). In the
late 9th century Northumbria became the Danish Kingdom of York, and around the same
time Galloway was settled by Vikings. There is evidence for Viking settlement at Whithorn, including carved crosses of the "Whithorn school." The new ruling class buried
their dead beside the old shrine of St. Ninian. Among the carved stones found here there
were at least 20 small crosses, used as headstones for graves dating from the Viking
period. Archaeological excavations in 1984 revealed a range of evidence from this period,
including a stake-built house similar to those found in Viking York and Dublin. This
was interpreted as part of a secular settlement on the edge of the monastic precinct.
Excavations also revealed extraordinary levels of craft working, with Whithorn as part
of a vigorous trade network. The Viking rule of Galloway seems to have come to an
end around 1100. By the 1120s Galloway dues were being paid to the Scottish king, Alexander I.[38]

In the middle of the 12th century, during the reign of King David I of Scotland
(1124–1153), Fergus, Lord of Galloway (d. 1161) founded a priory at Whithorn for a community of Premonstratensian canons. Whithorn became a place of pilgrimage, and the
most famous early pilgrim was King Robert the Bruce (1306–1329). In March and April
1329, crippled by the illness which killed him (possibly leprosy), he traveled around Galloway until he reached Whithorn in early April. On his journey he visited a number of
healing wells. He is recorded at being at Kirkmaiden, in the Rinns of Galloway, which
diverts from a direct route from the north to Whithorn. He is said to have visited Munt-
loch Well on Kilbuie Moss, where an abundance of water would heal the sick, but dryness
would indicate no hope. St. Medan's well, which is probably one of three wells marked
near St. Medana's cave, was also said to have healing powers attached to it and would
have been within visiting distance of Bruce on his journey.[39]

James IV of Scotland (1488–1513) was also a regular visitor to Whithorn. He began
his association with the shrine early, as in 1473 his mother, Queen Margaret and his
father, James III, made a thanksgiving pilgrimage to the shrine for the safe delivery of
their son. James IV's first pilgrimage recorded in the Treasurer's Accounts occurred in
1491 and annual pilgrimages became a frequent part of the life of the royal court. These
were split between Whithorn, usually in the summer, and the shrine of St. Duthac at

Tain in the north, which took place in the autumn. The *Treasurer Accounts* indicate much hunting and hawking occurred along the way. Payments along the way on these pilgrimages were made in the form of alms, or to those who entertained and provided help or accommodation for the royal pilgrims.[40]

St. Kentigern of Glasgow

Glasgow seems to have been founded in the 12th century, but before that there was an early kingdom near Glasgow known as *Alt Clut* ("Clyde Rock"), or Strathclyde. *Alt Clut*, now known as Dumbarton ("Fort of the Britons"), is on the River Clyde to the west of Glasgow and is mentioned by Bede in his *Ecclesiastical History*. In describing the western of the two arms of the sea which divided the Picts from the Britons—that is, the Firths of Forth and Clyde—Bede writes "there is up to the present a strongly defended political center of the Britons called Alcluith" (Book 1, Chapter 1). Elsewhere he calls it *urbs Alcluith* ("city of Alcluith") and explains that *Alcluith* "means Clyde Rock in their language" (i.e., that of the Britons; *Petra Cluit* in Latin) "because it is beside the river of that name" (Book 1, Chapter 12). Adomnan, in his *Life* of St. Columba, also mentions a "King Roderc, son of Tothal, who reigned on the Rock of Cluaith" (Clyde Rock). In 870 CE, the Annals of Ulster record that two kings of the Norsemen, Olaf and Ivar, besieged the citadel for four months, and ultimately destroyed and plundered it, and this is the last we hear of the name.[41]

After Dumbarton Rock was destroyed by the Norsemen in 870, the kingdom of Strathclyde apparently moved to Govan, now a district in the southwest of Glasgow. New archaeological discoveries in and around Govan Old parish church now suggest that Govan—11 miles upstream from Dumbarton—was the principal royal center of Strathclyde during the period. A major administrative center seems to have been constructed around the church of St. Constantine, which housed a royal burial cult, perhaps dedicated to Constantine I (d. 877), the son of the Pictish king Kenneth MacAlpin. Close to the church was an assembly place (an artificial mound known as the Doomster Hill), while across the Clyde was a royal residence at Partick.

The church at Govan is not old, but it houses a remarkable collection of 31 early medieval sculpted stones, mostly dating to the 10th or 11th century. They are all carved in a British style, which has affinities with Pictish, Scottish and Anglo-Norse traditions. Among the collection are several monumental crosses and a unique monolithic "sarcophagus" which presumably served as a reliquary. But most important are the grave stones 5 hog-backs and 21 recumbent slabs with interlace crosses. These elaborately treated monuments probably marked burials of the Strathclyde royal house.[42]

In the 12th century, the kingdom of Strathclyde was incorporated into Scotland, and the ecclesiastical focus switched to Glasgow, with the building of the first Glasgow Cathedral in the 12th century. The patron saint of the new cathedral was St. Kentigern, also known as St. Mungo. He supposedly lived in the 6th century and is known to us through the *Life* of the saint, written around 1185 by Jocelin of Furness, and based on an earlier *Fragmentary Life*. There is only one early reference to Kentigern. A clerk of St. David's in southwest Wales, in compiling the earliest version of the *Annales Cambriae* ("Annals of Wales"), composed an entry for the year 612 or 613 that records the "Death of Conthigirn and Bishop Dyfrig."[43] This entry was probably written in the last decade of the

8th century, nearly 200 years after the deaths of Conthigirn and Dyfrig. The *Annales Cambriae* is mainly concerned with events relating to saints, bishops and kings, and since there is no record of a king called Conthigirn, we must assume he was a bishop or saint.

Clearly Kentigern's biographer knew very little about the actual Kentigern and came up with some fantastical details about the saint. According to the *Fragmentary Life*, Ewen, son of Queen Erwegende and King Ulien (in other words, Owain son of Urien Rheged), seduced Thaney, daughter of King Leudonus of Leudonia (Lothian). Ewen courted Thaney, but she refused to marry him. In punishment, her father made her work as a swineherd's servant. Ewen sent a female intermediary to persuade Thaney to love him, but when persuasion did not achieve his ends, he disguised himself as a girl and approached Thaney near a fountain. He tricked her into accompanying him to an isolated place, where he raped her. Thaney then conceived the son who would become St. Kentigern. In punishment for her pregnancy, her father had her thrown from a mountaintop, but she miraculously survived.[44]

The *Life* of Kentigern also contains a reference to a certain Lailoken, who may have been the inspiration for Merlin in Geoffrey of Monmouth's 12th century *History of the Kings of Britain* and *Life of Merlin*[45]:

> In the same year that Saint Kentigern was released from the affairs of men and departed into heaven, King Rederech, who has been named often, stayed for a longer time than usual in a royal village which is called Pertnech. A certain foolish man, who was called Laleocen, lived at his court, and he received his necessary sustenance and garments from the bountifulness of the king. For it is customary for the chief men of the earth and for sons of kings to be given to vain things and to retain with them men of the sort who are able to excite these lords and their households to jests and loud laughter by foolish words and gestures. But after the burial of Saint Kentigern, this man was himself afflicted with the most severe mourning, and he would not receive any comfort from anyone.
>
> When they sought why he grieved so inconsolably, he answered that his lord King Rederech and another of the first men of the land, named Morthec, would not be long in this life after the death of the holy bishop, but that they would succumb to fate in that present year and die. The deaths of those whom he mentioned that followed in that year clearly proved that the words of the fool were not spoken foolishly, but rather they were spoken prophetically.

King Rederech is Rhydderch Hael, king of Alt Clut (580–614) and Pertnech is Partick, an area of Glasgow on the north bank of the Clyde.

The cult of St. Kentigern was promoted by Jocelin, Bishop of Glasgow (1174–1199). Jocelin's most notable success was the development of a close relationship between the saint and the royal house. For William I (1165–1214), Kentigern was a personal intercessor second only to his commitment to Thomas Becket, to whom his new foundation at Arbroath was dedicated. Although it has been suggested that royal interest in the saint began to wane after William's death, Alexander II and III continued to be major patrons of Glasgow Cathedral throughout the 13th century. In a poignant act, Alexander III founded an altar dedicated to St. Kentigern in the nave of the cathedral in 1284, for the souls of his ancestors and family, including his recently deceased sons and daughter.[46]

High-status interest in the cult fluctuated during the following centuries, but there was an unbroken strand of popular support for Kentigern within the diocese of Glasgow throughout the period. Kentigern/Mungo was an increasingly common forename across southern Scotland in the late 15th and 16th centuries, appearing within urban groups and in the families of minor nobles.[47]

Kentigern was popularly known as Mungo ("My Dear One") and is referred to by both names in literary texts. In 1379 the English chronicler Thomas Walsingham, a monk in St. Albans Abbey, described Scottish raiders as praying to "God and St. Kentigern."[48] The Scottish poet David Lindsay (1490–1555), in a poem written in 1530, describes a funeral with Dominican Friars singing "St Mungo's matins" around the grave; and in another poem dating from 1550, the poet scorns people who "bring mad men, on foot and horse / And bring them to St. Mungo's cross."[49]

St. Æbbe of Coldingham (Berwickshire)

In the Northumbrian period St. Æbbe's monastery was at St. Abbs Head, but in 1098 King Edgar of Scotland asked the Benedictines at Durham to establish a foundation at Coldingham, on a site a little inland from the earlier monastery. By 1100 what is referred to as *The Old Church* had been built, covering much of the area of the church that stands today, though rather narrower than it. By 1147 this had developed into a priory under the authority of Durham. In 1216 Coldingham Priory was destroyed by King John of England. It was quickly rebuilt on a very much grander scale, incorporating a huge priory church.[50]

Coldingham Priory housed the shrine of St. Æbbe, but for the majority of pilgrims eager to solicit Æbbe's help their goal was not the saint's reliquary, which stood on the altar of the priory church, nor her tomb also located in the church, but a tiny oratory perched on top of the nearby headland overlooking the sea. It was here that Æbbe would invariably appear and heal those keeping nocturnal vigil.[51] A particular route was prescribed for the journey to the oratory. Six of the miracles depict pilgrims drinking and washing in a spring at the foot of the hill upon which the oratory stood (known today as Kirk Hill). They would typically visit the spring and then visit the oratory. One miracle recounts the story of a young girl who had lost her voice during a demonic attack[52]:

> Coming to the fountain which the local people call the fountain of the blessed Æbbe, she washed her mouth and face. Immediately it seemed that the blessed Æbbe placed a finger in her mouth and straightaway the bond of her tongue was loosed.... Coming at once to the oratory of the blessed Æbbe, she spent the night there in vigils and prayers.

Our Lady of Whitekirk (East Lothian)

In the 12th century Whitekirk church was simply a parish church dedicated to the Virgin Mary, but by 1300 miracles of healing were being performed at a nearby well and the church was eventually placed under the protection of James I (Canmore, *Parish Church, Whitekirk*). The number of miracles performed at this well was so great that in 1309 John Aberndley procured a shrine to be erected and dedicated to the Holy Mother. The well was about 242 yards northeast of the church; it was formerly held in great repute for the cure of barrenness, but has since dried up.[53] In 1413 the well received 15,653 visitors and offerings totaled 1,423 merks, or about 948 Scottish pounds.[54] Hostels for the accommodation of the large number of pilgrims visiting Our Lady's Well were built at Whitekirk by James I around 1430.[55] James IV (1488–1513) was a frequent visitor to Whitekirk—we read of him that "while profuse in his offerings generally there were certain shrines he never passed by unremembered when he happened to be in their neighbourhood—such was St. Mary of Hamer or Whitekirk." James IV was killed in the Battle of Flodden, fought against an English army in 1513 and Whitekirk suffered an eclipse. In 1537 James V gave his favorite Oliver Sinclair permission to pull down the pilgrims' houses and use the stones to build a house for himself.[56]

St. Margaret of Dunfermline (Fife)

Margaret was a member of the old dynasty of Wessex and England. She was the daughter of Edward Atheling and granddaughter of Edmund Ironside, who was briefly king in 1016 before being defeated by the Danish king Cnut, who ruled England from 1016 until 1035. After Edmund Ironside's death in 1016, Edward Atheling went into exile in Hungary, where he married and had three children, Margaret, Christine and Edgar. Edward Atheling returned to England in 1057 but died within two days of his arrival. Margaret and her siblings were then brought up by the king, Edward the Confessor. After the death of Harold at the Battle of Hastings, Margaret's young brother, Edgar Atheling, was acknowledged as king by many leading English prelates and nobles, but he was never crowned and soon submitted to the Norman conqueror, William I.

Edgar, along with his mother and sisters, fled to Scotland, where they were welcomed by Malcolm III "Canmore," who married Margaret in about 1070. Margaret founded a monastery at Dunfermline in Fife, the place where she had married Malcolm. It is probable that this was initially a daughter house of Canterbury, with Benedictine monks sent from England, but was raised to the status of an independent abbey in 1128. Margaret was herself buried in the church, which served henceforth as a mausoleum of the Scottish kings. The body of her husband, Malcolm Canmore was brought back from England, where he had been killed, to lie near his queen, while her sons Edgar, Alexander, and David I, were interred there, as was David's successor Malcolm IV.

In 1180 the monks of Dunfermline resolved "that they should move the tomb of St Margaret the queen from the place in which it was situated." They employed a skilled artist, named Ralph, to construct a reliquary; "To increase devotion to her, they had already employed an artist (*pictor*) called Ralph, a man of great reputation and most renowned as a creator of carvings. He prepared a reliquary (*theca*) for the blessed queen, covered with gold leaf and with carved images, as can still be seen from the object itself...." During the translation ceremony the monks lay prostrate in the choir, reciting the seven penitential psalms and the litany. Eventually the relics were re-enshrined "on the north side of the altar," elevated on a stone slab covered with a splendid cloth. It is known that at some point, possibly during the translation of 1250, Margaret's head was separated and enshrined in its own reliquary. The head shrine consisted of a gilded head-shaped case, which could be opened to reveal the partially pressed head of the saint.[57]

An account of Margaret's miracles was written in the 13th century, perhaps in advance of her canonization in 1249. One of Margaret's miracles concerns a girl possessed by a demon. A young girl and her mother are out one day when they hear the complaint of a young child. The mother orders the girl to find the child, but the girl objects. Finally, she is overruled:

> She ran quickly to the place where the voice had been heard and, while her mother watched, she lifted up a boy who was just like her brother, who had died a little time before. He said to her, "Sister, give me a kiss." She refused, saying "I know that you are my brother, but because you have gone the way

The ruined refectory of Dunfermline Abbey, founded by St. Margaret. October 14, 2011 (Kim Traynor, CCA-Share Alike 3.0 Unported).

of all flesh, I am not allowed to kiss you." As they argued, he grabbed the girl's throat with his left hand and pushed her between the shoulders with his right, knocking her down and then leaving ...

When he mother perceived all this, the bowels of maternal compassion were moved within her for her daughter, she was almost out of her mind with pain within and great anxiety, and she ran to her weeping and wailing, and found her possessed by a demon, prostrate on the ground and close to death, lacking speech or sensation. The she began to grieve and to sorrow, tearing her hair, ripping her clothes and like a roaring lioness she called out in tears to her servant, "Come, my servants, come and see if there is sorrow like my sorrow."

After being taken home, the unfortunate girl cries out, "I see the house full of men and women, boys and girls," adding "Behold how beautiful that queen is, how fair of face, how lovely in appearance, how sweet the song of those leading the choir." In desperation the parents take her to Dunfermline and place her "before the altar of St Margaret, the queen." The next day Margaret appears to the girl in a dream and instructs her to go to her tomb ("the place where my bones rested"). Once at the tomb, Margaret again appears to the girl in a dream, "taking her head in her hands and placing a finger in her throat, then, as she withdrew her finger, the girl said, 'Most holy mother, I give you deep thanks for the mercy you have shown me. I feel that I have recovered my senses and the power of speech. If you would be willing to touch the place where I was struck by the demon, I know that I would be completely restored to heath.'" Margaret, of course, heals the girl, who then expresses her gratitude by becoming a nun.[58]

St. Andrew of St. Andrews (Fife)

St. Andrew is the patron saint of Scotland, and his cult was probably introduced into Scotland by way of the kingdom of Northumbria. Andrew is mentioned in the gospels of Matthew, Mark and Luke as one of the twelve apostles, and is singled out as a fisherman in Matthew 4.18–20 (King James Version): "And Jesus, walking by the sea of Galilee, saw two brethren, Simon called Peter, and Andrew his brother, casting a net into the sea: for they were fishers. And he saith unto them, Follow me, and I will make you fishers of men. And they straightway left their nets, and followed him."

In the Gospel of John, Andrew plays a more important role. In this passage from the Gospel of John, John the Baptist announces in the presence of Andrew that Jesus is the Messiah (John 1:34–42):

> And I saw, and bare record that this is the Son of God. Again the next day after John stood, and two of his disciples; And looking upon Jesus as he walked, he saith, Behold the Lamb of God! And the two disciples heard him speak, and they followed Jesus. Then Jesus turned, and saw them following, and saith unto them, What seek ye? They said unto him, Rabbi, (which is to say, being interpreted, Master,) where dwellest thou? He saith unto them, Come and see. They came and saw where he dwelt, and abode with him that day: for it was about the tenth hour. One of the two which heard John speak, and followed him, was Andrew, Simon Peter's brother. He first findeth his own brother Simon, and saith unto him, We have found the Messiah, which is, being interpreted, the Christ. And he brought him to Jesus.

As a result, Andrew was claimed to be the first apostle of Jesus, and when the Roman Emperor Constantine in 330 CE established his new capital, Constantinople (now Istanbul), the relics of St. Andrew were transferred from Patras in Greece to the church of the Holy Apostles in Constantinople.

In 597 CE St. Augustine was sent by Pope Gregory the Great to convert the Anglo-Saxons of Kent to Christianity. Before he was dispatched to England, Augustine was prior of the monastery of St. Andrew in Rome, and one of the churches he built, at Rochester in Kent, was dedicated to St. Andrew. In 674 Wilfrid established a monastic church at Hexham in Northumbria dedicated to St. Andrew. The cult of St. Andrew probably reached Kinrymont (St. Andrews) on the east coast of Fife some time in the 8th or 9th century. The Irish Annals of Tigernach record the death in 747 of the abbot Tuathalan of *Cennrigmonaid* (Kinrymont).[59]

There are no remains of the early church, but in 1833, during the digging of a grave in the cemetery of the ruined St. Andrews Cathedral, several pieces of sculptured stone were unearthed. It soon became clear that these were the broken remains of what had once been an ancient coffin or sarcophagus. Only one of the long side-panels, three of the four cornerstones and one end-panel are complete. One of the figures on the side-panel represents the Israelite king David. He is killing a lion by pulling its jaws apart, a motif seen also in Irish and Anglo-Saxon sculpture. Another figure represents a mounted huntsman accompanied by hounds. He is tackling a ferocious beast that rears up at him on its hind legs. Below him is a man on foot armed with a spear and shield. Stags and other animals fill the remaining space on the panel. The monument is thought to have been carved between 750 and 850.[60] In addition, more than fifty fragments of small 8/9th century cross-slabs were found in excavating the foundations of the ruined church of St. Mary of the Rock.

St. Andrews Cathedral was built in 1158 and became the seat of the Archdiocese of

St. Andrews and the bishops and archbishops of St. Andrews, as well as the home to a priory of Augustinian canons. It fell into disuse and ruin after the Reformation in the 16th century. The ruins indicate that the building was approximately 391 feet long, which means it was the largest church to have been built in Scotland. The origins of the cult of St. Andrew were all but forgotten, and by the later Middle Ages it was claimed that a 4th century Greek monk called Regulus or Rule had been instructed in a vision to bring the relics of St. Andrew to Scotland. There he was welcomed by the Pictish king Oengus I (732–761). The story is fantastical, but it is possible that the cult of St. Andrew did begin in the 8th century when Oengus I was king.

St. Duthac of Tain (Ross-shire)

Duthac is thought to have been born in Tain in Ross-shire, in the Scottish Highlands, in about 1000 CE. He was educated in Ireland and went on to become a renowned preacher who attracted a considerable following. He was regarded as sufficiently important for his death to be reported in *The Annals of Ulster* for the year 1065. Tales of miracles soon grew up around the memory of Duthac. One story related how as a boy he had been sent to collect hot coals from the local smithy. The smith simply placed the hot coals in Duthac's lap, whereupon the boy carried them to his master without ill effect.

The ruins of the nave of St. Andrews Cathedral, the largest church built in Scotland. February 3, 2008 (Oliver Keenan, CCA 3.0).

In June 1253 St. Duthac's remains, said to have been uncorrupted by the passage of two centuries since his death, were returned to Tain and buried in the original St. Duthac's Chapel, built on the site of his birth. Its ruins lie on the north east side of the town, in the old town cemetery and near the golf club. This first chapel rapidly became a place of pilgrimage and of sanctuary. Robert the Bruce's family took shelter here en route to Orkney during his exile, but the Earl of Ross took them prisoner anyway, and handed them over to the English in 1307.

This idea of sanctuary also led to the chapel's destruction, in 1427. A local outlaw had pursued an enemy into the chapel and overcame the technicality of sanctuary by burning it down. St. Duthac's relics were then transferred to St. Duthac's Collegiate Church, in the center of Tain This had been built in 1360 on the site of an earlier church, part of which still remains in the churchyard. King James IV, when he was not visiting Whithorn, made at least 18 pilgrimages to the shrine of St. Duthac between 1493 and 1513.[61]

Duthac was an important regional saint, and a series of secular lordships had bolstered their hold in Ross by linking their power with St. Duthac's cult, his relics, and his shrine at Tain. In the 14th century the earls of Ross had ridden out to war wearing what was reputed to be St. Duthac's shirt. For most of the 15th century, control of the earldom of Ross was a matter of political dispute between the royal dynasty and the MacDonald lordship of the Isles. One element in the struggle for the support of the local communities was the Stewart monarch's veneration for St. Duthac, which goes some way to explaining James IV's regular pilgrimages to Tain.[62]

St. Magnus of Orkney

Magnus Erlendsson was the Norwegian Earl of Orkney from about 1108 to 1115. He was supposedly killed, on the orders of his cousin Hakon Palsson, by a blow to the head. This happened in the Easter period on the island of Egilsay, on April 16, possibly in 1115. A damaged skull, found with other bones on the south side of the choir of Kirkwall Cathedral in 1919, has been taken to be that of Magnus, its patron saint.[63]

The Old Norse *Orkneyinga Saga*, or *History of the Earls of Orkney*, composed around 1200 and revised around 1230, gives an account of the death of Magnus[64]:

> When God's friend was led to the blow, he said to Lifolf, "Stand in front of me, and strike me a great wound on the head, because it is not fitting to cut down chieftains like thieves..." ... After that he crossed himself, and bent under the blow, and his spirit passed to heaven.

The *Orkneyinga Saga* recounts that the site of Magnus' murder was originally rocky and overgrown, but after his death "God showed that he had suffered for righteousness' sake" and the area was miraculously transformed into a green field. Magnus' corpse was transferred to Birsay, possibly to the site of the present St. Magnus Kirk. From the day of his burial a bright, heavenly light was said to have been seen above Magnus' grave. This holy light was accompanied by a "heavenly fragrance." Before long, as the cult of Magnus grew, other stories began to spread, each detailing the miraculous happenings around about the Earl's gravesite. For example, a man called Thorkell who lived in Orkney "fell from his barley-rick right down to the ground and was maimed all down one side. He was taken to the shrine of the blessed earl Magnus and recovered his health there."[65]

Initially, the Bishop of Orkney, William the Old (d. 1168), tried to suppress the growing cult of Magnus, dismissing the alleged miracles and warning that it was "heresy to go about with such tales." But then, in an episode described in the *Orkneyinga Saga*, Bishop William was suddenly convinced of Magnus' holiness after being struck blind in his Birsay cathedral. Falling upon Magnus' grave, and praying, the bishop's sight was miraculously restored. Bishop William had Magnus' remains exhumed, washed and tested in consecrated fire. Their holiness confirmed, Magnus was proclaimed a saint and his remains enshrined above the Birsay kirk's altar. The relics stayed in Birsay "for a long time" until Magnus supposedly appeared to a Westray man, Gunni, in a dream. Magnus told Gunni that Bishop William should be told that Magnus wished to leave Birsay and move east to the growing town of Kirkwall on Orkney Mainland.[66]

The Saints of Papa Westray (Orkney Islands)

Papa Westray, also called Papay, is one of the most northern of the Orkney Islands, and its name links it to priests (*papar* means "priests, monks" in Old Norse, the language spoken by the Norwegians who settled in Orkney in the 9th century). There are two main ecclesiastical sites on Papay, St. Boniface's and St. Tredwell's, and both saints were traditionally members of the Northumbrian mission to Pictland in the 8th century. Boniface (also known as Curetan) is said to have been bishop of Rosemarkie from 690 to 710. He was one of the witnesses at the Synod of Birr in 697 which promulgated Adomnan's *Law of Innocents* protecting women and non-combatants in time of war. He is commemorated in the martyrologies of *Tallaght* (10th century) and *O'Gorman* (12th century). The legend or *Life* of Curetan is found under the name of Boniface in the early 16th century Breviary of Aberdeen. His festival is given as March 16 (the same day as for Curetan in the early martyrologies), and he is portrayed as a contemporary of Nechtan. Boniface is said to have been of Hebrew origin, descended from the sisters of Saints Peter and Andrew, and to have been ordained priest by the Patriarch of Jerusalem.[67]

According to the Aberdeen Breviary, Tredwell or Triduana also had eastern Mediterranean origins. She was born in the Greek city of Colosse, in what is now western Turkey, and traveled from Constantinople with St. Rule, who supposedly brought the bones of St. Andrew to Scotland in the 4th century. She settled at Rescobie near Forfar in Angus, but her beauty attracted the attentions of Nechtan, king of the Picts. To discourage these attentions, Triduana tore out her own eyes and gave them to Nechtan. Afterwards, she was associated with curing eye disorders. In the 12th century the Norse Earl of Orkney Harald Maddadsson punished bishop John of Caithness by having him blinded. According to the 13th century *Orkneyinga Saga*, John prayed to "Trøllhaena" (Tredwell), and later regained his sight when brought to her "resting place," possibly referring to St. Tredwell's on Papay.[68]

The 12th century church of St. Boniface lies close to an extensive Iron Age settlement, with a small stone-lined grave containing the skull and fragments of long bones, probably of a child, and a possible broch (a type of drystone roundhouse), which incorporated the grave into its south wall. In the 1920s a cross slab dating to around 700 CE was found in the graveyard of the church. The incised, compass-drawn cross, formed from interlacing segments of circles, set within a circle, recalls the St. Peter stone at Whithorn.[69] The St. Peter's stone at Whithorn bears an inscription LOCI PETRI APOSTOLI, "the *locus* (place) of the Apostle Peter," written in a style belonging to Merovingian Gaul. A *locus* is a place dedicated in honor of a saint, and the cross was originally found by the roadside.

The chapel of St. Tredwell also dates to the 12th century and was one of the most renowned pilgrimage centers of Orkney. Brand's statement that votive offerings of coins were still being made in the late 17th century was confirmed by Traill's excavation of 1880, when thirty coins, ranging from Charles II to George III, were found on the chapel floor. The chapel occupies a mound which could contain the remains of a broch, and a souterrain, possibly part of a post-broch settlement. The mound was dug into in 1883 by Traill who found a curved underground passage which apparently was traced to the point where it entered a circular building. There was a door to a corbelled cell in the right wall of this passage just before that point and a pair of door-checks immediately before this cell. A heap of charred grain was found in the passage, together with an iron spear-head and a ball of serpentine (a type of rock). A bone die from the site is in the collections of the Museum of Scotland, as is a bone playing disc and a bone ring. On the southwest side of the mound, a 38-foot length of curved and battered dry stone wall is exposed; it has a maximum height of 6 feet but its curvature is irregular and it could be part of the outer wall of a broch.[70]

Up until the early years of the 19th century, the people of Orkney regarded the waters of St. Tredwell's Loch in Papay as medicinal. As a result, the loch, and the 12th century St. Tredwell's Chapel, built on what was once an island but is now a peninsula, was one of Orkney's most visited pilgrimage sites. In 1700, in his *A Brief Description of Orkney, Zetland, Pightland Firth and Caithness*, the Rev. John Brand wrote that those seeking a cure would walk around the loch in complete silence—to talk to anyone, he noted, would prevent the cure from working. The circuits done, the "afflicted" would enter the water, or bathe the afflicted body part, making sure to leave an offering—usually a rag, piece of cloth, or money.[71]

Paganism in Late Medieval Christianity

The Anglo-Saxons converted to Christianity in the 7th century, although the Vikings briefly reintroduced paganism to England in the late 9th century. By the late Middle Ages, paganism was a very distant memory but, despite this, practices persisted in Christianity which can be linked to earlier pagan religious beliefs.

11

Pagan Magic in Late Medieval Christianity

St. Patrick's Purgatory

We are all familiar with the idea of Heaven and Hell, but Purgatory is less familiar to those of us who come from a Protestant background. The notion of Purgatory as a specific place did not emerge until the 13th century, with Pope Innocent IV (1243–1254), and the Second Council of Lyon (1274), but the idea had been around for much longer. The doctrine of Purgatory is based on *2 Maccabees* 12:42–45 (New Revised Standard Version Catholic Edition), which is recognized by Catholic and Orthodox churches, but not by Protestants:

> and they turned to supplication, praying that the sin that had been committed might be wholly blotted out. The noble Judas exhorted the people to keep themselves free from sin, for they had seen with their own eyes what had happened as the result of the sin of those who had fallen. He also took up a collection, man by man, to the amount of two thousand drachmas of silver, and sent it to Jerusalem to provide for a sin offering. In doing this he acted very well and honorably, taking account of the resurrection. For if he were not expecting that those who had fallen would rise again, it would have been superfluous and foolish to pray for the dead. But if he was looking to the splendid reward that is laid up for those who fall asleep in godliness, it was a holy and pious thought. Therefore he made atonement for the dead, so that they might be delivered from their sin.

St. Augustine of Hippo, writing in the early 5th century, said, in *The City of God*, that "temporary punishments are suffered by some in this life only, by others after death, by others both now and then; but all of them before that last and strictest judgment."[1] Pope Gregory the Great, writing in the late 6th century, said in his *Dialogues*[2]:

> we must believe that before the day of judgment there is a Purgatory fire for certain small sins: because our Saviour saith, that he which speaketh blasphemy against the holy Ghost, that it shall not be forgiven him, neither in this world, nor in the world to come. Out of which sentence we learn, that some sins are forgiven in this world, and some other may be pardoned in the next.

Bede, in his *Ecclesiastical History*, presents two visions of the Afterlife which include descriptions of Purgatory, but I'll just look at one of these visions, experienced by Fursey, an Irish monk who established a monastery at Burgh Castle in Norfolk, some time around 630. After establishing the monastery, says Bede,[3] he fell sick:

> he fell into a trance, and quitting his body from the evening till the cock crew, he was found worthy to behold the choirs of angels, and to hear the praises which are sung in heaven. He was wont to

declare, that among other things he distinctly heard this: "The saints shall advance from one virtue to another." And again, "The God of gods shall be seen in Sion." Being restored to his body at that time, and again taken from it three days after, he not only saw the greater joys of the blessed, but also extraordinary combats of evil spirits, who by frequent accusations wickedly endeavored to obstruct his journey to heaven; but the angels protecting him, all their endeavors were in vain.

Bede then elaborates on one of the visions that Fursey had when he was "lifted up on high":

he was ordered by the angels that conducted him to look back upon the world. Upon which, casting his eyes downward, he saw, as it were, a dark and obscure valley underneath him. He also saw four fires in the air, not far distant from each other. Then asking the angels, what fires those were? he was told, they were the fires which would kindle and consume the world. One of them was of falsehood, when we do not fulfil that which we promised in baptism, to renounce the Devil and all his works. The next of covetousness, when we prefer the riches of the world to the love of heavenly things. The third of discord, when we make no difficulty to offend the minds of out neighbors even in needless things. The fourth of iniquity, when we look upon it as no crime to rob and to defraud the weak. These fires, increasing by degrees, extended so as to meet one another, and being joined, became an immense flame. When it drew near, fearing for himself, he said to the angel, "Lord, behold the fire draws near me." The angel answered, "That which you did not kindle shall not burn you; for though this appears to be a terrible and great fire, yet it tries every man according to the merits of his works; for every man's concupiscence shall burn in the fire; for as every one burns in the body through unlawful pleasure, so when discharged of the body, he shall burn in the punishment which he has deserved."

Then he saw one of the three angels, who had been his conductors throughout both visions, go before and divide the flame of fire, whilst the other two, flying about on both sides, defended him from the danger of that fire. He also saw devils flying through the fire, raising conflagrations of wars against the just. Then followed accusations of the wicked spirits against him, the defense of the good angels in his favor, and a more extended view of the heavenly troops; as also of holy men of his own nation, who, as he had long since been informed, had been deservedly advanced to the degree of priesthood, from whom he heard many things that might be very salutary to himself, or to all others that would listen to them. When they had ended their discourse, and returned to heaven with the angelic spirits, the three angels remained with the blessed Fursey, of whom we have spoken before, and who were to bring him back to his body. And when they approached the aforesaid immense fire, the angel divided the flame, as he had done before; but when the man of God came to the passage so opened amidst the flames, the unclean spirits, laying hold of one of those whom they tormented in the fire, threw him at [Fursey], and, touching his shoulder and jaw, burned them. He knew the man, and called to mind that he had received his garment when he died; and the angel, immediately laying hold, threw him back into the fire, and the malignant enemy said, "Do not reject him whom you before received; for as you accepted the goods of him who was a sinner, so you must partake of his punishment." The angel replying, said, "He did not receive the same through avarice, but in order to save his soul." The fire ceased, and the angel, turning to him, added, "That which you kindled burned in you; for had you not received the money of this person that died in his sins, his punishment would not burn in you." And proceeding in his discourse, he gave him wholesome advice for what ought to be done towards the salvation of such as repented.

Being afterwards restored to his body, throughout the whole course of his life [Fursey] bore the mark of the fire which he had felt in his soul, visible to all men on his shoulder and jaw; and the flesh publicly showed, in a wonderful manner, what the soul had suffered in private.

The four fires kindled by falsehood, covetousness, discord and iniquity are presumably the "purifying fires" mentioned by St. Augustine of Hippo.

While the torments of the Anglo-Saxon Purgatory were real enough, its geography remained somewhat hazy. However, by the 12th century it had become a very real place which anyone could visit, called St. Patrick's Purgatory. The *Tractatus de Purgatorio Sancti Patricii* ("Treatise on St. Patrick's Purgatory") was written in 1180–84 by a monk who identifies himself as Henry de Saltrey, from the Cistercian abbey at Sawtry in Cambridge-shire, not far from Ramsey Abbey. The *Tractatus* relates the journey of an Irish knight Owein to St. Patrick's Purgatory, where he journeys through Purgatory and the Earthly Paradise. Among the most famous versions of the *Tractatus* are the late 12th century *Legend of the Purgatory of St. Patrick*, written in French by Marie de France, and a Middle English version from the 14th century preserved in the Auchinleck manuscript in the National Library of Scotland. The Middle English version begins with a vision experienced by St. Patrick[4]:

Saint Patrick felt such pity for the Irish folk, who lived in deadly sin and false belief, that he constantly besought them to turn to God and obey His law, but they were so full of wickedness that they scorned every word he spoke. They all said that they would not repent nor cease from evil unless he would undertake the adventure of going down into hell to bring them back tidings of the pain and woe which souls suffer there evermore. The saint was sorely dismayed upon hearing this, and, often, with fasting and prayer, he begged Jesus Christ to grant him the grace to find a way by which he might bring the people of Ireland out of bondage to the fiend, and lead them to believe in God Omnipotent.

Once, while he was in holy church, praying thus, he fell asleep before the altar, and began to dream of heaven's bliss; he thought that Jesus came to him and gave him a book such as no clerk can ever write, telling all manner of good tidings of heaven and earth and hell, and of God's mystery. Into his hand God put a fair staff, which to this day is called, in Ireland, God's staff. And God led him straight-way thence into a great desert where was a secret opening, grisly to see. Round it was, and black; in all the world it has no mate. When Saint Patrick saw that sight he was greatly troubled in his sleep, but God revealed to him that if a man who had sinned against the holy law and yet truly repented should do penance in this hole, a day and a night, his sins would be forgiven him. If the man were of good faith, steadfast in belief, he should see the strong pains of those who have sinned in this world, but should not suffer himself, and finally, he should behold the joy that lasts for aye in paradise. Then Jesus withdrew his gracious countenance and left Patrick there alone.

When the saint awoke he found God's tokens, and, taking them in his hand, he knelt to thank Jesus Christ for revealing to him how he might turn the Irish folk to amendment. On that spot, without delay, he had a fair abbey built, in the name of God and of our Lady. The abbey had no equal anywhere; solace and glee and rejoicing abounded for poor and for rich. White canons regular were placed there to serve God early and late and to be holy men. The book and the staff God gave him men may still see. In the east end of the abbey is that grisly hole, with a good stone wall all around it, and a gate with lock and key. That very spot is called the right entrance to Patrick's Purgatory, for in the times when this happened many a man went down to hell, as the story tells us, and suffered pain for his trespasses, and then returned again, through God's grace.

There is no indication where St. Patrick's Purgatory is, but Gerald of Wales, in his *Topography of Ireland* (published in 1188), is more specific[5]:

There is a lake in Ulster containing an island divided into two parts. In one of these stands a church of especial sanctity, and it is most agreeable and delightful, as well as beyond measure glorious for the visitations of angels and the multitude of the saints who visibly frequent it. The other part, being cov-ered with rugged crags, is reported to be the resort of devils only, and to be almost always the theatre on which crowds of evil spirits visibly perform their rites. This part of the island contains nine pits, and should any one perchance venture to spend the night in one of them (which has been done, we know, at times, by some rash men), he is immediately seized by the malignant spirits, who so severely torture him during the whole night, inflicting on him such unutterable sufferings by fire and water, and other torments of various kinds, that when morning comes scarcely any spark of life is found left in his wretched body. It is said that any one who has once submitted to these torments as a penance imposed upon him, will not afterwards undergo the pains of hell, unless he commit some sin of a deeper dye. This place is called by the natives the Purgatory of St. Patrick.

Gerald of Wales' "lake in Ulster" is Lough Derg in County Donegal, northwest Ireland, and most later accounts make it clear there was only one "cave," and that it was an artificial structure built of stone. It appears to have been around 15 feet long, 2 feet wide, and only 3 feet wide.[6]

The Middle English version mostly concerns the visit of a certain Owain to St. Patrick's Purgatory. According to the tale, he was a knight of Northumberland who lived in the days of King Stephen (1135–1154) and "was very sinful toward his Creator." In order to absolve himself of his sins, he decided to enter St. Patrick's Purgatory. In this extract, Owain has just been led to the cave entrance[7]:

Owain, left there in dread, began to lament and call upon God. Soon he heard a piteous cry; he could not have been more frightened if the heaven had fallen. When he had recovered from the fear caused by that cry, there came flocking in a crowd of fiends, fifty score or more, loathsome things altogether. Crowding around the knight they laughed him to scorn, saying that he had come in flesh and skin to win the joys of hell forever. The master fiend, falling upon his knees, said, "Welcome, Owain; thou art come to suffer penance for thy sins, but thou wilt get no benefit, for thou shalt have torments, hard and strong and tough enough because of thy deadly sins. Never hadst thou more mischance than thou shalt have in our dance when we begin our sport. However, if thou wilt do our bidding, since thou art dear to us, our whole company will bring thee back with tender love to the spot where thou didst leave the prior. If thou dost refuse, we shall prove to thee that thou hast served us many a year in pride and luxury, and all our company will thrust their hooks at thee." Owain answered, "I forsake your counsel, and will endure my penance." When the fiends heard this, they made a great fire in the hall,

St. Patrick's Purgatory. Chapel, bell tower and penitential beds on Station Island in Lough Derg, Ireland. The bell tower stand son a mound that is the site of the original cave. June 1, 2010 (Egardiner0, CCA-Share Alike 3.0 Unported).

and binding him fast, feet and hands, they cast him into the midst of it. He called upon our Lord, and at once the fire vanished; no coal nor spark was left, through the grace of God Almighty. As soon as the knight saw this he grew bolder, realizing that it was the treachery of the fiends to try his heart.

Owain then followed the "fiends" and witnessed people in torment:

Then the devils went out of the hall, leading the knight with them to a strange place, where nothing good entered, only hunger, thirst, and cold. He could see no tree, could hear no sound of wind, yet a cold blast blew that pierced his side. At last the fiends brought him to a valley where the knight thought he must have reached the deepest pit of hell. As he drew nearer, he looked about, for he heard screaming and groaning, and he saw a field full of men and women, each lying face downward, naked, and with deadly wounds. They lay prone on the earth, bound with iron bands, screaming and wailing, "Alas, alas, mercy, mercy, mercy, God Almighty!" Mercy there was none, but only sorrow of heart and grinding of teeth, which was a grisly sight. That sorrow and misery is punishment for the foul sin of sloth. Whosoever is slow in God's service may expect to lie in purgatory in such torment.

The punishments here were slight compared to some of the punishments that followed. Here is one example:

They then led him into a spot where men never did any good deeds, but only shameful and villainous ones. In the fourth field this was, full of torments. There were people hanging by the feet from burning iron hooks, others hung by the neck, the stomach, the back, and in other ways too numerous to mention. Some were hanging by the tongue, and their constant cry was "Alas!" and no other prayer. In a furnace with molten lead and burning brimstone boiling over the fire were many folk. Some lying on gridirons glowing against the flames were people whom Owain had once known, but who were now entirely changed through the penance they suffered. A wild fire surged among them, and all whom it seized, it burned, ten thousand souls and more. Those that hung by feet and neck were thieves, or the companions of thieves, and wrought men woe. Those that hung by the tongue and ever sang "Alas!" and cried so loudly were backbiters in their lives. Beware, man or wife, if thou art fond of chiding! All the places the knight came by were full of the pains of purgatory. Whosoever takes the name of God in vain, or bears any false witness, suffers strong pains there.

As mentioned previously, St. Patrick's Purgatory is in a cave on an island in Lough Derg and combines two places associated with the afterlife in prehistoric Britain. Caves were used for burial throughout the pagan period, including caves near Cheddar in Somerset, caves on Caldey Island off the coast of Pembrokeshire, the caves known as the Ryedale Windypits in North Yorkshire, and Sculptor's Cave on the Moray Firth in eastern Scotland. Water is also associated with burial—for example, the River Thames between London and Oxford, and the Cambridgeshire Fens. Victims of human sacrifice have also been found buried in peat bogs in Germanic lands, including the Netherlands (Yde Girl), Lower Saxony in Germany (Girl of the Uchter Moor), Schleswig-Holstein in Germany (Windeby I), the Jutland Peninsula in Demark (Tollund Man), and southwest Sweden (Bocksten Man).

The Cult of the Dead in Late Medieval England: Chantries and Charnel Chapels

The historian Eamon Duffy[8] speaks of a medieval "cult of the dead," which found its expression in many different ways, and was closely linked to the idea of Purgatory. Purgatory was place of punishment, but it was only temporary (though temporary might involve centuries or millennia!), and you could eventually hope to escape it through the prayers of the living. If you were wealthy, the best way to ensure that prayers were said for your soul after your death was to found a chantry chapel, that is, a chapel where masses were sung for souls in Purgatory, to speed their release from Purgatory and subsequent entry into Heaven (the word *chantry* is from Old French *chanterie*, "a mass sung for the dead"). Robert of Edwinstowe (Nottinghamshire), a chancery clerk of Edward III (1327–1377) said in the preamble to the foundation deed of the chantry which he established in his native town[9] :

> Amongst other means of restoring fallen humanity, the solemn celebration of Masses, in which for the well-being of the living and the repose of the departed, to God most High, the Father, His Son is offered, is to be judged highest in merit and of most power to draw down the mercy of God.

Only the wealthy could afford to found a chantry chapel, so the poor had to rely on other institutions. Charnel chapels are medieval ecclesiastical buildings, located within the confines of the cemetery of ecclesiastical complexes (including abbeys, cathedrals, hospitals, monasteries and parish churches). They were constructed in England from the early 13th century to the Reformation in the mid–16th century but the height of construction occurred in the 1300's. There are two forms of charnel chapel: free-standing, two-storied buildings and those built below churches. Both structural types primarily consist of a semi-subterranean vault or chamber for the purpose of storing disturbed and displaced bones from the surrounding graveyards. Free-standing examples had a chapel built directly on top of these partially underground chambers and in the majority of cases those charnel chapels built below churches were located under chapels within the church.[10]

Charnel chapels were not, as previously believed, merely storage locations for bones, but fulfilled a role similar to that of chantry chapels. Many of the charnel chapels were episcopal foundations, established by abbots and bishops. The foundation records state that these charnel chapels were built for the lay population of the associated community, seemingly in the same manner as private chantries were founded and served a particular family; charnel chapels appear to have been chantry chapels, for the "ordinary" people.

In the 1316 foundation charter for Norwich charnel chapel, it is stated that "in the Carnary beneath the said Chapel of St John we wish that human bones, completely stripped of flesh, be preserved seemly to the time of the general Resurrection." Given that blood was viewed as a contaminant to consecrated ground, the disturbance and disarticulation of a still fleshed corpse could have been tantamount to contamination of the graveyard. Even today in modern Catholic societies who practice charnelling, bones are generally not moved or brought above the earth until they are defleshed. The lack of evidence for disturbance prior to decomposition may reflect the medieval belief that a body may in some way retain an element of life while fleshed, that a soul may linger in the vicinity of its deceased body for up to a month, and the general acceptance that it took about a year for a body to fully decompose. It was decreed in 1299 by Pope Boniface VIII, that once bodies had returned to ash there was no objection to their being displaced from the grave or their being relocated.

Charnel chapels also clearly linked to confession, penance and prayer. The charnel chapel at Exeter Cathedral was built as a penance for murder, and it was dedicated to Edward the Confessor. It is recorded that one of the chantry priest's duty there was to help in hearing confession and imposing penances on parishioners.

In 1282 the Mayor of London and the commonality of the city paid for the "communal chantry" chapel to be built over the charnel chamber in the graveyard of St. Paul's

Cathedral. A chaplain was also to be maintained there who would pray for "all the faithful departed." In 1302 this chaplain was required to open the charnel house to pilgrims "who were to have access to the charnel house every Friday and on certain days, such as the Feast of the Dedication of the cathedral, three days after Whitsun, and the Feast of the Relics." By 1379 the charnel chapel was in need of repair and all those who contributed to restoring the charnel chapel were granted a "great pardon" by the Cathedral's archbishop. At Worcester the charnel chapel's priests' duties included daily masses for the dead. At Norwich, chaplains were also to pray for "all the dead in general; and in particular for the souls of all those whose bones were deposited in the vault of this charnel."

Rothwell Holy Trinity Church near Kettering in Northamptonshire houses one of only two known surviving and in situ medieval ossuaries in England. The ossuary is in the crypt near the south door and was discovered by chance in about 1700. The crypt has been reorganized so that the skulls are now displayed on shelves around the walls, and the thigh bones displayed in two large square piles in the center.

The other surviving ossuary is St. Leonard's Church in Hythe, Kent, which dates from about 1100. Hythe was one of the Cinque Ports (a confederation of five trading ports), at the height of her prosperity in the 12th and 13th centuries. At first the church had an unaisled Norman nave. This building, late in the 12th century, was given aisles and transepts. It was decided at some time not before about 1230 to rebuild the chancel longer and to have three stories of arcade, gallery and clerestory—the greatest possible rarity in a parish church. There were to be vaults in the aisles and a high vault, and this was built except for the vaults and the north wall above the arcade which were not finished until 1886 by J. L. Pearson. From outside, the chancel seems to rise like a grey cliff on its steep hillside site. The processional way through multi-shafted archways is now an ossuary, with about 8000 long bones and 590 skulls, representing the remains of about 4000 people, and mainly dating from the 14th and 15th century.[11]

The Norwich charnel house, now part of Norwich School was founded by John Salmon Bishop of Norwich, who died in 1325. The upper charnel chapel is now the schoolroom and was dedicated to the honor of St. John the Evangelist. In this, the *custos* or master, and chaplains with him, served daily; underneath was the lower charnel chapel, and charnel-house itself; all which is now used for a vault or cellar: this chapel was dedicated to the same saint. Here the keeper of the lower charnel "officiated daily, as they all did, for the souls of Salomon, his father, Amy, his mother, his own soul, and those of all the departed Bishops of Norwich in particular; all the dead in general; and in particular for the souls of all those whose bones were deposited in the vault of this charnel; in which, with the leave of the sacrist, who kept the key of the vault, the bones of all such as were buried in Norwich might be brought into it, if dry and clean from flesh, there to be decently reserved till the last day."[12] The building today is known as the Carnary Chapel (*carnary* was another name for charnel house).

At Bury St. Edmunds a Chapel of the Charnel was founded in the 13th century by Abbot John de Northwold. Now roofless, the walls both inside and outside are covered with memorial tablets, mostly dating from the first half of the 14th century. The charnel house stood in the abbey cemetery; its vaulted crypt used for storing human skeletal remains.[13]

Charnel chapels were entirely Christian, of course, but they do recall earlier pagan practices. In the Iron Age one common form of burial was excarnation, or de-fleshing, in which the body is allowed to decompose, and the "dry" bones are then given a second burial. This practice was widespread, and has been observed at Danebury hillfort in Hampshire, Wilsford Shaft near Amesbury in Wiltshire, Glastonbury Lake Village in Somerset, and Godwin Ridge in the Cambridgeshire Fens.

The Walking Dead

THE THREE DEAD KINGS

The Church taught that after death all souls went to Heaven, Hell or Purgatory, but this did not stop medieval Britons from envisaging alternative fates for the soul. In the early 15th century Middle English poem *The Three Dead Kings*, attributed to the Shropshire priest John Audelay, the unnamed narrator describes seeing a boar hunt. Three kings are following the hunt; they lose their way in mist and are separated from their retainers. Suddenly three walking corpses appear[14]:

> And out of the grove, three men come in view:
> Shadowy phantoms, fated to show,
> With legs long and lean, and limbs all askew,
> Their liver and lights all foetid.

The kings are terrified but show a range of reactions to the three dead men, ranging from a desire to flee to a resolve to face them. The three corpses, in response, state that they are not demons, but the three kings' forefathers:

> "Fiends? Demons? Nay! You're mistaken!
> We're your fathers—salt of the earth—soon forgotten
> As you flourish like leaves on the linden,
> Holding lordships of towns from Lorne to London.
> Those who doubt your decree, or don't do your bidding,
> You beat and bind, or defraud for a flogging.
> Look! The worms use my bowel for a womb, all writhing,
> Each ribboned like the rope my shroud is a-binding.
> With this rope I am bound
> Though the world once esteemed
> Me. My carrion was found
> Kissable once. But you—unsound
> Masters—say no mass, leave us unredeemed!"

The story originated in France with the 13th century Flemish poet Baudouin de Condé and his work *The Three Dead and the Three Living*, and was common in medieval art, especially in churches, both in France and England. Paintings of the three living and the three dead are known in English churches from places as far apart as Tarrant Crawford in Dorset, Alton in Staffordshire, Paston in Norfolk, and Wensley in North Yorkshire.[15]

MEDIEVAL GHOSTS

It is a small step from living corpses to ghosts, and ghost stories began circulating in the 12th century. In his *Courtier's Trifles*, the Welsh writer Walter Map recounts how "a knight of Northumberland was seated alone in his house after dinner in summer about the tenth hour, and lo! his father, who had died long before, approached him clad in a foul and ragged shroud." The knight believed that the apparition was a devil and drove it from the threshold, but then the ghost spoke, revealing his identity and entreating his son to fetch the priest. When he arrived the ghost exclaimed, "I am that wretch whom you long ago excommunicated unnamed, with many more, for unrighteous withholding of tithes; but the common prayers of the church and alms of the faithful have, by God's grace, so helped me that I am permitted to ask for absolution." The priest duly administered this and the ghost walked back to the grave.[16]

William de Newburgh, an Augustinian canon from Newburgh Priory in North Yorkshire, writing around the same time, records a number of ghost stories in his *History of English Affairs*. One story seems rather similar to Walter Map's tale[17]:

> In these days a wonderful event befell in the county of Buckingham, which I, in the first instance, partially heard from certain friends, and was afterwards more fully informed of by Stephen, the venerable archdeacon of that province. A certain man died, and, according to custom, by the honorable exertion of his wife arid kindred, was laid in the tomb on the eve of the Lord's Ascension. On the following night, however, having entered the bed where his wife was reposing, he not only terrified her on awaking, but nearly crushed her by the insupportable weight of his body. The next night, also, he afflicted the astonished woman in the same manner, who, frightened at the danger, as the struggle of the third night drew near, took care to remain awake herself, and surround herself with watchful companions. Still he came; but being repulsed by the shouts of the watchers, and seeing that he was prevented from doing mischief, he departed. Thus driven off from his wife, he harassed in a similar manner his own brothers, who were dwelling in the same street; but they, following the cautious example of the woman, passed the nights in wakefulness with their companions, ready to meet and repel the expected danger. He appeared, notwithstanding, as if with the hope of surprising them should they be overcome with drowsiness; but being repelled by the carefulness and valor of the watchers, he rioted among the animals, both indoors and outdoors, as their wildness and unwonted movements testified.
>
> Having thus become a like serious nuisance to his friends and neighbors, he imposed upon all the same necessity for nocturnal watchfulness; and in that very street a general watch was kept in every house, each being fearful of his approach unawares. After having for some time rioted in this manner during the night-time alone, he began to wander abroad in daylight, formidable indeed to all, but visible only to a few; for oftentimes, on his encountering a number of persons, he would appear to one or two only though at the same time his presence was not concealed from the rest. At length the inhabitants, alarmed beyond measure, thought it advisable to seek counsel of the church; and they detailed the whole affair, with tearful lamentation, to the above-mentioned archdeacon, at a meeting of the clergy over which he was solemnly presiding.

The archdeacon wrote to Hugh, Bishop of Lincoln, who was then resident in London. The bishop consulted colleagues, who advised that the body of the deceased man should be dug up and burnt:

> This proceeding, however, appeared indecent and improper in the last degree to the reverend bishop, who shortly after addressed a letter of absolution, written with his own hand, to the archdeacon, in order that it might be demonstrated by inspection in what state the body of that man really was; and he commanded his tomb to be opened, and the letter having been laid upon his breast, to be again closed: so the sepulcher having been opened, the corpse was found as it had been placed there, and the charter of absolution having been deposited upon its breast, and the tomb once more closed, he was thenceforth never more seen to wander, nor permitted to inflict annoyance or terror upon any one.

FEAR OF THE WALKING DEAD

It seems that fear of the walking dead was very real in the Middle Ages. Wharram Percy is a deserted medieval village in the Ryedale district of North Yorkshire, not far from the border with East Yorkshire. Wharram Percy was a small, low-status rural agrarian

settlement, and in the medieval period it consisted of two facing rows of dwellings orientated approximately north–south. The shorter eastern row lay in a valley, together with
the church and its churchyard. The longer western row lay on a 30- to 50-foot-high plateau, separated from the eastern buildings by a steep escarpment. Human remains were
recovered in 1963–4 from a location now known as Site 2, a domestic context toward the
southern end of the western row of buildings, situated on the plateau. The assemblage
consists of 137 bones representing the substantially incomplete remains of a minimum
of at least ten individuals, ranging in age from 2 to 4 years to more than 50 years at death.
Both sexes are represented. Seventeen bones show a total of 76 perimortem [occurring
at or near the time of death] sharp force marks (mainly knife-marks); these marks are
confined to the upper body parts. A minimum of seventeen bones show evidence for
low-temperature burning, and six long bones show perimortem breakage. The radiocarbon dates center on the 11th–13th century CE.

The authors say that the marks on the bones could suggest cannibalism, but they
tend to favor an explanation involving revenant corpses (a revenant is a re-animated
corpse that arises from its grave). Belief in revenants was widespread in medieval northern
and western Europe. Revenants were usually malevolent, spreading disease and physically
assaulting the living. Textual accounts of revenants in England are known from the 11th
century onward, but they may represent more ancient folklore. Clerics were able to
accommodate beliefs in revenants within Christian theology, considering that it was
Satan who animated these corpses, but the predominant view seemed to associate
revenants with the individual whose corpse it was: reanimation arose as a result of a lin-
gering life-force in individuals who committed malign, evil deeds and projected strong
ill-will in life, or who experienced a sudden death leaving energy still unexpended. Methods of dealing with the undead involved physical and/or spiritual means, with an emphasis on the former. The most usual way was to dig up the body and subject it to mutilation
(particularly decapitation) and burning. For example, in the late 12th century, William
of Newburgh relates that, in Berwick (Scotland), a revenant corpse roamed at night, and
these visitations only ceased when local youths dug up the offending body, dismembered
it and burnt the pieces in a fire. In medieval texts, the revenant is a fleshed corpse rather
than a skeleton: it is only in the liminal period between death and the decay of the flesh
that the body poses a threat. Mutilation and burning represent efforts to destroy the
integrity of the corpse.[18]

Fear of the dead returning to life seems to have been widespread in Roman Britain
and in pagan Anglo-Saxon England, judging from the bodies found mutilated in Romano-
British and Anglo-Saxon cemeteries. In the case of Anglo-Saxon cemeteries, bodies buried
prone (face down), decapitated or weighed down with stones were interpreted as "cunning
women" (magical healers) who may also have been seen as witches. It is likely that Iron
Age Britons also feared the dead returning to haunt them: this may explain why at Danebury hillfort complete bodies were buried at the bottom of ditches, while skulls were placed
in the upper fills.

Shape-Shifting Ghosts in North Yorkshire

In around 1400 a monk from Byland Abbey in the Ryedale district of North Yorkshire
wrote down a series of ghost stories in Latin, which were discovered in the early 20th

century by the Cambridge don and writer of ghost stories, M.R. James, and have since been translated into English.

One striking feature of these stories is that several of the Byland Abbey ghosts are shape-changers, taking grotesque forms. In Story I, a man carrying a sack of beans meets "something like a horse rearing up on its hind legs with its forelegs in the air," which turns into "a whirling heap of hay with a light in the middle of it." The man exclaims, "God forbid you should harm me!," at which the apparition takes human shape, and explains who he is and why he haunts the spot. The man arranges for the spirit to be posthumously absolved and Masses sung, which frees him from his ghostly state.

In Story II, a tailor called Snowball, riding from Gilling to Ampleforth in North Yorkshire one night, encounters a crow with sparks of fire flashing from its sides, which flaps round his head and then knocks him off his horse; he draws his sword, "and it seemed to him he was attacking a peat-stack in a marsh"; then it reappears as a dog with a chain round its neck. At this stage Snowball successfully conjures the apparition by the Trinity and Christ's wounds to explain what it wants; it speaks from its guts rather than its tongue, and he can see through its mouth that all its innards are on fire. Whether it is still in dog-form or has turned human is not said. He promises to obtain a written absolution and lay it in the ghost's grave, and to arrange for numerous Masses for its repose. He then tries to send it away to Hodgebeck; it shrieks "No, no, no!," but consents to go to Byland Brink Hill. Some days later, having persuaded certain priests and friars in York to do what was required, Snowball goes to an agreed spot to summon the ghost and report progress; he protects himself with a circle and holy objects, as described earlier. This is just as well, since the ghost now appears as a goat which goes three times round the circle, bleating; he conjures it and it falls down flat, only to leap up again as a huge and hideous man, "as thin as one of the Dead Kings in the painting," before announcing that it will be allowed to enter Heaven next Monday. Not only is this ghost himself a shape-changer, he describes others which appear "like a thorn bush or a fire," like a huntsman, and "like a bull-calf without mouth, eyes, or ears."[19]

It is possible that medieval Britons believed in the possibility of human-animal transformation, and there is a striking example of such a transformation in the *Mabinogion*. After Gilfaethwy raped Math's footholder Goewin in the Fourth Branch *Math, Son of Mathonwy*, Math punished Gilfaethwy and Gwydion in an unusual way[20]:

> he took his magic wand and struck Gilfaethwy, turning him into a sizable hind. He seized [Gwydion] quickly—and though he would have liked to escape, he was not able. He was struck with the same magic wand, turning him into a stag.
>
> "Since you have been in league together, I will make you fare together and be mated. You will have the same nature as the beasts whose shapes you are in; and during this time, they will have offspring—so you will have them too. A year from today, come to me here."

One year later a stag, a hind and a sturdy fawn turned up at the court, and Math transformed the hind into a wild boar and the stag into a wild sow. A year later, a wild boar, a wild sow and a fine little piglet turned up at the court, and Math transformed the wild boar into a she-wolf, and the sow into a wolf. After a further year had passed, a wolf, a she-wolf and a sturdy wolf-cub turned up at court, and Math struck Gwydion and Gilfaethwy with his magic wand, returning them to their own shape.

This of course is a Welsh tale, but Germanic peoples may also have believed in human-animal transformation. Trajan's Column in Rome was completed in 113 CE to commemorate the Emperor Trajan's victory in the Dacian Wars, and scene 36 on Trajan's

Column depicts Germanic warriors (the Batavi were a Germanic tribe from the Nether-lands)[21]:

> On the relief, eight soldiers of the emperor's strike force wear Roman auxiliary uniforms: knee-breeches, tunics, mailshirts, and neckerchiefs. Their weapon of attack is the sword, with which Batavi tribesmen were wont to fight and with which, when they closed in for the shock attack, they stabbed their foes. Unlike other regular auxiliaries on the Column, however, these men sport strange headgear: four wear openwork crossband helmets, two wear broad-pawed bearskins, two others narrow-pawed wolfskins. Most of them are bearded, while most regular soldiers on the Column are clean-shaven.
>
> The wolfskins and bearskins seen here cover head and shoulders, leaving the arms free.... Like Her-akles, the warriors on the Column fasten their skins over the chest by crossing and knotting the animal's forelegs.

In the mid–1st century CE bear-hoods came into use among regular non–Germanic Roman auxiliaries, worn by eagle-bearers, standard-bearers and musicians. It is possible that Romans adopted bear-hoods from their northern neighbors. Roman soldiers "who killed Germanic bear-warriors may have stripped off their hoods as trophies and worn them as badges of bravery." The earliest known bear-hooded Roman standard-bearer is Pintaius of cohors V Asturum, whose gravestone at Bonn dates to the reign of Claudius (41–54 CE). The next one is Genialis, image-bearer of cohors VII Raetorum, whose grave-stone at Mainz dates to the time of Nero (54–68 CE).[22]

The warriors depicted on Trajan's Column may be compared to the *Berserkers* ("Bear-Warriors") of Norse legend. The earliest surviving reference to the term "berserker" is in *Haraldskvæði*, a skaldic poem composed by the Norwegian Thórbiörn Hornklofi in the late 9th century in honor of King Harald Fairhair, as *ulfheðnar* ("men clad in wolf skins"). This translation from the Haraldskvæði saga describes Harald's berserkers[23]:

> I'll ask of the berserks, you tasters of blood,
> Those intrepid heroes, how are they treated,
> Those who wade out into battle?
> Wolf-skinned they are called. In battle
> They bear bloody shields.
> Red with blood are their spears when they come to fight.
> They form a closed group.
> The prince in his wisdom puts trust in such men
> Who hack through enemy shields.

The "tasters of blood" in this passage are thought to be ravens, who feasted on the dead. The Icelandic historian and poet Snorri Sturluson (1179–1241) wrote the following descrip-tion of berserkers in his *Ynglinga saga*:

> His (Odin's) men rushed forwards without armour, were as mad as dogs or wolves, bit their shields, and were strong as bears or wild oxen, and killed people at a blow, but neither fire nor iron told upon them. This was called *Berserkergang*.

It seems likely that the Berserkers were believed to transform themselves, symbolically at least, into wild animals like wolves or bears.

Bending a Penny to a Saint

Henry VI never became a saint (the Reformation intervened), but he was a martyr, a victim of the War of the Roses, and soon became the object of a cult which casts a fascinating light on late medieval beliefs. Henry, who belonged to the House of Lancaster, became king in 1422 at the age of nine months, and assumed government in 1437. He was deposed in 1461 by Edward of York, who was crowned Edward IV; Edward IV was in turn deposed in 1470 by Henry but regained the throne in 1471. Henry was then imprisoned in the Tower of London, and died two weeks later, possibly murdered on the orders of Edward. He was initially buried at Chertsey Abbey in Surrey, but in 1485 his body was moved to St. George's Chapel Windsor.

An unofficial cult grew up around Henry, and miracles were soon being attributed to him. Robert Vertelet, a cripple cured at Henry VI's shrine, had dragged himself from Winchester to Windsor because "he had heard of the wide renown of the most devout King Henry, which had been spread abroad everywhere through the frequent occurrence of miracles done by him." The people of Westwell near Canterbury in August 1481 stood helpless round a millpond in which the miller's son was drowning, till someone "chanced to mention the glorious King Henry," and on invoking him the boy's body was recovered and revived.[24]

A mariner named Henry Walter from Guildford was grievously wounded in a sea battle during the reign of Richard III (1483–1485). Walter had an atrocious abdominal wound which festered so badly that the stench became intolerable to his shipmates, who put him out of the ship into a small boat on his own. After fifteen days of suffering he had a vision of Henry VI, whose miracles were at the time much in the public eye. He was dressed as a pilgrim, and had fifteen days' growth of beard like Walter, apparently

St. George's Chapel, Windsor Castle, where Henry VI was buried. March 21, 2010 (Aurelien Guichard, CCA-Share Alike 2.0 Generic).

as a mark of solidarity in suffering. Walter had a special devotion to St. Erasmus (an early Christian martyr), who under the name St. Elmo, protected ships in storms. On gazing around, he saw that "the holy martyr Erasmus ... lay near him, as if with the pain of his sufferings renewed, just as he is often represented in churches, being tortured by his executioners." From this vision "the man conceived great gladness of heart, and from that time entertained no little confidence that he could hope for recovery." No doubt Walter was thinking of the scene depicted in many paintings and altar-pieces where Erasmus lies on a table while his entrails are wound out on a nautical windlass.[25]

The Kentish man Edward Crump was skeptical about saints and miracles, but when he became afflicted with agonizing burning pains all over his body, his pious wife urged to him to have recourse to King Henry. He agreed and sent her to the closet to fetch a silver penny to bend; by the time she got back to his bed he had been cured. Katherine Bailey, a Cambridge woman blind in one eye, was kneeling at mass in the Austin Friars' church one day when a mysterious stranger bent over her and told her to bend a coin to King Henry. She had no purse with her but made a mental promise to do so at the earliest opportunity. When the priest raised the Host at the sacring (consecration of the Host) she could see it with both eyes and went home cured.[26] When Thomas Fuller of Hammersmith was unjustly condemned to death for sheep-stealing, he invoked Henry's help because "he considered him to be the most speedy succour of the oppressed, as the fame of his miracles showed." Henry appeared and placed his hand between Fuller's windpipe and the rope. Though apparently dead, Fuller revived in the cart taking him for burial, and was duly released.[27]

This practice of bending a silver penny as an offering is not unique to Henry VI. An account written in the 1160s or 1170 tells of a monk of Durham who injured his testicles in a riding accident and decided to seek help at the shrine of St. Cuthbert on Farne Island (the island where Cuthbert lived as a hermit). Drawing a penny from his purse, he vowed to carry it with him to St. Cuthbert on Farne Island, and he bent it in half so he should recognize it by that sign. On arrival at the church of Farne, he offered the bent penny and immediately began to recover. A penny bent in honor of St. Wulfstan of Worcester and tied around the neck of a struggling woman in the grip of insanity calmed her and prepared her for cure. After a woman in Sussex had given birth to what seemed to be a still-born baby, both she and her husband appealed to St. Richard of Chichester. The man said: "O blessed Richard, if you infuse the vital spirit into this boy through your merits, I will bring a wax image of this boy, along with the boy, to your tomb." He then made the sign of the cross on the boy's forehead and bent a penny over the boy to confirm the vow and honor the saint. Immediately the child showed signs of life. Pennies were also bent in honor of St. Thomas de Cantilupe of Hereford. A falcon belonging to the Worcestershire knight Geoffrey d'Arbitot was brought back to life by having a penny bent over it, and it was even possible to put out a dangerous fire by praying to the saint and bending a penny in the direction of the flames.[28]

The practice of bending a penny resembles practices in prehistoric Britain. In the Middle-Late Bronze Age swords were bent or broken before they were cast into the River Thames between London and Oxford or into Flag Fen in Cambridgeshire as offerings to the gods, and coins were bent before being offered to the gods at the Late Iron Age shrine on Hayling Island in Hampshire.

Grave Goods in Late Medieval England

In the pagan Anglo-Saxon cemeteries of Northumbria, East Anglia, Mercia and Wessex, the elite were buried with grave goods—but until recently it was thought that medieval Christians did not take goods with them into the next world. However, in the past 20 years many Christian cemeteries have been excavated, including the large cemetery at the hospital of St. Mary Spital, in the East End of London, with nearly 11,000 graves, and it has become clear that both priests and lay people were as well equipped for the afterlife as their prehistoric ancestors. So from the mid–11th into the 12th century, it became common to inter monks and nuns in their consecration clothing, and with the emblems of their religious status. Female skulls excavated from the nunnery of Clementhorpe, York, and the double monastery of Syon in Isleworth, Middlesex, showed evidence of staining from copper alloy pins, suggesting that nuns were buried in their headdresses. Abbots were buried in their full office regalia; the richness of the dress displayed in bishops' and archbishops' burials suggests that ecclesiastical corpses were dressed for a period of lying in state. Priests were buried with symbols of their clerical status: copies in wax, ceramic or metal of the vessels with which they officiated at the mass. Abbots, abbesses and bishops were buried with their croziers, the pastoral staffs symbolic of their office. Some of these seem to have been the actual staffs used by the deceased ecclesiastics. Others were specially made for funerary use, in base metal or, in a unique case from Chichester cathedral, in jet.[29]

Innovation in secular burials came slightly later. By 1200–1300 it was more common to place personal items on the corpse, including jewelry, domestic seals, coins, papal seals (bullae) spindle whorls and clothing. Fasteners are all that usually survive of clothes, but where preservation conditions are good, as at Hull Augustinian friary, we glimpse the richness of secular burial traditions. People sported embroidered and vividly colored wool and linen garments, high fashion tunics, breeches, a liripipe (a hood with a tail) and a variety of shoes that were everyday or best dress, rather than made for the grave.

Some of the most evocative grave goods may be linked to the doctrines of Purgatory and resurrection, and the resulting beliefs that both the body and soul of the deceased required continued care and protection. Apotropaic items (believed to avert evil) placed with the corpse were added when the body was washed and shrouded: for example, coins or stones placed in the mouth, crosses or papal bullae placed on the chest, and padlocks placed near the pelvis. Many talismans were placed with children, revealing that the family prepared the corpse for burial, and demonstrating their concern for its continued welfare. Examples include a pilgrim's badge buried with a child near the south porch of St. Augustine's, Canterbury; and a cross recovered from near the mouth of a child buried in the church of Pontefract Priory, Yorkshire.

Healing, whether connected with medical, spiritual or popular cures, was a persistent theme in the treatment of the medieval dead. Evidence of medical care is occasionally seen in items worn by the corpse, which were presumably believed to possess continued efficacy after death. These include copper alloy plates used to heal and protect joint injuries or disease, and a hernia truss from Merton Priory, southwest London. Certain materials used for mortuary objects were believed to have intrinsic healing properties. Particularly significant are the jet, amber and quartz items, valued as mortuary goods from prehistoric times onwards for their electrostatic and refractive properties. In the Middle Ages, the use of such materials was part of a mainstream belief in the healing power of gems to rebalance the humors, as set out in the 11th century lapidary written by Bishop Marbode of Rennes.

The End of the Saints

In the middle of the 16th century, under Henry VIII and his young son Edward VI, all the monasteries in England and Wales were dissolved, the Catholic mass was abolished, and England became a Protestant country. In the Middle Ages the Catholic church had kept supernatural forces under control with a variety of rituals, but the new Anglican church scorned the "magic" of the Catholic church. As a result, the fear of magic increased and led to a number of witchcraft trials, especially during the English Civil War of the mid–17th century.

12

Magic, Cunning-Folk and Witchcraft Trials in the Sixteenth and Seventeenth Centuries

Magic in the Middle Ages

THE "MAGIC" OF THE CHURCH

As the historian Keith Thomas points out, nearly every "primitive religion" is regarded by its adherents as a medium for obtaining supernatural power, and the history of early Christianity offers no exception to this rule. Conversions to the new religion were frequently assisted by the view of converts that they were acquiring not just a means of other-worldly salvation, but a new and more powerful magic. The Apostles of the early Church attracted followers by working miracles and performing supernatural cures. The claim to supernatural power was an essential element in the Anglo-Saxon Church's fight against paganism, and missionaries did not fail to stress the superiority of Christian prayers to heathen charms.

The medieval Church "thus found itself saddled with the tradition that the working of miracles was the most efficacious means of demonstrating its monopoly of the truth." By the 12th and 13th centuries the *Lives* of the saints related the miraculous achievements of holy men, and stressed how they could "prophesy the future, control the weather, provide protection against fire and flood, magically transport heavy objects, and bring relief to the sick."[1]

The shrines of the saints became objects of pilgrimage to which "the sick and the infirm made long and weary journeys in the confident expectation of obtaining a supernatural cure. Over 500 cures were associated with Becket and his shrine at Canterbury; and at the Holy Rood of Bromholm in Norfolk thirty-nine persons were said to have been raised from the dead and twelve cured of blindness." Holy relics became wonder-working fetishes, believed to have the power to cure illness and protect against danger; around 1426 "the Bishop of Durham's accounts contain a payment for signing sixteen cattle with St Wilfrid's signet to ward of the murrain."[2]

Images also had magical powers. The large mounted figure of the warrior saint Derfel at Llanderfel in Meirionydd protected men and cattle, rescued souls from Purgatory, and inflicted disease upon his enemies; Henry VIII's visitors, who had come to suppress the cult of St. Derfel, found five or six hundred worshippers at the shrine on the day they went there to pull it down.[3]

Saints were often called upon to cure diseases, but they could perform many functions. John Aubrey, writing in the late 17th century gives a "nostalgic description" of the role saints had once played in the daily lives of the Gloucestershire country folk[4]:

> At St Oswaldsdown and Fordedown…, the shepherds prayed at night and at morning to St Oswald (that was martyred there) to preserve their sheep safe in the fold.…When they went to bed they did rake up their fire and make a cross in the ashes and pray to God and St Osyth to deliver them from fire and water and from all misadventure. When the bread was put into the oven, they prayed to God and to St Stephen to send them a just batch and an even.

St. Oswald's Down is in the parish of Marshfield, which lies on the Gloucestershire/Wiltshire border; Aubrey is no doubt referring to a Bronze Age barrow called St. Oswald's Tump, traditionally associated with the martyrdom of the Northumbrian saint Oswald.

However, the Church did not simply rely on the supernatural powers of the saints but exercised other important powers. Liturgical books of the time "contained rituals devised to bless houses, cattle, crops, ships, tools, armour, wells and kilns. There were formulae for blessing men who were preparing to set off on a journey, to fight a duel, to engage in battle or to move into a new house." Such rituals usually involved "the presence of a priest and the employment of holy water and the sign of the cross."[5] Holy water could be used to "drive away evil spirits and pestilential vapours. It was a remedy against disease and sterility, and an instrument for blessing houses and food."[6] As late as 1543, when a storm burst over Canterbury, the inhabitants ran to church for holy water to sprinkle in their houses, so as to drive away the evil spirits in the air, and to protect their property against lightning.[7]

Holy amulets were also important in the Middle Ages. The most common of these amulets was the *agnus dei* ("lamb of god"), a small wax cake, originally made out of paschal candles and blessed by the Pope, bearing the image of the lamb and flag. This was intended to serve as a defense against the assaults of the Devil and as a preservative against thunder, lightning, fire, death, drowning, death in child-bed and similar dangers."[8]

The consecrated host used during the Mass was regarded as "an object of supernatural potency." The communicant "who did not swallow the bread, but carried it away from the church in his mouth, was widely believed to be in possession of an impressive source of magical power. He could use it to cure the blind or the feverish; he could carry it around with him as a general protection against ill fortune."[9]

There was a widespread belief in magic during the Middle Ages and the Church, through its various rituals, was able to offer to people the hope of protection from harmful magic. With the Reformation in the mid–16th century, this protection against harmful magic was withdrawn, in a way that left many people feeling vulnerable to the most malevolent form of magic, witchcraft.

The Reformation and Attitudes to Catholic "Magic"

In 1534 Henry VIII was declared supreme head of the Church of England instead of the Pope in Rome, and by the late 1530s all the monasteries in England and Wales had been dissolved. In 1549, during the reign of the boy-king Edward VI, the English Book of Common Prayer replaced the Latin Mass, and England was well on the way to becoming a Protestant country. The extreme Protestant view of Catholic ritual was summed up by those early Protestants, the Lollards, in their *Twelve Conclusions* of 1395[10]:

> The exorcisms or hallowings, made in the Church, of wine, bread, and wax, water, salt and oil and incense, the stone of the altar, upon vestments, mitre, cross, and pilgrims' staves, be the very practice of necromancy, rather than of the holy theology. This conclusion is proved thus. For by such exorcisms creatures be charged to be of higher virtue than their own kind, and we see nothing of change in no such creature, that is so charmed, but by false belief, the which is the principle of the Devil's craft.

Such views were repeated after the Reformation. James Calfhill, Archdeacon of Colchester and Bishop-designate of Worcester, who died in 1570, asked rhetorically: who were "the vilest witches and sorcerers of the earth," if not "the priests that consecrate crosses and ashes, water and salt, oil and cream, boughs and bones, stocks and stones; that christen bells that hang in the steeple; that conjure worms that creep in the field; that give St. John's Gospel to hang about men's necks?" John Jewel, Bishop of Salisbury (1522–1571) wondered how the "conjuration" of the agnus dei could endow it with the power to preserve its wearer from lightning and tempest. Of what avail was" a mere piece of wax against a storm sent by God?"[11] Protestant reformers were particularly critical of the Mass: what was transubstantiation, they asked, "but a spurious piece of legerdemain"— "the pretence of a power, plainly magical, of changing the elements in such a sort as all the magicians of Pharaoh could never do, nor had the face to attempt the like, it being so beyond all credibility."[12]

Protestants were also suspicious of prayers, since prayers were often like magic spells. This idea was expressed by the late 16th century Puritan Richard Greenham, when he explained that parishioners should not assume that their ministers could give them immediate relief when their consciences were troubled. This, he wrote, is "a coming rather as it were to a magician (who, by an incantation of words, makes silly souls look for health) rather than to the minister of God, whose words being most angelical comfort, not until, and so much as, it pleaseth the Lord to give a blessing unto them; which sometime he doth deny, because we come to them with too great an opinion of them; as they were wise men [i.e., wizards]."[13]

Holy Wells and the Persistence of Catholic "Magic" After the Reformation

However, some of the traditions of the Catholic past lingered on. Many of the old holy wells, for example, retained their semi-magical associations, even though Protestants preferred to regard them as medicinal springs working by natural means. A good example of a holy well with supposed medicinal properties is the Chalice Well at Glastonbury in Somerset. In the mid–18th century the water from a spring, which had been used by the abbey for centuries as a water supply, suddenly became a miracle cure for a variety of complaints. The spring water is mildly chalybeate (that is, it contains salts of iron) and the dissolved iron oxidizes on contact with the atmosphere leaving a red deposit in the channel, as water flows down the valley to the west of Glastonbury Tor. In places this deposit gives the appearance of clots of blood leading to its name, the Red or Blood Spring. Joseph is said to have buried the cruets (and/or Grail) in the vicinity of the spring which thereafter provided a constant flow of water tinged red by the healing blood of

Christ. Because of this association with Joseph the spring is also known as the Holy Well or Chalice Well and the hill above the spring as Chalice Hill.

The waters of the spring became a miracle cure when Matthew Chancellor of North Wootton had a dream in 1750 which sounds very much like a medieval vision. Chancellor had suffered with asthma for 30 years until, around the middle of October 1750, he had a violent fit during the night. He swore on oath that he subsequently fell asleep and dreamt that he was in Glastonbury, in the horse track some way above Chaingate. Here he saw some of the clearest water he had ever seen in his life and knelt down to drink. As he stood up again he sensed someone standing before him who instructed him to drink a glass full of the water issuing from an adjacent freestone shoot [a sloping channel for conveying water to a lower level]. He was told that if he did this for the following seven Sunday mornings, before he had eaten and without being seen, he would be cured. He asked why seven days and was told that the world was made in six and on the seventh God rested and blessed this day above all other days. He was further told that the water came from holy ground where many saints and martyrs had been buried. According to his sworn statement, Chancellor followed the instructions carefully and went the following Sunday to Glastonbury where he found the freestone shoot exactly as seen in his dream. Unfortunately, there was little water flowing in the shoot and he had to dip his glass three times into the hole below it in order to drink the equivalent of a full glass! However, he persevered for seven Sundays as directed and was completely cured. His story appeared in the *Gentleman Magazine* of 1751 and people began flocking to Glastonbury to drink the waters of the spring. A spa was opened in 1753, but was not a success, for by 1779 the waters had "entirely lost their reputation."[14]

Other wells remained places of pilgrimage. Pilgrimages, sometimes very large ones, were made to St. Winifred's well at Holywell in northeast Wales throughout the 17th century and it was not only recusants (those who remained loyal to the Pope and the Catholic Church) who went there in search of a cure. When a man was found dead at the well in 1630 after having made scoffing remarks about its supposed powers a local jury brought in a verdict of death by divine judgement.[15]

In 1589 the people of Clynnog Fawr on the Llyn Peninsula still observed the feast day of St. Beuno; they sacrificed bulls in Beuno's honor, and gave other offerings to him as well, thinking him the most powerful of all the saints. In fact, people continued to come from far and wide to ask for Beuno's help with their sick livestock and other concerns for many years afterward. Beuno's well was also thought to have special powers to cure sickness.[16] St. Beuno's well lies by the old roadside around 200 yards to the west of the church. The village, and well, now bypassed, lay on the principal pilgrims' route to Bardsey and would have been an important stop on their journey. The well was traditionally resorted to for the treatment of sick children, in particular those suffering from epilepsy and rickets. It was also claimed to cure impotence. After bathing the patient was carried to St. Beuno's chapel and laid on rushes overnight on Beuno's tomb, a plain altar like structure that stood in the center of the chapel before Beuno's shrine. If they slept, then the cure would be effective. The custom was still in place at least until the 18th century, since Pennant remarks, in his *Tour in Wales*: "I myself once saw on it (the tomb) a feather bed on which a poor paralytic from Merioneddshire had lain the whole night after undergoing the same ceremony."[17]

St. Eilian's well at Llaneilian (Anglesey) was very well visited as a healing well for many years. It had the advantage of requiring that a financial donation (usually a groat,

Chalice Well, Glastonbury, which for a brief period in the 18th century was thought to cure asthma. The water has a reddish hue because of iron oxide deposits (Spsmiler).

or four pennies) was made for a cure to work, and the parish grew wealthy on the payments from pilgrims. A chest, dating from the early 17th century, Cyff Eilian can still be seen in the church into which groats were placed. It was opened annually and apparently yielded sums of the order of 300 pounds a year. Later the well developed a reputation as a cursing well. A number of such wells exist in the region, the most famous now being another Ffynnon Eilian near Conwy. A number of cursing rituals grew up. Most commonly at this location the would-be curser paid the well custodian to engrave the name or initials on a slate with a pin, the pin would then be bent and thrown into the well. The typical witch's method of making a dummy of the person to be cursed and piercing or drowning the dummy were also carried out. Such a marked slate and dummy were found close to the well in 1925 and are now in the museum at Bangor.[18]

Ffynnon Eilian near Colwyn Bay in Conwy is the most famous cursing well in Wales. It was said to have sprung up in the 6th century at the place where St. Eilian prayed for water when overcome by thirst while on a journey. He also prayed that whoever came to the well with faith would obtain his wish, though he was probably not thinking of evil wishes. Ffynnon Eilian was originally a healing well, but from the late 18th century it gained a wide reputation as a cursing well and became a lucrative business for the people who ran it: in the early 19th century the owner was earning nearly £300 a year from both cursers and cursees. Various names of those who profited are on record, but the most famous was tailor John Evans, known as Jack Ffynnon Eilian, who twice went to prison for his involvement in the cursing business in the early 19th century.

An involved ritual had to be performed when laying or lifting a curse at Ffynnon Eilian. To lay a curse, the victim's name was written in a book, and his/her initials scratched on a slate, or written on parchment which was folded in lead to which a piece of slate was tied, and then placed in the well while curses were uttered verbally. Alternatively, a pin was thrown into the well while the victim was named. The well-guardian read some passages from the Bible, then handed the curser a cup of water, some of which was drunk, and the rest was thrown over the curser's head. He or she spoke the curse which they wished for, while the ritual was repeated twice more. Sometimes a wax effigy with pins stuck into it was used, and the well-guardian would speak secret curses, the effigy being dipped three times and then left in the well. It would seem that there was no hard and fast ritual which must always be followed: the well-guardian may have varied the ritual according to his or her whim, or according to what the curser was able to pay. Whatever form the ritual took, it seems to have impressed both cursers and cursees, or else neither would have paid the large sums which they did. To curse someone cost one shilling, and ten shillings was charged to lift a curse; in 1820 five shillings was charged for a curse, and fifteen shillings to lift it. The rituals for lifting curses were equally involved and included a reading of psalms and other Bible texts, walking three times round the well, and the emptying of the well by the guardian so that the lead and slate with his/her initials could be found and removed. Sometimes the slate was ground into dust, mixed with salt, and burned on the fire. The cursee also had to take some well water home and drink it while reading psalms.[19]

The Rise of Miracle-Working Sects During the Civil War and the Protectorate (1640–1660)

The Reformation had done away with all the rituals which had apparently kept people safe from harmful magic and abolished the saints' cults which had played such a crucial role in the health and well-being of many believers. So what happened during the English Civil War, the subsequent execution of James I, and the years of the Commonwealth, was not surprising. This period began in 1640 when the Long Parliament convened; the Long Parliament sat during the Civil War (1642–1651) and the Protectorate under Oliver Cromwell and his son Richard (1653–59); it was only dissolved in 1660 after Charles II became king. During this time of political upheaval, Protestant sects proliferated, and one reason for this is that many sects claimed to provide "that supernatural solution to earthly problems which the makers of the Protestant Reformation had so sternly rejected."[20] The sects "revived the miracle-working aspect of medieval Catholicism without its Roman and hierarchical features. They practised prophesying and faith-healing; they generated a widespread faith in the possibilities of unaccompanied prayer for healing the sick and for accomplishing other miraculous feats; they even claimed to raise people from the dead."[21]

Among the Protestant sects, the Baptists based their healing on James 5:14 ("Is any sick among you? Let him call for the elders of the church; and let them pray over him, anointing him with oil in the name of the Lord"). The Baptist minister Hanserd Knollys (1599–1691) resolved to take no more medicine, but to be anointed and prayed over by his colleagues. With William Kiffin he attempted to restore sight to the blind by prayer and holy oil. A Sandwich tailor was encouraged by a vision in 1647 to attempt the miraculous healing of the sick and blind.[22] But the Quakers were the greatest miracle-workers. Over 150 cures were attributed to their leader George Fox alone, and many other Friends boasted similar healing powers. Several emulated the Ranter John Robins, who had been credited with the power to raise the dead. James Nayler was said in 1656 to have claimed to have resurrected the widow Dorcas Erbury in Exeter gaol.[23]

Practitioners of Magic: Cunning Men and Wise Women

With the saints no longer offering miraculous cures, many people had recourse to the "traditional dispenser of magical remedies"—the village wizard or "wise man," variously known through the 16th and 17th centuries as "cunning men," "wise women," "charmers," "blessers," "conjurers," "sorcerers" or "witches." Traditional folk medicine was a "mixture of common-sensical remedies, based on the accumulated experience of nursing and midwifery, combined with inherited lore about the healing properties of plants and minerals. But it also included certain types of ritual healing, in which prayers, charms or spells accompanied the medicine, or even formed the sole means of treatment."[24]

A great deal of magical healing in the late Middle Ages and Early Modern Period "reflected the old belief in the curative powers of the medieval Church." In 1528 the wise woman Margaret Hunt described her methods before the Commissary of London. First, she ascertained the names of the sick persons. Then she knelt and prayed to the Blessed Trinity to heal them from all their wicked enemies. Then she told them to say for nine consecutive nights five Paternosters ("Our Father"), five Aves ("Hail Mary") and a Creed, followed by three more Paternosters, three Aves and three Creeds "in the worship of Saint Spirit." At bedtime they were to repeat one Paternoster, one Ave and one Creed in worship of St. Ive, to save them from all envy. For the ague she prescribed various herbs. For sores she also recommended herbs but taken with a little holy water and some prayers.[25]

The pronunciation of Catholic prayers in Latin long remained a common ingredient in the magical treatment of illness. For example, in 1557 a certain Cowdale of Maidstone in Kent confessed to healing people by such prayers alone, regardless of the type of sickness involved. He simply prescribed five Paternosters, five Aves and a Creed, to be said in honor of the Holy Ghost and Our Lady.[26]

Often the cunning man or wise woman would diagnose a supernatural cause for the patient's illness, saying that he or she had been "overlooked" or "forspoken," that is to say, bewitched. There were a number of remedies for this. In 1622 when the London healer Robert Booker informed a patient that he had been bewitched, he anointed him with oil and pronounced a charm: "Three biters have bit him—heart, tongue and eye; three better shall help him presently—God the Father, God the Son, and God the Holy Spirit." This was a standard formula and indicated the three supposed sources of witchcraft—concealed malevolence ("heart"), bitter words ("tongue"), and ocular fascination ("eye").[27]

The first modern study of cunning men and wise women was produced by the historian Keith Thomas in his 1971 work *Religion and the Decline of Magic: Studies in Popular Beliefs in Sixteenth and Seventeenth Century England*. More recently, in 2003, the historian Owen Davies updated Thomas's work with his *Popular Magic: Cunning-folk in English*

History (he prefers the gender-neutral term *cunning-folk*). Davies points out that *cunning* comes from the Old English *cunnan* "to know," although in Anglo-Saxon times cunning-folk were referred to as *wiccan* "witches."[28] The first mention of witches in English law is in the time of King Alfred, who decreed that "women who are wont to practise enchantments, and magicians and witches, do not allow them to live." His guide was the passage in Exodus 22:18, which commanded: "Thou shalt not suffer a witch to live."

From the 12th century there were no specific secular laws against magic, but the activities of cunning-folk continued to be seen as a problem by the authorities and surviving ecclesiastical documents and state papers show that resort to those who practiced magic was widespread. There were particular fears in elite circles about its use in aiding political intrigues. The most famous such case was that of Eleanor Cobham, duchess of Gloucester, who in 1441 was tried for using magic against Henry VI. To achieve her purposes, she was accused of hiring the services of an astronomer and astrologer named Roger Bolingbrooke, Thomas Southwell, a canon of St. Stephen's chapel, Westminster, and a cunning-woman named Margerie Jourdayne. The latter was further accused of supplying the duchess with love potions and was burned at Smithfield for treason.[29]

The case of Eleanor Cobham shows that cunning women were not simply healers, but also provided love potions. In the Middle Ages, the activities of cunning-folk were regulated by ecclesiastical courts, and a case involving love potions was heard at Durham. In October 1446 the "official" of the priory and convent of Durham heard evidence against Mariot de Belton and Isabella Brome, who were accused of telling women they could magically procure husbands for them. In 1492 the commissary's court of the London diocese heard how Richard Laukiston had offered to find a rich husband for a widow named Margaret Geffrey. Laukiston was going to achieve this by applying to a "cunning man that by his cunning can cause a woman to have any man that she hath favour to."[30]

Indeed cunning-folk had a wide repertoire of activities, including thief detection. and many of the cases heard by ecclesiastical courts involved accusations of deception leveled against cunning-folk who promised to detect thieves. In 1375 John Porter of Clerkenwell (London) prosecuted John Chestre for having failed to discover a thief who had stolen some valuables. Chestre admitted that "he often exercised that art," and claimed to have successfully restored £15 stolen from a man at Garlickhithe. The plaintiff and defendant agreed on a settlement, and the court ruled that, because the defendant's art was held to be a deception to the public, he must swear not to exercise it in future.[31]

In 1382 Robert Berewold was accused of defamation and deceit. He had been asked to identify the thief who stole a mazer (drinking bowl) from a house in St. Mildred Poultry in the City of London. Like Chestre he divined by "turning the loaf." A wooden peg was sunk into the top of a loaf of bread and four knives were placed in the sides. When a list of names was gone through, either verbally or mentally, the loaf turned at the name of the thief. In this manner Berwold fixed upon a woman named Johanna Wolsy, who subsequently accused him of "maliciously lying" and causing a public scandal. For his punishment he was put in the pillory with the incriminating loaf hung round his neck and was made to go to church on the following Sunday at the hour of mass and confess his crime before Johanna's fellow parishioners and other neighbors.[32]

The first attempt to regulate cunning-folk came with the Witchcraft Act of 1542. Although it made provision for those who used "witchcrafts, enchantments, and sorceries to the destruction of their neighbours persons and goods," that is witches as later defined, its main target were those who took "upon them to declare and tell where things lost or stolen should become," those who practiced invocations and conjurations to "get knowledge for their own lucre in what place treasure of gold and silver should or might be found," and those who "provoke any person to unlawful love." The penalty for such activities was death. There is no record of anyone dying because of the act, and it was repealed less than six years later under Edward VI.[33]

A new Witchcraft Act was passed in 1563, directed like the previous act against cunning-folk but with no death penalty for a first offence—those convicted were to face one year's imprisonment and four stints in the pillory.[34] The 1563 act "sparked a fiery zeal of repression—but not against those who were the original targets of the law. It was witches, those who thought to use their powers for nothing else than malicious harm against man and beast, who subsequently felt its full force."[35]

There were numerous books of magic in the Middle Ages, but they were in Latin, and few cunning-folk could read them. The first book of magic in English was a mid–16th century translation of Albertus Magnus's *Book of Secrets*, which described the magical properties of stones, herbs and beasts. However, it was only during the Interregnum, the period between the execution of Charles I (1649) and the accession of his son Charles II (1660), that translations of the most important source book. of magic began to appear (Davies, p.121). The most significant of these was Robert Turner's 1655 translation of the *Fourth Book of Occult Philosophy*. This key textbook of practical demonic magic was spuriously attributed to Cornelius Agrippa, a German writer on the occult, who flourished in the early 16th century. It soon became one of the most notorious magical books in Europe—in the preface to his *Daemonologie* James I noted that those "who would know what are the particular rites and curiosities of these black arts ... he will find it in the Fourth book of Agrippa."[36]

Ironically, one of the books most useful to cunning-folk was Reginald Scot's *Discoverie of Witchcraft* (1584), which was actually skeptical of witchcraft. In order to expose their fraudulent activities and show what "notorious blasphemie" necromancers and conjurors committed, Scot elucidated in great detail a wide range of charms, talismans and rituals. These included an inventory of the names, shapes and powers of the principal devils and spirits used in conjurations. Scot further provided directions on how to call up spirits and illustrated these with diagrams of magic circles and the characters and seals of the angels.[37]

From Cunning-Folk to Witches and Witchcraft Trials

It is clear that before and after the Reformation many people in England believed in magic, that magic was part of the repertory of cunning-folk, and that many diseases were believed to occur because the patient was bewitched. So it is not surprising that some people should be accused of being witches, especially during the upheavals before and after the execution of James I, and before the restoration of Charles II.

In the matter of witchcraft, the most influential book in the Late Middle Ages was the *Malleus maleficarum* ("Hammer of Witches"), published in 1486 in the German city of Speyer by Heinrich Kramer, a Dominican theologian and inquisitor. The book was written at a time when Kramer and his fellow inquisitor Jacob Sprenger were encountering resistance in their efforts to prosecute witches in the area of upper Germany and the Rhineland. In 1484 they secured a bull from Pope Innocent VIII confirming their authority to proceed against witches in these areas. The bull was included as a preface to this work, which was intended to make authorities aware of the threat posed by witchcraft and to provide a manual for inquisitors who would try them. The treatise went into fifteen printings between 1486 and 1520 and another nineteen printings between 1569 and 1669, which was the most intense period of witch-hunting in Europe.[38]

By the mid–16th century the early modern European stereotype of witchcraft had been fully formed. This stereotype combined many different elements: "Ideas of maleficent magic performed through the power of the Devil, demonic temptation, the negotiation of a pact with the Devil, the collective worship of the Devil at the sabbath, the performance of amoral and anti–Christian activities at the sabbath, the nocturnal flight of witches, and their metamorphosis into beasts had all been integrated into a frightening depiction of the witch and her activities."[39] A number of treatises of witchcraft were written between 1570 and 1700, including two by British Protestants—the English theologian William Perkins, and the Scottish cleric James Hutchinson. In his treatise *The Damned Art of Witchcraft*, written around 1602, Perkins insisted that the pact with the Devil, rather than the practice of harmful magic, was the essence of the crime of witchcraft—even though the witchcraft statute of 1563 defined the crime exclusively in terms of *maleficium* ("evildoing"), and in most English cases of witchcraft villagers simply accused their neighbors of harming them by magical means.[40] In 1697 the Scottish minister James Hutchinson preached a sermon which touched on the culpability of children in witchcraft trials (he blamed the parents), and came close to advocating torture to extract confessions from those accused of witchcraft.[41]

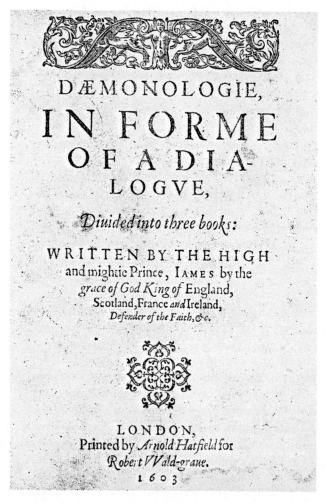

The title page of James I's book on witchcraft, written in 1597 (Wellcome Images, CCA 4.0 International).

However, not everyone believed in witchcraft. Reginald Scot, in his *Discoverie of Witchcraft* (1584) argued there was no biblical foundation for witch-hunting and offered four reasons why he was skeptical about witchcraft. Firstly, he showed that poor women who begged for charity and had been estranged from their neighbors were most likely to be accused of witchcraft. Secondly, not only was there no biblical foundation to the belief in witchcraft, but it was idolatrous to attribute powers to witches. Thirdly, he demonstrated that the crimes attributed to witches could be prosecuted using laws that were already in force. Finally, he used philosophy and science to establish the impossibility of the deeds confessed by witches.[42]

Perhaps the most famous British treatise on witchcraft was the one written by James VI of Scotland in 1597 that was widely circulated not only in Scotland but in England, where he became king in 1603 (as James I). James had had a personal experience with witchcraft in 1590, when a conspiracy of witches had allegedly tried to prevent the arrival of his bride, Princess Anne of Demark, in Scotland. The witches had allegedly also tried to use witchcraft to murder him. James' treatise on witchcraft was intended mainly as a response to skeptical witchcraft treatises written by Jonathan Weyer in 1563 and Reginald Scot. The most widely cited part of the treatise is its final chapter, which deals with the discovery and punishment of witches. The king

> takes a hard line regarding the punishment of offenders, including those who counsel witches. The only exception he allows is that of children [bairns] who have not reached the age of reason. James urges the appropriate caution of judicial authorities in adjudicating witchcraft cases, lest the innocent suffer, but the seriousness of the crime leads him to permit the testimony of children, wives, and confessing witches. He also allows the use of spectral evidence (the visions afflicted persons saw of the witches as they were allegedly causing them harm), the pricking of witches to detect the Devil's mark, and the swimming of witches (the old water ordeal).[43]

Witchcraft Trials in England

AGNES WATERHOUSE OF HATFIELD PEVERELL (ESSEX)

As I said earlier, the end of the Roman Catholic mass, rites, monasteries and saints left people feeling vulnerable to harmful magic, and it is perhaps no coincidence that many witchcraft trials were associated with towns or villages which, until the 1530s, had ancient monasteries with powerful protector saints. Agnes Waterhouse was the first woman executed for witchcraft in England. In 1566, she was accused of witchcraft along with two other women: Elizabeth Francis and Joan Waterhouse. All three women were from the same town, Hatfield Peverell in Essex, which for over 400 years, until 1536, had been the home of the Priory of St. Mary the Virgin, a cell of St. Albans Abbey. She confessed to having been a witch and that her familiar was a cat (later turned into a toad) by the name of Satan, sometimes spelled Sathan, which originally belonged to Elizabeth Francis. Agnes was put on trial in Chelmsford, Essex, England, in 1566 for using witchcraft to cause illness to William Fynne, who died on November 1, 1565. She was also charged with using sorcery to kill livestock, cause illness, as well as bring about the death of her husband. Her eighteen-year-old daughter Joan Waterhouse was also accused (but found not guilty) of the same crime. Joan Waterhouse's testimony ultimately helped to convict the two other women. Two days after the trial finished, Agnes was hanged.[44]

THE WITCHES OF WARBOYS (CAMBRIDGESHIRE)

Warboys is a village in Cambridgeshire, not far from the site of Ramsey Abbey (dissolved in 1539), which produced a famous case of witchcraft between 1589 and 1593, involving the Puritan Throckmorton family. Puritanism began in the late sixteenth century and was essentially a drive to reform the Church of England even further in the direction of Continental Protestantism, such as the Calvinism of Geneva. Puritans insisted that Biblical injunctions should be followed to the letter, including the instruction in the Book of Exodus, "Thou shalt not suffer a witch to live." Paranoid fear of witchcraft became a defining feature of Puritan belief, since Puritans believed that the devil was out to get the "godly" in the midst of a godless generation.[45]

The first allegations of witchcraft were made in November 1589 by Jane Throckmorton, the ten-year-old daughter of Robert Throckmorton, the Squire of Warboys, when she started suffering from fits. She accused the 76-year-old Alice Samuel of being the cause, and this was soon echoed by Jane's four sisters and some household servants who began exhibiting similar symptoms. The Squire was a close friend of Sir Henry Cromwell, one of the wealthiest commoners in England and, when Lady Cromwell came to visit in March 1590, she also accused Alice Samuel of being a witch. Lady Cromwell reportedly grabbed a pair of scissors and cut a lock of hair off Alice and gave it to Mrs. Throckmorton to burn (a folk remedy believed to weaken a witch's power). That night, Lady Cromwell had nightmares, became ill and later died in 1592. The local parson persuaded Alice to confess to witchcraft in 1592, but she recanted the very next day. However, she confessed again when brought before the Bishop of Lincoln and was taken to Huntingdon where she was imprisoned with her daughter, Agnes, and her husband, John. All three were tried in April 1593 for the murder by witchcraft of Lady Cromwell. Alice's words to Lady Cromwell ("Madam, why do you use me thus? I never did you any harm as yet") were used against her at the trial, and all three were found guilty and hanged.[46]

A WITCHCRAFT TRIAL AT BURY ST. EDMUNDS (SUFFOLK)

The most famous witchcraft trial at Bury St. Edmunds, until 1540 home to the shrine of St. Edmund, took place in 1645, during the English Civil War, at the instigation of Matthew Hopkins, the self-proclaimed Witchfinder General. On August 27, 1645, no fewer than 18 witches were hanged, among them John Lowes, Susanna Smith, Prissilla Collit, and Susanna Stegold.

John Lowes was around 80 years of age and was the vicar of Brandston in Suffolk. A graduate from St. Johns College in Cambridge, Lowes maintained the traditional norms that were present in England in 1645. His claim was that he was trying to "reform" his parish from what he called bad vices. Members of his parish eventually became upset with his self assertion and contemptuous disregard for local expectations. Lowes had a complex legal history with his accusers since 1614 including past accusations of witchcraft. This suggests that Lowes and his accusers had consistent bad blood between them that boiled over once Matthew Hopkins, the witch-finder general arrived. It is also relevant that the people of Suffolk were in a region that strongly supported Parliamentary forces during the English Civil War. Being on the side of change and reform, the people of Suffolk turned to the accusation of witchcraft to remove an allegedly corrupt minister.

Susanna Smith was accused of infanticide. Susanna was living in a time of harsh economic conditions during Europe in the middle of the 17th century. Likely, the birth of her children only increased the strain of surviving with enough resources to support herself and her family. Whether or not Susanna actually committed infanticide and harmed one or more of her children is not known. However, it is known that she confessed that she had been tempted to commit infanticide to ease the pain of poverty.

Prissilla Collit was also accused of infanticide and confessed to making a deal with the Devil—in return, the Devil offered her ten shillings. Like Susanna, Prissilla was in the lower class that was subject to poverty in the harsh economic times. Her covenant with the Devil while ill twelve years before her arrest shows how poverty took a toll on early modern Europeans. Likely malnourished and unable to work, Prissilla would have been unable to actively earn money or food for her family. Prissilla openly confessed that if her other child had not removed her baby from near the fire; the baby would have burned to death, as she had planned after she left the baby by the fire. The historian Louise Jackson suggests that women like Prissilla, were empowered to turn to witchcraft and the devil as a way to escape poverty. For instance, it was commonly feared and believed at this time that a covenant with the devil could bring one material gain.

Susanna Stegold was accused of killing her husband. She confessed to the court that she was in an unhappy marriage in which she was beaten regularly. English common law at this time permitted a man to beat his wife as long as it wasn't fatal. The woman was expected accept the beatings as their due. The confessions undoubtedly show that Stegold was looking for and wanted a way out of her marriage. After receiving regular beatings from her husband, Stegold likely imagined harmful thoughts back at the man who treated her poorly. Stegold's confession that she killed a pig through malicious thought represents another theme of witchcraft in early modern England. It brings light to the idea that some women may have believed they actually made covenants with the devil to improve their well being. Stegold told her captors that she first realized she had witchcraft powers when a pig died after she wished it would stop eating.[47]

THE WITCHES OF PENDLE HILL (LANCASHIRE)

The trials of the Pendle witches in 1612 are among the most famous witch trials in English history. The twelve that were accused lived in the area surrounding Pendle Hill in Lancashire, and were charged with the murders of ten people by the use of witchcraft. All but two were tried at Lancaster Assizes on August 18–19, 1612; one was tried at York Assizes on July 27, 1612, and another died in prison. Six of the Pendle witches came from one of two families, each at the time headed by a woman in her eighties: Elizabeth Southerns (also known as Demdike), her daughter Elizabeth Device, and her grandchildren James and Alizon Device; Anne Whittle (also known as Chattox), and her daughter Anne Redferne.

At the end of the 16th century Lancashire was regarded by the authorities as a wild and lawless region: an area "fabled for its theft, violence and sexual laxity, where the church was honoured without much understanding of its doctrines by the common people." The nearby Cistercian abbey at Whalley had been dissolved by Henry VIII in 1537, a move strongly resisted by the local people, over whose lives the abbey had until then exerted a powerful influence. Despite the abbey's closure, and the execution of its abbot, the people of Pendle remained largely faithful to their Catholic beliefs and were quick to revert to Catholicism on Queen Mary's accession to the throne in 1553. When Elizabeth I came to the throne in 1558, Catholic priests had to once again go into hiding, but in remote areas such as Pendle they continued to celebrate the Mass in secret.

In early 1612, the year of the trials, every justice of the peace (JP) in Lancashire was ordered to compile a list of recusants in their area, i.e., those who refused to attend the English Church and to take communion, a criminal offence at that time. Roger Nowell of Read Hall, on the edge of Pendle Forest, was the JP for Pendle. It was against this background of seeking out religious nonconformists that, in March 1612, Nowell investigated a complaint made to him by the family of John Law, a peddler, who claimed to have been injured by witchcraft. Many of those who subsequently became implicated as the investigation progressed did indeed consider themselves to be witches, in the sense of being village healers who practiced magic, probably in return for payment, but such men and women were common in 16th-century rural England, an accepted part of village life.

The event which sparked the JP's investigation occurred on March 21, 1612. On her way to Trawden Forest, Demdike's granddaughter, Alizon Device, encountered John Law, a peddler from Halifax, and asked him for some pins. Seventeenth-century metal pins were handmade and relatively expensive, but they were frequently needed for magical purposes, such as in healing—particularly for treating warts—divination, and for love magic, which may have been why Alizon was so keen to get hold of them and why Law was so reluctant to sell them to her. Whether she meant to buy them, as she claimed, and Law refused to undo his pack for such a small transaction, or whether she had no money and was begging for them, as Law's son Abraham claimed, is unclear. A few minutes after their encounter Alizon saw Law stumble and fall, perhaps because he suffered a stroke; he managed to regain his feet and reach a nearby inn. Initially Law made no accusations against Alizon, but she appears to have been convinced of her own powers; when Abraham Law took her to visit his father a few days after the incident, she reportedly confessed and asked for his forgiveness.

Alizon Device, her mother Elizabeth, and her brother James were summoned to appear before Nowell on March 30, 1612. Alizon confessed that she had sold her soul to the Devil, and that she had told him to lame John Law after he had called her a thief. Her brother, James, stated that his sister had also confessed to bewitching a local child. Elizabeth was more reluctant to speak, admitting only that her mother, Demdike, had a mark on her body, something that many, including Nowell, would have regarded as having been left by the Devil after he had sucked her blood. When questioned about Anne Whittle (Chattox), Alizon accused Chattox of murdering four men by witchcraft, and of killing her father, John Device, who had died in 1601. She claimed that her father had been so frightened of Old Chattox that he had agreed to give her 8 pounds of oatmeal each year in return for her promise not to hurt his family. The meal was handed over annually until the year before John's death; on his deathbed John claimed that his sickness had been caused by Chattox because they had not paid for protection.

On April 2, 1612, Demdike, Chattox, and Chattox's daughter Anne Redferne, were summoned to appear before Nowell. Both Demdike and Chattox were by then blind and in their eighties, and both provided Nowell with damaging confessions. Demdike claimed that she had given her soul to the Devil 20 years previously, and Chattox that she had given her soul to "a Thing like a Christian man," on his promise that "she would not lack anything and would get any revenge she desired." Based on the evidence and confessions he had obtained, Nowell committed Demdike, Chattox, Anne Redferne and Alizon Device to Lancaster Gaol, to be tried for *maleficium*—causing harm by witchcraft—at the next assizes.

The committal and subsequent trial of the four women might have been the end of the matter, had it not been for a meeting organized by Elizabeth Device at Malkin Tower, the home of the Demdikes, held on Good Friday, April 10, 1612. To feed the party, James Device stole a neighbor's sheep. Friends and others sympathetic to the family attended, and when word of it reached Roger Nowell, he decided to investigate. On April 27, 1612, an inquiry was held before Nowell and another magistrate, Nicholas Bannister, to determine the purpose of the meeting at Malkin Tower, who had attended, and what had happened there. As a result of the inquiry, eight more people were accused of witchcraft and committed for trial: Elizabeth Device, James Device, Alice Nutter, Katherine Hewitt,

Statue of the Pendle Witch Alice Nutter in Roughlee, Lancashire. August 20, 2012 (Graham Demaline, CCA-Share Alike 3.0 Unported).

John Bulcock, Jane Bulcock, Alice Grey and Jennet Preston. Preston lived across the border in Yorkshire, so she was sent for trial at York Assizes; the others were sent to Lancaster Gaol, to join the four already imprisoned there.[48]

WITCHCRAFT IN STANLEY, NEAR CHIPPENHAM (WILTSHIRE)

According to the Chancery Proceedings of May 29, 1565, Edward Baynton, Esquire, and Agnes, his wife, complained that whereas Agnes Mylles, widow, late of Stanley, in Wiltshire "not having God before her eyes but being seduced with a devilish instigation by using of Sorcerer's charms and witchcraft," about the Friday before Palm Sunday feloniously by witchcraft murdered Wyllyam Baynton, an infant, the only son and heir apparent of Edward and Agnes Baynton. And as Agnes Mylles confessed diverse times before John Bishop of Sarum, George Penruddock and John Hooper, Esquires, justices of the peace in Wilts, and other justices and witnesses, that she did the same murder by the procurement and enticement of Dorothy, wife of Henry Baynton, Gentleman, to whom and to the heirs male of his body the greater portion of the complainant's lands are to remain on his dying without issue male, the said Henry now having by Dorothy three sons and two daughters to whom the said land is entailed. Agnes was tried at Salisbury, and hanged at Fisherton Anger near Salisbury, the site of the local gaol.[49]

Stanley near Chippenham in northwest Wiltshire was for almost four centuries until 1536 the home of the Cistercian abbey of Stanley, not far from the Romano-British temple at Nettleton dedicated to Apollo the Hound-Lord.

WITCHCRAFT IN SALISBURY (WILTSHIRE)

Anne Bodenham of Fisherton Anger, on the western outskirts of Salisbury, was the wife of a clothier who had lived "in good fashion," and in her old age she taught children to read. She had, it seems, been in earlier life an apt pupil of Dr. Lambe and had learned from him the practice of magic lore. She drew magic circles, saw visions of people in a glass, possessed numerous charms and incantations, and, above all, kept a wonderful magic book. She attempted to find lost money, to tell the future, and to cure disease; indeed, she had a varied repertoire of occult performances.

She did all these things for money and roused no antagonism in her community until she was unfortunate enough to have dealings with a maid-servant in a Wiltshire family. How Anne Bodenham became implicated in the affair is unclear—the American historian Wallace Notestein says that it is "impossible to get behind the few hints given us by the cautious writer." The members of the family, evidently one of some standing in Wiltshire, became involved in a quarrel among themselves. It was believed, indeed, by neighbors that there had been a conspiracy on the part of some of the family to poison the mother-in-law. At all events, a maid in the family was imprisoned for participation in such a plot. It was then that Anne Bodenham first came into the story. The maid, to judge from the few data we have, in order to distract attention from her own doings, made a confession that she had signed a book of the Devil's with her own blood, all at the instigation of Anne Bodenham. Moreover, Anne, she said, had offered to send her to London in two hours. This was communicated to a justice of the peace, who promptly took the accused woman into custody. The maid-servant, successful thus far, began to simulate fits and to lay the blame for them on Mistress Anne. Questioned as to what she conceived her condition, she replied, "Oh very damnable, very wretched." She could see the Devil, she said, on the housetop looking at her. These fancies passed as facts, and the accused woman was put to the usual humiliations. She was searched, examined, and urged to confess. The narrator of the story made effort after effort to wring from her an admission of her guilt, but she slipped out of all his traps. Against her accuser she was very bitter. "She hath undone me ... that am an honest woman, 'twill break my Husband's heart, he grieves to see me in these Irons: I did once live in good fashion."

The case was turned over by the justices of the peace to the assizes at Salisbury, where Chief Baron John Wylde of the exchequer presided. The testimony of the maid was brought in, as well as the other proofs. All we know of the trial is that Anne was condemned, and that Judge Wylde was so well satisfied with his work that he urged Edmund Bower, who had begun an account of the case, but had hesitated to expose himself to "this Censorious Age," to go on with his booklet. That detestable individual had followed the case closely. After the condemnation he labored with the woman to make her confess. But no acknowledgment of guilt could be wrung from the "high-spirited Mistress Bodenham," even when the would-be father confessor held out to her the false hope of mercy. She made a will giving gifts to thirty people, declared she had been robbed by her maids in prison, lamented over her husband's sorrow, and requested that she be buried under the gallows. When the officer told her she must go with him to the place of execution, she replied, "Be you ready, I am ready." The narrator closes the account with some moral reflections.[50] She was hanged around 1650, during the time of the Civil War.

Fisherton Anger is not far from Wilton, the home of the cult of St. Edith until the Reformation, and close to Salisbury Cathedral, which by the late 15th century had a shrine to St. Oswald, and a cult of the Virgin Mary which attracted visitors from as far afield as Ghent in Belgium.[51]

WITCHCRAFT IN CORNWALL

Seventeenth century Cornwall was witness to a dozen or so witch trials, held at the Assize courts at Launceston. For example, in the 1650s more than 25 people were sent to Launceston Gaol when a woman, accused by her neighbors of being a witch, implicated others in her alleged practice of the dark arts. Some of them were executed at that time. In 1671 Isaac Pearce was accused of laming Honor Teague by witchcraft. A little later in 1675, Mary Glasson was accused of murdering 11-year-old Isabella Hockin of Camborne by witchcraft. Most dramatic perhaps were the cases of Jane Nicholas and Mary Guy, in 1686 and 1696 respectively, who were accused of bewitching two children and of tormenting them to the point that they suffered from fits, and vomited pins, nails, and other assorted objects, which were produced in court as evidence. The boy at the center of the 1686 case claimed that Jane Nicholas "very often appeared to him, sometimes in [her own shape]; at other times like a *Cat*; whereupon the Boy would shriek, and cry out that he would not see her, laying his hands over his Eyes and Mouth, and would say with a loud voice, she is putting things into my Mouth, she will Choke me, she will Poison me." One of the towers of Launceston Castle was formerly known as the "Witch's Tower," owing to the belief that witches were burned at its base, though under English law those convicted of witchcraft were hanged.[52]

Saveock Water is a hamlet in the middle of Cornwall, between Perranporth, with its cult of St. Piran, and Glasney College, Penryn, a center of the Cornish language until

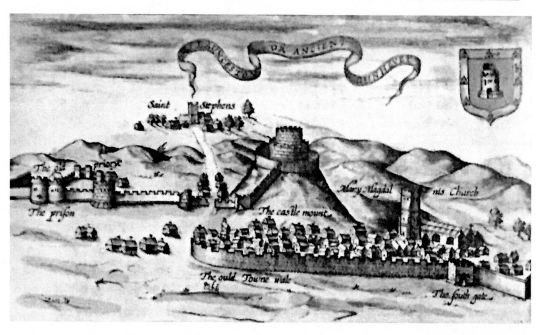

A 1611 depiction of Launceston town and castle, where witchcraft trials were held in the 17th century (*The Theatre of the Empire of Great Britain*, by John Speed, 1611).

1548. For the last 17 years Saveock water has been the site of an archaeological dig, led by Jacqui Wood, which has uncovered a Mesolithic camp, a Neolithic ritual area, and a Bronze Age metalworking area, and pagan pits which date from the 1640s to the 1970s.[53] These pagan pits show that there were people in Cornwall who considered themselves to be witches or, more likely, cunning-folk.

Jacqui Wood is an experimental archaeologist, and she was digging up the ground to create an ancient kind of furnace when she discovered a clay floor. In 2001 she gathered together some archaeology students to investigate the clay floor. As the group peeled off layers of turf, they discovered the clay floor was an extensive man-made platform—probably a foundation for a group of ancient dwellings. Based on flint fragments embedded in the clay, a Danish specialist dated the site to the late Mesolithic, around 8,500 years ago.

But as Wood and her team excavated the platform over the next few seasons, unusual features began to emerge. They came across strange rectangular holes, about 15 by 10 inches, in the clay. "At first we thought they must be postholes or something," says Wood. But the first of the holes, about 6 inches deep, was lined with white feathers. The pits cut through the clay platform, so Wood knew that they had to date to a later time, but only a radiocarbon test could determine the date. "We guessed it might have been a bird-plucking pit, a common farming practice at the turn of the 19th century," says Wood.

But that couldn't be the case—Wood found that the feathers were still attached to the skin, which had been laid in the pit with the feathers facing inward. A bird expert from the local zoo confirmed they came from a swan. On top of the swan skin, Wood found a pile of pebbles and a number of claws from different birds. She later learned that the stones came from a coastal region 15 miles away, though no one knows why they were brought from so far. Someone had gone to considerable trouble to gather the contents of this pit. That season, Wood and her colleagues found eight pits, two of which contained odd collections of bird parts, and six of which had been emptied, but with a few tell-tale feathers and stones left behind.

More unusual finds came in 2005. Sandwiched between two of the rectangular pits was a round pit with a swan-feather lining. On top of the swan feathers nestled 55 eggs, seven of which contained chicks that would have been close to hatching. The shells of the eggs had dissolved, but the moist environment had preserved their membranes. Remains of magpies—birds associated with luck and superstition even today—had been placed on each side of the eggs. By that time Wood was convinced that only witchcraft could explain her unusual finds, but no one had ever heard of anything like this. Radiocarbon tests revealed the swan skins dated to around 1640 CE, the time of civil war in England and a very dangerous period to be practicing witchcraft. And yet witchcraft remained popular, says Marion Gibson of Exeter University, a specialist on 16th- and 17th-century paganism. "Every village would have had people thought to be skilled in magic in one way or another and people in the area would go to them for their specialist services, just as we might go to a lawyer or plumber today."

Not far from the three pits, Wood and her colleagues uncovered the remains of a spring-fed pool, carefully lined with white quartz, and containing 128 textile scraps, six medieval straight pins, shoe parts, heather branches (associated with luck), fingernail clippings, human hair, and part of an iron cauldron. "Two of the pieces of fabric contained wool and silk, indicating they originally belonged to someone of high status," says Wood. Others were coarser and may have come from those of lower status. Further excavation uncovered a stone-lined drain and a second pool that only fills in winter.

Wood realized that the pools were much older than their contents, and that this site may have been special to people for thousands of years. Based on stratigraphic evidence, she believes the quartz-lined pools date from around 4000 BCE, in the Neolithic. "The white quartz would have made the pools glow in the moonlight, and we think they may have been very special, a place of ritual for people in those times," she speculates.

Wood's 2008 field season brought more unusual discoveries. "We have been uncovering some extraordinary animal pits," says Wood. One was lined with the skin of a black cat and contained 22 eggs, all with chicks close to hatching, in addition to cat claws, teeth, and whiskers. Another held a dog skin, dog teeth, and a baked pig jaw. The week prior to my arrival, Wood's students uncovered a pit that contained a mysterious seven-inch iron disk with a swan skin on one side and animal fur on the other. The biggest shock of all came from the radiocarbon dates for these pits. The cat pit dated to the 18th century, while the dog pit dated to the 1950s. It is not clear whether the pits were the work of a single family or a countrywide guild of witches. One lead came from a conversation between a member of Wood's excavation team and some locals in a pub. They recalled that there was a family, the Burnetts, reputed to be witches, that lived near Wood's house. Two sisters resided there until the 1980s, so it is possible the dog pit could have been their work.[54]

The significance of the swan feathers in the pits is unknown, but Jacqui Wood believes that the feathers were an offering to St. Bridget or St. Bride, the patron saint of brides, who has a swan as her symbol. It is said that offerings to her were placed at the branches of three rivers, and this area used to be called Threewaters—after Saveock water, Blackwater and Chacewater. Jacqui Wood's theory is that if you got married and did not get pregnant in the first year, you might make an offering to St. Bride of a feather pit. If you finally got pregnant, you had to go back to the pit, take out the contents and burn them to set the spirit of the swan free. If you never got pregnant then the pit remained untouched.[55]

Witchcraft Trials and Cunning-Folk

Although cunning-folk practiced magic, it seems that that cunning-folk were rarely accused of witchcraft. A London cunning-woman, Joan Peterson, one of the few practitioners to be hanged, was convicted in 1652 for bewitching Christopher Wilson. He had been to her for a cure but had failed to pay for services rendered. In retaliation she threatened, "You had been better you had given me my money for you shall be ten times worse than ever you were." The worried Wilson subsequently fell into strange fits and became very sick.

Another case involved Ursula Kemp, a cunning-woman of St. Osyth in Essex, home until 1539 to a well-known priory of Augustinian canons. Ursula Kemp had treated a woman named Grace Thurlow, who suffered from "a lameness in her bones," and was promised twelve pence as payment. Five weeks later, Kemp went to see Thurlow, who was now feeling much better, and asked her for the money. Thurlow reneged on her promise, saying "she was a poor and needy woman and had no money." Kemp then asked for some cheese instead, but Thurlow said she had none to give. The frustrated Kemp swore she "woulde be even with her," and the next day Thurlow was taken lame. Kemp was subsequently accused of putting a spell on her, even though she had stressed on an earlier occasion that although "she could unwitch" she could "not witch." She was convicted of witchcraft and hanged in 1582.[56]

Witchcraft in Wales

Soothsayers in Medieval Wales

The Welsh obviously believed in ritual curses, but apparently, they also believed that certain people could foretell the future. In Chapter 16 of his *Description of Wales* ("Concerning the soothsayers of this nation, and persons as it were possessed"), the Welsh-Norman cleric Gerald of Wales describes a group of people he calls awenyddion[57]:

> There are certain persons in Cambria, whom you will find nowhere else, called Awenyddion, or people inspired; when consulted upon any doubtful event, they roar out violently, are rendered beside themselves, and become, as it were, possessed by a spirit. They do not deliver the answer to what is required in a connected manner; but the person who skilfully observes them, will find, after many preambles, and many nugatory and incoherent, though ornamented speeches, the desired explanation conveyed in some turn of a word: they are then roused from their ecstasy, as from a deep sleep, and, as it were, by violence compelled to return to their proper senses. After having answered the questions, they do not recover till violently shaken by other people; nor can they remember the replies they have given. If consulted a second or third time upon the same point, they will make use of expressions totally different; perhaps they speak by the means of fanatic and ignorant spirits. These gifts are usually conferred upon them in dreams: some seem to have sweet milk or honey poured on their lips; others fancy that a written schedule is applied to their mouths and on awaking they publicly declare that they have received this gift.... They invoke, during their prophecies, the true and living God, and the Holy Trinity, and pray that they may not by their sins be prevented from finding the truth.—*Gwen Ellis of Betws yn Rhos (Conwy, North Wales)*

There were few witchcraft trials in Wales, and one of them involved a woman called Ellis. Gwen Ellis (Gwen ferch Ellis) was born in Llandyrnog in the Vale of Clwyd and spent her childhood in the commote (district) of Yale (Ial) near Wrexham. In 1588 she and her second husband (a miller) went to live at the mill in Llaneilian yn Rhos. When her husband died she married a third time, a man from Betws yn Rhos. By profession Gwen was a weaver but she had a talent for healing, and by the use of herbs she healed both people and their animals. Her incantations always began with the words "in the names of the father, the son and the Holy Ghost," and were more likely folk prayers than "spells." Because of her abilities, the rich and powerful sought her help as well as ordinary folk.

At some point, Gwen became involved with a Jane Conway of Marle near the town of Conwy, who seems to have had some quarrel with Thomas Mostyn of Gloddaeth Hall, Llandudno. When a charm, written backwards, was found in the parlor of magistrate Thomas Mostyn's home, Ellis was accused of putting it there to bewitch him. So in 1594 at the age of 42 she found herself in Flint Jail accused of witchcraft being questioned by the Bishop of St. Asaph. Later that year a formal investigation was held in Llansanffraid Church, near the town of Conwy; five men and two women gave evidence against her. She was accused of driving a child insane and, worst of all, killing a man through witchcraft. Witnesses claimed that she had a familiar, a bad temper and a sharp tongue. Accusations accumulated, the most serious of which was that she murdered one Lewis ap John by witchcraft. On the last count she was found guilty and sentenced to death. She was found guilty and hanged in Denbigh Town Square in late 1594.[58] Interestingly, the story of Gwen Ellis took place in an area which had once been dominated by Basingwerk Abbey and St. Winefride's well at Holywell, where pilgrimages were still being made in the 17th century.

Witchcraft in Scotland

THE WITCHES OF NORTH BERWICK (EAST LOTHIAN)

There were numerous witchcraft trials in Scotland, no doubt inspired by James VI's *Daemonologie*. The North Berwick witch trials (which were instigated by James VI himself) ran for two years from 1590 to 1592 and implicated at least seventy people from southern Scotland, including several nobles of the Scottish court. The suspected witches were accused of holding their covens on the Auld Kirk Green in the village of North Berwick, which is not far from Whitekirk, where there was a well-known shrine to Our Lady, much frequented by James IV of Scotland until his death in 1513.

As part of the background to the trials, a year or so prior to these events, King James VI of Scotland, who had initially been quite lenient toward witchcraft, experienced terrible storms while sailing to Copenhagen to marry Princess Anne of Denmark and was forced to take refuge on the coast of Norway for some time. More storms greeted their return journey, and the admiral of the escorting Danish fleet (among others) blamed the storm on witchcraft. These events drastically changed James' views toward witchcraft, and he became single-minded in his persecution of witchcraft in Scotland, later writing *Daemonologie* and instructing his followers that they must denounce and prosecute any supporters or practitioners of witchcraft.

In 1590, a young servant called Gilly (or Gellie) Duncan, from the small town of Tranent near Edinburgh had been arrested for suspected witchcraft after some of her healing cures were branded as miraculous and the work of a witch. Initially, Gellie obstinately refused to confess to any dealings with the Devil but, after protracted torture and after the discovery of a so-called "Devil's mark" on her neck, she confessed to being a witch and having sold her soul to the Devil, and effecting all her cures by his aid. Under further torture, she named various accomplices, including Dr. John Fian (a local school master and alleged coven leader and wizard), Agnes Sampson (a respected local midwife and healer), Barbara Napier (the widow of Earl Archibald of Angus), Francis Stewart (the 1st Earl of Bothwell, and the King's cousin) and Euphemia Maclean (the daughter of the Lord Cliftonhall). Ultimately, Gilly was burned at the stake.

In all, about seventy people were accused of witchcraft, although it is not known exactly how many were executed. Many confessed under torture to having met with the Devil in the North Berwick churchyard at night, and to devoting themselves to doing evil, including attempts to poison the King and other members of his household, and to sink the King's ship. Specific confessions claimed that, on Halloween of 1590, the Devil had the witches dig up corpses and cut off different joints or organs which were then attached to a dead cat and thrown into the sea in order to call up the storm which had nearly shipwrecked the King's ship. Some attested that the Devil had incited them to these acts because he considered King James his greatest enemy (an admission that James found particularly flattering). The confessions were all suspiciously similar and were all extracted by torture.

One particularly gruesome account was that of Agnes Sampson, who was examined by King James himself at his palace of Holyrood House. She was fastened to the wall of her cell by a "witch's bridle," an iron instrument with four sharp prongs forced into the mouth, so that two prongs pressed against the tongue, and the two others against the cheeks. She was kept without sleep, thrown with a rope around her head, and only after these ordeals did Agnes Sampson confess to the fifty-three indictments against her. She was finally strangled and burned as a witch.[59]

THE WITCHES OF ABERDEEN

Aberdeen was founded in the 12th century, and until 1690 St. Machar's Cathedral was the seat of a bishop; Aberdeen was also home to a Carmelite Friary and a Dominican Friary, both destroyed at the time of the Reformation. One of the most interesting witchcraft cases in Aberdeen happened from 1596 and concerned a whole family[60]:

The mother, Jane Wishart, was brought to trial and eventually convicted on 18 points of witchcraft, although the total number of charges brought against her exceeded 30 and covered a period of over 20 years. The charges included casting a spell on a fisherman who then took to his bed and "lay bedsick for one month." The earliest charge related to an incident when five men caught her coming out of the yard of Adam Mair, one of her neighbours, at two in the morning. The men woke up Adam's wife to tell her what they had discovered and, later that day at about two or three o'clock in the afternoon, two of the men were found drowned in the Auld Wattergang at the Links where they had gone to wash themselves. Two others who had seen Janet leave her neighbour's house subsequently offered the testimony against her. Janet's son-in-law, John Allan testified against her following an incident when he hit his wife and was chastised by Janet. Following this, a brown dog started to come into his bedroom and attack him, although it left his wife alone. This continued until John threatened to complain to the minister and the Kirk Session. Eight days before Janet was apprehended there was heard a rumbling noise in her house which frightened her next door neighbour who thought his house might fall over. This, too, was attributed to Janet's supernatural powers and formed one of the points of witchcraft on which she was convicted.

Janet's son, Thomas Leyis, was found guilty of being a ringleader and convicted on three accounts of witchcraft. He is said to have presided at a meeting held at midnight in the Castlegate when many witches convened at the Market and Fish crosses "under the conduct and guiding of the devil present with them." These people all danced and played instruments about the crosses and Thomas was accused of being foremost amongst them and of hitting Kathren Mitchell "because she spoilt the dance and ran not so fast as the rest." According to the records, both Janet and Thomas were strangled and burnt.

On the 22nd of March the same year John Leyis (Janet's husband) and their three daughters, Elspet, Janet and Violet were also accused of sorcery. They were absolved on all counts of witchcraft but found guilty of being in the company of Janet and Thomas and acting as their accomplices. As a result they were banished from Aberdeen and the surrounding area and were forbidden to come within 10 miles of the burgh. Unfortunately the dittays [indictments] for each of these trials no longer exist but Aberdeen's City Archives do still have the original dittay for the trial of Isobel Strathauchyn—also known as Isobel Skuddie. She was found guilty of witchcraft and burned in March 1597. The charges against her included making up a love charm and gathering up bones in Dyce churchyard, boiling them in water and then taking the water and washing William Symmer of Hatton of Fintray. Thereafter she caused William's mother to take the bones and throw them in to the River Don, which when she did "caused the water to rumble in such a manner as [if] all the hills had fallen therein."

DEMONIC POSSESSION IN ERSKINE (RENFREWSHIRE)

In August 1696 Christian, the 11-year-old daughter of John Shaw, the laird of Bargarran, in the parish of Erskine, to the west of Glasgow, began to experience fits and bodily contortions; her body became stiff and motionless, and her tongue protruded at great length. She experienced temporary deafness, blindness and an inability to speak. She regurgitated hair, straw, coal cinders the size of chestnuts, gravel, pins, feathers of wild fowl and bones of various sorts. At times her head twisted around, as if her neck bone had been dissolved. Her stomach "swelled like a drum, as like a woman with child." At times she had difficulty breathing and felt as if she was being choked. During some of her fits she took off all her clothes. Witnesses claimed that on a number of occasions she was carried through her house "with such a swift and unaccountable motion that it was not in the power of any to prevent her—her feet not touching the ground." She also conversed with invisible specters.

While experiencing her fits, Christian Shaw accused Katherine Campbell, one of the maids in the house, and Agnes Nasmith, described by her neighbors as "an old woman, ignorant, and of a malicious disposition, addicted to threatenings," of having caused her suffering by witchcraft. She later added others to the list of accused culprits. The entire affair was eventually referred to the privy council, which commissioned Lord Blantyre and eight other members of the local elite to interrogate and imprison persons suspected of witchcraft and to examine witnesses. The resulting precognitions (preliminary examinations), which were not taken on oath, led to the confessions of Elizabeth Anderson (aged 17), James Lindsay (aged 14), and Thomas Lindsay (a minor), all grandchildren of Jean Fulton, and the naming of accomplices who had allegedly gathered with the Devil. All in all, 24 persons were indicted for witchcraft. On April 5, a commission of justiciary granted by the privy council authorized a trial of seven of these persons. All seven were tried and executed at Paisley in May.[61] Paisley was the home of the Cluniac abbey of Paisley, founded around 1163 and burned by Reformers in 1561.

CUNNING-FOLK AND CHARMERS IN SCOTLAND

The terms "charmer" and "charming" were used in the Scottish court records to denote those acts of magic that did not cause harm but were nevertheless "superstitious" and sinful in the eyes of the authorities. As a category of offence then it was distinguishable from "witchcraft." This distinction between good and bad magic undoubtedly mirrored popular perceptions, although at a popular level charming was not considered as "superstitious." Yet in the court records the distinction was not always made. A number of the items of healing in Thomas Grieve's dittay [charge] of 1623, for example, were not described as charming but in such terms as "curing, by devillery and Witchcraft," which reflected the Calvinistic conception of popular magic.[62]

Scottish charmers used "charms," and one of the oldest examples is the verse against sprains used by the Orkney charmer Catherine Carrie in 1616 which went: "bone to bone, synnew to synnew, and flesche to flesche, and bluid to bluid." This type of charm usually began with Christ's mishap when riding, as in this example used by Janet Brown in 1643[63]:

> Our Lord forth raide;
> His foal's foot slade;
> Our Lord down lighted;
> His foal's foot righted;
> Saying Flesh to Flesh, blood to blood,
> And bane to bane
> In Our Lord his name.

In Scotland the charmer would sometimes tie a piece of thread around the injured part while murmuring the verse.[64]

Cunning-folk in England were rarely tried for witchcraft, but they were in Scotland. The classic case is Agnes Sampson, who was one of those tried and executed in the North Berwick witch trials. Of the 53 charges brought against her over half concerned healing and divination. Item 21, for example, concerned "the healing of the laird of Reidshill's son by witchcraft, whom the chirurgeons had given over," and Item 27 for curing a child by "gripping him and speaking some words of charming."[65]

Scottish healers used various techniques to cure their patients. As in England, herbs were widely used to treat disease. Christian Lewinston prescribed that one patient be bathed with red nettles and lovage and be rubbed with lovage and butter. For heart sickness she told a patient to drink broom and chamomile in white wine. Another healer gave a bewitched man a herbal drink mixed with butter and saffron. The use of threads was another common technique. This either involved tying thread around the affected part of the body or passing the sick person or animal through a skein of yarn. Thomas Grieve cured William Beveridge of a "grievous sickness" by making him pass through the yarn several times and then burning it in a big fire.

The use of water from holy wells and south-running streams or rivers was also a prominent feature of Scottish healing. Grieve cured David Chalmers by making him wear a shirt washed in south-running water and making certain crosses or signs over him. Isobel Haldane washed one child in water she had brought in silence from St. Carol's Well, Ruthven (Aberdeenshire). One particular ritual involving water stands out, according to the historian Owen Davies[66]—an "intriguing and highly unusual ritual use of hot stones to divine and cure." Davies says he has found "no parallels elsewhere to the technique employed by Katherine Craigie to treat the husband of Janet Craigie." She placed three stones, representing a hill spirit, water spirit and a kirk spirit, in a fire. She left them there to bake for a whole day and then after sunset placed them under the threshold of the door overnight. Before sunrise, she took up the stones, still hot presumably, and placed them in a vessel full of water. From examining the reaction, she declared, "it is a kirk spirit which troubleth Robbie your husband." She was then directed to wash her husband with water from the vessel.

The story of the three stones recalls a miracle performed by St. Columba when he was among the Picts of eastern Scotland in the 6th century. He was visiting the Pictish king Bridei son of Maelchon in Inverness, and in his *Life of St. Columba*, Adomnan describes the visit as follows[67]:

> The fact is said to have taken place near the fortress of King Brude (near Inverness). When the saint himself was chanting the evening hymns with a few of the brethren, as usual, outside the king's fortifications, some Druids, coming near to them, did all they could to prevent God's praises being sung in the midst of a pagan nation. On seeing this, the saint began to sing the 44th Psalm, and at the same moment so wonderfully loud, like pealing thunder, did his voice become, that king and people were struck with terror and amazement.

While St. Columba was visiting Bridei, he begged Broichan the Druid to free "a certain Scotic female slave." When Broichan refused, the saint warned him, in the presence of the king, that if he did not free the slave, he would die before St. Columba left the province. The saint then left the royal palace and proceeded to the River Ness:

> from this stream he took a white pebble, and showing it to his companions said to them: "Behold this white pebble by which God will effect the cure of many diseases among this heathen nation."
>
> Having thus spoken, he instantly added, "Broichan is chastised grievously at this moment, for an angel being sent from heaven, and striking him severely, hath broken into many pieces the glass cup in his hand from which he was drinking, and hath left him gasping deeply for breath, and half dead. Let us await here a short time, for two of the king's messengers, who have been sent after us in haste, to request us to return quickly and help the dying Broichan, who, now that he is thus terribly punished, consenteth to set the girl free."

Two horsemen then rode up and told them that Broichan was seriously ill, and that the king was begging St. Columba to cure his foster-father Broichan.

> Having heard these words of the messengers, St. Columba sent two of his companions to the king with the pebble which he had blessed, and said to them: "If Broichan shall first promise to set the maiden free, then at once immerse this little stone in water, and let him drink from it and he shall be instantly cured; but if he break his vow and refuse to liberate her, he shall die that instant."
>
> The two persons, in obedience to the saint's instructions, proceeded to the palace, and announced to the king the words of the venerable man. When they were made known to the king and his tutor Broichan, they were so dismayed that they immediately liberated the captive and delivered her to the saint's messengers. The pebble was then immersed in water, and in a wonderful manner, contrary to the laws of nature, the stone floated on the water like a nut or an apple, nor, as it had been blessed by the holy man, could it be submerged. Broichan drank from the stone as it floated on the water, and instantly returning from the verge of death recovered his perfect health and soundness of body.

So it seems that stones were thought to possess magical properties from at least the 6th century. Katherine Craigie was from Rousay, a small island in the Orkney Islands, and there stones were even more significant. Pictish painted pebbles, dating from the 2nd to 8th centuries CE, have been found on broch sites which had an extensive post-broch occupation (brochs are Iron Age drystone roundhouses). The pebbles are often painted with dots and wavy lines, and sometimes with small circles, pentacles, crescents and triangles.[68]

Conclusion

Magic has long played an important part in British life since at least the Iron Age, when amulets were made from human bones, often skull bones. Indeed, skulls were often buried in pits and ditches of important settlements like Danebury hillfort in Hampshire and may well have had a magical function. However, the first clear-cut magic in Britain was the use of curse tablets, which came with the Romans, and seem to be most common in western Britain (Somerset, Gloucestershire and southeast Wales). Skulls continued to play a significant role in burial rituals with the decapitated burials of southern England. More clearly magical were the prone (face down) burials of Roman Britain designed to prevent the dead from returning to haunt the living.

It was only with the coming of Christianity in the 5th and 6th century (Wales and Scotland) and the 7th century (Anglo-Saxon England) that the British acquired a voice, and it became clear how widely magic was used. Curses were used in charters granting land to monasteries or individuals; there were written spells and charms like the *Æcerbot*, designed to improve fields which were not productive, spells or charms against diseases such as the one against rheumatism from *Lacnunga*; and there seems to have been a widespread belief in witches and witchcraft. There is little documentary evidence for Anglo-Saxon witchcraft, but women buried in early Anglo-Saxon cemeteries are often found with beaver-tooth pendants or cowrie shells, or bags with unusual objects, and the Anglo-Saxon scholar Andrew Reynolds speculates that these were cunning-women (witches) who were able to offer a variety of magical services.

The Church was opposed to witches and witchcraft and offered their own form of "magic"—the miracles performed by saints through the help of God. The Church, of course, did not regards the saints' miracles as magic, but the Reformation certainly did, and condemned all forms of "magic" practiced by the Catholic Church. But magic thrived, especially among the cunning-folk, who offered a variety of services including the treatment of common ailments. The new Protestant church continued to condemn magic, and this led to a series of witchcraft trials, often involving older women.

Cunning-folk or witches certainly existed, as we can see from the finds at Saveock Water in Cornwall. In fact, there is some evidence that there continued to be "witches" at Saveock Water as late as the 1950s. We can dismiss this as rural superstition, but in reality magic is not far from all our lives, especially—but not solely!—in children's books. Indeed, magic is still a fact of life in many parts of the world. Many years ago, I was teaching English in Malawi, a small country in southern Africa. In the newspaper I saw several reports of people who had been beaten up because they had allegedly "tied up the rain"—this was at the start of the rainy season, and it had apparently rained in one village but not in the neighboring village. It seems to me that the 16th and 17th century British people who accused their neighbors of being witches must have thought in a similar way—and that was after a thousand years of Christianity (compare this with Malawi, where Christianity was introduced just over a century ago). Perhaps this kind of magic no longer exists in Western societies, but the popularity of the Harry Potter books suggests that we rather wish it did.

Chapter Notes

Introduction

1. Muhammad A. Dandamayev, "Magi," in Ehsan Yarshater (ed.), *Encyclopedia Iranica*, at the website http://www.iranicaonline.org/articles/magi.
2. Matthew W. Dickie, *Magic and Magicians in the Greco-Roman World* (Taylor & Francis e-library, 2005).
3. *Ibid.*
4. Richard Kieckhefer, *Magic in the Middle Ages* (Cambridge, UK: Cambridge University Press, 2000), 22.
5. *Ibid.*, 47.
6. *Ibid.*
7. *Ibid.*, 48.
8. *Ibid.*, 21.
9. *Ibid.*, 25.

Chapter 1

1. Richard Kieckhefer, *Magic in the Middle Ages* (Cambridge, UK: Cambridge University Press, 2000), 85.
2. British Museum, *Hounslwo Boar Figurine*.
3. Dennis Harding, *Death and Burial in Iron Age Britain* (Oxford, UK: Oxford University Press, 2015), 186.
4. Mike Pitts, "News: All Cannings Cross," *British Archaeology* 74 (January 2004).
5. Pastscape, *All Cannings Cross*.
6. John Barrett and David McOmish, *All Cannings Cross*.
7. Ian Armit, *Headhunting and the Body in Iron Age Europe* (Cambridge, UK: Cambridge University Press, 2012), 6.
8. Andrew Lawson, *Potterne 1982–5* (Salisbury, UK: Trust for Wessex Archaeology, 2000), 4.
9. Pastscape, *Monument No. 211644*.
10. Ian Armit, *Headhunting and the Body*, 6.
11. Jacqueline McKinley, "Human Bone," in Andrew Lawson, *Potterne 1982–5*, 98.
12. *Ibid.*, 100.
13. David McOmish, "East Chisenbury: Ritual and Rubbish at the British Bronze Age-Iron Age Transition," *Antiquity* (March 1996).
14. Barry Cunliffe, "Understanding Hillforts: Have We Progressed?," in Andrew Payne, Mark Corney and Barry Cunliffe, *The Wessex Hillforts Project* (London; English Heritage, 2006), 159.

15. Maud Cunnington, "Lidbury Camp," *Wiltshire Archaeological and Natural History Magazine* 40 (1917), 17–19.
16. *Ibid.*, 22.
17. *Ibid.*, 25.
18. Maud Cunnington, "Excavations in Yarnbury Castle Camp," *Wiltshire Archaeological and Natural History Magazine* 46 (1933), 203.
19. Pastscape, *Yarnbury Castle*.
20. Maud Cunnington, "Excavations in Yarnbury Castle Camp," 202.
21. *Ibid.*, 202–203.
22. *Ibid.*, 206.
23. *Ibid.*, 207.
24. Jodie Lewis, "Upwards at 45 Degrees: The Use of Vertical Caves During the Neolithic and Early Bronze Age on Mendip, Somerset," *Capra* 2 (2000).
25. Pastscape, *Wilsford Shaft*.
26. Paul Ashbee, Martin Bell and Edwina Proudfoot, *Wilsford Shaft: Excavations 1960–62* (London: English Heritage, 1989), 126.
27. *Ibid.*, 68.
28. Chris Ellis and Andrew B. Powell, *An Iron Age Settlement Outside Battlesbury Hillfort, Warminster and Sites Along the Southern Range Road* (Salisbury, Wiltshire: Wessex Archaeology, 2008), 50.
29. *Ibid.*, 135–6.
30. *Ibid.*, XV22.
31. *Ibid.*, 71–6.
32. *Ibid.*, 81–2.
33. *Ibid.*, 34–5.
34. Pastscape, *Danebury*.
35. Barry Cunliffe, "Landscape with People," in Kate Flint and Howard Morphy, *Culture, Landscape and the Environment* (Oxford, UK: Oxford University Press, 2000), 126.
36. *Ibid.*, 128.
37. Miranda Green, *Animals in Celtic Life and Myth* (London: Routledge, 1998), 119.
38. Barry Cunliffe, *Danebury: An Iron Age Hillfort in Hampshire Vol. 6. a Hillfort Community in Perspective* (London: Council for British Archaeology, 1995), 77.
39. D. Serjeantson and J. Morris, "Ravens and Crows in Iron Age and Roman Britain," *Oxford Journal of Archaeology* 30 (2011), 91.
40. Chris Webster, *The Archaeology of South West England* (Taunton: Somerset County Council, 2008), 133–4.
41. Arthur Bulleid and Harold St. George Gray, *The*

Glastonbury Lake Village (Glastonbury, UK: The Glastonbury Antiquarian Society, 1917), 405.

42. *Ibid.*, 676.

43. Christopher Evans, "Delivering Bodies Unto Waters: A Late Bronze Age Mid-Stream Midden Settlement and Iron Age Ritual Complex in the Fens," *The Antiquaries Journal* 93 (2013), 63.

44. *Ibid.*, 63–7.

45. *Ibid.*, 67.

46. *Ibid.*, 76.

47. Robert Hertz, "A Contribution to the Study of the Collective Representation of Death," in Robert Hertz, *Death and the Right Hand*, trans. Rodney and Claudia Needham (London: Cohen and West, 1960).

48. Rebecca Redfern, "New Evidence for Iron Age Secondary Burial Practice and Bone Modification from Gussage All Saints and Maiden Castle (Dorset, England)," *Oxford Journal of Archaeology* 27 (2008), 286.

49. *Ibid.*, 291.

50. J. Barber, "Bronze Age Farms and Iron Age Farm Mounds of the Outer Hebrides," *Scottish Archaeological Internet Reports* 3 (2003), 140.

51. *Ibid.*, 90.

52. Ian Armit, *Headhunting and the Body*, 205.

53. David Keys, "Iron Age Chariot and Horse Found Buried Together in Yorkshire," *The Independent* (Thursday 30 March 2017).

Chapter 2

1. Bryan P. Levack, *The Witchcraft Sourcebook* (New York: Routledge, 2004), 29.

2. *Ibid.*, 31.

3. Lucius Apuleius, *The Golden Ass*, Book 2, trans. A.S. Kline, at the website Poetry in Translation, http://www.poetryintranslation.com/PITBR/Latin/TheGoldenAssII.htm.

4. Horace, "Epode V," in *The Epodes and Carmen Saeculare*, trans. A.S. Kline, at the website Poetry in Translation, http://www.poetryintranslation.com/PITBR/Latin/HoraceEpodesAndCarmenSaeculare.htm#anchor_Toc98670053.

5. Bryan P. Levack, *The Witchcraft Sourcebook*, 38.

6. Tacitus, *Annals*, trans. John Jackson (Cambridge, MA: Harvard University Press, 1931), Book 2, Chapter 69.

7. Pliny the Younger, *Letters by Pliny the Younger*, trans. William Melmoth (New York: P.F. Collier & Son, 1909–14), Letter LXXXIII to Sura.

8. Tacitus, *Annals*, Book 14, Chapter 30.

9. Coflein, *Llyn Cerrig Bach*.

10. Tacitus, *Annals*, Book 14, Chapter 30.

11. *Ibid.*, Book 14, Chapter 33.

12. *Ibid.*, Book 14, Chapter 35.

13. Cassius Dio, *Roman History*, trans. Earnest Cary (Cambridge, MA: Harvard University Press, 1914–1927), Book 62.

14. Martin Barber, *Pre-Christian Cemeteries* (London: English Heritage, 2011), 4.

15. Dorothy Watts, *Religion in Late Roman Britain* (London: Routledge, 1998), 74.

16. Jacqueline McKinley, "Human Bone," in Kirsten Egging Dinwiddy, *A Late Roman Cemetery at Little Keep. Dorchester, Dorset* (Salisbury, Wiltshire: Wessex Archaeology, 2007).

17. Giles Clarke, *Pre-Roman and Roman Winchester: The Roman Cemetery at Lankhills* (Oxford, UK: Oxford University Press, 1979), 141.

18. *Ibid.*, 142.

19. *Ibid.*, 192.

20. "Winterbourne Down," *Wiltshire Archaeological and Natural History Magazine* 58 (1962), 470.

21. Gaynor Western, *Osteological Analysis of Human Remains from Sainsbury's Site, St. Johns, Worcester* (Wisbech, UK: Ossafreelance, 2009).

22. T. Anderson, "Two Decapitations from Roman Towcester," *Journal of Osteoarchaeology* 11 (2001), 400–405.

23. Neil McGavin, "A Roman Cemetery and Trackway at Stanton Harcourt," *Oxoniensia* 45 (1980), 112–123.

24. Katie Tucker, "Whence This Severance of the Head?": The Osteology and Archaeology of Human Decapitation in Britain (Ph.D. diss., University of Winchester, 2012), 221–230.

25. Belinda Crerar, *Contextualising Deviancy: A Regional Approach to Decapitated Inhumation in Late Roman Britain* (Ph.D. diss., University of Cambridge, 2012), 169.

26. *Ibid.*, 169–170.

27. *Ibid.*, 93–94.

28. *Ibid.*, 104.

29. Alison Taylor, "Aspects of Deviant Burial in Roman Britain," in Eileen M. Murphy, *Deviant Burial in the Archaeological Record* (Oxford, UK: Oxbow Books, 2008), 160.

30. *Ibid.*, 167.

31. *Ibid.*, 170.

32. Pastscape, *Jordan Hill Roman Temple*.

33. *Hamble*, at the website Curse Tablets from Roman Britain, http://curses.csad.ox.ac.uk/index.shtml.

34. T.F.C. Blagg, *Research on Roman Britain, 1960–1989* (London: Society for the Promotion of Roman Studies, 1989), 224.

35. South Elmham and District Local History Group, *Newsletter* 27 (May 2011), 15.

36. Anthony King and Grahame Soffe, "Internal Organisation and Deposition at the Iron Age Temple on Hayling Island (Hampshire)," in J. Collis (ed.), *Society and Settlement in Iron Age Europe* (Sheffield, UK: Sheffield Academic Press, 2001), 111–124.

37. *Hayling Island Romano-British Temple*, at the website Roman Britain, http://roman-britain.co.uk/places/hayling_island.htm.

38. John Valentin and Stephen Robinson, "Excavations in 1999 on Land Adjacent to Wayside Farm, Nursteed Road, Devizes," *Wiltshire Archaeological and Natural History Magazine* 95 (2002), 152–153.

39. *Ibid.*, 194, 208.

40. *Ibid.*, 184.

41. *Ibid.*, 188.

42. *Ibid.*, 189.

43. *Ibid.*, 195–196.

44. *Ibid.*, 207.

45. *Ibid.*, 167.

46. Pastscape, *Monument No. 209294*.

47. *Brean Down*, at the website Curse Tablets from Roman Britain.

48. *Pagans Hill*, at the website Curse Tablets from Roman Britain.

49. Ranko Matasovic, "'Sun' and 'Moon' in Celtic and Indo-European," *Celto-Slavica* 2 (2009), 152–162.

50. Sandra Billington and Miranda Green, *The Concept of the Goddess* (London: Routledge, 2002), 35.

51. Wikipedia, *Bath Curse Tablets*.

52. British Museum, *Bronze Spoons*.

53. Pastscape, *West Hill Romano-Celtic Complex.*

54. *Uley*, at the website Curse Tablets from Roman Britain.

55. *Lydney*, at the website Curse Tablets from Roman Britain.

56. M.J.T. Lewis, *Temples in Roman Britain* (Cambridge, UK: Cambridge University Press, 1966), 89.

57. *Lydney*, at the website Curse Tablets from Roman Britain.

58. *Caerleon*, at the website Curse Tablets from Roman Britain.

59. Wessex Archaeology, *Springhead*, at the website www.wessexarch.co.uk/projects/kent/springhead/index.html.

60. Ralph Haeussler, "From Tomb to Temple: On the Role of Hero Cults in Local Religions in Gaul and Britain in the Iron Age and Roman Period," in J. Alberto Arenas-Esteban (ed.), *Celtic Religion Across Space and Time* (Toledo, ESP: Junta de Comunidades de Castilla-La Mancha, 2010), 214.

61. Pastscape, *Duroliponte.*

62. David Hall and John Coles, *Fenland Survey: An Essay in Landscape and Persistence* (London: English Heritage, 1994), 114.

63. Christopher Evans, "Delivering Bodies Unto Waters: A Late Bronze Age Mid-Stream Midden Settlement and Iron Age Ritual Complex in the Fens," *The Antiquaries Journal* 93 (2013), 69.

64. Alex Mullen, "New Thoughts on British Latin: A Curse Tablet from Red Hill, Ratcliffe-on-Soar (Nottinghamshire)," *Zeitschrift Für Papyrologie Und Epigraphik* 187 (2013), 267.

65. Lincolnshire Museums, *Gods and Goddesses of Roman Ancaster*, at the website https://www.thecollectionmuseum.com/assets/downloads/IS_arch_8_gods_and_goddesses_of_roman_ancaster.pdf.

66. Steve Roskams, Cath Neal, Jane Richardson and Ruth Leary, "A Late Roman Well at Heslington East: Ritual or Routine Practices," *Internet Archaeology* 34 (2013).

67. Pastscape, *Coventinas Well.*

68. Lindsey Allason-Jones, "Coventina's Well," in Sandra Billington and Miranda Green, *The Concept of the Goddess*, 107–108.

69. The Trimontium Trust, *Newstead Project*, http://www.trimontium.org.uk/wb/pages/fort/finds/newstead-project.php.

70. Ian Armit and Rick Schulting, "An Iron Age Decapitation from the Sculptor's Cave, Covesea, Northeast Scotland," *Past* 55 (April 2007), 1–2.

Chapter 3

1. Gildas, *On the Ruin and Conquest of Britain*, trans. Hugh Williams (London: Cymmrodorion, 1899), Chapter 22.

2. *Ibid.*, Chapter 23.

3. N.J. Higham, *The English Conquest* (Manchester, UK: Manchester University Press, 1994), 40.

4. Gildas, *On the Ruin and Conquest of Britain*, Chapter 24.

5. Tacitus, *Germania*, trans. Alfred John Church and William Jackson Brodribb (London: Macmillan, 1877), Chapter 10.

6. Kathryn Bernick (ed.), *Hidden Dimensions: The Cultural Significance of Wetland Archaeology* (Vancouver, BC: UBC Press, 1998), 75.

7. Jan Oloffson and Egil Josefson, "Horse Sacrifice at Eketorp Fort, Sweden," *Expedition* 49.1 (2007), 28–34.

8. Anne Monikander, "Borderland-Stalkers and Stalking Horses: Horse Sacrifice as Liminal Activity in the Early Iron Age," *Current Swedish Archaeology* 14 (2006), 143–158.

9. Dalum Hjallese Debate Club, *Denmark's History—Roman Iron Age*, at the website http://www.dandebat.dk/eng-dk-historie11.htm.

10. Anne Monikander, "Borderland-Stalkers and Stalking Horses: Horse Sacrifice as Liminal Activity in the Early Iron Age."

11. Carla Nayland, *Sutton Hoo Mound 17: The Horse and His Boy*, at the website http://www.carlanayland.org/essays/sutton_hoo_mound_17.htm.

12. Mildenhall and District Museum, *The Lakenheath Warrior*, at the website https://mildenhallmuseum.co.uk/collections/lakenheath-warrior/.

13. Tacitus, *Germania*, Chapter 45.

14. H.R. Ellis Davidson, *Myths and Symbols in Pagan Europe* (Syracuse, NY: Syracuse University Press, 1988), 49.

15. Wikipedia, *Benty Grange Helmet.*

16. Wikipedia, *Pioneer Helmet.*

17. Seamus Heaney, *Beowulf* (London: Faber and Faber, 2000).

18. Sarah Foster, "Religion and Landscape—How the Conversion Affected the Anglo-Saxon Landscape and Its Role in Anglo-Saxon Ideology," *The University of Newcastle School of Historical Studies Postgraduate Forum E-Journal* 6 (2007/08), 5–6.

19. *Harrow Hill*, at the website Sussex Archaeology and Folklore, http://www.sussexarch.org.uk/saaf/harrowhill.html.

20. Sarah Semple, "Defining the OE *Hearg*: A Preliminary Archaeological and Topographic Examination of *Hearg* Place Names and Their Hinterlands," *Early Medieval Europe* 15 (2007), 375–377.

21. *Ibid.*, 377.

22. *Ibid.*, 381.

23. *Ibid.*, 379.

24. Howard Williams, "Ancient Landscapes and the Dead: The Reuse of Prehistoric and Roman Monuments as Early Anglo-Saxon Burial Sites," *Medieval Archaeology* 41 (1997), 6–7.

25. *Ibid.*, 7.

26. *Ibid.*, 9.

27. Seamus Heaney, *Beowulf.*

28. Richard Morris, *The Blickling Homilies of the Tenth Century* (Cambridge, Ontario: In Parentheses Publications, 2000),105.

29. Brenda Danet and Bryna Bogoch, "'Whoever Alters This, May God Turn His Face from Him on the Day of Judgement': Curses in Anglo-Saxon Legal Documents," *The Journal of American Folklore* 105 (1992), 132–133.

30. Petra Hofmann, *Infernal Imagery in Anglo-Saxon Charters* (Ph.D. diss., University of St. Andrews, 2008), 36.

31. *Ibid.*, 39.

32. *Ibid.*, 42.

33. *Ibid.*, 80.

34. Brenda Danet and Bryna Bogoch, "'Whoever Alters This, May God Turn His Face from Him on the Day of Judgement': Curses in Anglo-Saxon Legal Documents," 142.

35. Gotfrid Storms, *Anglo-Saxon Magic* (The Hague: Springer, 1948), 173–177.

36. *Ibid.*, 177.

37. J.B. Rives, *Agricola and Germania* (London: Penguin, 2010).

38. Rory McTurk, *A Companion to Old Norse-Icelandic Literature and Culture* (Malden, MA: Blackwell Publishing, 2005), 304.

39. Wikipedia, *Oseberg Ship.*

40. Rory McTurk, *A Companion to Old Norse-Icelandic Literature and Culture*, 304.

41. Maria Kvilhaug, *Roots of the Bronze Age*, at the LadyoftheLabyrinth's Old Norse Mythology Website, http://freya.theladyofthelabyrinth.com/?page_id=89.

42. Gotfrid Storms, *Anglo-Saxon Magic*, 141–143.

43. Seamus Heaney, *Beowulf.*

44. Andrew Reynolds, *Anglo-Saxon Deviant Burial Customs* (Oxford, UK: Oxford University Press, 2009), 5.

45. A Clerk of Oxford (Eleanor Parker), *Ramsey the Rich*, http://aclerkofoxford.blogspot.co.uk/2015/11/ramsey-rich.html.

46. J.A. Giles, *William of Malmesbury's Chronicle of the Kings of England* (London: H.G. Bohn, 1847), 230–232.

47. Andrew Reynolds, *Anglo-Saxon Deviant Burial Customs*, 77.

48. *Ibid.*, 93.

49. *Ibid.*, 84.

50. *Ibid.*, 95.

51. *Ibid.*, 190.

52. *Ibid.*, 198.

53. *Ibid.*

54. Martin Carver, "The Anglo-Saxon Cunning Woman," *History Extra* (September 12, 2016).

55. Walter W. Skeat, *Aelfric's Lives of the Saints* (London: Early English Text Society, 1881), 371

56. *Ibid.*, 373.

57. *Ibid.*, 375.

58. John Frankis, *From Old English to Old Norse* (Oxford, UK: The Society for the Study of Medieval Languages and Literature, 2016), 79.

Chapter 4

1. John Koch, *Celtic Culture: A Historical Encyclopedia* (Santa Barbara, CA: ABC-CLIO, 2006), 585.

2. Dominic Powlesland, *25 Years of Archaeological Research on the Sands and Gravels of Heslerton*, http://www.landscaperesearchcentre.org/html/25_years_digging.html.

3. Sam Lucy, *The Anglo-Saxon Way of Death* (Stroud, UK: Sutton, 2000), 92.

4. Sam Lucy, *The Early Anglo-Saxon Cemeteries of East Yorkshire* (Oxford, UK: British Archaeological Reports, 1998), 109.

5. Andrew Reynolds, *Anglo-Saxon Deviant Burial Customs* (Oxford, UK: Oxford University Press, 2009), 202.

6. Stephen J. Sherlock and Martin G. Welch, *An Anglo-Saxon Cemetery at Norton, Cleveland* (London: Council for British Archaeology, 1992), 26–27.

7. Bede, *Ecclesiastical History of the English Nation* (London: J.M. Dent; New York: E.P. Dutton, 1910), Book, 1, Chapter 34.

8. *Ibid.*, Book 2, Chapter 13.

9. Ashmolean Museum, *Anglo-Saxon Cemetery at Sancton, Yorkshire.*

10. Sarah Semple and Howard Williams, *Anglo-Saxon Studies in Archaeology and History 14: Early Medieval Mortuary Practices* (Oxford, UK: Oxbow Books, 2007), xcviii.

11. J.A. Giles, "Nennius's History of the Britons," in *Six Old English Chronicles* (London: Henry G. Bohn, 1848), Chapter 63.

12. *Ibid.*, Chapter 57.

13. Martin Grimmer, "The Exogamous Marriages of Oswiu of Northumbria," *Heroic Age* 9 (2006).

14. Bede, *Ecclesiastical History of the English Nation*, Book 1, Chapter 22.

15. Pastscape, *Catterick Roman Town.*

16. Barry C. Burnham and John Wacher, *The Small Towns of Roman Britain* (Berkeley: University of California Press, 1990), 116–117.

17. Pastscape, *Monument No. 1200574.*

18. Paul Frodsham, "Forgetting *Gefrin*: Elements of the Past in the Past at Yeavering," in Paul Frodsham, Peter Topping, and Dave Cowley (eds.), *We Were Always Chasing Time: Papers Presented to Keith Blood* (Newcastle upon Tyne, Northern Archaeology Group, 1999), 191–207.

19. Bede, *Ecclesiastical History of the English Nation*, Book 2, Chapter 20.

20. Canmore, *Iona, Early Christian Monastery.*

21. Bede, *Ecclesiastical History of the English Nation*, Book 3, Chapter 2.

22. William Reeves (ed.), *Life of Saint Columba, Founder of Hy. Written by Adamnan, Ninth Abbot of That Monastery* (Edinburgh: Edmonston and Douglas, 1874), Book 1, Chapter 1.

23. English Heritage, *Significance of Lindisfarne Priory.*

24. Bede, *Ecclesiastical History of the English Nation*, Book 3, Chapter 12.

25. Wikipedia, *Bamburgh Castle.*

26. Bede, *Ecclesiastical History of the English Nation*, Book 3, Chapter 25.

27. Michelle Ziegler, "Anglian Whitby," *Heroic Age* 2 (Autumn/Winter 1999).

28. Neil Holbrook and Alan Thomas, "An Early-Medieval Monastic Cemetery at Llandough, Glamorgan: Excavations in 1994," *Medieval Archaeology* 49 (2005), 37.

29. Bede, *Ecclesiastical History of the English Nation*, Book 4, Chapter 24.

30. Albert S. Cook, "The Name Caedmon," *PMLA* 6 (1891), 9–28.

31. Bede, *Ecclesiastical History of the English Nation*, Book 4, Chapter 26.

32. Alex Woolf, "Dun Nechtain, Fortriu and the Geography of the Picts," *The Scottish Historical Review* 85 (2006), 182–201.

33. Bede, *Ecclesiastical History of the English Nation*, Book 3, Chapter 9.

34. *Ibid.*, Book 3, Chapter 11.

35. *Ibid.*, Book 4, Chapter 27.

36. Pastscape. *Monument No. 8298.*

37. Bede, *Ecclesiastical History of the English Nation*, Book 4, Chapter 30.

38. *Ibid.*, Book 4, Chapter 32.

39. Bede, "The Life and Miracles of St Cuthbert," in J.A. Giles, *Ecclesiastical History of the English Nation* (London: J.M. Dent; New York: E.P. Dutton, 1910), Chapter 10.

40. Wikipedia, *Cuthbert.*

41. Pastscape, *Hexham Priory.*

42. Bede, *Ecclesiastical History of the English Nation*, Book 5, Chapter 3.

43. *Ibid.*, Book 5, Chapter 2.

44. A. P. Baggs, L. M. Brown, G. C. F. Forster, I. Hall, R. E. Horrox, G. H. R. Kent and D. Neave, "Medieval Beverley: Beverley and St John," in K.J. Allison (ed.), *A History of the County of York East Riding: Volume 6, the Borough and Liberties of Beverley*, at the website British History Online http://www.british-history.ac.uk/vch/yorks/east/vol6/pp2-11.

45. Pastscape, *Ripon Minster.*

46. Bede, *Ecclesiastical History of the English Nation*, Book 5, Chapter 19.

47. *Ibid.*, Book 3, Chapter 23.

48. *Ibid.*, Book 4, Chapter 19.

49. Canmore, *St Abb's Head, Kirk Hill.*

50. Canmore, *Catch-A-Penny.*

51. Bede, *Ecclesiastical History of the English Nation*, Book 3, Chapter 4.

52. Canmore, *Whithorn, Bruce Street, Whithorn Priory.*

53. Whithorn Priory and Museum, *The Latinus Stone.*

54. Canmore, *Whithorn, Bruce Street, Whithorn Priory.*

55. Alan Thacker, "Lindisfarne and the Origins of the Cult of St Cuthbert," in Gerald Bonner, David Rollason and Clare Stancliffe (eds.), *St Cuthbert: His Cult and His Community to AD 1200* (Woodbridge, UK: Boydell and Brewer, 2002), 107.

56. W.W. MacQueen, "Miracula Nynie Episcopi," *Transactions of the Dumfriesshire and Galloway Natural History and Antiquarian Society* 38 (1959–60), 21–57.

57. *The York Helmet*, at the website http://www.historyofyork.org.uk/themes/anglo-saxon/the-york-helmet.

58. British Library, *Lindisfarne Gospels.*

59. British Museum, *The Franks Casket/The Auzon Casket.*

60. *Ibid.*

61. Wikipedia, *Wayland the Smith.*

62. Michael Alexander, *A History of English Literature* (Peterborough, Ontario: Broadview Press, 2002), 24.

63. Wikipedia, *Wudga.*

Chapter 5

1. Pastscape, *Spong Hill Saxon Cemetery.*

2. Neil Price (ed.), *The Archaeology of Shamanism* (London: Routledge, 2001), 197–198.

3. Norfolk Heritage Explorer, *Multi-Period Activity at the Boneyard, Sedgeford.*

4. John Davies, "Norfolk: Land of Boudicca," *Current Archaeology* (September 11, 2009).

5. Jacek Fisiak, Peter Trudgill, *East Anglian English* (Woodbridge, UK: Boydell and Brewer, 2001), 41.

6. Barbara Green and Ian Stead, "The Snettisham Treasure," *Current Archaeology* (May 24, 2007).

7. Bede, *Ecclesiastical History of the English Nation* (London: J.M. Dent; New York: E.P. Dutton, 1910), Book 2, Chapter 15.

8. *Ibid.*, Book 2, Chapter 5.

9. British Museum, *The Sutton Hoo Ship Burial.*

10. British Museum, *The Sutton Hoo Helmet.*

11. British Museum, *Who Was Buried at Sutton Hoo?*

12. Seamus Heaney, *Beowulf* (London: Faber and Faber, 2000).

13. Wikipedia, *Vendel.*

14. Andrew Reynolds, "Anglo-Saxon Human Sacrifice at Cuddesdon and Sutton Hoo?," *Papers from the Institute of Archaeology* 7 (1996), 23–30.

15. Bede, *Ecclesiastical History of the English Nation*, Book 3, Chapter 22.

16. Pastscape, *Monument No. 1598275.*

17. Keith Wade, *A History of Archaeology in Ipswich and Its Anglo-Saxon Origins*, at the website http://ipswichat.org.uk/AboutUs/History.aspx.

18. Bede, *Ecclesiastical History of the English Nation*, Book 3, Chapter 18.

19. *Ibid.*, Book 2, Chapter 15.

20. *Ibid.*, Book 3, Chapter 19.

21. *Ibid.*, Book 3, Chapter 7.

22. *Ibid.*, Book 4, Chapter 19.

23. *Ibid.*, Book 2, Chapter 20.

24. *Ibid.*, Book 3, Chapter 24.

25. J.A. Giles, "Nennius's History of the Britons," in *Si Old English Chronicles* (London: Henry G. Bohn, 1848), Chapter 65.

26. Bede, *Ecclesiastical History of the English Nation*, Book 3, Chapter 24.

27. Sarah Semple and Howard Williams, *Anglo-Saxon Studies in Archaeology and History 14: Early Medieval Mortuary Practices* (Oxford, UK: Oxbow Books, 2007), xcviii.

28. Elizabeth O'Brien, *Post-Roman Britain to Anglo-Saxon England: The Burial Evidence Reviewed* (Ph.D. Diss., University of Oxford, 1996), 208.

29. Peter Liddle, "An Anglo-Saxon Cemetery at Wanlip, Leicestershire," *Transactions of the Leicestershire Archaeological and Historical Society*, Volume 55 (1979–80), 11–21.

30. Peter Liddle and Samantha Middleton, "An Anglo-Saxon Cemetery at Wigston Magna, Leicestershire," *Transactions of the Leicestershire Archaeological and Historical Society*, Volume 68 (1994), 64–86.

31. Bede, *Ecclesiastical History of the English Nation*, Book 3, Chapter 21.

32. *Ibid.*, Book 3, Chapter 24.

33. Pastscape, *Peterborough Abbey.*

34. Pastscape, *Church of All Saints.*

35. John Koch, *Celtic Culture: A Historical Encyclopedia* (Santa Barbara, CA: ABC-CLIO, 2006), 360.

36. Lichfield District Council, *Lichfield City Conservation Area Appraisal.*

37. Bede, *Ecclesiastical History of the English Nation*, Book 4, Chapter 3.

38. Charles Wycliffe Goodwin, *The Anglo-Saxon Version of the Life of St. Guthlac* (London: J.R. Smith, 1848), 21.

39. *Ibid.*, 27.

40. Pastscape, *Monument No. 1408333.*

41. *The Find*, at the Staffordshire Hoard website, http://www.staffordshirehoard.org.uk/about.

42. *Biblical Inscription*, at the Staffordshire Hoard website, http://www.staffordshirehoard.org.uk/staritems/the-biblical-inscription.

43. Michelle P. Brown, *The Manuscript Context for the Inscription*, at the website of the Portable Antiquities Scheme, https://finds.org.uk/staffshoardsymposium/papers/michellebrown.

44. Nicholas Brooks, *The Staffordshire Hoard and the Mercian Royal Court*, at the website of the Portable Antiquities Scheme, https://finds.org.uk/staffshoardsymposium/papers/nicholasbrooks.

Chapter 6

1. Bede, *Ecclesiastical History of the English Nation* (London: J.M. Dent; New York: E.P. Dutton, 1910), Book 2, Chapter 5.

2. *Ibid.*, Book 3, Chapter 7.

3. Daniel G. Russo, *Town Origins and Development in Early England, C.400–950 A.D.* (Westport, CT: Greenwood, 1998),109–110.

4. Nicholas Doggett, "The Anglo-Saxon See and the Cathedral of Dorchester-On-Thames: The Evidence Reconsidered," *Oxoniensia* 51 (1986), 50.

5. Pastscape, *Monument No. 338479.*

6. Bede, *Ecclesiastical History of the English Nation*, Book 3, Chapter 7*ibid.*

7. *Ibid.*

8. *Ibid.*, Book 4, Chapter 15.

9. *Ibid.*

10. *Ibid.*, Book 5, Chapter 7.

11. Alex Woolf, "Apartheid and Economics in Anglo-Saxon England," in N.J. Higham (ed.), *The Britons in Anglo-Saxon England* (Woodbridge, UK: The Boydell Press, 2007), 115–129.

12. Bede, *Ecclesiastical History of the English Nation*, Book 5, Chapter 18.

13. Martin Grimmer, "Saxon Bishop and Celtic King," *Heroic Age* 4 (2001).

14. Bede, *Ecclesiastical History of the English Nation*, Book 3, Chapter 28.

15. Pastscape, *Monument No. 231741.*

16. Gale R. Owen-Crocker, *Dress in Anglo-Saxon England* (Woodbridge, UK: The Boydell Press, 2004), 145.

17. Barbara Yorke, "The Oliver's Battery Hanging Bowl Burial from Winchester, and Its Place in the Early History of Wessex," in M. Henig and N. Ramsay (eds.), *Intersections: The Archaeology and History of Christianity in England, 400–1200. Essays in Honour of Martin Biddle and Birthe Kjølbye Biddle* (Oxford, UK: British Archaeological Reports, 2010), 77–86.

18. Rupert Bruce-Mitford, *The Corpus of Late Celtic Hanging Bowls* (Oxford, UK: Oxford University Press, 2005), 3.

19. Lloyd Robert Laing, *The Archaeology of Celtic Britain and Ireland* (Cambridge, UK: Cambridge University Press, 2006), 176.

20. Barbara Yorke, "The Oliver's Battery Hanging Bowl Burial from Winchester, and Its Place in the Early History of Wessex."

21. S.E. Kelly (ed.), *Charters of Malmesbury Abbey* (Oxford, UK: Oxford University Press, 2005), 2.

22. *Ibid.*, 2.

23. Martin Grimmer, "British Christian Continuity in Anglo-Saxon England: The Case of Sherborne/Lanprobi," *Journal of the Australian Early Medieval Association*, 1 (2005).

24. John Davey, *Dorset Historic Towns Survey: Sherborne* (Dorchester, UK: Dorset County Council, 2011), 27.

25. Willibald, "The Life of Saint Boniface," in Thomas F.X. Noble and Thomas Head (eds.), *Soldiers of Christ: Saints and Saints' Lives from Late Antiquity and the Early Middle Ages* (University Park: The Pennsylvania State University Press, 2000), 112.

26. Pastscape, *Monument No. 448316.*

27. Pastscape, *Church of St Mary Major.*

28. "A Letter to the Soldiers of Coroticus," in John Skinner, *The Confession of Saint Patrick* (New York: Doubleday, 1998).

29. Bede, *Ecclesiastical History of the English Nation*, Book 4, Chapter 23.

30. Historic England, *Portchester Castle.*

31. *Buried in Time—The Breamore Bucket*, at the website Hampshire Archaeology: Musings from a Hampshire Archaeologist, https://hampshirearchaeology.word press.com/2015/09/21/buried-in-time-the-breamore-bucket/.

32. Barbara Yorke, *Kings and Kingdoms of Early Anglo-Saxon England* (Taylor & Francis e-library, 2003), 27.

33. *Buried in Time—The Breamore Bucket*, at the website Hampshire Archaeology: Musings from a Hampshire Archaeologist.

34. Katie Hinds, *50 Finds from Hampshire: Objects from the Portable Antiquities Scheme* (Stroud, UK: Amberley Publishing, 2017).

35. Michael Swanton, *Anglo-Saxon Chronicle* (New York: Routledge, 1998), 16.

36. Pastscape, *Monument No. 217630.*

37. Pastscape, *Monument No. 217700.*

38. Dr. AD Russell, *Desk-Based Assessment of the Archaeological Potential of Land South of East Gomeldon Road, Gomeldon, Wiltshire* (Southampton, UK: Southampton City Council, 2017).

39. Nick Stoodley, *Collingbourne Ducis, Wiltshire: An Early Saxon Cemetery with Bed Burial*, http://www.wessexarch.co.uk/book/export/html/2315.

40. Kirsten Egging Dinwiddy and Nick Stoodley, *An Anglo-Saxon Cemetery at Collingbourne Ducis, Wiltshire* (Salisbury, UK: Wessex Archaeology, 2016), 4–39.

41. "Prehistoric Monuments and 150 Anglo-Saxon Graves Found at Bulford," *Current Archaeology* (April 15, 2016).

42. Mike Pitts, Alex Bayliss, Jacqueline McKinley, "An Anglo-Saxon Decapitation and Burial at Stonehenge," *Wiltshire Archaeological and Natural History Magazine* 95 (2002), 131–146.

43. F.K. Annable and B.N. Eagles, *The Anglo-Saxon Cemetery at Blacknall Field, Pewsey, Wiltshire* (Devizes, UK: Wiltshire Archaeological and Natural History Society, 2010), 1.

44. *Ibid.*, ix.

45. *Ibid.*, 68.

46. *Ibid.*, 81.

47. *Ibid.*, 83.

48. Andrew Reynolds, *Anglo-Saxon Deviant Burial Customs* (Oxford, UK: Oxford University Press, 2009), 78.

49. Paul C. Tubb, "Late Bronze Age/Early Iron Age Transition Sites in the Vale of Pewsey: The East Chisenbury Midden in Its Regional Context," *Wiltshire Archaeological and Natural History Magazine* 104 (2011), 44–61.

50. Sarah Semple and Howard Williams, "Excavation on Roundway Down," *Wiltshire Archaeological and Natural History Magazine* 94 (2001), 236–239.

51. Salisbury Museum, *Ford Warrior.*

52. Salisbury Museum, *Wilton Hanging Bowl.*

53. Howard Williams, *Death and Memory in Early Medieval Britain* (Cambridge, UK: Cambridge University Press, 2006), 27–29.

54. *Ibid.*, 31.

55. Wiltshire County Council, *Tisbury: Thumbnail History.*

56. H. F. Chettle, W. R. Powell, P. A. Spalding and P. M. Tillott, "Parishes: Bradford-On-Avon," in R.B. Pugh and Elizabeth Crittall (eds.) *A History of the County of*

Wiltshire: Volume 7. http://www.british-history.ac.uk/vch/wilts/vol7/pp4–51.

57. P. Rahtz, "The Dobunnic Area in Post-Roman Times," in M. Ecclestone, K.S. Gardner, N. Holbrook and A. Smith (eds.), *The Land of the Dobunni* (Heritage Marketing and Publications, 2003), 24–31.

58. David Farmer, *The Oxford Dictionary of Saints* (Oxford, UK: Oxford University Press, 2011), 101.

59. Pastscape, *Glastonbury Tor and St Michaels Churches.*

60. Martin Grimmer, "Saxon Bishop and Celtic King," *Heroic Age* 4 (2001).

61. Pastscape, *Monument No. 199898.*

62. Pastscape, *Monument No. 191207.*

63. Michael Garcia, *St Alban and the Cult of Saints in Late Antique Britain* (Ph.D. diss., University of Leeds, 2010), 200.

64. Pastscape, *Monument No. 188644.*

65. Clare Gathercole, *An Archaeological Assessment of Wells* (Taunton, UK: Somerset County Council. 2003), 7–8.

66. *Ibid.*

67. Michael Swanton, *Anglo-Saxon Chronicle,* 40.

68. William of Malmesbury, *Chronicle of the Kings of England,* trans. the Rev. John Sharpe (London: George Bell and Sons, 1904), Book 1, Chapter 2.

69. Clare Gathercole, *An Archaeological Assessment of Glastonbury* (Taunton, UK: Somerset County Council, 2003), 29.

70. Michael Lapidge, *Anglo-Latin Literature 900–1066* (London: The Hambledon Press, 1972), 419.

71. M.C. Siraut, A.T. Thacker and Elizabeth Williamson, "Glastonbury Abbey," in R.W. Dunning (ed.), *A History of the County of Somerset Volume 9: Glastonbury and Street,* http://www.british-history.ac.uk/vch/som/vol9/pp11–16.

72. John Allan, "A Window into the Material World of Glastonbury Abbey—The Pottery Collection," in *Rediscovering Glastonbury Abbey Excavations: Symposium at Glastonbury Abbey, 9 June 2011.* http://www.glastonburyabbeysymposium.com/summary.php?&id=1016&rpn=summaries.

73. University of Reading, Trustees of Glastonbury Abbey, *Glastonbury Abbey: Archaeological Excavations 1904–1979* [data-set]. York: Archaeology Data Service [distributor], 2015. https://doi.org/10.5284/1022585.

Chapter 7

1. Michael Swanton, *Anglo-Saxon Chronicle* (Routledge: New York, 1998), 62.

2. *Ibid.,* 58.

3. *Ibid.,* 60.

4. *Ibid.,* 63.

5. *Ibid.,* 64.

6. *Ibid.,* 68.

7. Janet Laughland Nelson, *The Annals of St-Bertin* (Manchester, UK: Manchester University Press, 1991), 92.

8. T.D. Kendrick, *A History of the Vikings* (Mineola, NY: Dover Publications, 2004), 208.

9. Michael Swanton, *Anglo-Saxon Chronicle,* 70.

10. Antonia Gransden, *Legends, Tradition and History in Medieval England* (London: Bloomsbury, 1992), 84–85.

11. Martin Biddle and Birthe Kjølbye-Biddle, "Repton and the Vikings," *Antiquity* 66 (1992), 36–51.

12. Barry M. Marsden, "The Vikings in Derbyshire," *Derbyshire Life & Countryside* (March and April 2007).

13. *Ibid.*

14. Historic England, *Viking Barrow Cemetery in Heath Wood.*

15. Michael Swanton, *Anglo-Saxon Chronicle,* 76.

16. *Ibid.,* 93.

17. *Ibid.,* 96.

18. James Ingram, *The Anglo-Saxon Chronicle* (London: Everyman, 1912), at the Online Medieval & Classical Library, http://omacl.org/Anglo/part3.html.

19. *Ibid.*

20. Andrew Rogerson, "Vikings and the New East Anglian Towns," *British Archaeology* 35 (June 1998).

21. James Albone, *An Archaeological Resource Assessment of Anglo-Saxon Lincolnshire,* http://archaeologydataservice.ac.uk/researchframeworks/eastmidlands/attach/County-assessments/AngloSaxonLincs.pdf.

22. Christine Mahanny and David Roffe, *Stamford: The Development of an Anglo-Scandinavian Borough,* in D.A.E. Pelteret (ed.), *Anglo-Norman Studies 5: Proceedings of the Battle Conference 1982* (New York: Garland Reference Library of the Humanities, 2000), 387–417.

23. Norfolk Heritage Explorer, *Parish Summary: South Lopham.*

24. Dr. Caitlin Green, *Pagan Pendants, Sceptres, Lead Tablets & Runic Inscriptions: Some Interesting Recent Finds from Lincolnshire,* http://www.caitlingreen.org/2014/12/pendants-sceptres-tablets-runes.html.

25. Phil Mcmahon, *An Extensive Urban Survey: Ramsbury* (Trowbridge, UK: Wiltshire County Council, 2004), 7.

26. James Ingram, *The Anglo-Saxon Chronicle.*

27. *Ibid.*

28. Richard Hall. "A Kingdom Too Far: York in the Early Tenth Century," in N.J. Higham and D.H. Hill (eds.), *Edward the Elder: 899–924* (London: Routledge, 2001), 194.

29. *Ibid.,* 194–195.

30. *Jorvik Artefact Gallery,* at the website http://jorvik-viking-centre.co.uk/about-jorvik/gallery/.

31. Thomas Dubois, *Nordic Religions in the Viking Age* (Philadelphia: University of Pennsylvania Press, 1999), 150.

32. Portable Antiquities Scheme, *Pendant LANCUM-ED9222.*

33. *Hogbacks: Stone Carved Viking Monuments Generally Accepted as Grave Markers,* at the website The Vintage News, https://www.thevintagenews.com/2017/01/25/hogbacks-stone-carved-viking-monuments-generally-accepted-as-grave-markers/.

34. Howard Williams, *Brompton: Hogbacks and More,* at the website Archaeodeath, https://howardwilliamsblog.wordpress.com/2015/01/13/brompton-hogbacks-and-more/.

35. Michael Swanton, *Anglo-Saxon Chronicle,* 82.

36. James P. Carley, *Glastonbury Abbey: The Holy House at the Head of the Moors Adventurous* (Glastonbury, UK: Gothic Image Publications, 1996).

37. Michael Lapidge, *The Cult of St Swithun* (Oxford, UK: Oxford University Press, 2003), 11.

38. *Ibid.,* 8.

39. Walter W. Skeat, *Ælfric's Lives of Saints* (London: Early English Text Society, 1881–5), at the website http://www.indiana.edu/~dmdhist/swithin.html.

40. James Ingram, *The Anglo-Saxon Chronicle.*

41. *Ibid.*

42. D.W. Rollason, "The Cults of Murdered Royal

Saints in Anglo-Saxon England," *Anglo-Saxon England* 11 (1982), 2.

43. Susan J. Ridyard, *The Royal Saints of Anglo-Saxon England* (Cambridge, UK: Cambridge University Press, 1988), 156.

44. Jacobus de Voragine, *The Golden Legend: Lives of the Saints* (London: Catholic Way Publishing, 2015).

45. Patricia Healy Wasyliw, *Martyrdom, Murder and Magic* (New York: Peter Lang, 2008), 78–79.

46. Michael Winterbottom, *William of Malmesbury: Gesta Pontificum Anglorum: The History of the English Bishops* (Oxford, UK: Clarendon Press, 2007), 260.

47. John Crook, *English Medieval Shrines* (Woodbridge, UK: Boydell Press, 2011), 104.

48. James Ingram, *The Anglo-Saxon Chronicle.*

49. Nadia Durrani, "Mass burials in England attest to a turbulent time, and perhaps a notorious medieval massacre," *Archaeology* (Tuesday, October 01, 2013).

50. Jan Ragnar Hagland and Bruce Watson, "Fact or Folklore: The Viking Attack on London Bridge," *London Archaeologist* (Spring 2005), 331.

51. *Ibid.*, 328.

Chapter 8

1. James Ingram, *The Anglo-Saxon Chronicle* (London: Everyman, 1912).

2. Michael Swanton, Stephen Knight and Thomas H. Ohlgren, *Hereward the Wake: Introduction*, University of Rochester TEAMS Middle English Texts, http://d.lib.rochester.edu/teams/text/hereward-the-wake-introduction.

3. Michael Swanton, Stephen Knight and Thomas H. Ohlgren, *Hereward the Wake*, Chapter 25. University of Rochester TEAMS Middle English Texts, http://d.lib.rochester.edu/teams/text/hereward-the-wake.

4. James Ingram, the *Anglo-Saxon Chronicle.*

5. *The Medieval Walking Dead*, at the website Medievalists.net, http://www.medievalists.net/2013/10/the-medieval-walking-dead/; Jean-Claude Schmitt, *Ghosts in the Middle Ages* (Chicago: Chicago University Press, 1998), 100.

6. Tacitus, *Germania*, trans. Alfred John Church and William Jackson Brodribb (London: Macmillan, 1877), Chapter 43.

7. John Lindow, *Norse Mythology: A Guide to Gods, Heroes, Rituals and Belief* (Oxford: Oxford University Press, 2001), 104–105.

8. Peter Herring, *St Michael's Mount, Cornwall: Reports on Archaeological Works, 1995–1998* (Truro, UK: CAU Report, 2000), 120–121.

9. John Whitaker, *The Ancient Cathedral of Cornwall* (London: John Stockdale, 1804), 102.

10. Peter Herring, *St Michael's Mount, Cornwall: Reports on Archaeological Works, 1995–1998*, 122.

11. Victoria County History, *The Monastery of St Michael's Mount*, at the website VCH Explore, https://www.victoriacountyhistory.ac.uk/explore/items/monastery-st-michaels-mount.

12. J.R. Fletcher, *A Short History of St Michael's Mount Cornwall* (Redditch, UK: Read Books Ltd, 2013).

13. Historic England, *St Piran's Oratory and Associated Early Medieval Cemetery.*

14. *St Piran's Old Church, Cornwall*, at the website http://www.cornwall-calling.co.uk/churches/st-piran-old-church.htm.

15. Liz Woods, *Cornish Feasts and Festivals* (Penzance, UK: Alison Hodge, 2013), 24.

16. Pru Manning and Peter Stead, "Excavation of an Early Christian Cemetery at Althea Library, Padstow," *Cornish Archaeology* 41–42 (2002–3), 80.

17. Graeme Kirkham, *Bodmin: Historic Characterisation for Regeneration* (Truro, UK: Cornwall County Council, 2005), 13–14.

18. *Ibid.*, 15–16.

19. David, Farmer, *The Oxford Dictionary of Saints* (Oxford, UK: Oxford University Press, 2011) 397.

20. Pastscape, *St Sidwells Well.*

21. Simon Bastone Associates Ltd., *Discovery of Medieval Well at Development at 3 Well Street, Exeter, Devon*, http://www.sb-a.co.uk/news/discovery-medieval-well-development-3-well-street-exeter-devon.

22. *Relic of Pilgrimage to a Holy Well*, at the website Devon Live http://www.devonlive.com/relic-pilgrimage-holy/story-18798727-detail/story.html.

23. Michael Winterbottom, *William of Malmesbury: Gesta Pontificum Anglorum: The History of the English Bishops* (Oxford, UK: Clarendon Press, 2007), 291–293.

24. *In the Shadow of a Giant … St. Augustine's Well of Cerne*, at the website HolyandHealingWells https://insearchofholywellsandhealingsprings.com/2015/01/19/in-the-shadow-of-a-giant-st-augustines-well-of-cerne/.

25. Pastscape, *Shaftesbury Abbey Church.*

26. "House of Benedictine Nuns: The Abbey of Shaftesbury," in William Page (ed.), *A History of the County of Dorset: Volume 2*, http://www.british-history.ac.uk/vch/dorset/vol2/pp73–79.

27. Susan Ridyard, *The Royal Saints of Anglo-Saxon England* (Cambridge, UK: Cambridge University Press, 1988), 84.

28. *Ibid.*, 147.

29. *Ibid.*, 152.

30. *Ibid.*, 150.

31. *Ibid.*, 156.

32. Stephanie Hollis, *Writing the Wilton Women* (Turnhout, Belgium: Brepols, 2004), 38.

33. *Ibid.*, 42–43.

34. *Ibid.*, 41.

35. Phil Mcmahon, *An Extensive Urban Survey: Amesbury* (Trowbridge, UK: Wiltshire County Council, 2004), 6.

36. "Houses of Benedictine Nuns: Abbey, Later Priory, of Amesbury," in R.B. Pugh and Elizabeth Crittall (eds.), *A History of the County of Wiltshire: Volume 3*, http://www.british-history.ac.uk/vch/wilts/vol3/pp242–259.

37. John Crook, *English Medieval Shrines* (Woodbridge, UK: Boydell Press, 2011), 119–120.

38. Gerald of Wales, *On the Instruction of Princes*, trans. John William Sutton, University of Rochester, The Camelot Project, http://d.lib.rochester.edu/camelot/text/gerald-of-wales-arthurs-tomb.

39. David Farmer, *The Oxford Dictionary of Saints*, 279.

40. Richard W. Barber, *Myths and Legends of the British Isles* (Woodbridge, UK: Boydell and Brewer, 1999), 385.

41. Valerie M. Lagorio, "The Evolving Legend of St Joseph of Glastonbury," in James P. Carley (ed.), *Glastonbury Abbey and the Arthurian Tradition* (Cambridge, UK: D.S. Brewer, 2001), 79.

42. David Farmer, *The Oxford Dictionary of Saints*, 201.

43. Wikipedia, *Frithuswith.*

44. Christopher Scull, "Excavations in the Cloister of St Frideswide's Priory, 1985," *Oxoniensia* 53 (1988), 21–74.

45. John Blair, "Thornbury, Binsey: A Probable Defensive Enclosure Associated with Saint Frideswide," *Oxoniensia* 53 (1988), 3–20.

46. Pastscape, *St Margarets Well.*

47. Oxford Diocese Pilgrim Project, *St Margaret of Antioch, Binsey,* https://www.oxford.anglican.org/wp-content/uploads/2013/02/St-Margarets-Binsey.pdf.

48. David Farmer, *The Oxford Dictionary of Saints,* 279.

49. *St Kenelm's Well, Winchcombe,* at the website HolyandHealingWells, https://insearchofholywellsandhealingsprings.com/2012/03/19/st-kenelms-well-at-winchcombe/.

50. Geoffrey Chaucer, *The Nun's Priests's Tale,* ed. and trans. Gerard NeCastro, at the website eChaucer, http://ummutility.umm.maine.edu/necastro/chaucer/translation/ct/21npt.html.

51. Michael Swanton, *Anglo-Saxon Chronicle* (Routledge: New York, 1998), 54.

52. Ian Bapty and Keith Ray, *Offa's Dyke: Landscape and Hegemony in Eighth Century Britain* (Oxford, UK: Oxbow, 2014).

53. Pastscape, *Freens Court.*

54. Pastscape, *Lichfield Cathedral.*

55. David Farmer, *The Oxford Dictionary of Saints,* 86.

56. *The Relics of St Chad,* at the website of St. Chad's, Birmingham, http://www.stchadscathedral.org.uk/cathedral/relics-of-st-chad/.

57. Michael Garcia, *St Alban and the Cult of Saints in Late Antique Britain* (Ph.D. diss., University of Leeds, 2010), 48–50.

58. *Ibid.,* 56.

59. Pastscape, *St Albans Abbey.*

60. Pastscape, *Bury St Edmunds Abbey.*

61. Diana Greenway and Jane Sayers, *Jocelin of Brakelond: Chronicle of the Abbey of Bury St Edmunds* (Oxford, UK: Oxford University Press, 1989), xiii.

62. Diana Webb, *Pilgrimage in Medieval England* (London: Hambledon Continuum, 2007), 118.

63. *Ibid.,* 128.

64. Christopher Fletcher, *Richard II: Manhood, Youth and Politics* (Oxford, UK: Oxford University Press, 2008), clxxxiv.

65. Pastscape, *Ramsey Abbey.*

66. Diana Webb, *Pilgrimage in Medieval England,* 25.

67. *Ibid.,* 26.

68. *Ibid.,* 42.

69. Pastscape, *Monument No. 369565.*

70. Pastscape, *St Johns Minster Church Beverley.*

71. Susan E. Wilson, *The Life and After-Life of St John of Beverley* (Aldershot, UK and Burlington, VT: Ashgate, 1988), 107.

72. Alban Butler, *The Lives of the Fathers, Martyrs and Principal Saints* (London: A. Wilson, 1821), 109.

73. Diana Webb, *Pilgrimage in Medieval England,* 113.

74. *Ibid.,* 128.

75. A Clerk of Oxford (Eleanor Parker), *Some Miracles of John of Beverley,* http://aclerkofoxford.blogspot.co.uk/2013/05/two-miracles-of-st-john-of-beverley.html.

76. Edward Lovett, "The Whitby Snake-Ammonite Myth," *Folklore* 16 (1905), 333–334.

77. Ambrose Riesinger, *The Esoteric Codex: Incorrupt Saints* (Raleigh, NC: Lulu, 2015), 113.

78. David Farmer, *The Oxford Dictionary of Saints,* 109.

79. Sally Crumplin, *Rewriting History in the Cult of St Cuthbert from the Ninth to the Twelfth Centuries* (Ph.D. diss., University of St. Andrews, 2004), 275.

80. The Megalithic Portal, *St Cuthbert's Well (Northumberland),* http://www.megalithic.co.uk/article.php?sid=8292.

Chapter 9

1. Katie Newell, *Historic Characterisation for Regeneration: Penryn* (Truro: Cornwall County Council, 2005), 1.

2. *Ibid.,* 20.

3. Historic England, *College Known as Glasney College, Penryn.*

4. Pastscape, *Old Sarum Castle.*

5. Pastscape, *Old Sarum Cathedral.*

6. Christian Frost, *Time, Space, and Order: The Making of Medieval Salisbury* (Oxford: Peter Lang, 2009), 107–108.

7. Eamon Duffy, *The Stripping of the Altars* (New Haven: Yale University Press, 2005), 190.

8. J.H. Ross and Meryl Jancey, "The Miracles of St Thomas of Hereford," *British Medical Journal* 295 (19–26 December 1987), 1590.

9. *Ibid.,* 1592.

10. Jussi Hanska, "The Hanging of William Cragh: Anatomy of a Miracle," *Journal of Medieval History* 27 (2001), 124–125.

11. *Ibid.,* 126.

12. *Ibid.,* 128.

13. *Ibid.,* 129.

14. *Ibid.,* 130.

15. *Ibid.,* 133.

16. *Ibid.,* 133.

17. *Ibid.,* 134.

18. Thomas Kerslake, "Vestiges of the Supremacy of Mercia in the South of England," *Transactions of the Bristol and Gloucestershire Archaeological Society* (1879), 62.

19. Diana Webb, *Pilgrimage in Medieval England* (London: Hambledon Continuum, 2007), 74–75.

20. Edward Grim, *The Murder of Thomas Becket,* Fordham University Medieval Sourcebook, https://sourcebooks.fordham.edu/source/Grim-becket.asp.

21. Michael Green, *St Thomas Becket* (Leominster, UK: Gracewing, 2004), 75.

22. *Ibid.,* 78–79.

23. John Steane, *The Archaeology of the Medieval English Monarchy* (London: Routledge, 2003), 189.

24. John Britton, *The History and Antiquities of the Metropolitan Church of Canterbury* (London: M.A. Nattali, 1836), 57.

25. Alban Butler, *The Lives of the Saints Complete Edition* (London: Catholic Way Publishing, 2015).

26. Clive Paine, "The Chapel and Well of Our Lady of Woolpit," *Proceedings of the Suffolk Institute of Archaeology and History* 38 (1993), 8.

27. Diana Webb, *Pilgrimage in Medieval England,* 99–100.

28. J.C. Dickinson, *The Shrine of Our Lady at Walsingham* (Cambridge, UK: Cambridge University Press, 1956), 4–9.

29. Robert Bartlett, *Why Can the Dead Do Such Great Things? Saints and Worshippers from the Martyrs to the*

Reformation (Princeton, NJ: Princeton University Press, 2013), 41.

30. Carol Rumsen, "Poem of the Week: A Lament for Our Lady's Shrine at Walsingham," *The Guardian* (February 23, 2011).

31. "Houses of Cluniac Monks: The Priory of Bromholm," in William Page (ed.), *A History of the County of Norfolk: Volume 2*, http://www.british-history.ac.uk/vch/norf/vol2/pp359–363.

32. The Rev. Edmund Venables, "The Shrine and Head of St Hugh of Lincoln," *The Archaeological Journal* 50 (1893), 37.

33. *Ibid.*, 39.

34. *Ibid.*, 40.

35. *Ibid.*, 42.

36. *Ibid.*, 44.

37. *Ibid.*, 45.

38. *Ibid.*, 49.

39. Our Lady of Lincoln, *Parish History*, http://www.ourladyoflincoln.com/history.

40. "Friaries: The White Friars of Doncaster," in William Page (ed.). *A History of the County of York: Volume 3*, http://www.british-history.ac.uk/vch/yorks/vol3/pp267–270.

41. Christopher Norton, *St. William of York* (Woodbridge, UK: Boydell and Brewer, 2006), 147.

42. *Ibid.*, 149.

43. *Ibid.*, 150.

44. *Ibid.*, 152.

45. Pastscape, *Rievaulx Abbey*.

46. Wikipedia, *Aelred of Rievaulx*.

47. Wolfgang Riehle, *The Secret Within: Hermits, Recluses and Spiritual Outsiders in Medieval England* (Ithaca, NY: Cornell University Press, 2014).

48. "Houses of Benedictine Monks: Priory of St John Baptist & St Godric, Finchale," in William Page (ed.), *A History of the County of Durham: Volume 2*, http://www.british-history.ac.uk/vch/durham/vol2/pp103-105.

49. Diana Webb, *Pilgrimage in Medieval England*, 55.

50. A Clerk of Oxford (Eleanor Parker), *The Songs of Godric of Finchale*, http://aclerkofoxford.blogspot.co.uk/2012/05/songs-of-godric-of-finchale.html.

51. Matthew Champion, *Medieval Graffiti: The Lost Voices of England's Churches* (London: Ebury Press, 2015).

52. Clarck Drieshen, "Frying Pans, Forks and Fever: Medieval Book Curses," *British Library Medieval Manuscripts Blog* (May 23, 2017), http://blogs.bl.uk/digitisedmanuscripts/2017/05/frying-pans-forks-and-fever-medieval-book-curses.html.

53. Matthew Champion, *Medieval Graffiti: The Lost Voices of England's Churches.*

54. Matthew Champion, "Wishing on the Walls: The Medieval Graffiti Curses of Norwich Cathedral," *Norfolk Archaeology* 46 (2014), 61–66.

Chapter 10

1. J. Wyn Evans and Jonathan M. Wooding, *St David of Wales: Church, State, Nation* (Woodbridge, UK: Boydell and Brewer, 2007), 127.

2. *Ibid.*, 129.

3. *Ibid.*, 113.

4. John Reuben Davies, "Cathedrals and the Cult of Saints in Eleventh- and Twelfth-Century Wales," in Paul Dalton, Charles Insley, Louise J. Wilkinson (eds.), *Cathedrals, Communities and Conflict in the Anglo-Norman World* (Woodbridge, UK: Boydell and Brewer, 2011), 99–100.

5. *Ibid.*, 102.

6. *Ibid.*, 113–114.

7. Castles of Wales, *St Non's Chapel & Holy Well*, http://www.castlewales.com/stnon.html.

8. "Vita Sancti Bernachius: The Life of St Brynach," in A.W. Wade-Evans, *Vitae Sanctorum Britanniae Et Genealogiae* (Cardiff, UK: University of Wales Press, 1944), http://www.maryjones.us/ctexts/brynach.html.

9. Castles of Wales, *The Nevern Cross and Church*, http://www.castlewales.com/nevern_cross.html.

10. Elizabeth Rees, *Celtic Sites and Their Saints* (London: Bloomsbury, 2003), 94.

11. University College London, *CISP Database: Capel Anelog.*

12. "Welsh Pilgrimages," *The Tablet* (September 29,1923).

13. Will Parker, *The Mabinogi of Branwen*, http://www.mabinogi.net/branwen.htm.

14. Wales Directory, *St Beuno's Church*, http://www.walesdirectory.co.uk/Ancient_Churches/St_Beunos_Church.htm.

15. "Life of St Beuno," in Oliver Davies, *Celtic Spirituality* (Mahwah, NJ: Paulist Press, 1999), 212.

16. Coflein, *Caer Gybi Roman Fort.*

17. John Roberts, *Land at Ty Mawr, Holyhead, Anglesey* (Bangor, UK: Gwynedd Archaeological Trust, 2004).

18. Well Hopper, *Clorach Wells*, https://wellhopper.wordpress.com/2016/10/15/clorach-wells/.

19. Roy Fry and Tristan Gray Hulse, "Holywell, Clwyd," *SOURCE—The Holy Wells Journal*, Issue 1 (Autumn 1994).

20. *Ibid.*

21. Coflein, *Group of Four Inscribed Stones in Gwytherin Churchyard.*

22. "Life of St Beuno," in Oliver Davies, *Celtic Spirituality*, 214.

23. Roy Fry and Tristan Gray Hulse, "Holywell, Clwyd."

24. Wirt Sikes, *British Goblins: Welsh Folk-Lore, Fairy Mythology, Legends and Traditions* (London: Sampson Low, Marston, Searle & Rivington, 1880),161.

25. Glamorgan-Gwent Archaeological Trust, *Historic Landscape Characterisation: Llancarfan.*

26. John Reuben Davies, *The Book of Llandaf and the Norman Church in Wales* (Woodbridge, UK: The Boydell Press, 2003), 15.

27. Madeleine Gray, *The Lives of St Cadoc and St Winifred*, at the website WalesOnline, http://www.walesonline.co.uk/news/wales-news/madeleine-gray-lives-st-cadoc-1846984.

28. Jane Cartwright, *Feminine Sanctity and Spirituality in Medieval Wales* (Cardiff, UK: University of Wales Press, 2008), 55.

29. *Ibid.*, 56.

30. Wikipedia, *Penrhys.*

31. Jane Cartwright, *Feminine Sanctity and Spirituality in Medieval Wales*, 57.

32. Madeleine Gray, *The Lives of St Cadoc and St Winifred.*

33. "The Life of Saint Cadog," in A.W. Wade-Evans, *Vitae Sanctorum at Genealogiae.*

34. Well Hopper, *Ffynnon Eilian, Llaneilian*, https://wellhopper.wordpress.com/2012/09/13/ffynnon-elian-llaneilian/.

35. "Vita Sancti Kebii: The Life of St. Cybi," in A.W. Wade-Evans, *Vitae Sanctorum Britanniae Et Genealogiae.*

36. Will Parker, *The Mabinogi of Math*, http://www.mabinogi.net/math.htm.

37. Rachel Bromwich, *Trioedd Ynys Prydein: Triads of the Island of Britain* (Cardiff, UK: University of Wales Press, 2014), 8403–8410.

38. The Whithorn Trust, *Viking Age*, http://www.whithorn.com/timeline/viking-age/.

39. Catriona McMillan, *The Whithorn Pilgrimage: A Report* (Whithorn, UK: The Whithorn Trust, 2013), 11–12.

40. *Ibid.*, 12–13.

41. L. Alcock and E.A. Alcock, "Reconnaissance Excavations on Early Historic Fortifications and Other Royal Sites in Scotland, 1974–84: 4, Excavations at Alt Clut, Clyde Rock, Strathclyde, 1974–75," *Proceedings of the Society of Antiquaries of Scotland* 120 (1990), 98–99.

42. Stephen Driscoll, "Kingdom of Strathclyde's Final Chapter," *British Archaeology* 27 (September 1997).

43. John Reuben Davies, "Bishop Kentigern Among the Britons," Steve Boardman, John Reuben Davies and Eila Williamson (eds.), *Saints' Cults in the Celtic World* (Woodbridge, UK: Boydell Press, 2013), 68.

44. Joseph L. Duggan, *The Romances of Chretien De Troyes* (New Haven: Yale University Press, 2008), 232.

45. Cynthia Whiddon Green, *Jocelyn, a Monk of Furness: The Life of Kentigern (Mungo)*, at the website http://legacy.fordham.edu/halsall/basis/jocelyn-lifeofkentigern.asp.

46. Thomas Turpie, *Scottish Saints Cults and Pilgrimage from the Black Death to the Reformation, C.1349–1560* (Ph.D. diss., University of Edinburgh, 2011), 172–173.

47. *Ibid.*, 195.

48. *Ibid.*, 178.

49. *Ibid.*, 196–197.

50. Undiscovered Scotland, *Coldingham Priory*, http://www.undiscoveredscotland.co.uk/coldingham/coldinghampriory/index.html.

51. Hilary Powell, "Pilgrimage, Performance and Miracle Cures in the Twelfth-Century *Miracula* of St Æbbe," in Effie Gemi-Iordanou, Stephen Gordon, Robert Matthew, Ellen McInnes and Rhiannon Pettitt (eds.), *Medicine, Healing and Performance* (Oxford: Oxbow, 2014), 74.

52. *Ibid.*, 77.

53. Canmore, *Our Lady's Well, Whitekirk*.

54. James Rattue, *The Living Streams: Holy Wells in Historical Context* (Woodbridge, UK: The Boydell Press, 1995), 82.

55. Canmore, *Whitekirk, Pilgrims' Houses*.

56. James Tindal Soutter, "The Church of St. Mary, Whitekirk," *Church Service Annual* 8 (1935–6), 28–36.

57. Sheila Pitcairn, *Place of Pilgrimage: Saint Margaret's Shrine Dunfermline Abbey* (Dunfermline, UK: Pitcairn Publications, n.d).

58. Catherine Keene, "Envisioning a Saint: Visions in the Miracles of St Margaret of Scotland," in Margaret Cotter-Lynch and Brad Herzog (eds.), *Reading Memory and Identity in the Texts of Medieval Holy Women* (New York: Palgrave Macmillan, 2012), 61–62.

59. Ursual Hall, "Andrew," in *The Oxford Dictionary of National Biography*. http://www.oxforddnb.com/index/60/101060305/.

60. *The St Andrews Sarcophagus*, at the website Senchus: Notes on Early Medieval Scotland, https://senchus.wordpress.com/2011/10/31/the-st-andrews-sarcophagus/.

61. Undiscovered Scotland, *Saint Duthac*, http://www.undiscoveredscotland.co.uk/usbiography/d/stduthac.html.

62. Katie Stevenson, *Chivalry and Knighthood in Scotland, 1424–1513* (Woodbridge, UK: The Boydell Press, 2006), 118.

63. Judith Jesch and Theya Molleson, "The Death of Magnus Erlendsson and the Relics of St Magnus," in Olwyn Owen (ed.), *The World of the Orkneyinga Saga* (Orkney: Orcadian Limited, 2005), 127.

64. *Ibid.*, 131.

65. Lars Boje Mortensen (ed.). *The Making of Christian Myths in the Pereiphery of Latin Christendom* (Copenhagen: Museum Tusculanum Press, 2006), 68.

66. *Magnus—The Martyr of Orkney*, at the website Orkneyjar: the heritage of the orkney islands, http://www.orkneyjar.com/history/stmagnus/index.html.

67. Ann Williams, Alfred P. Smyth and D.P. Kirby, *A Biographical Dictionary of Dark Age Britain* (London: Seaby, 1991), 94.

68. A.S. Cowper, *St Triduana in Caithness*, http://caithness.org/atoz/churches/ballachly/index.htm.

69. *Papa Westray* at the website *The Papar Project*, http://www.paparproject.org.uk/orkney2.html.

70. Canmore, *Papa Westray, St Tredwell's Chapel*.

71. *St Tredwell's Loch, Papay*, at the website Orkneyjar, http://www.orkneyjar.com/tradition/sacredwater/tredwell.htm.

Chapter 11

1. Augustine of Hippo, *The City of God*, trans. Marcus Dods (Edinburgh, UK: T. and T. Clark, 1913), Book 21, Chapter 13.

2. Gregory the Great, *Dialogues*, trans. P.W. (London: Philip Lee Warner, 1811), Book 4, Chapter 39.

3. Bede, *Ecclesiastical History of the English Nation* (London: J.M. Dent; New York: E.P. Dutton, 1910), Book 3, Chapter 19.

4. Matha Hale Shackford, "The Purgatory of Saint Patrick," in *Legends and Satires from Medieval Literature* (Boston: Ginn and Company, 1913).

5. *Giraldus Cambrensis: The Topography of Ireland*, trans. Thomas Forester (Cambridge, Ontario: In parentheses Publications, 2000), 35.

6. Michael P. Carroll, *Irish Pilgrimage: Holy Wells and Popular Catholic Devotion* (Baltimore: Johns Hopkins University Press, 1999), 82.

7. Martha Hale Shackford, "The Purgatory of Saint Patrick."

8. Eamon Duffy, *The Stripping of the Altars: Traditional Religion in England 1400–1580* (New Haven: Yale University Press, 2005), 302.

9. Miss K.L. Wood-Legh, "Some Aspects of the History of Chantries in the Later Middle Ages," *Transactions of the Royal Historical Society* 8 (1946), 48.

10. Jennifer N. Crangle, "The Rothwell Charnel Chapel and Ossuary Project," *Past Horizons* (August 3, 2013).

11. Pastscape, *St Leonards Church*.

12. Frances Blomefield, "City of Norwich, Chapter 41: Of the Cathedral Precinct, the Charnel House," in *An Essay Towards a Topographical History of the County of Norfolk: Volume 4 the History of the City and County of Norwich, Part II*, http://www.british-history.ac.uk/topographical-hist-norfolk/vol4/pp55–62.

13. Pastscape, *Chapel of the Charnel*.

14. Giles Watson, *The Three Dead Kings*, http://

gileswatson.deviantart.com/art/The-Three-Dead-Kings-306948886.

15. Anne Marshall, *The Three Living and the Three Dead: A Medieval Morality*, http://www.paintedchurch.org/ldintro.htm.

16. C.S. Watkins, *History and the Supernatural in Medieval England* (Cambridge, UK: Cambridge University Press, 2007), 186–187.

17. William de Newburgh, "History of English Affairs," trans. Joseph Stevenson, in *The Church Historians of England* (London: Seeley's, 1861), Book 5, Chapter 22.

18. S. Mays, R. Fryer, A.W.G. Pike, M.J. Cooper, P. Marshall, "A Multi-Disciplinary Study of a Burnt and Mutilated Assemblage of Human Remains from a Deserted Mediaeval Village in England," *Journal of Archaeological Science: Reports* (2017).

19. Jacqueline Simpson, "Repentant Soul or Walking Corpse? Debatable Apparitions in Medieval England," *Folklore* 114 (2003), 397–398.

20. Will Parker, *The Mabinogi of Math*, http://www.mabinogi.net/math.htm.

21. Michael Speidel, *Ancient Germanic Warriors* (London and New York: Routledge, 2004), 14.

22. *Ibid.*, 36.

23. Wikipedia, *Berserker*.

24. Eamon Duffy, *The Stripping of the Altars*, 169.

25. *Ibid.*, 170.

26. *Ibid.*, 184.

27. *Ibid.*, 188.

28. Robert Bartlett, *Why Can the Dead Do Such Great Things? Sains and Worshippers from the Martyrs to the Reformation* (Princeton, NJ: Princeton University Press, 2013), 355.

29. Roberta Gilchrist, "Requiem for a Lost Age," *British Archaeology* 84 (September/October 2005).

Chapter 12

1. Keith Thomas, *Religion and the Decline of Magic: Studies in Popular Beliefs in Sixteenth- and Seventeenth-Century England* (London: Penguin, 1991), 628.

2. *Ibid.*, 641.

3. *Ibid.*, 647.

4. *Ibid.*, 678.

5. *Ibid.*, 692.

6. *Ibid.*, 699.

7. *Ibid.*, 705.

8. *Ibid.*, 720.

9. *Ibid.*, 792.

10. *The Twelve Conclusions of the Lollards*, at the website http://sites.fas.harvard.edu/~chaucer/special/varia/lollards/lollconc.htm.

11. Keith Thomas, *Religion and the Decline of Magic: Studies in Popular Beliefs in Sixteenth- and Seventeenth-Century England*, 1132.

12. *Ibid.*, 1147.

13. *Ibid.*, 1296.

14. J.D. Mather, "'Wonder-Working Water': The History and Hydrogeology of the Chalice Well and Other Glastonbury Springs," *Geoscience in South-West England* 12 (2009), 115–124.

15. Keith Thomas, *Religion and the Decline of Magic: Studies in Popular Beliefs in Sixteenth- and Seventeenth-Century England*, 1459.

16. *A New History of Wales: Katharine Olson Debates Reformation in Wales—A Hidden History?*, at the website WalesOnline, http://www.walesonline.co.uk/news/wales-news/new-history-wales-katharine-olson-1899471.

17. Well Hopper, *Ffynnon Beuno, Clynnog Fawr*, https://wellhopper.wordpress.com/2013/01/23/ffynnon-beuno-clynnog-fawr/.

18. Well Hopper, *Ffynnon Eilian, Llaneilian*, https://wellhopper.wordpress.com/2012/09/13/ffynnon-elian-llaneilian/.

19. Janet Bord, "Cursing Not Curing: The Darker Side of Holy Wells," *Source* Issue 4 (Summer 1995).

20. Keith Thomas, *Religion and the Decline of Magic: Studies in Popular Beliefs in Sixteenth- and Seventeenth-Century England*, 2509.

21. *Ibid.*, 2515.

22. *Ibid.*, 2529.

23. *Ibid.*, 2536.

24. *Ibid.*, 3427.

25. *Ibid.*, 3433.

26. *Ibid.*, 3440.

27. *Ibid.*, 3593.

28. Owen Davies, *Popular Magic: Cunning-Folk in English History* (London: Hambledon Continuum, 2003), VIII

29. *Ibid.*, 1.

30. *Ibid.*, 2.

31. *Ibid.*

32. *Ibid.*, 2–3.

33. *Ibid.*, 4–5.

34. *Ibid.*, 6–7.

35. *Ibid.*, 7.

36. *Ibid.*, 123.

37. *Ibid.*, 125.

38. Bryan P. Levack, |*The Witchcraft Sourcebook* (New York: Routledge, 2004), 73.

39. *Ibid.*, 85.

40. *Ibid.*, 110.

41. *Ibid.*, 129.

42. *Ibid.*, 301.

43. *Ibid.*,, 156.

44. Wikipedia, *Agnes Waterhouse*.

45. Francis Young, *Witchcraft in Cambridgeshire*, Talk delivered to Fulbourn History Society (16th October 2014).

46. *Witches of Warboys Witch Trials (England 1589–1593)*, at the website http://www.witchcraftandwitches.com/trials_warboys.html.

47. Caroline Boswell, *Suffolk Witch Trials: The Witch Persecutions of Suffolk, England in 1645*, at the website https://sites.google.com/site/witchcraftin1645/suffolk-witch-trials.

48. Wikipedia, *Pendle Witches*.

49. E.M. Thompson, "The Murder of William Baynton by Reputed Witchcraft," *Wiltshire Notes & Queries*, Volume 4 (1902–1904), 72–73.

50. Wallace Notestein, *A History of Witchcraft in England from 1558 to 1718* (Washington, D.C.: The American Historical Association, 1911), 211–213.

51. Edmund Waterton, *Pietas Mariana Britannica: A History of English Devotion to Our Blessed Ladye* (London: St. Joseph's Catholic Library, 1879), 419.

52. Jason Semmens, *Witchcraft in Cornwall*, at the website artcornwall.org, http://www.artcornwall.org/features/witchcraft_in_cornwall.htm.

53. "Saveock Water Archaeology," *Current Archaeology* (April 5, 2017).

54. Kate Ravilious, "Witches of Cornwall," *Archaeology* Volume 61 Number 6 (November/December 2008).

55. Jacqui Wood, *Secret Bird Worshiping Cult at*

Saveock, at the website Saveock Water Archaeology, http://www.archaeologyonline.org/Site%20-%20Area%20Feather%20Pits.html.

56. Owen Davies, *Popular Magic: Cunning-Folk in English History*, 12.

57. Giraldus Cambrensis, *The Itinerary Through Wales and the Description of Wales* (London: J.M. Dent & Co; New York: E.P. Dutton & Co., 1908).

58. *Gwen Ferch Ellis (1542–1594)*, at the website of The Parish of Llansanffraid Glan Conwy in the Diocese of St. Asaph, http://parish.churchinwales.org.uk/a065/history-en/gwen-ferch-elis-1542-1594/; Owen Davies, "Witches in the Dock: 10 of Britain's Most Infamous Witch Trials," *BBC History Magazine* (December 2012).

59. *North Berwick Witch Trials (Scotland, 1590–1592)*, at the website http://www.witchcraftandwitches.com/trials_north_berwick.html.

60. Aberdeen City Council, *Witches and Witchcraft in Aberdeen*, http://www.aberdeencity.gov.uk/education_learning/local_history/archives/loc_witches.asp.

61. Brian P. Levack, "Demonic Possession in Early Modern Scotland," in Julian Goodare, Lauren Martin and Joyce Miller, *Witchcraft and Belief in Early Modern Scotland* (Basingstone, UK: Palgrave Macmillan, 2008), 168.

62. Owen Davies, "A Comparative Perspective on Scottish Cunning-Folk and Charmers," in Julian Goodare, Lauren Martin and Joyce Miller, *Witchcraft and Belief in Early Modern Scotland*, 186.

63. *Ibid.*, 187.

64. *Ibid.*, 188.

65. *Ibid.*, 190.

66. *Ibid.* 197.

67. William Reeves (ed.), *Life of Saint Columba, Founder of Hy. Written by Adamnan, Ninth Abbot of That Monastery* (Edinburgh: Edmonston and Douglas, 1874), Book 2, Chapter 34.

68. Anna Ritchie, "Painted Pebbles in Early Scotland," *Proceedings of the Society of Antiquaries of Scotland* 104 (1971–72), 297–301.

Bibliography

Aberdeen City Council. *Witches and Witchcraft in Ab-erdeen*, http://www.aberdeencity.gov.uk/education_learning/local_history/archives/loc_witches.asp.

Albone, James. *An Archaeological Resource Assessment of Anglo-Saxon Lincolnshire*. http://archaeologydata service.ac.uk/researchframeworks/eastmidlands/attach/County-assessments/AngloSaxonLincs.pdf.

Alcock, L. and Alcock, E.A. "Reconnaissance Excavations on Early Historic Fortifications and Other Royal Sites in Scotland, 1974–84: 4, Excavations at Alt Clut, Clyde Rock, Strathclyde, 1974–75." *Proceedings of the Society of Antiquaries of Scotland* 120 (1990): 95–149.

Alexander, Michael. *A History of English Literature*. Peterborough, Ontario: Broadview Press, 2002.

Allan, John. "A Window into the Material World of Glastonbury Abbey—The Pottery Collection." in *Rediscovering Glastonbury Abbey Excavations: Symposium at Glastonbury Abbey, 9 June 2011*. http://www.glastonburyabbeysymposium.com/summary.php?&id=1016&rpn=summaries.

Allason-Jones, Lindsey. "Coventina's Well." In *The Concept of the Goddess*. Edited by Sandra Billington and Miranda Green. London: Routledge, 2002.

Anderson. T. "Two Decapitations from Roman Towcester." *Journal of Osteoarchaeology* 11 (2001): 400–405.

Anglo-Saxon Chronicle: Peterborough Manuscript. https://classesv2.yale.edu/access/content/user/haw6/Vikings/AS%20Chronicle%20Peterborough%20MS.html.

Annable, F.K., and Eagles, B.N. *The Anglo-Saxon Cemetery at Blacknall Field, Pewsey, Wiltshire*. Devizes, UK: Wiltshire Archaeological and Natural History Society, 2010.

Apuleius, Lucius. *The Golden Ass*. Translated by A.S. Kline. http://www.poetryintranslation.com/PITBR/Latin/TheGoldenAssII.htm.

Armit, Ian. *Headhunting and the Body in Iron Age Europe*. Cambridge, UK: Cambridge University Press, 2012.

Armit, Ian, and Schulting, Rick. "An Iron Age Decapitation from the Sculptor's Cave, Covesea, Northeast Scotland." *Past* 55 (April 2007): 1–2.

Ashbee, P., Bell M. and Proudfoot, E. *Wilsford Shaft: Excavations 1960–62*. London: English Heritage, 1989.

Augustine of Hippo. *The City of God*. Translated by Marcus Dods. Edinburgh, UK: T. and T. Clark, 1913.

Baggs, A.P., Brown, L.M., Forster, G.C.F., Hall, I., Horro, R.E., Kent, G.H.R. and Neave, D. "Medieval Beverley:

Beverley and St John." In *A History of the County of York East Riding: Volume 6, the Borough and Liberties of Beverley*. Edited by K.J. Allison. http://www.british-history.ac.uk/vch/yorks/east/vol6/pp2–11.

Bapty, Ian, and Ray, Keith. *Offa's Dyke: Landscape and Hegemony in Eighth Century Britain*. Oxford, UK: Oxbow, 2014.

Barber, J. "Bronze Age Farms and Iron Age Farm Mounds of the Outer Hebrides," *Scottish Archaeological Internet Reports* 3 (2003).

Barber, Richard W. *Myths and Legends of the British Isles*. Woodbridge, UK: Boydell and Brewer, 1999.

Bartlett, Robert. *Why Can the Dead Do Such Great Things? Saints and Worshippers from the Martyrs to the Reformation*. Princeton, NJ: Princeton University Press, 2013.

Bede, *Ecclesiastical History of the English Nation*. London: J.M. Dent; New York: E.P. Dutton, 1910.

Bernick, Kathryn. *Hidden Dimensions: The Cultural Significance of Wetland Archaeology*. Vancouver, BC: UBC Press, 1998.

Biddle, Martin, and Kjølbye-Biddle, Birthe. "Repton and the Vikings." *Antiquity* 66 (1992): 36–51.

Blagg, T.F.C. *Research on Roman Britain, 1960–1989*. London: Society for the Promotion of Roman Studies, 1989.

Blair, John. "Thornbury, Binsey: A Probable Defensive Enclosure Associated with Saint Frideswide." *Oxoniensia* 53 (1988): 3–20.

Blomefield, Frances. "City of Norwich, Chapter 41: Of the Cathedral Precinct, the Charnel House." In *An Essay Towards a Topographical History of the County of Norfolk: Volume 4 the History of the City and County of Norwich, Part II*. http://www.british-history.ac.uk/topographical-hist-norfolk/vol4/pp55-62.

Bord, Janet. "Cursing Not Curing: The Darker Side of Holy Wells." *Source* Issue 4 (Summer 1995).

Boswell, Caroline. *Suffolk Witch Trials: The Witch Persecutions of Suffolk, England in 1645*. https://sites.google.com/site/witchcraftin1645/suffolk-witch-trials.

Britton, John. *The History and Antiquities of the Metropolitan Church of Canterbury*. London: M.A. Nattali, 1836.

Bromwich, Rachel. *Trioedd Ynys Prydein: Triads of the Island of Britain*. Cardiff, UK: University of Wales Press, 2014.

Brooks, Nicholas. *The Staffordshire Hoard and the Mercian Royal Court*. https://finds.org.uk/staffshoard symposium/papers/nicholasbrooks.

Brown, Michelle P. *The Manuscript Context for the Inscription*. https://finds.org.uk/staffshoardsymposium/papers/michellebrown.

Bruce-Mitford, Rupert. *The Corpus of Late Celtic Hanging Bowls*. Oxford, UK: Oxford University Press, 2005.

Bulleid, Arthur and Gray, Harold St. George, *The Glastonbury Lake Village*. Glastonbury, UK: The Glastonbury Antiquarian Society, 1917.

Burnham, Barry C. and Wacher, John. *The Small Towns of Roman Britain*. Berkeley and Los Angeles, CA: University of California Press, 1990.

Butler, Alban. *The Lives of the Fathers, Martyrs and Principal Saints*. London: A. Wilson, 1821.

Carley, James P. *Glastonbury Abbey: The Holy House at the Head of the Moors Adventurous*. Glastonbury, UK: Gothic Image Publications, 1996.

Carroll, Michael P. *Irish Pilgrimage: Holy Wells and Popular Catholic Devotion*. Baltimore: The Johns Hopkins University Press, 1999.

Cartwright, Jane. *Feminine Sanctity and Spirituality in Medieval Wales*. Cardiff, UK: University of Wales Press, 2008.

Carver, Martin. "The Anglo-Saxon Cunning Woman," *History Extra* (Monday 12th September 2016).

Cassius Dio. *Roman History*. Translated by Earnest Cary. Cambridge, MA: Harvard University Press, 1914–1927.

Champion, Matthew. *Medieval Graffiti: The Lost Voices of England's Churches*. London: Ebury Press, 2015.

Champion, Matthew. "Wishing on the Walls: The Medieval Graffiti Curses of Norwich Cathedral." *Norfolk Archaeology* 46 (2014): 61–66.

Chaucer, Geoffrey. *The Nun's Priest's Tale*. Edited and translated by Gerard NeCastro. http://ummutility.umm.maine.edu/necastro/chaucer/translation/ct/21npt.html.

Chettle, H.F., Powell, W.R., Spalding, P.A. and Tillott, P.M. "Parishes: Bradford-On-Avon." In *A History of the County of Wiltshire: Volume 7*. Edited by R.B. Pugh and Elizabeth Crittall. http://www.british-history.ac.uk/vch/wilts/vol7/pp4–51.

Clarke, Giles. *Pre-Roman and Roman Winchester: The Roman Cemetery at Lankhills*. Oxford, UK: Oxford University Press, 1979.

A Clerk of Oxford (Eleanor Parker). *Ramsey the Rich*. http://aclerkofoxford.blogspot.co.uk/2015/11/ramsey-rich.html.

A Clerk of Oxford (Eleanor Parker), *Some Miracles of John of Beverley*, http://aclerkofoxford.blogspot.co.uk/2013/05/two-miracles-of-st-john-of-beverley.html.

A Clerk of Oxford (Eleanor Parker), *The Songs of Godric of Finchale*, http://aclerkofoxford.blogspot.co.uk/2012/05/songs-of-godric-of-finchale.html.

Cook, Albert S. "The Name Caedmon." *PMLA* 6 (1891): 9–28.

Cowper, A.S. *St Triduana in Caithness*. http://caithness.org/atoz/churches/ballachly/index.htm.

Crangle, Jennifer N. "The Rothwell Charnel Chapel and Ossuary Project." *Past Horizons* (August 3, 2013.

Crerar, Belinda. *Contextualising Deviancy: A Regional Approach to Decapitated Inhumation in Late Roman Britain*. Ph.D. diss., University of Cambridge, 2012.

Crook, John. *English Medieval Shrines*. Woodbridge, UK: Boydell Press, 2011.

Crumplin, Sally. *Rewriting History in the Cult of St Cuthbert from the Ninth to the Twelfth Centuries*. Ph.D. diss., University of St. Andrews, 2004.

Cunliffe, Barry. *Danebury: An Iron Age Hillfort in Hampshire Vol. 6. a Hillfort Community in Perspective*. London: Council for British Archaeology, 1995.

Cunliffe, Barry. "Landscape with People." In *Culture, Landscape and the Environment*. Edited by Kate Flint and Howard Morphy. Oxford, UK: Oxford University Press, 2000.

Cunliffe, Barry. "Understanding Hillforts: Have We Progressed?" In *The Wessex Hillforts Project*. Edited by Andrew Payne, Mark Corney and Barry Cunliffe. London: English Heritage, 2006.

Cunnington, Maud. "Lidbury Camp." *Wiltshire Archaeological and Natural History Magazine* 40 (1917): 12–36.

Cunnington, Maud. "Excavations in Yarnbury Castle Camp." *Wiltshire Archaeological and Natural History Magazine* 46 (1933): 198–213.

Dandamayev, Muhammad A., "Magi." In *Encyclopedia Iranica*. Edited by Ehsan Yarshater. http://www.iranicaonline.org/articles/magi.

Danet, Brenda, and Bogoch, Bryna. "Whoever Alters This, May God Turn His Face from Him on the Day of Judgement": Curses in Anglo-Saxon Legal Documents." *The Journal of American Folklore* 105 (1992): 132–165.

Davey, John. *Dorset Historic Towns Survey: Sherborne*. Dorchester, UK: Dorset County Council, 2011.

Davidson, H.R. Ellis. *Myths and Symbols in Pagan Europe*. Syracuse, NY: Syracuse University Press, 1988.

Davies, John. "Norfolk: Land of Boudicca," *Current Archaeology* (Sep 11, 2009).

Davies, John Reuben. "Bishop Kentigern Among the Britons." In *Saints' Cults in the Celtic World*. Edited by Steve Boardman, John Reuben Davies and Eila Williamson. Woodbridge, UK: Boydell Press, 2013.

Davies, John Reuben. *The Book of Llandaf and the Norman Church in Wales*. Woodbridge, UK: The Boydell Press, 2003.

Davies, John Reuben. "Cathedrals and the Cult of Saints in Eleventh- and Twelfth-Century Wales." In *Cathedrals, Communities and Conflict in the Anglo-Norman World*. Edited by Paul Dalton, Charles Insley, Louise J. Wilkinson. Woodbridge, UK: Boydell and Brewer, 2011.

Davies, Oliver. *Celtic Spirituality*. Mahwah, NJ: Paulist Press, 1999.

Davies, Owen. "A Comparative Perspective on Scottish Cunning-Folk and Charmers." In *Witchcraft and Belief in Early Modern Scotland*. Edited by Julian Goodare, Lauren Martin and Joyce Miller. Basingstone, UK: Palgrave Macmillan, 2008.

Davies, Owen. *Popular Magic: Cunning-Folk in English History*. London: Hambledon Continuum, 2003.

Davies, Owen. "Witches in the Dock: 10 of Britain's Most Infamous Witch Trials." *BBC History Magazine* (December 2012).

Dickie, Matthew W. *Magic and Magicians in the Greco-Roman World*. Taylor & Francis e-library, 2005.

Dickinson, J.C. *The Shrine of Our Lady at Walsingham*. Cambridge, UK: Cambridge University Press, 1956.

Dinwiddy, Kirsten Egging. *A Late Roman Cemetery at Little Keep, Dorchester, Dorset*. Salisbury, UK: Wessex Archaeology, 2007.

Dinwiddy, Kirsten Egging, and Stoodley, Nick. *An Anglo-Saxon Cemetery at Collingbourne Ducis, Wiltshire*. Salisbury, UK: Wessex Archaeology, 2016.

Doggett, Nicholas. "The Anglo-Saxon See and the Cathedral of Dorchester-On-Thames: The Evidence Reconsidered." *Oxoniensia* 51 (1986): 49–61.

Drieshen, Clarck. "Frying Pans, Forks and Fever: Medieval Book Curses." *British Library Medieval Manuscripts Blog* (23 May 2017). http://blogs.bl.uk/digitisedmanuscripts/2017/05/frying-pans-forks-and-fever-medieval-book-curses.html.

Driscoll, Stephen. "Kingdom of Strath'clyde's Final Chapter." *British Archaeology* 27 (September 1997).

Dubois, Thomas. *Nordic Religions in the Viking Age.* Philadelphia, PA: University of Pennsylvania Press, 1999.

Duffy, Eamon. *The Stripping of the Altars.* New Haven: Yale University Press, 2005.

Duggan, Joseph L. *The Romances of Chretien De Troyes.* New Haven, CT: Yale University Press, 2008.

Durrani, Nadia. "Mass Burials in England Attest to a Turbulent Time, and Perhaps a Notorious Medieval Massacre." *Archaeology* (Tuesday, October 01, 2013).

Ellis, Chris, and Powell, Andrew B. *An Iron Age Settlement Outside Battlesbury Hillfort, Warminster and Sites Along the Southern Range Road.* Salisbury, UK: Wessex Archaeology, 2008.

Evans, Christopher. "Delivering Bodies Unto Waters: A Late Bronze Age Mid-Stream Midden Settlement and Iron Age Ritual Complex in the Fens." *The Antiquaries Journal* 93 (2013): 55–79.

Evans, J. Wyn, and Wooding, Jonathan M. *St David of Wales: Church, State, Nation.* Woodbridge, UK: Boydell and Brewer, 2007.

Farmer, David. *The Oxford Dictionary of Saints.* Oxford, UK: Oxford University Press, 2011.

Fisiak, Jacek, and Trudgill, Peter. *East Anglian English.* Woodbridge, UK: Boydell and Brewer, 2001.

Fletcher, Christopher. *Richard II: Manhood, Youth and Politics.* Oxford, UK: Oxford University Press, 2008.

Fletcher, J.R. *A Short History of St Michael's Mount Cornwall.* Redditch, UK: Read Books Ltd, 2013.

Foster, Sarah. "Religion and Landscape—How the Conversion Affected the Anglo-Saxon Landscape and Its Role in Anglo-Saxon Ideology." *The University of Newcastle School of Historical Studies Postgraduate Forum E-Journal* 6 (2007/08): 5–6.

Frankis, John. *From Old English to Old Norse.* Oxford, UK: The Society for the Study of Medieval Languages and Literature, 2016.

"Friaries: The White Friars of Doncaster." In *A History of the County of York: Volume 3.* Edited by William Page. http://www.british-history.ac.uk/vch/yorks/vol3/pp267–270.

Frodsham, Paul. "Forgetting *Gefrin*: Elements of the Past in the Past at Yeavering." In *We Were Always Chasing Time. Papers Presented to Keith Blood.* Edited by Paul Frodsham, Peter Topping, and Dave Cowley. Newcastle upon Tyne, Northern Archaeology Group, 1999.

Frost, Christian. *Time, Space, and Order: The Making of Medieval Salisbury.* Oxford: Peter Lang, 2009.

Fry, Roy, and Hulse, Tristan Gray. "Holywell, Clwyd." *SOURCE—the Holy Wells Journal* Issue 1 (Autumn 1994).

Garcia, Michael. *St Alban and the Cult of Saints in Late Antique Britain.* Ph.D. diss., University of Leeds, 2010.

Gathercole, Clare. *An Archaeological Assessment of Glastonbury.* Taunton, UK: Somerset County Council, 2003.

Gathercole, Clare. *An Archaeological Assessment of Wells.* Taunton, UK: Somerset County Council. 2003.

Gerald of Wales. *Giraldus Cambrensis: The Topography of Ireland.* Translated by Thomas Forester. Cambridge, Ontario: In parentheses Publications, 2000.

Gerald of Wales. *On the Instruction of Princes.* Translated by John William Sutton. University of Rochester, The Camelot Project. http://d.lib.rochester.edu/camelot/text/gerald-of-wales-arthurs-tomb.

Gilchrist, Roberta. "Requiem for a Lost Age." *British Archaeology* 84 (September/October 2005).

Gildas. *On the Ruin and Conquest of Britain.* Translated by Hugh Williams. London: Cymmrodorion, 1899.

Giles, J.A., "Nennius's History of the Britons." In *Six Old English Chronicles.* London: Henry G. Bohn, 1848.

Giles, J.A. *William of Malmesbury's Chronicle of the Kings of England.* London: H.G. Bohn, 1847.

Giraldus Cambrensis (Gerald of Wales). *The Itinerary Through Wales and the Description of Wales.* London: J.M. Dent & Co; New York: E.P. Dutton & Co., 1908.

Goodwin, Charles Wycliffe. *The Anglo-Saxon Version of the Life of St. Guthlac.* London: J.R. Smith, 1848.

Gransden, Antonia. *Legends, Tradition and History in Medieval England.* London: Bloomsbury, 1992.

Gray, Madeleine. *The Lives of St Cadoc and St Winifred.* http://www.walesonline.co.uk/news/wales-news/madeleine-gray-lives-st-cadoc-1846984.

Green, Barbara, and Stead, Ian. "The Snettisham Treasure." *Current Archaeology* (May 24, 2007).

Green, Caitlin. *Pagan Pendants, Sceptres, Lead Tablets & Runic Inscriptions: Some Interesting Recent Finds from Lincolnshire.* http://www.caitlingreen.org/2014/12/pendants-sceptres-tablets-runes.html.

Green, Cynthia Whiddon. *Jocelyn, a Monk of Furness: The Life of Kentigern (Mungo).* http://legacy.fordham.edu/halsall/basis/jocelyn-lifeofkentigern.asp.

Green, Michael. *St Thomas Becket.* Leominster, UK: Gracewing, 2004.

Green, Miranda. *Animals in Celtic Life and Myth.* London: Routledge, 1998.

Green, Miranda. "The Celtic Goddess as Healer." In *The Concept of the Goddess.* Edited by Sanda Billington and Miranda Green. London: Routledge, 2002.

Greenway, Diana, and Sayers, Jane. *Jocelin of Brakelond: Chronicle of the Abbey of Bury St Edmunds.* Oxford, UK: Oxford University Press, 1989.

Gregory the Great. *Dialogues.* Translated by P.W. London: Philip Lee Warner, 1811.

Grim, Edward. *The Murder of Thomas Becket.* https://sourcebooks.fordham.edu/source/Grim-becket.asp.

Grimmer, Martin. "British Christian Continuity in Anglo-Saxon England: The Case of Sherborne/*Lanprobi*." *Journal of the Australian Early Medieval Association*, 1 (2005).

Grimmer, Martin. "The Exogamous Marriages of Oswiu of Northumbria." *Heroic Age* 9 (2006).

Grimmer, Martin. "Saxon Bishop and Celtic King," *Heroic Age* 4 (2001).

Gwen Ferch Ellis. http://parish.churchinwales.org.uk/a065/history-en/gwen-ferch-elis-1542–1594/

Haeussler, Ralph. "From Tomb to Temple: On the Role of Hero Cults in Local Religions in Gaul and Britain in the Iron Age and Roman Period." In *Celtic Religion Across Space and Time.* Edited by J. Alberto Arenas-Esteban. Junta de Comunidades de Castilla-La Mancha, 2010.

Hagland, Jan Ragnar, and Watson, Bruce. "Fact or Folklore: The Viking Attack on London Bridge." *London Archaeologist* (Spring 2005): 328–333.

Hall, David, and Coles, John. *Fenland Survey: An Essay in Landscape and Persistence.* London: English Heritage, 1994.

Hall, Richard. "A Kingdom Too Far: York in the Early

Tenth Century." In *Edward the Elder: 899–924*. Edited by N.J. Higham and D.H. Hill. London: Routledge, 2001.

Hall, Ursula. "Andrew," in *The Oxford Dictionary of National Biography*. http://www.oxforddnb.com/index/60/101060305/

Hanska, Jussi. "The Hanging of William Cragh: Anatomy of a Miracle." *Journal of Medieval History* 27 (2001): 121–138.

Harding, Dennis. *Death and Burial in Iron Age Britain*. Oxford, UK: Oxford University Press. 2015.

Heaney, Seamus. *Beowulf*. London: Faber & Faber, 2000.

Herring, Peter. *St Michael's Mount, Cornwall: Reports on Archaeological Works, 1995–1998*. Truro, UK: CAU Report, 2000.

Hertz, Robert. "A Contribution to the Study of the Collective Representation of Death." In *Death and the Right Hand*. Translated by Rodney and Claudia Needham. London; Cohen and West, 1960.

Higham, N.J. *The English Conquest*. Manchester, UK: Manchester University Press, 1994.

Hinds, Katie. *50 Finds from Hampshire: Objects from the Portable Antiquities Scheme*. Stroud, UK: Amberley Publishing, 2017.

Hoffmann, Petra. *Infernal Imagery in Anglo-Saxon Charters*. Ph.D. Diss., University of St. Andrews, 2008.

Holbrook, Neil, and Thomas, Alan. "An Early-Medieval Monastic Cemetery at Llandough, Glamorgan: Excavations in 1994," *Medieval Archaeology* 49 (2005): 1–92.

Hollis, Stephanie. *Writing the Wilton Women*. Turnhout, Belgium: Brepols, 2004.

HolyandHealingWells. *In the Shadow of a Giant…St. Augustine's Well of Cerne*. https://insearchofholywellsandhealingsprings.com/2015/01/19/in-the-shadow-of-a-giant-st-augustines-well-of-cerne/

HolyandHealingWells. *St Kenelm's Well, Winchcombe*. https://insearchofholywellsandhealingsprings.com/2012/03/19/st-kenelms-well-at-winchcombe/

Horace, "Epode V." In *The Epodes and Carmen Saeculare*. Translated by A.S. Kline. http://www.poetryintranslation.com/PITBR/Latin/HoraceEpodesAndCarmenSaeculare.htm#anchor_Toc98670053.

"House of Benedictine Nuns: The Abbey of Shaftesbury." In *A History of the County of Dorset: Volume 2*. Edited by William Page. http://www.british-history.ac.uk/vch/dorset/vol2/pp73–79.

"Houses of Benedictine Monks: Priory of St John Baptist & St Godric, Finchale." In *A History of the County of Durham: Volume 2*. Edited by William Page. http://www.british-history.ac.uk/vch/durham/vol2/pp103-105.

"Houses of Benedictine Nuns: Abbey, Later Priory, of Amesbury." In *A History of the County of Wiltshire: Volume 3*. Edited by R.B. Pugh and Elizabeth Crittall. http://www.british-history.ac.uk/vch/wilts/vol3/pp242-259.

"Houses of Cluniac Monks: The Priory of Bromholm." In *A History of the County of Norfolk: Volume 2*. Edited by William Page. http://www.british-history.ac.uk/vch/norf/vol2/pp359-363.

Ingram, James. *The Anglo-Saxon Chronicle*. London: Everyman, 1912.

Jesch, Judith, and Molleson, Theya. "The Death of Magnus Erlendsson and the Relics of St Magnus." In *The World of the Orkneyinga Saga*. Edited by Olwyn Owen. Orkney, UK: Orcadian Limited, 2005.

Keene, Catherine. "Envisioning a Saint: Visions in the Miracles of St Margaret of Scotland." In *Reading Memory and Identity in the Texts of Medieval Holy Women*. Edited by in Margaret Cotter-Lynch and Brad Herzog. New York: Palgrave Macmillan, 2012.

Kelly, S.E. *Charters of Malmesbury Abbey*. Oxford, UK: Oxford University Press, 2005.

Kendrick, T.D. *A History of the Vikings*. Mineola, NY: Dover Publications, 2004.

Kerslake, Thomas. "Vestiges of the Supremacy of Mercia in the South of England." *Transactions of the Bristol and Gloucestershire Archaeological Society* (1879): 1–63.

Keys, David. "Iron Age Chariot and Horse Found Buried Together in Yorkshire," *The Independent* (Thursday 30 March 2017).

Kiekhefer, Richard. *Magic in the Middle Ages*. Cambridge, UK: Cambridge University Press, 2000.

King, Anthony, and Soffe, Grahame. "Internal Organisation and Deposition at the Iron Age Temple on Hayling Island (Hampshire)." In *Society and Settlement in Iron Age Europe*. Edited by J. Collis. Sheffield, UK: Sheffield Academic Press, 2001.

Kirkham, Graeme. *Bodmin: Historic Characterisation for Regeneration*. Truro, UK: Cornwall County Council, 2005.

Koch, John. *Celtic Culture: A Historical Encyclopedia*. Santa Barbara, CA: ABC-CLIO, 2006.

Kvilhaug, Maria. *Roots of the Bronze Age*. http://freya.theladyofthelabyrinth.com/?page_id=89.

Lagorio, Valerie M. "The Evolving Legend of St Joseph of Glastonbury." In *Glastonbury Abbey and the Arthurian Tradition*. Edited by James P. Carley. Cambridge, UK: D.S. Brewer, 2001.

Laing, Lloyd Robert. *The Archaeology of Celtic Britain and Ireland*. Cambridge, UK: Cambridge University Press, 2006.

Lapidge, Michael. *Anglo-Latin Literature 900–1066*. London: The Hambledon Press, 1972.

Lapidge, Michael. *The Cult of St Swithun*. Oxford, UK: Oxford University Press, 2003.

Lawson, Andrew. *Potterne 1982–5*. Salisbury, UK: Trust for Wessex Archaeology, 2000.

Levack, Bryan P. "Demonic Possession in Early Modern Scotland." In *Witchcraft and Belief in Early Modern Scotland*. Edited by Julian Goodare, Lauren Martin and Joyce Miller. Basingstone, UK: Palgrave Macmillan, 2008.

Levack, Bryan, P. *The Witchcraft Sourcebook*. New York: Routledge, 2004.

Lewis, Jodie. "Upwards at 45 Degrees: The Use of Vertical Caves During the Neolithic and Early Bronze Age on Mendip, Somerset." *Capra* 2 (2000).

Lewis, M.J.T. *Temples in Roman Britain*. Cambridge, UK: Cambridge University Press, 1969.

Liddle, Peter. "An Anglo-Saxon Cemetery at Wanlip, Leicestershire." *Transactions of the Leicestershire Archaeological and Historical Society* 55 (1979–80): 11–21.

Liddle, Peter, and Middleton, Samantha. "An Anglo-Saxon Cemetery at Wigston Magna, Leicestershire." *Transactions of the Leicestershire Archaeological and Historical Society* 68 (1994): 64–86.

Lindow, John. *Norse Mythology: A Guide to Gods, Heroes, Rituals and Belief*. Oxford: Oxford University Press, 2001.

Lovett, Edward. "The Whitby Snake-Ammonite Myth," *Folklore* 16 (1905): 333–334.

Lucy, Sam. *The Anglo-Saxon Way of Death*. Stroud, UK: Sutton, 2000.

Lucy, Sam. *The Early Anglo-Saxon Cemeteries of East Yorkshire*. Oxford, UK: British Archaeological Reports, 1998.

MacQueen, W.W. Miracula Nynie Episcopi. *Transactions of the Dumfriesshire and Galloway Natural History and Antiquarian Society* 38 (1959–60): 21–57.

Mahanny, Christine, and Roffe, David. *Stamford: The Development of an Anglo-Scandinavian Borough*. In *Anglo-Norman Studies 5: Proceedings of the Battle Conference 1982*. Edited by D.A.E. Pelteret. New York: Garland Reference Library of the Humanities, 2000.

Manning, Pru, and Stead, Peter. "Excavation of an Early Christian Cemetery at Althea Library, Padstow." *Cornish Archaeology* 41–42 (2002–3): 80–106.

Marsden, Barry M. "The Vikings in Derbyshire." *Derbyshire Life & Countryside* (March & April 2007).

Marshall, Anne. *The Three Living and the Three Dead: A Medieval Morality*, http://www.paintedchurch.org/ldintro.htm.

Matasovic, Ranko. "'Sun' and 'Moon' in Celtic and Indo-European." *Celto-Slavica* 2 (2009): 152–162.

Mather, J.D. "'Wonder-Working Water': The History and Hydrogeology of the Chalice Well and Other Glastonbury Springs." *Geoscience in South-West England* 12 (2009): 115–124.

Mays, S., Fryer, R., Pike, A.W.G., Cooper, M.J., Marshall, P. "A Multi-Disciplinary Study of a Burnt and Mutilated Assemblage of Human Remains from a Deserted Mediaeval Village in England." *Journal of Archaeological Science: Reports* (2017).

McGavin, Neil. "A Roman Cemetery and Trackway at Stanton Harcourt." *Oxoniensia* 45 (1980): 112–123.

Mcmahon, Phil. *An Extensive Urban Survey: Amesbury*. Trowbridge, UK: Wiltshire County Council, 2004.

Mcmahon, Phil. *An Extensive Urban Survey: Ramsbury*. Trowbridge, UK: Wiltshire County Council, 2004.

McMillan, Catriona. *The Whithorn Pilgrimage: A Report*. Whithorn, UK: The Whithorn Trust, 2013.

McOmish, David. "East Cisenbury: Ritual Nd Rubbish at the British Bronze Age-Iron Age Transition." *Antiquity* 70 (March 1996): 68–76.

Mcturk, Rory. *A Companion to Old Norse-Icelandic Literature and Culture*. Malden, MA: Blackwell Publishing, 2005.

Monikander, Anne. "Borderland-Stalkers and Stalking Horses: Horse Sacrifice as Liminal Activity in the Early Iron Age." *Current Swedish Archaeology* 14 (2006): 143–158.

Morris, Richard. *The Blickling Homilies of the Tenth Century*. Cambridge, Ontario: In parentheses Publications, 2000.

Mortensen, Lars Boje. *The Making of Christian Myths in the Periphery of Latin Christendom*. Copenhagen: Museum Tusculanum Press, 2006.

Mullen, Alex. "New Thoughts on British Latin: A Curse Tablet from Red Hill, Ratcliffe-On-Soar (Nottinghamshire)." *Zeitschrift Für Papyrologie Und Epigraphik* 187 (2013): 266–272.

Nayland, Carla. *Sutton Hoo Mound 17: The Horse and His Boy*. http://www.carlanayland.org/essays/sutton_hoo_mound_17.htm.

Nelson, Janet Laughland. *The Annals of St-Bertin*. Manchester, UK: Manchester University Press, 1991.

Newell, Katie. *Historic Characterisation for Regeneration: Penryn*. Truro: Cornwall County Council, 2005.

North Berwick Witch Trials (Scotland, 1590–1592). http://www.witchcraftandwitches.com/trials_north_berwick.html.

Norton, Christopher. *St. William of York*. Woodbridge, UK: Boydell and Brewer, 2006.

Notestein, Wallace. *A History of Witchcraft in England from 1558 to 1718*. Washington, D.C.: The American Historical Association, 1911.

O'Brien, Elizabeth. *Post-Roman Britain to Anglo-Saxon England: The Burial Evidence Reviewed*. Ph.D. diss., University of Oxford, 1996.

Oloffson, Jan, and Josefson, Egil. "Horse Sacrifice at Eketorp Fort, Sweden." *Expedition* 49.1 (2007): 28–34.

Olson, Katharine. *A New History of Wales: Katharine Olson Debates Reformation in Wales—A Hidden History?* http://www.walesonline.co.uk/news/wales-news/new-history-wales-katharine-olson-1899471.

Owen-Crocker, Gale. *Dress in Anglo-Saxon England*. Woodbridge, UK: The Boydell Press, 2004.

Paine, Clive. "The Chapel and Well of Our Lady of Woolpit." *Proceedings of the Suffolk Institute of Archaeology and History* 38 (1993): 8–12.

Parker, Will. *The Mabinogi of Branwen*. http://www.mabinogi.net/branwen.htm.

Parker, Will. *The Mabinogi of Math*. http://www.mabinogi.net/math.htm.

Pitcairn, Sheila. *Place of Pilgrimage: Saint Margaret's Shrine Dunfermline Abbey*. Dunfermline, UK: Pitcairn Publications, n.d.

Pitts, M., Bayliss, A. and McKinley, J. "An Anglo-Saxon Decapitation and Burial at Stonehenge." *Wiltshire Archaeological and Natural History Magazine* 95 (2002): 131–146.

Pitts, Mike. "News; All Cannings Cross." *British Archaeology* 74 (January 2004).

Pliny the Younger. *Letters by Pliny the Younger*. Translated by William Melmoth. New York: P.F. Collier & Son, 1909–14.

Powell, Hilary. "Pilgrimage, Performance and Miracle Cures in the Twelfth-Century *Miracula* of St Æbbe." In *Medicine, Healing and Performance*. Edited by Effie Gemi-Iordanou, Stephen Gordon, Robert Matthew, Ellen McInnes and Rhiannon Pettitt. Oxford: Oxbow, 2014.

Powlesland, Dominic. *25 Years of Archaeological Research on the Sands and Gravels of Heslerton*. http://www.landscaperesearchcentre.org/html/25_years_digging.html.

Price, Neil. *The Archaeology of Shamanism*. London: Routledge, 2001.

Rahtz, P. The Dobunnic Area in Post-Roman Times." In *The Land of the Dobunni*. Edited by M. Ecclestone, K.S. Gardner, N. Holbrook and A. Smith. Heritage Marketing and Publications, 2003.

Rattue, James. *The Living Streams: Holy Wells in Historical Context*. Woodbridge, UK: The Boydell Press, 1995.

Ravilious, Kate. "Witches of Cornwall." *Archaeology* Volume 61 Number 6 (November/December 2008).

Redfern, Rebecca. "New Evidence for Iron Age Secondary Burial Practice and Bone Modification from Gussage All Saints and Maiden Castle (Dorset, England)," *Oxford Journal of Archaeology* 27 (2008): 281–301.

Rees, Elizabeth. *Celtic Sites and Their Saints*. London: Bloomsbury, 2003.

Reeves, William. *Life of Saint Columba, Founder of Hy. Written by Adamnan, Ninth Abbot of That Monastery*. Edinburgh: Edmonston and Douglas, 1874.

Reynolds, Andrew. *Anglo-Saxon Deviant Burial Customs*. Oxford, UK: Oxford University Press, 2009.

Reynolds, Andrew. "Anglo-Saxon Human Sacrifice at

Cuddesdon and Sutton Hoo?" *Papers from the Institute of Archaeology* 7 (1996): 23–30.

Ridyard, Susan J. *The Royal Saints of Anglo-Saxon England*. Cambridge, UK: Cambridge University Press, 1988.

Riehle, Wolfgang. *The Secret Within: Hermits, Recluses and Spiritual Outsiders in Medieval England*. Ithaca, NY: Cornell University Press, 2014.

Riesinger, Ambrose. *The Esoteric Codex: Incorrupt Saints*. Raleigh, NC: Lulu, 2015.

Ritchie, Anna. "Painted Pebbles in Early Scotland." *Proceedings of the Society of Antiquaries of Scotland* 104 (1971–72): 297–301.

Rives, J.B. *Agricola and Germania*. London: Penguin, 2010.

Roberts, John. *Land at Ty Mawr, Holyhead, Anglesey*. Bangor, UK: Gwynedd Archaeological Trust, 2004.

Rogerson, Andrew. "Vikings and the New East Anglian Towns." *British Archaeology* 35 (June 1998).

Rollason, D.W. "The Cults of Murdered Royal Saints in Anglo-Saxon England." *Anglo-Saxon England* 11 (1982): 1–22.

Roskams, S., Neal, C., Richardson, J. and Leary, R. "A Late Roman Well at Heslington East: Ritual or Routine Practices," *Internet Archaeology* 34 (2013).

Ross, J.H., and Jancey, Meryl. "The Miracles of St Thomas of Hereford." *British Medical Journal* 295 (19–26 December 1987).

Rumsen, Carol. "Poem of the Week: A Lament for Our Lady's Shrine at Walsingham." *The Guardian* (Wednesday 23 February 2011).

Russell, A.D. *Desk-Based Assessment of the Archaeological Potential of Land South of East Gomeldon Road, Gomeldon, Wiltshire*. Southampton, UK: Southampton City Council, 2017.

Russo, Daniel, G. *Town Origins and Development in Early England, C.400–950 A.D.* Westport, CT: Greenwood, 1998.

"Saveock Water Archaeology." *Current Archaeology* (Apr 05, 2017).

Schmitt, Jean-Claude. *Ghosts in the Middle Ages*. Chicago, IL: Chicago University Press, 1998.

Scull, Christopher. "Excavations in the Cloister of St Frideswide's Priory, 1985." *Oxoniensia* 53 (1988): 21–74.

Semmens, Jason. *Witchcraft in Cornwall*. http://www.artcornwall.org/features/witchcraft_in_cornwall.htm.

Semple, Sarah. "Defining the OE *Hearg*: A Preliminary Archaeological and Topographic Examination of *Hearg* Place Names and Their Hinterlands." *Early Medieval Europe* 15 (2007): 364–385.

Semple, Sarah, and Williams, Howard. *Anglo-Saxon Studies in Archaeology and History 14: Early Medieval Mortuary Practices*. Oxford, UK: Oxbow Books, 2007.

Semple, Sarah, and Williams, Howard. "Excavation on Roundway Down," *Wiltshire Archaeological and Natural History Magazine* 94 (2001): 236–239.

Serjeantson, D., and Morris, J. "Ravens and Crows in Iron Age and Roman Britain." *Oxford Journal of Archaeology* 30 (2011): 85–107.

Shackford, Martha Hale. "The Purgatory of Saint Patrick." In *Legends and Satires from Medieval Literature*. Boston and New York, Ginn and company, 1913.

Sherlock, Stephen J., and Welch, Martin G. *An Anglo-Saxon Cemetery at Norton, Cleveland*. London: Council for British Archaeology, 1992.

Sikes, Wirt. *British Goblins: Welsh Folk-Lore, Fairy Mythology, Legends and Traditions*. London: Sampson Low, Marston, Searle & Rivington, 1880.

Simpson, Jacqueline. "Repentant Soul or Walking Corpse? Debatable Apparitions in Medieval England." *Folklore* 114 (2003): 389–402.

Siraut, M.C., Thacker, A.T. and Williamson, E. "Glastonbury Abbey." In *A History of the County of Somerset Volume 9: Glastonbury and Street*. Edited by R.W. Dunning. http://www.british-history.ac.uk/vch/som/vol9/pp11-16.

Skeat, Walter W. *Aelfric's Lives of the Saints*. London: Early English Text Society, 1881.

Skinner, John. *The Confession of Saint Patrick*. New York: Doubleday, 1998.

Soutter, James Tindal. "The Church of St. Mary, Whitekirk," *Church Service Annual* 8 (1935–6): 28–36.

Speidel, Michael. *Ancient Germanic Warriors*. London: Routledge, 2004.

Steane, John. *The Archaeology of the Medieval English Monarchy*. London: Routledge, 2003.

Stevenson, Katie. *Chivalry and Knighthood in Scotland, 1424–1513*. Woodbridge, UK: The Boydell Press, 2006.

Storms, Gotfrid. *Anglo-Saxon Magic*. The Hague: Springer, 1948.

Stoodley, Nick. *Collingbourne Ducis, Wiltshire: An Early Saxon Cemetery with Bed Burial*. http://www.wessexarch.co.uk/book/export/html/2315.

Swanton, M., Knight, S. and Ohlgren, Thomas H. *Hereward the Wake*. University of Rochester TEAMS Middle English Texts, http://d.lib.rochester.edu/teams/text/hereward-the-wake.

Swanton, Michael. *Anglo-Saxon Chronicle*. New York: Routledge, 1998.

Tacitus. *Annals*. Translated by John Jackson. Cambridge, MA: Harvard University Press, 1931.

Tacitus. *Germania*. Translated by Alfred John Church and William Jackson Brodribb. London, New York: Macmillan, 1877.

Taylor, Alison. "Aspects of Deviant Burial in Roman Britain." In *Deviant Burial in the Archaeological Record*. Edited by Eileen M. Murphy. Oxford, UK: Oxbow Books, 2008.

Thacker, Alan. "Lindisfarne and the Origins of the Cult of St Cuthbert." In *St Cuthbert: His Cult and His Community to AD 1200*. Edited by Gerald Bonner, David Rollason and Clare Stancliffe. Woodbridge, UK: Boydell and Brewer, 2002.

Thomas, Keith. *Religion and the Decline of Magic: Studies in Popular Beliefs in Sixteenth- and Seventeenth-Century England*. London: Penguin, 1991.

Thompson, E.M. "The Murder of William Baynton by Reputed Witchcraft." *Wiltshire Notes & Queries*, Volume 4 (1902–1904).

Tubb, Paul C. "Late Bronze Age/Early Iron Age Transition Sites in the Vale of Pewsey: The East Chisenbury Midden in Its Regional Context." *Wiltshire Archaeological and Natural History Magazine* 104 (2011): 44–61.

Tucker, Katie. *"Whence This Severance of the Head?": The Osteology and Archaeology of Human Decapitation in Britain*. Ph.D. diss., University of Winchester, 2012.

Turpie, Thomas. *Scottish Saints Cults and Pilgrimage from the Black Death to the Reformation, C.1349–1560*. Ph.D. diss., University of Edinburgh, 2011.

University of Reading, Trustees of Glastonbury Abbey. *Glastonbury Abbey: Archaeological Excavations 1904–1979* [data-set]. York: Archaeology Data Service [distributor], 2015. https://doi.org/10.5284/1022585.

Valentin, John, and Robinson, Stephen. "Excavations in

1999 on Land Adjacent to Wayside Farm, Nursteed Road, Devizes." *Wiltshire Archaeological and Natural History Magazine* 95 (2002): 147–213.

Venables, the Rev. Edmund. "The Shrine and Head of St Hugh of Lincoln." *The Archaeological Journal* 50 (1893): 37–61.

Victoria County History. *The Monastery of St Michael's Mount.* https://www.victoriacountyhistory.ac.uk/explore/items/monastery-st-michaels-mount.

Voragine, Jacobus de. *The Golden Legend: Lives of the Saints.* London: Catholic Way Publishing, 2015.

Wade, Keith. *A History of Archaeology in Ipswich and Its Anglo-Saxon Origins.* http://ipswichat.org.uk/AboutUs/History.aspx.

Wade-Evans, A.W. *Vitae Sanctorum Britanniae Et Genealogiae.* Cardiff, UK: University of Wales Press, 1944.

Wasyliw, Patricia Healy. *Martyrdom, Murder and Magic.* New York: Peter Lang, 2008.

Waterton, Edmund. *Pietas Mariana Britannica: A History of English Devotion to Our Blessed Ladye.* London: St. Joseph's Catholic Library, 1879.

Watkins, C.S. *History and the Supernatural in Medieval England.* Cambridge, UK: Cambridge University Press, 2007.

Watson, Giles. *The Three Dead Kings.* http://gileswatson.deviantart.com/art/The-Three-Dead-Kings-306948886.

Watts, Dorothy. *Religion in Late Roman Britain.* London: Routledge, 1998.

Webb, Diana. *Pilgrimage in Medieval England.* London: Hambledon Continuum, 2007.

Webster, Chris. *The Archaeology of South West England.* Taunton, UK: Somerset County Council, 2008.

Well Hopper. *Clorach Wells.* https://wellhopper.wordpress.com/2016/10/15/clorach-wells/

Well Hopper. *Ffynnon Beuno, Clynnog Fawr.* https://wellhopper.wordpress.com/2013/01/23/ffynnon-beuno-clynnog-fawr/.

Well Hopper. *Ffynnon Eilian, Llaneilian.* https://wellhopper.wordpress.com/2012/09/13/ffynnon-elian-llaneilian/.

Western, Gaynor. *Osteological Analysis of Human Remains from Sainsbury's Site, St. Johns, Worcester.* Wisbech, UK: Ossafreelance, 2009.

Whitaker, John. *The Ancient Cathedral of Cornwall.* London: John Stockdale, 1804.

William de Newburgh. "History of English Affairs." Translated by Joseph Stevenson. In *The Church Historians of England.* London: Seeley's, 1861.

Williams, Ann, Smyth, Alfred P. and Kirby, D.P. *A Biographical Dictionary of Dark Age Britain.* London: Seaby, 1991.

Williams, Howard. "Ancient Landscapes and the Dead: The Reuse of Prehistoric and Roman Monuments as Early Anglo-Saxon Burial Sites," *Medieval Archaeology* 41 (1997): 1–32.

Williams, Howard. *Brompton: Hogbacks and More.* https://howardwilliamsblog.wordpress.com/2015/01/13/brompton-hogbacks-and-more/

Williams, Howard. *Death and Memory in Early Medieval Britain.* Cambridge, UK: Cambridge University Press, 2006.

Willibald. "The Life of Saint Boniface." In *Soldiers of Christ: Saints and Saints' Lives from Late Antiquity and the Early Middle Ages.* Edited by Thomas F.X. Noble and Thomas Head. University Park, PA: The Pennsylvania State University Press, 2000.

Wilson, Susan E. *The Life and After-Life of St John of Beverley.* Aldershot, UK and Burlington, VT: Ashgate, 1988.

Winterbottom, Michael. *William of Malmesbury: Gesta Pontificum Anglorum: The History of the English Bishops.* Oxford, UK: Clarendon Press, 2007.

Witches of Warboys Witch Trials (England 1589–1593). http://www.witchcraftandwitches.com/trials_warboys.html.

Wood, Jacqui. *Secret Bird Worshiping Cult at Saveock.* http://www.archaeologyonline.org/Site%20-%20Area%20Feather%20Pits.html.

Wood-Legh, K.L. "Some Aspects of the History of Chantries in the Later Middle Ages." *Transactions of the Royal Historical Society* 8 (1946): 47–60.

Woods, Liz. *Cornish Feasts and Festivals.* Penzance, UK: Alison Hodge, 2013.

Woolf, Alex. "Apartheid and Economics in Anglo-Saxon England." In *The Britons in Anglo-Saxon England.* Edited by N.J. Higham. Woodbridge, UK: The Boydell Press, 2007).

Woolf, Alex. "Dun Nechtain, Fortriu and the Geography of the Picts," *The Scottish Historical Review* 85 (2006): 182–201.

Young, Framcis. *Witchcraft in Cambridgeshire.* Talk delivered to Fulbourn History Society (16th October 2014).

Yorke, Barbara. *Kings and Kingdoms of Early Anglo-Saxon England.* Taylor & Francis e-library, 2003.

Yorke, Barbara. "The Oliver's Battery Hanging Bowl Burial from Winchester, and Its Place in the Early History of Wessex." In *Intersections: The Archaeology and History of Christianity in England, 400–1200. Essays in Honour of Martin Biddle and Birthe Kjølbye Biddle.* Edited by M. Henig and N. Ramsay. Oxford, UK: British Archaeological Reports, 2010.

Ziegler, Michelle. "Anglian Whitby," *Heroic Age* 2 (Autumn/Winter 1999).

Index

Æcerbot 50–53
Ælfric 59
Aelred of Rievaul 168–169
Æthelred (Unready) 126–129
Æthelwold (bishop) 122,
Aldhelm (bishop) 96, 126, 143
Alfred (king) 111–112, 113–114
All Cannings Cross 7–8
Amesbury Abbey 125–126, 142–143
amulets 7, 8, 14, 58–59, 61, 86, 116, 216
Ancaster 39
Anglesey 22–24

Baptists 220–221
Bardsey Island 178
Bath (Somerset) 33–34
Battlesbury Bowl 11–12
Berkeley (witch of) 55–56
Berserkers 210
Birinus (bishop) 93
boars (paganism) 46–46
Boudica 24
Bradford on Avon 104–105
Breamore 99
Brean Down 31–32
Bromholm Priory 166, 215
Bulford 101–102
Bury St. Edmunds 84, 111, 147, 226–227

Cædmon 66
Cædwalla (king) 94–95
Caerleon 35
Cambridge 37–38
Catterick 63
Celtic Christianity 105–107
Cenwalh (king) 94
Cerdic (Wessex) 98
Chalice Well 218–219
chantry chapels 203–204
charnel chapels 204–206
Cnut (king) 129
Collingbourne Ducis 100–101
Coventina's Well 40

cowrie shells 58, 101
cunning folk 221–223, 232, 234, 238–239
cunning women 58–59, 61, 101, 221
curses, ritual 17, 28–29, 32, 33, 34, 35, 38, 49–50, 171–174, 184–188
Cynegils (king) 93

Danebury 12–13, 15–16
Danelaw 114
decapitated burials 25–27, 56
Discoverie of Witchcraft 224–225
Dommoc (Dunwich) 84
Dorchester (Dorset) 25
Dorchester (Thames) 93–94
druids 22

East Chisenbury 9
Ecgfrith (king) 66–67
Edward the Elder 114–115
Edwin (king) 61–62
Egbert (king) 109–110
Ely 85
excarnation 15
Exeter 98

Five Boroughs 114–118
Franks Casket 75–78
Fursey 84, 199–200

ghosts 21–22, 206–207, 208–209
Gildas 42
Glasney Collge 154
Glastonbury 13–14, 106, 107–108, 121–123, 143–144, 217–218
Godric of Finchale 169–171
Godwin Ridge 14–15
Gosforth cross 120
grave goods 213–214

Haddenham 38
Hædde (bishop) 93, 95–96
hanging bowls 97, 103–104

Hayling Island 29–30
hearg (temple) 47–48
Hellequin's Army 136–137
Henry VI (saint) 210–212
Hereward the Wake 131–134
Heslington East 39–40
Hjortspring boat 44
hogback stones 120–121
Holywell (Wales) 182–183, 218
Hornish Point 15–16
horses (paganism) 43–46, 80–81, 86–87

Illerup Adal 44
Ine (king) 95
Iona (monastery) 64

James VI 225, 235
Jordan Hill 28

Lacnunga 53–54
Lakenheath 45–46
Lidbury Camp 10
Lincoln 116, 166–167
Lindisfarne Gospels 75
Lydney Park 35

Mabinogion 178–179, 185–188, 209
Malleus maleficarum 223–224
Malmesbury 97

Nerthus (goddess) 52–53
Nettleton Shrub 31
Newstead Fort 40–41
Nodens (god) 35

Oliver's Battery 97
Orderic Vitalis 135–136
Oswiu (king) 65–66
Our Lady shrines: Doncaster 167–168; Lincoln 166–167; Penrhys (Wales) 183–184; Walsingham 164–166; Whitekirk (Scotland) 191–192; Woolpit 163–164

Pagans Hill 32–33
Papa Westray 197–198
Peada of Mercia 87
Penda of Mercia 85–86
Peterborough Abbey 87, 134–135
Pewsey 102–103
Pocklington 16
Potterne 8–9
prone burials 27, 56, 61, 101, 103
purgatory 199

Quakers 221

Rædwald (king) 81
Ramsey Abbey 54, 111
Repton (Vikings) 111–113

St. Æbbe 73, 191
St. Æthelberht 146, 160
St. Alban 147
St. Albans (town) 37, 147
St. Andrew 194–195
St. Augustine's Well 140
St. Beuno 179, 218
St. Brice's Day 127–128
St. Brynach 176–177
St. Cadoc 183, 184–185
St. Chad 88–89, 146–147
St. Columba 65, 239
St. Cuthbert 67–70, 152–153
St. Cybi 180, 185
St. David 175–176
St. Derfel 215–216
St. Duthac 195–196
St. Edith 140–142
St. Edmund 111, 147–150
St. Edward 124–125, 140–141
St. Etheldreda 84–85

St. Frideswide 144–145
St. Guthlac 89–90
St. Hilda 72–73, 152
St. Hugh of Lincoln 166–167
St. Ivo 150–151
St. John of Beverley 70–71, 151–152
St. Kenelm 145–146
St. Kentigern 189–191
St. Magnus 196–197
St. Margaret 192–193
St. Melor 125–126
St. Michael's Mount 137
St. Ninian 73–74, 188–189
St. Osmund 154–157
St. Oswald 64–65, 67, 216
St. Patrick's Purgatory 200–203
St. Petroc 138–139
St. Piran 137–138
St. Sidwell 139
St. Swithun 123–124
St. Thomas Becket 161–163
St. Thomas Cantilupe 157–160
St. Wilfrid 71
St. William York 168
St. Winefride 180–183
Salisbury 100, 154–157, 230–231
Saveock Water 231–234
Sculptor's Cave 41
shape-shifters 209–210
Sherborne 97–98
Sigeberht (king) 84
Skedemosse Bog 43
spells/charms 50–54, 221–223, 238–239
Spong Hill 80
Springhead 35–37
Staffordshire Hoard 91–92
Stanton Harcourt 26

Stonehenge 102
Sutton Hoo 44–45, 81–83
Swein Forkbeard 128–129

Thor's hammer 116–118, 120
Three Dead Kings 206
Tisbury 104
Towcester 26

Uley 34

walking dead 207–208
Wayside Farm 30–31
Wells (Somerset) 107, 118
wergeld 95
Whitby 65–66
Wild Hunt 134–137
Wilsford Shaft 10–11
Wilton 103–104
Winchester 25, 96–97
Winterbourne Down 25
witchcraft 18–21, 54–56, 59, 133–134, 222–225, 231–234
witchcraft trials: Aberdeen 236–237; Bury St. Edmunds 226–227; Conwy (Wales) 235; Erskine 237; Hatfield Peverell 225; Launceston 231; North Berwick 235–236; Pendle Hill 227–230; St. Osyth 235; Salisbury 230–231; Stanley 230; Warboys 225–226
Worcester 26

Yarnbury Castle 10
Yeavering 63
York 62, 74, 119–120
York Helmet 74–75